WILLS, PROBATE AND ADMINISTRATION

WILLS, PROBATE AND ADMINISTRATION

Sheila L Bramley LLB (London), Solicitor

Robin E Riddett, Solicitor

1997

Published by
Jordan Publishing Limited
21 St Thomas Street
Bristol BS1 6JS

© The College of Law 1997

Crown copyright is reproduced with the permission
of the Controller of Her Majesty's Stationery Office.

All rights reserved. No part of this publication may be
reproduced, stored in a retrieval system, or transmitted in
any way or by any means, including photocopying or recording,
without the written permission of the copyright holder,
application for which should be addressed to the publisher.

British Library Cataloguing-in-Publication Data
A catalogue record for this book is available from the British Library.

ISSN 1352–4569
ISBN 0 85308 433 5

Photoset by Pentacor PLC, High Wycombe, Buckinghamshire
Printed in Great Britain by Hobbs The Printers Ltd of Southampton

PREFACE

This is the fifth edition of a book which was originally written and edited by a team from Guildford comprising the current authors, Angela Applegate, Carol Jeffers and Paula McWhirter.

The intention is to give a comprehensive introduction to the legal and taxation implications of drafting wills and administering estates. A practical approach is adopted throughout, and relevant law is referred to in context. The law which is relevant both to will drafting and to probate and administration is grouped together, for convenience, in Part II of the book.

For the sake of brevity, the masculine pronoun is used throughout to include the feminine.

The permission of the Inland Revenue to reproduce various tax forms is acknowledged with thanks. In addition, the authors and publishers are grateful to the Capital Taxes Office of the Inland Revenue, The Law Society and The Solicitor's Law Stationery Society Ltd for giving their kind permission to reproduce their materials in this book.

The authors extend their thanks to Paul Brearley, Forms Adviser to the Capital Taxes Office of the Inland Revenue, for his help in updating this book.

The model precedents which appear in this book are based on precedents contained in Volume 42 of the *Encyclopaedia of Forms and Precedents* 5th edn (Butterworths) and Pettitt and Riddett *Will Draftsman's Handbook* 7th edn (Longman, 1995).

The law is stated as at 31 March 1997.

SHEILA BRAMLEY
ROBIN RIDDETT
Guildford

CONTENTS

PREFACE		v
TABLE OF CASES		xiii
TABLE OF STATUTES		xv
TABLE OF STATUTORY INSTRUMENTS		xvii
ABBREVIATIONS		xix

PART I	**DRAFTING THE WILL**		1
Chapter 1	INTRODUCTION		3
	1.1	The importance of a valid and effective will	3
	1.2	Death testate, intestate or partially intestate	3
	1.3	Disposing of property other than by will/intestacy rules	4
	1.4	Tax	4
	1.5	Personal representatives	4
	1.6	Grant of representation	5
	1.7	Conclusion	5
Chapter 2	THE FUNCTION AND SCOPE OF A WILL		7
	2.1	What is a will?	7
	2.2	Who may make a will?	7
	2.3	Why make a will?	7
	2.4	What property passes by the will/intestacy rules?	9
	2.5	Succession and tax	10
Chapter 3	FORM AND CONTENT OF A WILL: BACKGROUND		11
	3.1	Introduction	11
	3.2	The draftsman's aim	11
	3.3	Drafting style	11
	3.4	Use of precedents	13
	3.5	Basic structure of a will	13
	3.6	Is a trust required?	13
	3.7	Codicils	14
Chapter 4	FORM AND CONTENT OF A WILL: EXAMPLES		15
	4.1	Introduction	15
	4.2	Mark King's will	15
	4.3	Julia Gold's will	18
	4.4	Codicil to Mark King's will	23
Chapter 5	COMMENCEMENT AND REVOCATION CLAUSES, AND DISPOSAL OF BODY		25
	5.1	Commencement	25
	5.2	The revocation clause	26
	5.3	Directions about disposal of body	26
Chapter 6	APPOINTMENT OF EXECUTORS AND TRUSTEES		29
	6.1	Why appoint executors?	29

	6.2 Are trustees also required?	29
	6.3 Dual capacity and transition	29
	6.4 How many to choose	29
	6.5 Whom to choose	30
	6.6 Individuals	30
	6.7 Solicitors or other professionals	32
	6.8 Trust corporations	35
	6.9 The Public Trustee	36
Chapter 7	**APPOINTMENT OF GUARDIANS**	37
	7.1 Introduction	37
	7.2 Method of appointment	37
	7.3 Effect of appointment	37
	7.4 Practical considerations	38
Chapter 8	**LEGACIES AND DEVISES**	39
	8.1 Introduction	39
	8.2 Types of gift	39
	8.3 General drafting considerations	40
	8.4 Specific gifts	43
	8.5 Pecuniary legacies	47
Chapter 9	**GIFTS OF RESIDUE**	49
	9.1 Drafting considerations	49
	9.2 Gift of residue: absolute interests	51
	9.3 Gift of residue: life interest	55
Chapter 10	**ADMINISTRATIVE PROVISIONS**	57
	10.1 Introduction	57
	10.2 Provisions concerning the administration of the estate	57
	10.3 Provisions concerning the administration of a trust	59
	10.4 Trusts of land	65
	10.5 The apportionment rules	66
	10.6 Miscellaneous additional powers	68
	10.7 Selecting the appropriate powers	69
Chapter 11	**TAKING INSTRUCTIONS: GENERAL MATTERS**	71
	11.1 The role of the solicitor	71
	11.2 Is there an existing will?	72
	11.3 The testator's property	72
	11.4 Planning the will	73
	11.5 Carrying out instructions	74
Chapter 12	**TAKING INSTRUCTIONS: TAX CONSIDERATIONS**	75
	12.1 Introduction	75
	12.2 Estimating the potential tax bill	75
	12.3 Lifetime gifts	76
	12.4 Planning the will	77
Chapter 13	**REQUIREMENTS FOR A VALID WILL**	81
	13.1 Introduction	81
	13.2 Capacity	81
	13.3 Intention	82
	13.4 Formalities for execution	85
	13.5 Choice of witnesses	87

		13.6 Alterations	89
Chapter 14		REVOCATION	91
		14.1 Introduction	91
		14.2 Mutual wills	91
		14.3 Methods of revocation	91
PART II		LAW COMMON TO WILLS, PROBATE AND ADMINISTRATION	95
Chapter 15		FAILURE OF GIFTS BY WILL	97
		15.1 Introduction	97
		15.2 Ademption	97
		15.3 Lapse	98
		15.4 Failure of contingency	100
		15.5 Divorce	101
		15.6 Uncertainty	101
		15.7 Beneficiary witnesses will	102
		15.8 Disclaimer	102
		15.9 Abatement	102
		15.10 Perpetuity and accumulations	102
Chapter 16		INTESTACY	103
		16.1 Introduction	103
		16.2 Structure of the intestacy rules	104
		16.3 Spouse and issue	106
		16.4 Intestate survived by spouse and parents, brothers or sisters or their issue	111
		16.5 Intestate survived by spouse and no other close relatives	112
		16.6 Distribution where there is no surviving spouse	113
		16.7 Intestacy and LPA 1925, s 184	114
Chapter 17		THE INHERITANCE (PROVISION FOR FAMILY AND DEPENDANTS) ACT 1975	115
		17.1 Introduction	115
		17.2 The right to bring a claim	116
		17.3 Application by the surviving spouse	117
		17.4 Application by a former spouse	118
		17.5 Application by a child of the deceased	118
		17.6 Application by a person treated as a child of the family	119
		17.7 Application by a person being maintained by the deceased immediately before his death	120
		17.8 Application by a cohabitee	121
		17.9 Orders and their effect	121
		17.10 Anti-avoidance provisions	124
		17.11 Summary of points to bear in mind in the office	124
		17.12 Standing search	125
Chapter 18		INHERITANCE TAX	127
		18.1 Introduction	127
		18.2 When is IHT chargeable?	127
		18.3 How to calculate IHT on death: a summary	128
		18.4 Step 1: identify the estate	129
		18.5 Step 2: value the estate	132

	18.6	Step 3: apply any relevant exemptions	133
	18.7	Step 4: apply business and agricultural property reliefs (if relevant)	136
	18.8	Step 5: calculate tax at the appropriate rate	137
	18.9	Liability for IHT on death	140
	18.10	Time for payment of IHT on death	142
	18.11	Burden of IHT on death	144
	18.12	Example of the application of IHT to an estate on death	145
	18.13	Lifetime transfers	147
Chapter 19		**FINANCIAL SERVICES: PROBATE PRACTICE**	153
	19.1	Introduction	153
	19.2	Estate administration	153
	19.3	Discrete investment business?	156
	19.4	Advising the beneficiaries	156
PART III		**PROBATE AND ADMINISTRATION**	159
Chapter 20		**PROBATE PRACTICE AND PROCEDURE**	161
	20.1	Introduction	161
	20.2	The solicitor's clients and duties	161
	20.3	First steps after receiving instructions	162
	20.4	Preparing to obtain a grant of representation	163
	20.5	Probate business	164
	20.6	Necessity for a grant of representation	165
	20.7	Application for grant	167
	20.8	Post-death variation or disclaimer	169
	20.9	Conclusion	169
Chapter 21		**COMPLETING THE INLAND REVENUE ACCOUNT**	171
	21.1	Introduction	171
	21.2	The requirement for an Inland Revenue account	174
	21.3	Points common to the completion of Forms IHT 202 and IHT 200	175
	21.4	Form IHT 202	179
	21.5	Form IHT 200	184
	21.6	Action following completion of account	206
Chapter 22		**OATHS: THE BACKGROUND LAW**	207
	22.1	Introduction	207
	22.2	Oath for executors	208
	22.3	Oath for administrators with will annexed	210
	22.4	Oath for administrators	214
	22.5	Effect of grant	218
	22.6	Limited grants	218
	22.7	The chain of representation and grant de bonis non administratis	220
	22.8	Caveats and citations	222
Chapter 23		**COMPLETING THE OATH**	225
	23.1	Introduction	225
	23.2	Oath for executors	225
	23.3	Oath for administrators with will annexed	231
	23.4	Oath for administrators	234
	23.5	Conclusion	237

Chapter 24	ADMINISTRATION OF AN ESTATE	239
	24.1 Introduction	239
	24.2 Duties of the PRs	239
	24.3 Record keeping and estate accounts	241
	24.4 File management and time organisation	241
Chapter 25	ADMINISTRATIVE POWERS OF PRS	245
	25.1 Introduction	245
	25.2 Description of the powers	245
	25.3 Sources of the powers	245
	25.4 PRs' powers considered in Chapter 10	246
	25.5 Other statutory powers	246
	25.6 Exercise of powers by PRs	248
Chapter 26	COLLECTING THE DECEASED'S ASSETS	249
	26.1 Duties of the PRs	249
	26.2 Methods of collection	249
	26.3 Devolution of assets on the PRs	249
Chapter 27	PAYING THE DECEASED'S FUNERAL AND TESTAMENTARY EXPENSES AND DEBTS	253
	27.1 Preliminary considerations	253
	27.2 Funeral and testamentary expenses and debts	254
	27.3 PRs' duty to pay debts	254
	27.4 Protection against unknown claims	255
	27.5 Administration of assets: solvent estate	256
	27.6 Contrary provision in the will	257
	27.7 No contrary provision in the will	258
	27.8 The insolvent estate	263
Chapter 28	DISTRIBUTING THE LEGACIES	265
	28.1 Introduction	265
	28.2 Construction of the will	265
	28.3 Identity of beneficiaries	266
	28.4 Classification of gifts	268
	28.5 Specific legacies	268
	28.6 Pecuniary legacies	269
	28.7 Incidence of pecuniary legacies	270
	28.8 Time for payment of pecuniary legacies	272
	28.9 Intestacy or partial intestacy	272
Chapter 29	COMPLETING THE ADMINISTRATION AND DISTRIBUTING THE RESIDUARY ESTATE	273
	29.1 Introduction	273
	29.2 Adjusting the IHT assessment	273
	29.3 Inland Revenue corrective account	276
	29.4 IHT clearance certificate	276
	29.5 Income tax and CGT	277
	29.6 Transferring assets to residuary beneficiaries	282
	29.7 Estate accounts	284
Chapter 30	POST-DEATH VARIATIONS AND DISCLAIMERS	287
	30.1 Introduction	287
	30.2 Disclaimer	287

	30.3 Variation	290
	30.4 IHT planning aspects of variations	292
Appendix 1	RODNEY PARKS DECEASED	295
	Attendance Note	295
	Oath for Administrators (with Will)	296
Appendix 2	ALISTAIR DAVIS DECEASED	299
	Attendance Note	299
	Inland Revenue Account for Inheritance Tax (Form IHT 202)	301
	Oath for Administrators	305
Appendix 3	ROSEMARY JONES DECEASED	307
	Attendance Note	307
	Inland Revenue Account for Inheritance Tax (Form IHT 200)	309
	Oath for Executors	321
	Corrective Account for Estate Duty, Capital Transfer Tax or Inheritance Tax (Form Cap D3)	323
	Form 301A	327
	Inland Revenue Capital Transfer Tax/IHTA 1984 (Form 30)	329
Appendix 4	FREDERICK SMITH DECEASED	331
	Estate capital account	331
	Estate income account	332
	Beneficiary's account	332
Appendix 5	EXTRACTS FROM THE NON-CONTENTIOUS PROBATE RULES 1987 (AS AMENDED)	333
Appendix 6	FAMILY DIVISION PRACTICE DIRECTION OF 19 APRIL 1988	337

INDEX 339

TABLE OF CASES

References in the right-hand column are to paragraph numbers.

Allhusen v Whittell (1867) LR 4 Eq 295	10.5.3, 10.5.5
Banks v Goodfellow (1870) LR 5 QB 549	13.2.2
Benjamin, Re [1902] 1 Ch 723	24.2.6
Coventry (deceased), Re; Coventry v Coventry [1980] Ch 461, CA	17.5.1
Everest (deceased), Re [1975] Fam 44	14.3.3
Hobbs v Knight (1838) 1 Curt 768	14.3.3
Howe v Dartmouth (1820) 7 Ves 137	10.5.2, 10.5.5
Kecskemeti v Rubens Rabin & Co (1992) *The Times*, 31 December	11.1.6
Kenward v Adams (1975) *The Times*, 29 November	13.2.3
Practice Direction of 19 April 1988	App 6
Recher's Will Trusts, Re; National Westminster Bank v National Anti-Vivisection Society [1972] Ch 526	8.3.3
Ross v Caunters [1980] Ch 297	11.1.6, 13.5.4
Saunders v Vautier (1841) 4 Beav 115	10.3.8
Sinclair (deceased), Re; Lloyd's Bank v Imperial Cancer Research Fund [1988] Ch 446, CA	15.5
Tankard, Re [1942] Ch 29	25.5.6, 27.3
White and Another v Jones and Another [1995] 2 AC 207, HL	11.5
Wintle v Nye [1959] 1 WLR 284, HL	13.3.2

TABLE OF STATUTES

References in the right-hand column are to paragraph numbers.

Administration of Estates Act 1925	9.1.4, 10.1.1, 16.1
s 7	22.7.2
s 25	23.2, 24.2.1
s 33	16.2.1, 28.7.1
(7)	28.7.1
s 34	18.6.3
(3)	8.3.2, 27.5.1, 27.5.2, 27.6.1, 27.7.2
s 35	8.4.5, 8.4.6, 27.5.2, 27.6.1
(1)	27.7.1, 27.7.2
s 36(4)	29.6.4
(6)	29.6.4
ss 39–44	25.3.1
s 39(1)	25.5.4
s 41	4.3.2, 10.2.2, 16.2.1, 25.4.2
s 42	8.3.3, 10.2.4, 25.5.5, 29.6.3
(2)	28.3.2
s 44	25.5.6, 28.8.1
s 46	16.2.1, 16.2.2, 16.2.3, 22.4.3
s 47	16.2.3
(1)	16.3.8
s 47A	16.3.5
s 55(1)(ix)	27.7.2
(x)	8.4.1, 8.5, 16.3.3
Sch 1, Pt II	27.5.2, 27.7.2, 28.5.2, 28.7.1
Administration of Estates Act 1971	
s 9	24.2.1
Administration of Estates (Small Payments) Act 1965	20.6.1, 21.1.3, 21.3.3, 26.2
Administration of Justice Act 1982	14.3.2, 15.5
s 17	13.4.1
s 20	28.2.1
s 21	28.2.1
Adoption Act 1976	9.2.2
s 39	28.3.2
s 45	28.3.3
Anatomy Act 1984	5.3
Apportionment Act 1870	
s 2	10.5.4, 10.5.5, 10.7.2, 10.7.3, 10.7.4
Children Act 1989	2.2.3
s 5(3)	7.2
(7)	7.3
Family Law Reform Act 1969	
s 3	13.2.1
s 15	28.3.1
Family Law Reform Act 1987	9.2.2, 28.3.4
Pt I	App 6
Pt II	App 6
s 1	App 6
(1)	28.3.1
s 18	App 6
(2)	16.6.2, 22.4.1
s 19(1)	28.3.1
s 21	App 6
Finance Act 1986	18.4.3
s 103	21.5.8
Financial Services Act 1986	19.1, 19.3, 19.4
Sch 1, Pt III	19.2
Human Tissue Act 1961	5.3
Inheritance (Provision for Family and Dependants) Act 1975	14.3.2, 17.1, 17.2, 23.2
s 1	17.4
(1)	17.2.2
(2)	17.2.3
(a),(b)	17.2.3
(3)	17.2.2, 17.7
s 2	17.8.1, 17.8.2
s 3	17.2.4
(1)	17.2.4, 17.3.2, 17.4.2, 17.5.2, 17.6.2, 17.7.2
(5),(6)	17.2.4
s 4	17.2.1
s 25	17.8.2
Inheritance Tax Act 1984	18.1
s 1	18.2
s 2	18.2
s 3A	18.2.1
s 4(2)	18.5.6
s 5(1)	18.4.1
(5)	18.5.4
s 7(1)	18.8.2
s 18	18.6.1
s 23(1)	18.6.2
s 38	18.6.3
(3)	18.6.3
s 49(1)	18.4.2
s 92	18.7.1
s 105	18.7.1
s 113A	18.13.1
s 113B	18.13.1
s 116	18.7.2
s 142	30.2.2, 20.3.2
s 160	18.5.1
s 162	18.5.4
s 171	18.5.2
ss 178–189	29.2.4
s 179	29.2.4
ss 190–198	29.2.4
s 200	18.9.2
(1)(c)	18.9.2
s 211	18.11.2, 27.7.3
(3)	18.11.3

Intestates' Estates Act 1952
  s 5 — 16.3.6

Law of Property Act 1925
  s 21 — 10.2.4
  s 184 — 9.2.1, 15.5.2, 15.5.3, 16.7, 18.4.5
Law of Property (Miscellaneous Provisions) Act 1994
  s 16 — 25.6.3
Law Reform (Succession) Act 1995 — 15.5, 16.1.4, 16.3.3, 17.2.2
  s 3 — 14.3.2
Legitimacy Act 1976
  s 5(3) — 28.3.3
    (4) — 28.3.3
  s 7 — 28.3.3

Married Women's Property Act 1882 — 21.1.3, 21.5.2
  s 11 — 2.4.3, 20.6.2, 26.3.2
Matrimonial Causes Act 1973
  s 18(2) — 16.3.1

Powers of Attorney Act 1971
  s 9 — 25.5.2

Settled Land Act 1925 — 9.1.3, 22.6.3, 23.2
Supreme Court Act 1981
  s 28 — 20.5.2
  s 114 — 22.3.4, 22.7.1

Taxation of Chargeable Gains Act 1992 — 29.1
  s 62 — 30.2.2, 30.3.2
    (4) — 29.5.4
  s 64(2) — 29.5.4

Trustee Act 1925 — 10.1.1, 25.3.1
  s 19 — 10.2.3, 25.4.2
  s 23(1),(2) — 25.5.1
  s 25 — 25.5.2
  s 27 — 24.2.5, 24.2.6, 24.4.1, 27.4, 28.3.4
  s 30(2) — 25.5.3
  s 31 — 10.3.5, 10.3.7, 10.4.1, 25.2.2, 25.4.2
    (1) — 10.3.5
      (ii) — 10.3.5
    (2) — 10.3.5
  s 32 — 10.3.6, 10.3.7, 25.2.2, 25.4.2
    (1)(a)–(c) — 10.3.6
  s 61 — 24.2.4
Trustee Investment Act 1961 — 10.1.1, 10.3.2, 10.3.3, 25.3.1, 25.4.2
Trusts of Land and Appointment of Trustees Act 1996 — 9.1.3, 9.2.4, 10.3.4, 10.4.1
  s 2 — 23.2
  s 4 — 9.2.4
  s 6(3) — 10.3.3
  s 11 — 10.4.2
  s 12 — 10.4.3
  s 19 — 10.3.3

Wills Act 1837
  s 1 — App 5
  s 7 — 13.2.1
  s 9 — 2.1.1, 13.4.1, 13.4.3, 20.7.1, App 5
  s 15 — 6.7.2, 13.5.2, 15.7
  s 18 — 14.3.2
    (3),(4) — 14.3.2
  s 18A — 6.4, 14.3.2, 15.5, 22.2.2, 22.3.1
  s 20 — 14.3.1, 14.3.3
  s 21 — 13.6.1, App 5
  s 24 — 8.4.1, 15.2.3
  s 33 — 9.2.3, 15.3.5, 28.3.5
    (2) — 15.3.5
  s 114 — App 5
Wills Act 1968
  s 1 — 13.5.3

TABLE OF STATUTORY INSTRUMENTS

References in the right-hand column are to paragraph numbers.

Administration of Insolvent Estates of Deceased Persons Order 1986, SI 1986/1999	27.8.3
Intestate Succession (Interest and Capitalisation Order) 1977, SI 1977/1491	16.3.5
Land Registration Rules 1925, SI 1925/1093	29.6.4
Non-Contentious Probate Rules 1987, SI 1987/2024	20.7.2
rr 12–17	App 5
r 20	20.2.2, 22.3.2, 22.4.2, 22.7.1, 22.7.3, 22.8.2, 23.3.2, App 5
(7)	22.2.4
r 22	20.2.2, 22.4.1, 22.4.2, 22.4.3, 22.4.5, 22.7.1, 22.7.3, 22.8.2, 23.4, App 5
r 25	App 5
r 27	App 5
(4)	22.3.4
(5)	22.3.3
r 32	22.6.4
r 44	22.8.1
r 46	22.8.2, App 5
Solicitors' Incorporated Practice Rules 1988	6.7.1
Solicitors' Investment Business Rules 1995	19.1, 19.2.4, 19.4
r 10(1)	19.3
Solicitors' Practice Rules 1990	
r 1	6.7.1

ABBREVIATIONS

STATUTORY MATERIAL

AEA 1925	Administration of Estates Act 1925
AEA 1971	Administration of Estates Act 1971
IHTA	Inheritance Tax Act 1984
I(PFD)A	Inheritance (Provision for Family and Dependants) Act 1975
LPA 1925	Law of Property Act 1925
SLA 1925	Settled Land Act 1925
TA 1925	Trustee Act 1925
TIA 1961	Trustee Investments Act 1961
TLATA 1996	Trusts of Land and Appointment of Trustees Act 1996
NCPR	Non-Contentious Probate Rules 1987
SIBR	Solicitors' Investment Business Rules 1995

BOOKS

'Barlow, King and King'	Barlow, King and King *Wills, Administration and Taxation* 6th edn (Sweet & Maxwell, 1994)
'Butterworths WPA Service'	*Wills, Probate and Administration* (Butterworths)
'Encyclopaedia of Forms and Precedents'	*Encyclopaedia of Forms and Precedents* 5th edn (Butterworths)
'Mellows'	Mellows *The Law of Succession* 5th edn (Butterworths, 1993)
'Orange Tax Handbook'	*Orange Tax Handbook 1997–98* (Butterworths)
'Parker's Precedents'	Parker *Modern Will Precedents* 2nd edn (Butterworths, 1987)
'Parry and Clark'	Parry and Clark *Law of Succession* 10th edn (Sweet & Maxwell, 1995)
'Tristram and Coote'	Tristram and Coote *Probate Practice* 28th edn (Butterworths, 1995)
'Whitehouse'	Whitehouse *Revenue Law: Principles and Practice* 14th edn (Butterworths, 1996)
'Will Draftsman's Handbook'	Pettitt and Riddett *Will Draftsman's Handbook* 7th edn (Longman, 1995)
'Williams on Wills'	Williams *Wills* 7th edn (Butterworths, 1995)
'Yellow Tax Handbook'	*Yellow Tax Handbook 1997–98* (Butterworths)

PART I

DRAFTING THE WILL

CONTENTS

Chapter 1 provides an overview of wills, probate and administration, so that drafting the will can be understood in context; it also introduces useful terminology.

As a preliminary to detailed will drafting, Chapters 2 to 4 deal with the nature and function of a will/codicil, introduce some general drafting considerations, examine structure and content in outline and analyse the text of two wills and one codicil.

Once the reader is familiar with standard layout and terminology, Chapters 5 to 10 examine in detail the legal and practical considerations governing the selection and drafting of appropriate clauses for the client's will/codicil.

Chapters 11 and 12 then deal with taking instructions from the client, to ensure that a suitable combination of correctly drafted clauses is used.

Finally, Chapters 13 and 14 deal with matters affecting the validity of the will/codicil and its ability to take effect on the testator's death.

TEXTBOOKS

For precedents, Volume 42 of the Encyclopaedia of Forms and Precedents, Parker's Precedents and the Will Draftsman's Handbook are recommended.

Barlow, King and King is a useful textbook for students and contains material relevant to Part I.

If an academic textbook is required for detail covered in Chapters 13 and 14, see Mellows or Parry and Clark.

A recognised specialist text in this area is Williams on Wills.

Chapter 1

INTRODUCTION

1.1　THE IMPORTANCE OF A VALID AND EFFECTIVE WILL

It is always important to ascertain whether or not the deceased left a valid and effective will, because the presence or absence of such a will affects what happens to the deceased's property (known as his 'estate') after his death.

1.2　DEATH TESTATE, INTESTATE OR PARTIALLY INTESTATE

When a person dies, he dies:

(1) testate; or
(2) intestate (ie totally intestate); or
(3) partially intestate.

1.2.1　Testate

The deceased dies testate if:

(1) he left a valid will, ie one which complies with all the formal rules (see Chapter 13); and
(2) that will disposes effectively of all those items of the deceased's property which are capable of being inherited under a will (see **2.4** for a detailed explanation of which types of property are capable of passing under a will and which are not).

1.2.2　Intestate

The deceased dies intestate if:

(1) he left no will; or
(2) he left a will which is invalid (see Chapter 13) or which does not take effect for some reason (see **14.3.2**).

If the deceased dies intestate, all those items of his property which could have passed by will (had there been one) are instead inherited according to a set of statutory rules known as the intestacy rules (see Chapter 16).

1.2.3　Partially intestate

The deceased dies partially intestate if:

(1) he left a valid will; but
(2) this will does not dispose of all of those items of the deceased's property which are capable of passing under a will.

If the deceased dies partially intestate, any property that is effectively dealt with by the will is inherited according to the provisions of that will. The remaining property (which is known as 'undisposed of' property) is inherited according to the intestacy rules.

Chapter 1 contents
The importance of a valid and effective will
Death testate, intestate or partially intestate
Disposing of property other than by will/intestacy rules
Tax
Personal representatives
Grant of representation
Conclusion

1.3 DISPOSING OF PROPERTY OTHER THAN BY WILL/INTESTACY RULES

Some types of property are never capable of being inherited under a will or the intestacy rules. Such items are inherited according to their own relevant rule of succession (see **2.4**), whether the deceased died testate, intestate or partially intestate.

1.4 TAX

Taxation takes an important place in will drafting, probate and administration of estates. The principal tax concerned is inheritance tax (IHT) but capital gains tax (CGT) and income tax are also relevant. IHT is covered in Chapter 18 and referred to extensively in other chapters. CGT and income tax are covered in less detail, mainly in **29.5**. Reference should also be made to the relevant chapters in the LPC Resource Book *Pervasive Topics* (Jordans, 1997), Part I.

1.5 PERSONAL REPRESENTATIVES

1.5.1 Role

The deceased's PRs are the people responsible for his affairs after his death. They must administer and wind up his estate. Broadly this involves:

(1) collecting in the deceased's assets;
(2) paying off all his debts and liabilities (including any IHT due from his estate);
(3) working out who is entitled to inherit the remaining property; and
(4) distributing the correct property to the right beneficiaries at the appropriate time.

The PRs often employ a solicitor to advise and assist in this work, or the solicitor may himself be a PR.

One PR is sufficient in certain cases, but it is usual to have two. Although there may be no limit on the number of PRs entitled to act, no more than four can take out a grant of representation.

1.5.2 Appointment

In a will, it is usual for one or more executors to be appointed (as described in Chapter 6). If the deceased died intestate, or there are no executors appointed in the will who are able and willing to act, the court will appoint administrators in accordance with statutory rules (Chapter 22). The administrators will normally be those who are entitled to the estate on intestacy or (if there is a will) the residuary beneficiaries.

Executors and administrators are collectively known as 'personal representatives' (PRs).

1.6 GRANT OF REPRESENTATION

Regardless of whether they are executors or administrators, the PRs must obtain an appropriate grant of representation in order to prove their right to administer the deceased's estate.

The three most common grants of representation are:

(1) grant of probate;
(2) grant of letters of administration with the will annexed;
(3) grant of letters of administration (ie simple administration with no will annexed).

1.6.1 Grant of probate

If the deceased made a valid and effective will and in it appointed executors who are still able and willing to act at his death, the executors will apply for a grant of probate. The grant confirms their right to administer the estate.

1.6.2 Grant of letters of administration with the will annexed

If the deceased made a valid will which takes effect at death, but no executors were appointed in it or those appointed are not able or willing to act at his death, then administrators will apply for a grant of letters of administration with the will annexed. The grant confers on the administrators the right to administer the estate.

1.6.3 Grant of letters of administration

If the deceased did not leave a valid will, then administrators will apply for a grant of letters of administration. Again, this confers on the administrators the right to administer the estate.

1.7 CONCLUSION

The examples set out below illustrate simply how all the basic concepts may link together and they provide a foundation for the study of wills, probate and administration. It should be assumed in each case that all the deceased's property was capable of passing under a will.

Example 1
John dies testate (ie leaving a valid and effective will which disposes of all his property which was capable of passing by will). In the will he has appointed executors who are able and willing to act at his death. The executors obtain a grant of probate, wind up the estate and distribute it in accordance with the provisions of John's will.

Example 2
Sarah dies without leaving a valid will (ie she dies intestate). Her administrators obtain a grant of letters of administration. They wind up the estate and distribute the property which would have been capable of passing by will (had there been one) in accordance with the intestacy rules.

Example 3

Anne dies leaving a valid will appointing her husband as executor, and leaving a gift of £10,000 to her sister and the rest of her property to her husband. Her sister survives her, but her husband died some time before her. Her husband cannot benefit under her will nor can he act as executor. This means that Anne has died partially intestate (because the property left to her husband is 'undisposed of') and there are no executors able and willing to act.

Her administrators obtain a grant of letters of administration with the will annexed and wind up the estate. This will include giving £10,000 to Anne's sister under the terms of her will and distributing the rest of the property which would have been capable of passing by will in accordance with the intestacy rules.

Chapter 2

THE FUNCTION AND SCOPE OF A WILL

2.1 WHAT IS A WILL?

A will is a declaration made in prescribed form of the intentions of the testator which are to take effect on his death and which remain revocable until then. To make a valid will a person must have the necessary capacity and intention, and the will must satisfy certain statutory formalities. Thus, a will has special characteristics.

2.1.1 Formalities

The formalities required for a valid will are prescribed by the Wills Act 1837, s 9 (as substituted). In general, a will must be in writing and must be signed by the testator. Two people must witness the signature, signing their own names to show that they have done so. The details of these formal requirements are considered in Chapter 13.

2.1.2 A will takes effect on death

During the testator's lifetime the people named in his will have no interest in his property and the testator remains free to dispose of it. If property specifically given away by will is no longer owned by the testator at his death, the gift will normally fail: technically it is 'adeemed' (see **15.2**). If a person to whom property is left by will dies before the testator the gift will also normally fail, or 'lapse' (see **15.3**).

2.1.3 A will is revocable

A will may be revoked:

(1) by a later will;
(2) by destruction, if the testator intends by destroying his will to revoke it; or
(3) automatically by marriage.

Further details are contained in Chapter 14.

2.2 WHO MAY MAKE A WILL?

In order to make a will, a person must generally be at least 18 years old and must have the required mental capacity to make a will. He must also know and approve the contents of his particular will. Details are contained in Chapter 13.

2.3 WHY MAKE A WILL?

2.3.1 Avoiding the intestacy rules

When a person dies intestate, the property which would have passed under his will is distributed according to the terms of the intestacy rules. The property is shared between the nearest relatives of the deceased (or 'next of kin') on terms prescribed

Chapter 2 contents
What is a will?
Who may make a will?
Why make a will?
What property passes by the will/intestacy rules?
Succession and tax

by the rules (see Chapter 16). These provisions may not accord with the wishes of the intestate.

In a will, a testator may direct who is to take his property and the terms on which it is to be taken. For example, if the testator wishes to prevent a beneficiary from receiving property at the age of 18, the gift may be made conditional ('contingent') on the beneficiary reaching a later age (eg 21 or 25).

Property may be disposed of 'absolutely' or through a trust created expressly in the will. Trusts are appropriate where, for example, the testator wishes to leave property contingently (as above) or to persons in succession (such as to his wife for her lifetime with remainder to his children). Trusts are considered in Chapter 9.

2.3.2 Appointing executors and trustees

When a person dies intestate, his estate is administered by administrators who are appointed by the court according to statutory rules. Usually the effect of these rules is that one or more of the people entitled to the estate on intestacy will be appointed as administrator(s). If any property in the estate is to be held on a continuing trust (perhaps because the beneficiary is a minor) the administrators will also act as trustees.

In a will, the testator may exercise his own choice by appointing executors to administer his estate and trustees to administer any trust he may create in that will. Usually the same people are appointed to be both executors and trustees (see Chapter 6).

2.3.3 Appointing guardians

The Children Act 1989 provides that guardians may be appointed by will. This is important for a testator who has children under the age of 18 (see Chapter 7).

In the absence of an express appointment, the court will appoint guardians for children under the age of 18 whose parents have died.

2.3.4 Extending the statutory powers of executors and trustees

Administrators and trustees of trusts arising under the intestacy rules have only the powers conferred by statute. In some cases, these powers may be unduly restrictive and expensive to operate. Making a will provides an opportunity to consider the statutory powers of the executors and trustees and extend them where appropriate (see Chapter 10).

2.3.5 Tax considerations

Making a will provides an opportunity for the testator to distribute his property in such a way as to mitigate the burden of tax on death. Further details are considered in Chapter 12.

2.3.6 Directions for burial and disposal of body

Some testators wish to express a preference in the will as to the burial and disposal of their body (see **5.3**).

2.4 WHAT PROPERTY PASSES BY THE WILL/INTESTACY RULES?

If a testator makes a will in which he disposes of all his estate, the will operates on his death to dispose of most types of property which he then owns. Thus a gift of 'all my estate to X' would include property held in the sole name of the testator at the time of his death in a variety of different forms, such as cash, money in bank and building society accounts, stocks and shares and other investments, land and chattels. If an individual does not dispose of such property by will, it passes on his death according to the intestacy rules.

However, there are some types of property which pass on death independently of the terms of the will or the intestacy rules.

2.4.1 Joint property

Where property is held by more than one person as joint tenants in equity, on the death of one joint tenant his interest passes by survivorship to the surviving joint tenant(s).

Example
George makes a will leaving all his estate to a charity. He and his brother Harry have a joint bank account and own a house as joint tenants in equity. On George's death his interests in the house and the bank account pass automatically to Harry, not to the charity under the terms of George's will.

Where land is held by more than one person as tenants in common, the share of each tenant in common passes on his death under his will (or under the intestacy rules).

2.4.2 Nominated property

Where an individual has deposited money with certain particular institutions, he may, exceptionally, dispose of the property on death by means of a nomination. A nomination is a direction to the institution to pay the money in the account, on the death of the investor, to a chosen ('nominated') third party. The statutory provisions which permit these disposals apply to deposits not exceeding £5,000 in certain trustee savings banks, friendly societies and industrial and provident societies. Similar provisions which permitted nomination of National Savings Certificates and National Savings Bank accounts were withdrawn from 1 May 1981. Nominations of such National Savings made before that date remain valid.

If an individual has an account to which these provisions apply and has made a nomination, on his death the property passes to the chosen nominee regardless of the terms of the will (if any) or intestacy rules. If no nomination has been made, the money in the account will pass under the will or intestacy in the usual way.

2.4.3 Insurance policies

Where a person takes out a simple policy of life assurance, the benefit of that policy belongs to him. On his death, the policy matures and the insurance company will pay the proceeds to his PRs who will distribute the money according to the terms of his will or the intestacy rules.

However, a life assurance policy may be taken out for the benefit of specified individuals. This may be done under the terms of the Married Women's Property Act 1882, s 11. Under this section, a person taking out a life assurance policy on his own life may express the policy to be for the benefit of his spouse and/or children. This creates a trust in favour of the named beneficiaries. Alternatively, the policy may be expressly written in trust for named beneficiaries. In either case, the benefit of the policy does not belong to the life assured. On death, the policy matures and the insurance company will pay the proceeds to the named beneficiaries (or to trustees for them) regardless of the terms of the deceased's will.

2.4.4 Pension benefits

Many pension schemes provide for the payment of benefits if an employee dies 'in service'. Commonly, a lump sum calculated on the basis of the employee's salary at the time of his death is paid by the trustees of the pension fund at their discretion to members of his family. Such a scheme usually allows the employee to indicate to the trustees which people he would like to benefit. The employee's choice is not binding on the pension fund trustees, but they will normally abide by his wishes.

Such pension benefits do not belong to the employee during his lifetime and pass on his death independently of the terms of his will.

2.5 SUCCESSION AND TAX

Property which falls outside an estate for succession purposes may nevertheless form part of the estate for tax purposes. Discretionary pension benefits and insurance policies in trust have the advantage of falling outside an estate for IHT purposes (see **12.4.3**). Joint tenancies and nominated property are included in the estate for IHT purposes. In the case of joint property, it will be the value of the deceased's share that is included in the value of his estate for IHT (see **18.5.3**).

Chapter 3

FORM AND CONTENT OF A WILL: BACKGROUND

3.1 INTRODUCTION

This chapter introduces the basic form and structure of a will and a codicil. General matters (eg the draftsman's aim when creating a will/codicil, drafting style, use of precedents) are considered here by way of introduction to Chapter 4, where examples of wills and a codicil are examined in outline. In this chapter and Chapter 4, the intention is to familiarise the reader with structure and outline content only.

Chapters 5 to 10 (inclusive) consider in detail the legal content and drafting implications of a wide range of specimen clauses.

Chapter 3 contents
Introduction
The draftsman's aim
Drafting style
Use of precedents
Basic structure of a will
Is a trust required?
Codicils

3.2 THE DRAFTSMAN'S AIM

The draftsman's aim is to produce a valid document which, at the testator's death, will dispose effectively of all the property which is capable of being passed by will in accordance with the testator's wishes. The will must therefore be clear, comprehensive and unambiguous.

The aim is also to anticipate and identify all foreseeable events and potential problems which may arise after the will has been executed and to ensure that the will specifies exactly what is to be done should the events occur or problems arise.

The provisions must be precise to ensure certainty and yet flexible so as to accommodate future changes in family and property circumstances. It is important to avoid loopholes which might give rise to disputes after the testator's death.

A solicitor should advise his client to review and update his will if his family or financial circumstances change in the future, but every will should be drafted to cater for the more predictable possibilities (eg the birth of more children or divorce) in case the client fails to revise his will before death. It does not matter if those events do not in fact occur (rendering the provisions superfluous). However, if such an event did occur and there was no provision in the will to cater for it, the draftsman's omission could create serious difficulties and dispute.

3.3 DRAFTING STYLE

3.3.1 'Traditional' versus 'plain English'

Drafting style is a personal matter. Many solicitors favour the 'traditional' style while others incline to the more streamlined 'plain English' approach. Both views have their merits.

The traditional style uses many clauses whose meaning and effect have been tested through the courts and are therefore not open to doubt; the drawback is that documents prepared in this way tend to be longer and less comprehensible to the client than their 'plain English' equivalents. Clients may also find the use of words such as 'hereby' and 'hereinbeforementioned' confusing.

By contrast, 'plain English' wills tend to be shorter and more accessible for a lay client, but there is a risk that the desire to express complex legal matters in concise, simple language may lead to ambiguity.

It is possible to use a blend of the two styles. Many firms now have their own 'in-house' style guide based on precedents.

Whatever style is adopted, it is important for the draftsman to be consistent in the use of words and phrases.

3.3.2 Punctuation

By tradition, wills are generally drafted without punctuation. The view taken in the past (and still supported by many draftsmen) was that punctuation might lead to ambiguities and cause problems in construing a will.

It is not mandatory to follow this convention and some draftsmen now include punctuation as they believe it makes a will easier to read and understand.

The essential rule when including punctuation is to ensure that it is used correctly. Incorrect punctuation is worse than no punctuation.

3.3.3 Capital letters and numbers

Some words and phrases in the will may be set out in capital letters. The aim behind this is to provide 'markers' in the will of important matters or phrases (eg the testator's name, the revocation clause, the name of the executor(s) and the beginning of each new gift or important instruction). It is a matter of personal style as to which words (if any) are 'highlighted' in this way.

It is generally accepted that it is easier to read and refer to clauses in a will if they are numbered.

3.3.4 Stylistic alternatives versus legal alternatives

When selecting the wording for some clauses (eg the opening words and the revocation clause) the draftsman's choice is simply one of style between different ways of achieving the same legal result for his client. However, for other clauses the client (preferably with the benefit of professional advice) must make a choice between alternative and entirely different legal results (eg should the beneficiary or the estate pay any tax which may be due on a particular gift?); once that decision has been made the draftsman can then select appropriate words to achieve the desired result.

3.3.5 Problems where the will is 'silent'

If the wording of the will does not expressly state what is to happen in a given situation, then the law will impose a particular result, which may or may not be what the client actually wanted (or would have wanted if he had been given the opportunity to express his wishes). Even if the client is content with the effect of the general law and does not want to change it, the draftsman should still specify the position expressly in the will.

3.3.6 Achieving the desired result

It is essential that a solicitor drafts with care all the clauses in the will and, where appropriate, he must explain the legal and practical alternatives to his client. The client should know the advantages, disadvantages and consequences of each option as they apply to his affairs so that he can make an informed decision. If the solicitor drafts without discussing the issues with his client, he may produce an unwanted result, thus breaching one of his fundamental professional duties, namely to ensure that the will carries out his client's intentions. It is essential to combine a sound knowledge of drafting with careful interviewing and advice when taking instructions.

3.4 USE OF PRECEDENTS

Precedent books (and collections of 'in-house' style precedents used by some firms) are invaluable as a guide and 'inspiration' in drafting. Precedents provide a guide to the options available when drafting clauses on standard matters and they offer inspiration when producing a novel clause to deal with a situation peculiar to one client.

Before using a precedent, the draftsman should analyse the wording phrase by phrase in order to identify exactly what the clause caters for and why. He must understand the precedent in order to recognise when and how to use or adapt it. Thus it is useful to approach each clause with the following four questions in mind:

(1) What issue(s) must be addressed in this type of clause?
(2) What options are there in relation to each issue?
(3) What legal or practical factors should be taken into account in deciding which option (if more than one) best suits the issue(s)?
(4) What wording will achieve the desired result?

3.5 BASIC STRUCTURE OF A WILL

All wills should generally contain the following:

(1) opening words;
(2) revocation clause;
(3) date;
(4) appointment of executors;
(5) legacies and/or gift of residue;
(6) attestation clause.

Whilst these clauses may be sufficient for a simple will, a more complex will generally requires additional provisions.

3.6 IS A TRUST REQUIRED?

In the case of a simple will there may be no need to create an express trust. Mark King's will (**4.2**) is an example of such a will.

By contrast, where the gifts in the will may give rise to a continuing trust, express trust provisions should be included. Julia Gold's will (**4.3**) provides an example. For further details, see **9.1.2**.

3.7 CODICILS

3.7.1 Nature and purpose

A codicil is a 'postscript' to a will and is used generally to make minor changes to a testator's existing will, for example to increase or decrease the amount of a pecuniary legacy, to substitute one beneficiary for another, or to add further gifts. If there are to be several amendments and/or complex changes, the solicitor will usually advise the testator to execute a new will instead of a codicil.

A codicil is designed to be read in conjunction with the will to which it must carefully cross-refer. In order to be valid, a codicil (like a will) must comply with the requirements relating to capacity, intention and formalities (see Chapter 13).

3.7.2 Legal significance of a codicil

A codicil 'republishes' the will to which it expressly refers, ie the will takes effect as if it had been executed on the date on which the codicil was executed, with all the changes introduced by the codicil included. Similarly, a second or subsequent codicil republishes any previous codicil which has already republished the original will. This republication can have far reaching effects on the way in which references to people and property are construed, and therefore the draftsman should always consider carefully the impact that the codicil's republication will have on the wording of the original will.

Chapter 4

FORM AND CONTENT OF A WILL: EXAMPLES

4.1 INTRODUCTION

In this chapter, specimens of two wills and one codicil have been set out with a commentary for each. They are examples of the basic structure and outline content of a will or codicil, and illustrate the general principles described in Chapter 3. The specimens are referred to as:

(1) 'Mark King's will' (**4.2**);
(2) 'Julia Gold's will' (**4.3**);
(3) 'Codicil to Mark King's will' (**4.4**).

Chapter 4 contents
Introduction
Mark King's will
Julia Gold's will
Codicil to Mark King's will

4.2 MARK KING'S WILL

4.2.1 Background

Mark King, a teacher from Weyford, has instructed his solicitor to draft his will. He wants to leave all his property (apart from three individual gifts) to his sister, Frances, and for her to administer his estate. He wishes to leave: his grand piano to his cousin, John; all his books to his brother-in-law, Leo; and £5,000 to his godson, Philip, who is a minor.

4.2.2 Text

I MARK KING of 20 High Street Weyford Blankshire Teacher HEREBY REVOKE all former wills and codicils AND DECLARE this to be my last Will and Testament which I make this   day of   199[ ]

1. I APPOINT my sister FRANCES WHITE of 18 Riverside Walk Weyford Blankshire to be my executrix
2. I GIVE my grand piano to my cousin John Crown of 83 Market Row Upton Blankshire free of all taxes and all costs of packing carriage and insurance incurred for the purpose of giving effect to this gift
3. I GIVE all the books I own at the date of my death free of all taxes to my brother-in-law Leo White of 18 Riverside Walk aforesaid
4. I GIVE to my Godson Philip Smith of 12 Acacia Drive Littleminster Blankshire the sum of five thousand pounds (£5000.00) free of all taxes absolutely AND I DIRECT that if he has not attained the age of 18 years at the time when the said legacy is payable my executrix may pay the legacy to his parent or guardian or to him personally if he has attained the age of 16 years and that their respective receipts shall be a full discharge to her

5. I GIVE all the rest of my estate both real and personal whatsoever and wheresoever SUBJECT TO the payment of my debts and funeral and testamentary expenses and legacies to my said sister

SIGNED by the above-named   )
MARK KING in our joint presence)
and then by us in his   )

4.2.3 Commentary

Opening words

The identity of the testator is clearly established by his full name, address and occupation.

The testator expressly revokes (ie cancels) any wills or codicils he may have made earlier.

The testator indicates his understanding of the nature of this document by referring to it as his 'last Will and Testament'.

Details of the day/month/year are left blank in the draft. They will be inserted when the testator executes the document to give it the formal status of a valid will capable of taking effect on his death.

Clause 1

In Clause 1 the testator appoints a single executrix (the female equivalent of an executor) who is clearly identified by her full name and address. One executor/trix is sufficient in some situations, but it is more usual to appoint two people as executors or a firm or institution which cannot die (see Chapter 6).

Clause 2

The gift of the piano is a specific legacy, recognisable by the use of the word 'my' (see **8.2.1**).

The beneficiary is clearly identified by full name and address.

When drafting any gift in a will, it is good practice to specify whether or not the beneficiary will be required to pay any tax (ie IHT) which may fall due when this property passes under the will at the deceased's death (see **8.3.2**). Here the testator has indicated that the beneficiary, John, will not have to pay any such tax; the estate will pay it instead.

When drafting the gift of a bulky and/or valuable item, it is good practice to specify whether or not the beneficiary will have to pay any expenses such as packing/transport/insurance which may be necessary to implement the gift of such an item. In this case, the estate, and not the beneficiary, will pay them.

Clause 3

The gift of books is another specific legacy. It differs from the gift of a single item in Clause 2 in that it is expressed in such a way that the actual number of books owned by Mark may increase or decrease but the collection will still meet the description contained in the clause. Such a gift may be described as a 'generic' specific legacy.

The clause defines precisely what property will pass under this clause (ie all the books that Mark owns when he dies, as opposed to only those books that he owned at the time when he executed his will). This example shows how the careful wording of a clause can avoid uncertainty and/or potential problems when construing the will after the testator's death. The draftsman must consciously select the correct words to implement the testator's intention; otherwise underlying legal rules may produce an unintended effect on what happens to the property.

The books are given free of all taxes. See Clause 2 above to discover the effect of the wording on Leo.

The testator did not specify whether or not the beneficiary is to pay the costs of packing/transport/insurance and so underlying legal rules will apply: Leo will have to bear these expenses whether or not Mark intended this result (see **8.4.2**).

Clause 4

This gift is a pecuniary legacy (ie a gift of money).

It is also a general legacy because the executrix is not told which source of estate funds to use in paying the £5,000 (see **8.2.2**).

See Clause 2 to discover the effect of the words 'free of all taxes' on Philip.

Philip's gift is a vested (ie absolute) gift because he will be entitled to the gift if he is alive at the testator's death. The wording attaches no express condition which he must fulfil to qualify for the property. Even if the word 'absolutely' had been omitted, this gift would still be a vested gift.

Clause 4 ends with an infant receipt clause ('AND I DIRECT . . . discharge to her'). The draftsman has ascertained from Mark King that his godson, Philip, is a minor and it is possible that the beneficiary may still be under 18 when the testator dies. After the executrix has administered the estate and is ready to distribute the assets to the beneficiaries, she will want to know who can give her a valid receipt for Philip's £5,000 (ie a receipt to confirm that she has discharged this part of her obligations as a PR by handing the correct amount of money over to someone entitled to receive it). A minor cannot give a good receipt for capital, nor can the minor's parent or guardian do so on the minor's behalf, unless the will specifically permits this. Consequently, for convenience, Clause 4 includes an infant receipt clause.

Clause 5

Clause 5 is the residue clause (ie a gift of the rest of the estate) which is always the last gift in the will. It is usually the main gift of property in a will.

In this clause residue is defined to include both realty and personalty. Realty (or real property) is generally taken to mean freehold land; personalty (or personal property) generally covers all other property capable of passing by will, including chattels (ie movable property) and leasehold land.

The executrix is instructed firstly to pay off all the deceased's debts (ie any bills and/or tax owing when he died), the cost of his funeral and the testamentary expenses (ie expenses of administering the estate). Then she should pay the non-residuary legacies and finally transfer what remains of the property passing under this will ('net residue') to herself as residuary beneficiary.

Attestation clause

The will concludes with an attestation clause which describes how the will was executed. Such a clause plays an important part in complying with the formalities needed for a valid will. This is the shortest acceptable version of an attestation clause and is appropriate for use in most situations. In unusual cases (eg where a testator does not himself sign the will) the wording of the attestation clause must be adapted (see **13.3.2**).

4.2.4 Comments on drafting style

Punctuation and capital letters
This will adopts the convention of not using punctuation but does provide 'markers' by including some words and phrases in capital letters (see **3.3.3**).

Functional and superfluous words
Distinguish between superfluous words, which are perhaps being included out of habit to give a traditional legal flavour to the document, and other words which perform a legal function.

For example, in the opening words 'HEREBY' is not necessary. Mark King could have said simply: 'I REVOKE all former wills . . .' By adding 'HEREBY' he is effectively saying: 'by this will I am revoking all former wills', but this fact is obvious. Similarly instead of referring to 'the said legacy' in Clause 4, the words 'this legacy' would have had the same effect in linking the infant receipt clause to the £5,000 legacy.

By contrast, the word 'joint' in the attestation clause has an important function as it indicates that the witnesses were present at the same time when the testator executed his will. This is a statutory requirement for execution of a will (see **13.4.1**).

4.3 JULIA GOLD'S WILL

4.3.1 Background

Julia Gold, a civil servant from Weyford, has instructed her solicitor to draft her will. She is married to Michael and has three children, Ian and Carol (who are adults) and James (who is a minor). She also has a sister, Barbara, who has two children.

She wants to give a Victoria Cross won by her father to James when he reaches 25, and £1,000 to each of Barbara's children. The rest of her property is to go to her husband provided that he survives her. If he does not, she wants her children to have that property equally.

Her solicitor has encouraged her to consider what should happen to that property if not only her husband but any of her children should also die before she does. She has decided that if any such child has children who survive Julia and live to be 18 years old, they should take their dead parent's share, divided equally between them.

Her solicitor has advised her that in order to carry out her wishes it will be necessary to set up a trust of residue. Julia wants Michael, Ian and Carol to administer her estate and to act as trustees, and she would like them to have fairly extensive administrative powers.

4.3.2 Text

This is the last will of me, Julia Gold, civil servant of High Trees Farm, Longdale, Weyford, Blankshire

1. I revoke all former testamentary dispositions.
2. I desire that my body shall be cremated.
3. I appoint my husband, Michael Peter Gold, and my children Ian Gold and Carol Hill (hereinafter called 'my trustees', which expression where the context so admits shall include the trustees or trustee hereof for the time being) to be the executors and trustees of this my will.
4. I give free of tax and the cost of insurance to my youngest son James Gold on attaining the age of 25 years the Victoria Cross medal won by my father.
5. I give a legacy of £1,000 free of tax to each of the children of my sister Barbara Hunt who shall be living at my death.
6. My trustees shall hold the rest of my estate on trust either to sell it or (if they think fit and without being liable for loss) to retain all or any of it and:

    (a) to pay debts, tax, funeral, testamentary and administrative expenses and legacies;
    (b) to pay the residue to my husband absolutely, if he shall survive me by thirty days; but if he does not so survive me, or if this gift shall fail for any reason, then
    (c) to pay the residue to such of my children as shall survive me, and if more than one in equal shares, provided always that if any child of mine shall die in my lifetime, leaving a child or children living at my death who attains or attain the age of 18 years or marries or marry under that age, then such last mentioned child or children shall take by substitution (and if more than one in equal shares) that share of my residue which his, her or their parent would have taken if he or she had survived me.

7. My trustees shall have the following powers in addition to their powers under general law:

    (a) to pay to, or apply for the benefit of, any beneficiary as my trustees think fit the whole or any part of the income from that part of my estate to which he is entitled or may in future be entitled;
    (b) to pay to, or apply for the benefit of, any beneficiary as my trustees think fit the whole or any part of the capital to which that beneficiary is entitled or may in future be entitled; and I leave it to the discretion of my trustees as to whether any such beneficiary shall, on becoming absolutely entitled, bring into account any payments received under this sub-clause;
    (c) to exercise the power of appropriation conferred by section 41 of the Administration of Estates Act 1925 without obtaining any of the consents required by the wording of that section, and even though one or more of them may be beneficially interested in the appropriation;

(d) to invest as freely as if they were an absolute beneficial owner, and to use trust money in or towards the purchase or improvement or repair of property for occupation as a residence by a beneficiary;

(e) to insure any asset of my estate on such terms as they think fit, and to pay premiums out of income or capital, and to use any insurance money received either to restore the asset in question or as if this money were the proceeds of sale;

(f) in any case where they have an obligation or discretion under this my will or general law to pay income or capital to or for the benefit of an infant, to meet that obligation or exercise that discretion by paying either to a parent or guardian of the infant or to the infant personally, if he shall have attained the age of 16, so that their respective receipts shall be a full discharge to my trustees who shall not be required to see to the application of any payments so made.

In witness whereof I have hereunto set my hand this   day of   199[ ]

Signed by the above-named   )
Julia Gold as her last will   )
in the presence of us present)
at the same time who at her   )
request in her presence and   )
in the presence of each other)
have hereunto subscribed our)
names as witnesses   )

4.3.3 Commentary

Opening words and Clause 1

The testatrix is clearly identified and so is the nature of the document. The phrase 'last will' has the same effect as the phrase 'last will and testament' used in Mark King's will (see **4.2**).

The precise date on which the testatrix executes the will must appear somewhere in the text. In Mark King's will, the blanks for completion appeared as part of the opening words. In this will they appear in the last paragraph, immediately before the attestation clause.

There is an express revocation of any former wills or codicils (collectively known as testamentary dispositions) which appears in a separate clause (Clause 1), rather than as part of the opening words.

Clause 2

This testatrix has included a direction about the disposal of her body since she has a definite preference. Not all wills contain such a clause (see **5.3**).

Clause 3

The testatrix appoints her husband and her two adult children to be both executors (to administer her estate) and trustees (ie trustees of the trust to be created in the residue clause of the will). The trust will come into operation when the administration of the estate has been completed and it is usual and convenient to appoint the same people to fulfil both roles. The children named are adults; minor children would not have been an appropriate choice.

It is not necessary to give the full address of close family members where there is unlikely to be any difficulty over identifying and contacting them at the testatrix's death.

The executors and trustees are appointed by name, and then collectively defined as 'my trustees'. This is a convenient way of referring in later clauses to Michael, Ian and Carol in their dual role as executors and trustees. The definition is then widened to include any replacement or additional executor/trustee who may be appointed in the future.

Clause 4

This gift is a specific legacy of a particular item. It is a contingent gift (as opposed to a vested/absolute gift), because the beneficiary has to fulfil the express condition set out in the wording in order to qualify for the property. In this case the contingency is the commonly chosen condition of attaining a specified age.

When the executors have completed the administration of the estate, they will transfer the medal to James if he is already 25 at that stage. If not, they will hold it for him until he reaches the age of 25. If he survives Julia but dies before he is 25, the gift to him will fail and the medal will pass with the residue of Julia's estate.

The draftsman has also specified that the beneficiary will not be required to pay any IHT and/or insurance expenses relating to this gift. They will be paid out of the residue of the estate instead.

Clause 5

Clause 5 provides for each member of a carefully described class of people (ie those children of Julia's sister, Barbara, who are alive at Julia's death) to receive £1,000. It is a vested pecuniary legacy. The gift could have been made to named individuals, but it is preferable to describe them as members of a class, to avoid, for example, excluding a child born after the date of the will (see **9.2.2**).

Again the draftsman has specified that the beneficiaries will not have to pay any IHT due on their money.

As there appears to be a possibility of a minor being entitled to a legacy on Julia's death, an infant receipt clause is included (see Clause 7(f) in the will and commentary below).

Clause 6

Clause 6 creates an express trust of residue. The trustees are given a series of instructions. They are told to hold 'the rest of my estate' (a simple but adequate definition of residue) expressly on trust. They are given express powers either to sell or to retain the assets in the estate. The phrase 'without being liable for loss' means that a residuary beneficiary is not entitled to compensation if the trustees' decision not to sell reduces the value of the assets in residue.

As in Mark King's will, the first requirement is to pay all the deceased's debts, any tax bills and assorted expenses and then to pay the non-residuary legacies (given in Clauses 4 and 5). The remaining property passing under this will should be given to Julia's husband if he survives her by 30 days. This wording is known as a 'survivorship clause'. It allows a testator to control who will inherit the property if his 'first choice' beneficiary predeceases him or dies within a specified short time of him. In certain circumstances it carries IHT advantages and also permits greater administrative convenience (see **9.2.1**).

A substitutional gift should follow to cover the situation where the husband does not survive by the specified period or where the gift fails for any other reason (eg if Julia and Michael divorce after Julia has executed this will (see **15.5**)). The importance of this 'fallback' provision is to exercise control and prevent a partial intestacy occurring. This substitutional gift is to a carefully described class of people ('such of my children as shall survive me') instead of to her existing children by name, to cover the possibility that she might have more children before she dies and would want them included in this gift.

If the substitutional gift takes effect, then the net residue will be divided equally between Julia's surviving children in the form of vested/absolute gifts. However, there is a further express substitutional clause ('provided always ... had survived me'). This is designed to cover the situation where one or more of Julia's children predecease her but leave a child or children of their own who is or are still alive at Julia's death. The will specifies that, in this situation, any such grandchildren who fulfil the condition of age or marriage (since theirs is a contingent gift) will divide their own dead parent's share of residue equally amongst themselves. This is known as 'per stirpes' substitution of grandchildren (see **9.2.3**) and is an example of how the draftsman should anticipate possible future problems and include express provision to avoid them.

Whether or not some or all of the residue has to be held on trust will depend on how events unfold after Julia's death. The executors may be able to distribute all of the net residue as soon as the administration of the estate has been completed if all the residuary beneficiaries are absolutely entitled to it. However if, for example, one of Julia's children dies before her, leaving a son who is still under 18 at Julia's death, then when the executors distribute Julia's estate at the end of administration, they will hold that grandson's contingent share of net residue as trustees for him until he reaches 18 (or marries under 18) and becomes absolutely entitled to it.

Clause 7
This clause contains a series of express powers for the executors/trustees to facilitate their administration of the estate and any trust that may arise. These express powers in the will extend the powers which executors and trustees are given by statute.

Administrative powers are examined in detail in Chapter 10 and the paragraphs referred to below explain the meaning and purpose of each of the powers contained in Clause 7:

(a) application of income for maintenance (see **10.3.5**);
(b) advancement of capital (see **10.3.6**);
(c) appropriation (ie transferring an actual item, rather than its cash equivalent, to a beneficiary) (see **10.2.2**);
(d) investment (see **10.3.2**);
(e) insurance (see **10.2.3**);
(f) infant receipt clause (see **10.2.4**).

Attestation clause
This is an alternative and longer version of the normal attestation clause.

4.3.4 Comments on drafting style

Since Julia Gold's will is longer and more complex than Mark King's will (because it requires a trust of residue and various express administrative provisions), it uses traditional language but introduces punctuation as an aid to comprehension.

4.4 CODICIL TO MARK KING'S WILL

4.4.1 Background

Assume that Mark King executed his will as set out in **4.2.2** above on 12 April 1992 and that his godson, Philip, was killed in a road accident in December 1992. If Mark left his will unchanged, the gift of £5,000 to Philip would lapse because Philip would not be alive at Mark's death. The £5,000 originally intended for Philip would become part of the residue of Mark's estate and pass to Mark's sister because she is the residuary beneficiary under the will.

If Mark decided that he wanted the £5,000 to go to a local registered charity (the Weyford Endeavour League) instead of Frances, he could either execute a new will or, because only one clause of the will has to be amended by a minor alteration, make a codicil to his existing will.

If Mark decided to take the opportunity to review his existing will and to consider more complex provisions (eg to cater for the situation that would occur if his sister predeceased him), then he would be advised to make a new will because extra changes (eg to the clause appointing his executrix and also to the residue clause) would be needed. A wholesale revision of a will is best done through a new will.

The rest of this chapter assumes that Mark has decided on a short codicil.

4.4.2 Text

I Mark King of 20 High Street Weyford Blankshire teacher declare this to be a first codicil to my will dated 12 April 1992.

1. I revoke the legacy of £5000 given to my godson Philip Smith by clause 4 of my will and I now give the sum of £5000 to Weyford Endeavour League ('the Charity') for its general charitable purposes and I direct that the receipt of the person who appears to be the treasurer or other proper officer of the Charity shall be a sufficient discharge to my executrix and I further direct that if at my death the Charity has ceased to exist or has amalgamated with another charity or has changed its name my executrix shall pay this legacy to the charitable organisation which she in her discretion considers most nearly fulfils the objects of the Charity.
2. In all other respects I confirm my will.

In witness whereof I have hereunto set my hand this   day of 199[ ]

Signed by the above named Mark King	)
as a first codicil to his will dated	)
12 April 1992 in the	)
presence of us present at the same	)
time who at his request in his	)
presence and in the presence of each	)
other have hereunto subscribed our	)
names as witnesses	)

4.4.3 Commentary

Opening words

The testator and the nature of the document are both clearly identified and there is a specific reference to the will to which this codicil relates. Details of the date on which this codicil is executed will be completed at the end of the document.

Clause 1

The gift to Mark's godson Philip is expressly revoked with a cross-reference to the relevant clause in the original will.

The substitute gift to the charity is then set out. There is no need to specify who is to pay any IHT because gifts to charities are exempt from IHT. However, gifts to charities do require careful wording (see **8.3.3**) so that the clause contains instructions on who can give a valid receipt for the money on behalf of the charity and what is to happen to the money if the charity changes or goes out of existence at some time between the execution of this codicil and Mark King's death.

Note the definition of the Weyford Endeavour League as 'the Charity' and the precise references to it, as distinct from the general references to 'charity' or 'charitable'. Accurate use of upper and lower case letters is necessary.

Clause 2

Once the draftsman has set out the changes to the will, it is important to confirm expressly that all the other parts of the will are to remain unchanged.

Testimonium and attestation clause

The date could have appeared as part of the opening words but in this codicil it appears at the end as part of the testimonium ('In witness whereof ...'). An attestation clause (suitably amplified) is important to indicate compliance with the formalities for valid execution (see **13.4.3**).

Chapter 5

COMMENCEMENT AND REVOCATION CLAUSES, AND DISPOSAL OF BODY

5.1 COMMENCEMENT

SPECIMEN CLAUSES

(1) This is the last will and testament of me [*full name*] of [*current address*]

or (2) This will dated this [ ] day of [ ] 19[ ] is made by me [*full name*] of [*current address*]

or (3) I [*full name*] of [*current address*] revoke all former testamentary dispositions and declare this to be my last will which I make this [ ] day of [ ] 19 [ ].

COMMENTARY

Identifying the testator
The main purpose of this clause (also referred to as 'the opening words') is to identify the testator. It should therefore include the testator's full name and current address.

If the testator uses a name other than his real name or owns property in a different name (eg a married woman holding assets in her maiden name) it is helpful to include a phrase such as 'formerly known as ...' or 'sometimes known as ...' in order to simplify matters when applying for a grant of representation after the client's death.

Details of the testator's occupation or a description of his status (eg retired company director) are often included to help identify him beyond all doubt. Traditionally, non-working women were described by reference to their marital status eg 'spinster' or 'married woman'. This is now outmoded and likely to offend.

Identifying the document
A reference to the document as the testator's 'last will' or (more traditionally) his 'last will and testament' helps to demonstrate that the testator had the necessary 'general intention' to make a will. This is one of the requirements for a will to be valid (see **13.3**). There is no legal difference between these phrases but neither one of them of itself automatically revokes any earlier will or codicil, and so an express revocation clause should always be included in the will, either as part of the opening words (see specimen clause (3) above) or as a separate clause (see **5.2**).

Blanks for the date on which the will is to be executed should be included either in the opening words or at the end of the will.

Chapter 5 contents
Commencement
The revocation clause
Directions about disposal of body

Forthcoming marriage
If the testator is shortly to be married, he can (with appropriate wording) make a will expressly in expectation of that marriage, to circumvent the rule that a subsequent marriage automatically revokes any existing will (see **14.3.2**).

5.2 THE REVOCATION CLAUSE

SPECIMEN CLAUSES

(1) I [hereby] revoke all former wills

or (2) I [hereby] revoke all former [wills and] testamentary dispositions

COMMENTARY

Express revocation
A solicitor should always include an express revocation clause (either as part of the opening words or in a separate paragraph) in every will he prepares, even if he believes that he is drafting the client's very first will. The purpose of this precaution is to rule out doubt, should it transpire that an earlier will and/or codicil exists.

Without an express revocation clause, the current document would impliedly revoke any earlier will or codicil to the extent that it is inconsistent with, or merely repeats, the provisions of that earlier document. (For detailed explanation, see **14.3.1**.) Clearly, it is better to specify revocation expressly in all cases, rather than risk complex law affecting the will.

Terminology
In a revocation clause the word 'wills' includes 'codicils' and the phrase 'testamentary dispositions' includes wills, codicils and even privileged wills. (A privileged will is an informal will made by a soldier or airman on actual military service or a sailor at sea. Such a will need not comply with the normal rules and requirements for validity.) Generally, the draftsman's choice of wording for a revocation clause is entirely a matter of personal style unless he believes that it is important to cater for any earlier privileged will which the testator may have made.

5.3 DIRECTIONS ABOUT DISPOSAL OF BODY

SPECIMEN CLAUSES

(1) I desire that my body [shall not be cremated] [shall be buried in...]

or (2) I request that my body shall be cremated [at...] [and my ashes deposited at...] [or scattered at...]

or (3) I desire that my body or any part of it may be used for therapeutic purposes including corneal grafting and organ transplantation or for medical education or medical research in accordance with the provisions of the Human Tissue Act 1961 and the Anatomy Act 1984 [and in due course the institution receiving my body shall have it cremated]

COMMENTARY

Legal effect
These provisions, if included in the will, have no binding legal effect on the executors and for that reason are expressed as requests or directions only.

Practical considerations
Specimen Clause (3) may be adapted to specify a part or parts of the body that the testator wishes to donate for medical education, research or transplant.

If the testator does have any particular wishes or preference, it is sensible not only to include details in the will but also for him to carry an appropriate donor card and to notify his doctor and the executors and close family or friends who are most likely to be making the practical arrangements immediately after his death. Such separate, non-testamentary notification is sufficient, even without a clause in the will, but it can be reassuring for family and friends to see confirmation of these wishes after the testator's death as part of the formal will.

'Therapeutic purposes' involves use of the body or organ(s) for the treatment of a medical patient. 'Medical education' includes medical students' anatomy and dissection classes.

In the case of all donations to medical education and research or to transplant programmes there are various formalities to be completed on death. It is therefore helpful if the solicitor obtains the relevant forms and telephone numbers (of HM Inspector of Anatomy (medical education and research) and/or of the relevant section of the Department of Health (transplant programmes)) when preparing the will, and keeps them together with the will until needed.

Chapter 6

APPOINTMENT OF EXECUTORS AND TRUSTEES

6.1 WHY APPOINT EXECUTORS?

If an individual is taking the trouble to make a will, it is sensible for him to choose his own executors (or executor/trustees) and appoint them expressly in that will, instead of leaving it to persons eligible under the relevant statutory rules (see Chapter 22) to apply after his death to be his administrators.

6.2 ARE TRUSTEES ALSO REQUIRED?

If there is any possibility that, when the estate has been administered, the executors will not be able to distribute the residue of the estate to the beneficiaries (eg because they are minors), an express trust should be created.

If the will does not contain a trust, then the testator need only appoint one or more people to be his executor(s) to administer and distribute his estate; obviously he will not need any trustees. However, if a trust is to be created under the terms of the will, then the testator must appoint both executors to administer and distribute his estate and trustees to run the trust which will come into effect once administration is complete.

6.3 DUAL CAPACITY AND TRANSITION

If executors and trustees are required, it is usual and convenient to appoint the same people to undertake both roles. When the administration has been completed and the executors are distributing the estate, there is a transition. The executors transfer that part of the estate which is going to be held on trust over to themselves as trustees to hold on the express trusts set out in the wording of the will.

The trust will come to an end when:

(1) all the beneficiaries of the trust have become absolutely entitled (which may only happen over a period of time, eg as children grow up and fulfil an age-related contingency); and
(2) the trustees have obtained a good receipt for all the trust property showing that they have discharged their obligations regarding distribution by handing over the correct trust assets, in their correct shares, to the correct recipients.

6.4 HOW MANY TO CHOOSE

The testator can appoint any number of executors, but since a maximum of four people can take out the grant (see **22.2.4**) there is no advantage in appointing more than four.

Chapter 6 contents
Why appoint executors?
Are trustees also required?
Dual capacity and transition
How many to choose
Whom to choose
Individuals
Solicitors or other professionals
Trust corporations
The Public Trustee

One executor is sufficient to administer the estate. In a small, straightforward estate the major beneficiary is often appointed sole executor/trix. However, a single appointee (unless a firm or institution) might predecease the testator or die before completing the administration of the estate, and so testators often appoint at least two executors, and may even include provision for substitutes. In addition, if the testator's spouse is to be appointed as executor/trix (or one of several), then consideration should be given to the effect of a subsequent divorce on such an appointment (see **14.3.2**). The Wills Act 1837, s 18A (as substituted) provides that, in such a case, the will takes effect as if the appointment of the former spouse as executor or executor/trustee were omitted.

If the executors will also be trustees, it is convenient to appoint two executor/trustees because two trustees (or a trust corporation) are needed to give a good receipt for the proceeds of sale if land held subject to a trust is sold.

Under normal circumstances, the appointment of executors results in all the testator's property which is capable of passing under the will vesting in those executors on his death. However, it is possible for the testator to limit the appointment of executors to certain property only. The most obvious example would be where an academic, novelist, poet or playwright appoints a set of literary executors to administer his literary estate. He would usually also appoint general executors to be responsible for his general estate. The testator should be advised that such an appointment will affect probate; ie two grants will be required: one limited to the special property and one for the general estate (save and except the special property) (see **22.6.2**).

6.5 WHOM TO CHOOSE

The testator can appoint any combination of the following:

(1) individuals;
(2) solicitors or other professionals;
(3) banks or other trust corporations.

The solicitor may be asked to advise the testator on the relative advantages and disadvantages of the various alternatives appropriate to his circumstances, to enable the testator to make an informed choice.

The solicitor must be familiar with all the relevant legal and practical considerations and be able to draft an effective appointment clause.

Although the testator could in principle appoint the Public Trustee (see **6.9**), in normal circumstances this would not be an appropriate choice.

6.6 INDIVIDUALS

Suitability and willingness
The testator can choose relatives and/or friends whom he knows and trusts to do the job well, and who will probably already know the family and beneficiaries and will be able to communicate easily with them. It is important to choose someone who has the time and aptitude to fulfil the role and is able to cope with responsibility. It is sensible for a testator to consult his intended choices to check that they are prepared to act when he dies, otherwise unnecessary work and expense could result

after his death if it emerges that the chosen executors are not willing to be involved in the administration work.

If more than one executor is to be appointed, it is important that they are able to work together harmoniously. The testator should also bear in mind the possibility of jealousies among family and beneficiaries who are not selected.

Capacity to take a grant of probate

Although anyone can be appointed an executor, certain people (such as a minor, a bankrupt or a convicted criminal) cannot take out a grant of probate. It is therefore sensible for the testator not to choose such individuals, because to do so would only create unnecessary work and expense for the estate.

Cost to the estate

Unless he is also to be one of the beneficiaries, a private individual as executor will take only his expenses out of the estate (as opposed to charging for the work done and time spent). This might seem a clear advantage (ie keeping down the costs of administration), but the potential complication is that a private individual may not have sufficient expertise to complete the administration without employing a solicitor or other professional to help and advise. The professional's bill would then be an additional administration expense to be paid out of the estate.

SPECIMEN CLAUSES

(1) APPOINTMENT OF EXECUTORS

I appoint [full name] of [address] and [full name] of [address] to be the executors of my will

(2) APPOINTMENT OF EXECUTORS AND TRUSTEES

I appoint [full name] of [address] and [full name] of [address] (hereinafter called 'my Trustees' which expression shall include the trustees for the time being) to be the executors and trustees of my will

(3) APPOINTMENT INCLUDING SUBSTITUTION

I APPOINT [*full name*] of [*address*] and [*full name*] of [*address*] to be the executors and trustees of my will but in case one or both of them shall predecease me or shall renounce probate or refuse or be unable to act then I appoint [*full name*] of [*address*] and [*full name*] of [*address*] in that order to fill any vacancy which may arise AND I DECLARE that the expression 'my Trustees' shall include the executors and trustees for the time being

ALTERNATIVELY:

I appoint my [husband/wife] [*name*] to be the sole executor/executrix of my will but if this appointment shall fail for any reason then I appoint [*full name*] of [*address*] and [*full name*] of [*address*] to be the executors and trustees

6.7 SOLICITORS OR OTHER PROFESSIONALS

6.7.1 Legal and practical considerations

Professional executor or merely adviser?
The testator may appoint one or more professionals (such as solicitors or accountants) either as named individuals or as a firm to be his executor(s). It is important to distinguish clearly between a solicitor (or other professional) who is himself an executor (perhaps along with other professionals or lay individuals) and the solicitor who has merely been employed by the executors to help and advise on the administration.

Advantages and disadvantages
The obvious attraction of choosing professionals as executors is their experience and expertise. They may also be familiar with the testator's affairs, and possibly with the family and beneficiaries.

The disadvantage is that they will charge for their work. However, a non-professional executor will usually employ a solicitor to assist with the administration work and so there may be no significant difference in cost to the estate.

Professional conduct considerations
When a solicitor is advising a client about an appropriate choice of executor, the solicitor must be aware of his professional conduct obligations and, in particular, the Solicitors' Practice Rules 1990, r 1 which states:

> 'A solicitor shall not do anything in the course of practising as a solicitor, or permit another person to do anything on his or her behalf, which compromises or impairs or is likely to compromise or impair any of the following:
>
> (a) the solicitor's independence or integrity;
> (b) a person's freedom to instruct a solicitor of his or her choice;
> (c) the solicitor's duty to act in the best interests of the client;
> (d) the good repute of the solicitor or of the solicitors' profession;
> (e) the solicitor's proper standard of work;
> (f) the solicitor's duty to the Court.'

The solicitor is under a professional duty to give his client independent advice which is in the client's own best interests. The solicitor must not let self-interest distort his advice to his client. However, if the solicitor is careful to compare the relative advantages and disadvantages of himself (or his firm) as professional executors with other appropriate alternatives for the estate, he will not be in breach of his obligation to give impartial advice.

Appointing a firm rather than an individual
The testator may want a particular professional person to administer his estate (eg the solicitor he has known and consulted often over the years). Alternatively the testator can appoint that person's firm (rather than a named individual). The reason for taking the latter course is to avoid the gap which would arise if a named person was appointed but had died, retired or left the firm by the time of the testator's death.

The practical impact on the administration of appointing the firm instead of the individual will be minimal. If the individual is still with the firm, he will be able to act (and will probably delegate various aspects of the administration work to colleagues within the firm in the same way as he would have done even if appointed as a named individual). If the preferred individual is no longer available, then other partners from the firm will act.

Drafting

If the appointment is to be of a firm of professionals, the clause must be carefully worded to overcome two potential problems:

(1) The appointment of a firm is in fact the appointment of the partners as at the date the will is executed, unless the will specifies something different. It is more convenient to specify that the appointment is to be of the partners as at the date of the testator's death because this avoids the possible complication of some of the partners having died or retired or left the firm between the execution of the will and the testator's eventual death.

(2) The firm may change its name or amalgamate with another firm between the execution of the will and the date of the testator's death. It is helpful to specify what is to happen in such an event. Usually the testator will want to appoint the future partners of the firm in its new name and form.

It is also common for the testator to request that only two of the partners actually take the grant of probate, but this is not crucial because if the testator does not express any preference then this matter is simply left to the partners' discretion, and they would normally decide on an application for a grant by two of their number.

The draftsman should also consider the possible effect on the appointment if a solicitors' practice is later incorporated. Under the Solicitors' Incorporated Practice Rules 1988, solicitors may practise as a company limited by shares or as an unlimited company (subject to various conditions). An incorporated practice will, in effect, practise as a solicitor. If partners in a firm of solicitors are appointed as executors or executor/trustees (either by using the firm's name or by reference to their position as partners in the firm) and that practice is later incorporated, then it has been suggested that such an appointment would be rendered ineffective. Such a risk should be avoided.

SPECIMEN CLAUSE

> I appoint the partners at the date of my death [in the firm of] [incorporated solicitors' practice known as] [name] Solicitors of [address] or in the firm or incorporated solicitors' practice which at the date carries on its practice (hereinafter called 'My Trustees') to be the executors and trustees of my will and I express the wish that two and only two of them shall prove my will and act initially in its trusts.

6.7.2 Charging clause

Purpose

If a professional person or firm is to be an executor or executor/trustee, that person or firm will want to charge for their time and work involved. However, any executor or trustee is under a fiduciary duty not to profit from his appointment unless expressly permitted to do so. Therefore, the professional cannot charge his profit costs unless the will contains an express charging clause. Without such a clause he can reclaim only his out-of-pocket expenses like any non-professional executor.

If the will did not contain such a clause the professional would be unlikely to accept the appointment for commercial reasons. Inclusion of the clause does not oblige the professional to charge, but absence of it means that he is not entitled to charge even if he wants to. Consequently, if the testator wants a professional executor it is appropriate to leave open the opportunity for the professional to charge, by including a charging clause in the will. The draftsman must explain the purpose and effect of the clause to the testator and obtain his authority to include it.

Some firms always include a professional charging clause in every will, even where no professional is being appointed, to cover the possibility of a professional being appointed after the testator's death as an additional or replacement trustee.

Drafting
The wording of a charging clause should deal with the following three issues:

(1) authority for the professional to charge;
(2) an explanation of what type or types of work he will be entitled to charge for; and
(3) the rate at which he is permitted to charge.

To be commercially viable, the clause should allow a solicitor (or other professional) to charge at his normal commercial rate both for what the executor or executor/trustee does personally and also for any work delegated within his firm. The wording should expressly include both work which only a professional person is equipped to do and also the routine work which a lay person could have done.

> SPECIMEN CLAUSE
> I DECLARE THAT if any of my [Trustees] is a solicitor or other person engaged in any profession or business then that [trustee] shall be entitled to charge and be paid all his usual professional or other charges for any services provided or time spent by him or his firm in connection with the administration of my estate [or the trusts of my will] including anything which [a trustee] not engaged in a profession or business could have done personally and on the same basis as if he were not one of my [Trustees] but had been employed to carry out the work on their behalf

Position in the will
The charging clause is often included early in the will as part of the clause which appoints the professional executor. For example, **6.7.2** sets out a sample clause appointing a firm of solicitors, and the charging clause could be added as a continuation of that paragraph. Alternatively, the charging clause can be included separately towards the end of the will as one of the administrative powers (see **10.4.1**). The choice is a matter of personal stylistic preference.

Witnesses
If a professional executor has the benefit of a charging clause in the will, it is important that neither he nor any of his partners witness the will when the testator executes it. If any of them were to witness the will, the charging clause would be void. The Wills Act 1837, s 15 (see **13.5.2**) provides (inter alia) that a gift fails if the beneficiary witnesses the will; a charging clause is treated as a legacy for the purposes of s 15.

6.8 TRUST CORPORATIONS

6.8.1 Legal and practical considerations

Alone or jointly?

The testator can appoint a trust corporation to be his executor/trustee. The trust corporations most frequently appointed are the trustee departments of the major high street banks. Although technically a trust corporation could be appointed to act together with individuals and/or professionals as executors/trustees, it is more usual for a trust corporation to be appointed to act alone.

Advantages and disadvantages

A testator may be attracted to the idea of appointing a trust corporation if, for example, his estate is large or complex and will need detailed and/or long-term financial supervision (although other professionals can also provide such financial expertise).

When an individual is an executor/trustee, there is always a risk that the individual may die. The choice of an institution (or similarly a professional firm) which is unlikely to go out of business avoids this risk.

On the other hand the family and beneficiaries may find it less easy to communicate with a large impersonal body.

A bank's method of charging usually makes it a more expensive alternative. The bill for administering an estate is usually based on a percentage of the value of the estate plus, in some cases, a further management and/or activity fee, and is sometimes subject to minimum charges. There are often separate fees for trustee work.

6.8.2 Professional conduct considerations

Sometimes the testator will approach his bank direct in the first instance, and it will be the bank manager who approaches the solicitor on behalf of that testator, asking the solicitor to draft the will. It is important for the solicitor to remember in these circumstances that his client is the testator and not the bank.

Moreover, it is part of the solicitor's professional duty to ensure that any will he prepares complies with the testator's wishes. Thus when instructions have been received indirectly, via a bank or other third party, the solicitor should make direct contact with the testator, to confirm that those instructions do indeed accurately represent his wishes (see **11.1**). The solicitor may also need to give the client independent advice on various matters relating to the will.

6.8.3 Drafting and advice

If a trust corporation is to be appointed, the draftsman should always obtain the institution's own standard published clause dealing with the terms and conditions on which it is prepared to be appointed. He must then explain the significance of the wording to the testator and obtain his authority to include the clause in the will.

These standard clauses usually impose on the estate whatever are the corporation's last set of standard terms and conditions and scales of remuneration to be published before the date of the testator's death.

6.9 THE PUBLIC TRUSTEE

The office of Public Trustee was created primarily to provide a 'fallback' choice of executor in the absence of any other viable appointee, although there are restrictions on when the Public Trustee can act (eg he cannot normally accept an appointment which would entail running a business, or run a trust which is exclusively for religious or charitable purposes).

Although a testator can appoint the Public Trustee as executor, this would not be an appropriate option in most cases because a solicitor will normally be able to offer the same service more conveniently and at a more competitive rate.

Chapter 7

APPOINTMENT OF GUARDIANS

7.1 INTRODUCTION

If the testator has any minor children, he should consider who will be responsible for any of them who are still under 18 at his death. Equally, he may be concerned about any future children he might have who might be under 18 at his death.

The law of guardianship is governed by the Children Act 1989. The statutory references in this chapter are to that Act.

Chapter 7 contents
Introduction
Method of appointment
Effect of appointment
Practical considerations

7.2 METHOD OF APPOINTMENT

Under s 5(3), any parent who has parental responsibility for his child may appoint one or more individuals to be the child's guardian(s). An unmarried father does not have parental responsibility unless he acquires it by court order, or by formal agreement with the mother, or marries the mother.

The appointment must be made in writing, dated and signed by the parent. It need not be by will, but a clause in a will is sufficient (even if the will is signed by someone other than the testator, on his behalf and at his direction: see **13.4.1**).

The appointment can be revoked in writing, provided the revocation is signed and dated, and even if the original appointment was in a will. (Other changes to the will would have to be made more formally by codicil or another will.)

7.3 EFFECT OF APPOINTMENT

By virtue of s 5(7), the appointment generally takes effect on the appointing parent's death, provided that there is no surviving parent with parental responsibility for the child at that time.

If, at the appointor's death, the child does have a surviving parent with parental responsibility, the appointment generally takes effect only on the death of that parent (unless there was a sole residence order in favour of the appointor in force at death).

Where the parents are married and there has been no legal dispute over the children, both parents retain parental responsibility until their respective deaths. Therefore, in such cases, if a testator (eg the father) includes a clause in his will appointing a guardian for his minor children, the appointment will only take effect at his death if the other parent is by then already dead. If the mother survives, his appointment only takes effect on her eventual death.

If the mother has appointed a different person as guardian for the children, both appointees will share parental responsibility, but in normal cases it is clearly better to avoid such a situation (see **7.4**).

The position is different for unmarried parents.

The court retains overriding jurisdiction, which could be relevant in the case of an unresolved family dispute over the care of the minor children.

7.4 PRACTICAL CONSIDERATIONS

Clearly, it is preferable for spouses or cohabitees with parental responsibility to appoint the same people (perhaps a couple with experience of bringing up children) as guardians for their minor children. Parents often feel that members of the family or friends who are already well known to, and liked by, the children are the most appropriate choice.

In every case, it is important that the candidates be consulted in advance to ensure that they are willing to act, and also that sensible provision is made for the cost of the children's upbringing.

One common financial arrangement is to appoint the guardians (perhaps together with a solicitor or accountant) as the trustees of a trust fund set up by the will for the children, and to give the trustees suitable powers to draw on the capital and income of this fund to meet the needs and expenses of the children (see **10.3.4** and **10.3.5**).

SPECIMEN CLAUSE
> I appoint [*full name*] of [*address*] [and [*full name*] of [*address*] jointly] to be the guardian[s] of any of my children who are under eighteen [at the date of my death] [at the date of death of my husband/wife]

Chapter 8

LEGACIES AND DEVISES

8.1 INTRODUCTION

Legacies and devises are the traditional terms used to describe gifts of property. A 'legacy' normally describes a gift (or 'bequest') of chattels or pure personalty; a 'devise' is used with reference to land. The word 'gift' is equally acceptable.

8.2 TYPES OF GIFT

8.2.1 Specific

A specific legacy is a gift of a particular item, or group of items of property owned by the testator, distinguished in the will from other property of the same kind, for example: 'I give my ruby and pearl brooch to X'; 'I give all my jewellery to X'. The main characteristic of a specific legacy or devise is that such gifts are subject to the doctrine of ademption; ie they fail if the property no longer forms part of the testator's estate at the time of death, usually because he has sold it or given it away during his lifetime (see **8.4** and **15.2**).

8.2.2 General

A general legacy is a gift of property to be provided out of the testator's estate, whether or not the property described forms part of his estate on death. Thus a gift of '500 shares in ABC Ltd to X' is a general legacy because there is no indication that any specific holding of 500 shares in ABC Ltd is intended. If no such shares are owned by the testator when he dies, the PRs must acquire them using funds from the estate. Usually, general legacies take the form of gifts of money.

8.2.3 Demonstrative

A demonstrative legacy is a gift which is general in nature but is directed to be paid from a specific fund, for example 'I give £1,000 to X to be paid from my Lloyds Bank account'. Such a legacy is treated as a specific legacy to the extent that the specified fund is in existence at the death. If the fund is not in existence, the legacy does not adeem, but is payable from the estate like a general legacy.

8.2.4 Pecuniary

A pecuniary legacy is simply a gift of money. Pecuniary legacies are usually general ('£100 to X'), but they may be demonstrative ('£100 to X payable from my current bank account') or even specific ('the £100 in my safe to X').

For details of a special definition that may be given to the term 'pecuniary legacy' see **8.5**.

8.2.5 Residuary

A residuary gift is a gift of the testator's remaining property (ie property not included in the other legacies or devises). If no other legacies are given, a gift of the

Chapter 8 contents
Introduction
Types of gift
General drafting considerations
Specific gifts
Pecuniary legacies

whole estate is a residuary gift. It is usual to dispose of residuary realty and personalty by means of a single gift. Normally it is provided that all the debts, expenses and other legacies are to be paid out of residue before it is distributed. Gifts of residue are covered in detail in Chapter 9.

8.3 GENERAL DRAFTING CONSIDERATIONS

Certain matters should be considered when drafting any legacy or devise.

8.3.1 Possible failure of benefit

It is important to consider the possibility that a gift by will may fail, for example because the intended beneficiary dies before the testator (see Chapter 15). Such matters should be drawn to the testator's attention and clear instructions taken. It is often possible to prevent a gift from failing completely, for example by including substitutional provisions in the will that take effect if the original gift fails.

8.3.2 Providing for the payment of debts, expenses and IHT

It is important to have in mind the question of where the burden of liabilities will fall, ie which part of the estate should be used to pay the debts owed by the testator at the time of death, the expenses of administering the estate and any IHT payable by the PRs. (These liabilities are commonly referred to as 'debts, funeral and testamentary expenses'.) If the will is silent, the statutory order set out in the Administration of Estates Act 1925 (AEA 1925), s 34(3) applies (see **27.5.1**). The effect of the statutory provisions is that in most cases the burden of payment falls on residue, except that debts charged on specific property, such as mortgages, are payable from that property (see **8.4.6** and **27.7.1**). The will may vary the statutory order by showing a contrary intention. Even in cases where the testator does not wish to vary the statutory order, it is usual to make express provisions in the will in order to ensure that the testator's wishes are clear.

The following provisions are commonly made:

Gift 'free of tax'/'subject to tax'
Any gift other than a gift of residue may be expressed to be made 'free of tax'.

This means that the beneficiary is not to be required to pay any IHT on the property. Such an instruction does not alter the statutory provision which would not in any event require a beneficiary to pay the IHT (see **18.11.2**). Conversely, if a legacy is given 'subject to tax' then the beneficiary must bear the burden of the IHT on the property.

The decision whether or not to make a gift free of tax can affect the amount of IHT payable on an estate and this should be explained to a client if relevant (see **18.6.3**).

Residue 'subject to payment of debts, funeral and testamentary expenses'
It is usual to make express provision in the gift of residue for the payment of debts, expenses and IHT from the residue of the estate, even though the testator may be repeating what would happen in any event under the AEA 1925. However, in some unusual circumstances a provision such as this does change the statutory order (see **27.7.2**).

8.3.3 The identity of the beneficiary

Certainty

If the beneficiary cannot be identified from the description in the will, the gift may fail for uncertainty (see **15.6**). The draftsman should avoid problems of identification by naming the beneficiary accurately and including his address, or by describing the beneficiary (eg 'my son') and adding his name.

It is usually preferable to avoid making a gift to a single individual by description alone. A gift to 'my son' could cause problems if the testator has more than one son. Further difficulties may arise if the identity of the person who fits the description changes. A gift to 'my son's wife' is construed as a gift to the person who fits the description at the time the will is made and that person would, for example, take the gift even if divorced before the testator's death.

Children and young people

The testator must consider the age at which he wishes young beneficiaries to inherit property from his will; he should anticipate the problem that his executors will face if the beneficiary is too young to give a receipt for the property and, if he wishes to benefit the children of another individual (eg his brother's children), he must decide whether to restrict the gift to children now living or to extend it to future children. These matters are considered below.

VESTED OR CONTINGENT GIFT

A gift is vested if, by its terms, the entitlement of the beneficiary depends only on his being alive at the testator's death. If the beneficiary dies before obtaining possession of the gift (eg because of a delay in transferring it), the benefit of the gift devolves as part of the beneficiary's estate.

Suppose a will contains a legacy which provides 'I give £10,000 to my grandson John'. When the testator dies John is 3 years old. John has a vested interest in the legacy, and assuming the estate is large enough, he is now entitled to £10,000. The money belongs to him even if he dies before he is 18. Should this happen, it will form part of John's estate. Although entitled to the money, John may not actually receive it as, until 18, he cannot give the executors a valid receipt for it (see below).

A gift is contingent if, by its terms, it can take effect only if and when some future condition is satisfied (usually the attaining of a particular age). Such a gift will not vest until the condition is satisfied. If the beneficiary dies before attaining a vested interest, no benefit can accrue to his estate.

In the example above, John may claim his £10,000 as soon as he is 18. Only his inability to give a receipt prevents him from claiming the money earlier. The testator may wish to prevent John from receiving the money when he is 18. This can be done only by creating a contingent gift, such as 'I give £10,000 to my grandson John if he attains the age of 21'. In this case, John may claim the £10,000 only when the contingency is satisfied, ie when he is 21. If he dies before he is 21, the gift fails.

RECEIPT

Under the general law, a person who is under 18 cannot give a valid receipt for property. Without authority to the contrary, the executors must hold that property on trust for the minor until he attains 18.

If the gift is vested, the executors may appoint new trustees and transfer the property to those trustees under AEA 1925, s 42 (see **25.5.5**).

Alternatively, an infant receipt clause may be included in the will allowing the executors to accept the receipt of the beneficiary's parent or guardian, or even of the beneficiary himself at the age of, for example, 16 (see **10.2.4**). Even if such a provision is included, the executors are not obliged to hand over the property until the beneficiary is 18; they are merely relieved from liability if they do so.

GIFT BY NAME OR DESCRIPTION

The principles discussed in **9.2.2** relating to the testator's children apply equally to the children of any person, and reference should be made to that paragraph. Care should be taken when drafting a class gift (eg '£10,000 to my brother's children'), and it should be suggested to the testator that he restrict the gift to those members of the class living at his death (see **28.3.5**).

Charitable and other unincorporated associations

A gift to an institution may fail if the institution is not accurately named in the will. It is the duty of the draftsman to confirm the existence and name of the institution and not merely to rely on information given by the testator (*Re Recher's Will Trusts* [1972] Ch 526).

The draftsman should also anticipate the difficulty which the executors may experience in ascertaining who has authority to give a receipt for the legacy on behalf of the institution and the possibility that the institution may change its name or amalgamate.

SPECIMEN CLAUSE 1: LEGACY TO AN UNINCORPORATED ASSOCIATION (NON-CHARITABLE)

> I GIVE £1,000 free of tax to the Barchester and District Golf Club ('the Club') and I DECLARE that the receipt of the person who appears to be the Treasurer or other proper officer of the Club shall be a full discharge to my executors and I FURTHER DECLARE that if at my death the Club has changed its name or amalgamated with another association this gift shall not fail but shall take effect as a gift to the Club in its changed name or the association which results from such amalgamation.

COMMENTARY

As mentioned above, the gift will fail if the institution is not accurately named in the will.

The gift takes effect as a gift to members of the club for the time being. The receipt provision avoids any theoretical requirement for the executors to obtain receipts from every member of the club. The words 'appears to be' are intended to avoid any need for the executors to check that the treasurer has been properly appointed.

The final declaration is intended to save the gift from failure, which would otherwise result if the association changed its name or amalgamated before the testator's death.

SPECIMEN CLAUSE 2: LEGACY TO A CHARITY

> I give £[ ] to [*full name*] ('the Charity') for its general charitable purposes and I direct that the receipt of a person who appears to be the treasurer or other proper officer of the Charity shall be a sufficient discharge to my executors [and I further direct that if at my death the Charity has ceased to exist or amalgamated with another charity or has changed its name my

executors shall pay this legacy to the charitable organisation which in their discretion consider most nearly fulfils the objects of the Charity]

COMMENTARY

A gift to a particular named charity may be construed as a gift for the purposes of the charity. Even though the charity has ceased to exist, the purposes for which it was founded may still be able to be carried out. The property given to the charity would be applied for those purposes by means of a scheme from the Charity Commission. The words 'for its general charitable purposes' are intended to show that the gift is made for the purpose of the charity and not to the particular institution alone.

Even if the purposes of the charity do not continue, the gift may be saved by the cy-près doctrine. This allows charitable gifts which fail to be applied for other charitable purposes, provided that the testator has shown a 'charitable intention'. The words 'for its general charitable purposes' may also help to show that the testator has such an intention. However, the specific instructions in square brackets have the advantage of providing the executors with an alternative in the case of the charity failing. They may pay the legacy to another charity instead.

Again a receipt provision has been included, so that the executors need not investigate the appointment of the officer of the charity.

8.4 SPECIFIC GIFTS

In addition to the considerations listed in **8.3**, the following matters have particular relevance when drafting specific gifts.

8.4.1 Identity of the property

Certainty
Care must be taken in drafting specific gifts to describe the property as clearly and accurately as possible. If the property cannot be identified from the description in the will, the gift may fail for uncertainty (see **15.6**).

Ademption
The effect of the doctrine of ademption on specific gifts should be explained to the testator so that alternative provisions may be considered. Details of the doctrine and its effect are in **15.2**. The examples below concern specific gifts of chattels; specific gifts of land are considered separately in **8.4.6**.

SPECIMEN CLAUSE 1

I give to [*full name*] my 1952 Daimler motor car, registration number SN 384.

COMMENTARY

The car has been clearly described to avoid uncertainty. Care must be taken to ensure that the description is accurate, as an error of detail could cause the gift to adeem. The testator's intention here is to give only the particular car described, regardless of the fact that the gift will adeem if the car has been replaced at the time of death.

SPECIMEN CLAUSE 2

I give to [*full name*] any motor car which I may own at the date of my death.

COMMENTARY

This clause seeks to avoid the danger of ademption by defining the property given as at the date of death. Although the Wills Act 1837, s 24 provides that a will 'speaks from death' with regard to property, a simple gift of 'my car' is likely to be construed as showing a contrary intention. Thus such a gift would be construed as referring only to the car owned by the testator at the date of the will and would adeem if it had been sold and replaced with another car before the death (see **15.2**).

SPECIMEN CLAUSE 3

I give to [*full name*] all my personal chattels as defined by the Administration of Estates Act 1925, s 55(1)(x) [except those which are specifically bequeathed by this will or by any codicil to it] [and also any car which I own at my death notwithstanding that it may be used wholly or partly for business purposes]

COMMENTARY

Under the Wills Act 1837, s 24 this gift operates to pass all property fitting the description owned by the testator at the date of death. The definition of personal chattels contained in the AEA 1925, s 55(1)(x) and applicable on intestacy is commonly adopted in this way. The section is set out at **16.3.3**.

The draftsman should consider whether the statutory definition is appropriate in the circumstances. Any items not clearly included in the definition but which are intended to pass with the chattels (such as chattels used for business purposes) should be specifically mentioned as in the specimen clause. The advantage of referring to a full and well-established statutory definition must be weighed against the possible disadvantage to the testator that the will cannot be fully understood without reference to the statute.

8.4.2 Costs of transfer

Specific legatees bear the burden of any costs of insuring, packing and transporting the property left to them in the will unless the will provides to the contrary. These costs may be considerable, particularly in the case of large or valuable chattels, and the testator may prefer them to be paid from residue. A provision may be included in the gift to vary the usual rule by making the gift free of costs of transfer. An example appears in Clause 2 of Mark King's will (see **4.2.2**).

8.4.3 Gift of chattels to be distributed between a number of beneficiaries

Where the testator wishes to give a large number of small specific legacies it may be preferable to avoid including a long and detailed list in the will. The following two specimen clauses offer different approaches to the problem. In the first, a list of the testator's wishes is incorporated into the will. In the second, the chattels are given to the executor with a request that he distribute them to the intended beneficiaries.

SPECIMEN CLAUSE 1: INCORPORATION BY REFERENCE
> I give to the people named in a list prepared and signed by me and dated [*date*] the items of my personal chattels respectively described in the said list opposite their respective names

COMMENTARY

A document may be incorporated into a will by reference provided that it is clearly identified in the will, is in existence at the date of the will and is described in the will as being already in existence. This clause complies with the above requirements provided the date of the list is prior to the date of execution of the will. The effect is that the list forms part of the will and is admitted to probate with the will. Incorporation by reference is not generally to be recommended in view of the various risks involved; for example the list may be lost, or the testator may attempt to substitute a later list, thereby invalidating the gifts.

SPECIMEN CLAUSE 2: 'PRECATORY TRUST'
> I give to [*my executor*] all my chattels and effects of household personal or domestic use or ornament and it is my wish (without imposing any trust or legal obligation upon him) that he should distribute such chattels and effects in accordance with any directions I give to him in any letter or memorandum signed by me

COMMENTARY

This alternative provision is generally described as a 'precatory trust', although this term is misleading as the intention is to avoid creating any trust or binding obligation. The chattels are given to the executor (or a beneficiary) who has only a moral obligation to distribute them according to the testator's expressed wishes. Such a provision avoids the need for a long list of legacies, allows the testator to change his mind after the will is made and may avoid the danger of dispute between the beneficiaries. The disadvantage is that the directions are unenforceable, so the testator has no guarantee that his wishes will be observed. Care should be taken in drafting such a provision to ensure that no trust is created and that any list referred to is not accidentally incorporated into the will.

8.4.4 Gift of chattels to be divided by agreement between beneficiaries

The testator may wish to leave the beneficiaries to decide on the division between themselves. The obvious danger is that they may find it difficult to reach an agreement. Any provision involving a division of chattels should include arrangements for the resolution of any dispute between the beneficiaries.

SPECIMEN CLAUSE
> I give all my personal chattels to my grandchildren living at my death in equal shares to be divided between them as they shall agree but so that in default of agreement such division shall be made by my Trustees in their absolute discretion and according to their estimation of the values of the several articles and shall be final and binding

8.4.5 Gift of shares

Gifts of shares give rise to drafting difficulties because of the danger that the shares held at the date of the will may change as a result of bonus issues, rights issues or reconstruction of the company's capital.

SPECIMEN CLAUSE

(1) I give to [full name] all shares in ABC plc to which I may be beneficially entitled at the time of my death

[(2) Any charge on the shares existing at my death shall be paid out of my residuary estate]

[(3) If any of the shares in ABC plc which I own at the date of this will are as a result of takeover amalgamation or reconstruction represented at the date of my death by a different holding whether in ABC plc or in any other company paragraph (1) above shall take effect as a gift of that holding]

COMMENTARY

Because of the problems caused by the possibility of share holdings changing between the date of the will and the date of death, it is usually preferable to avoid a precise description of the shares held at the date of the will.

Paragraph (2) counters the effect of AEA 1925, s 35 which provides that debts charged on particular assets are payable from those assets (see **27.7.1**). The will provides instead that any such liabilities are to be paid from residue and not by the specific beneficiary.

Paragraph (3) avoids the difficulty of deciding whether a gift of shares has been adeemed when the company is taken over or amalgamated, with the result that the holding is replaced with shares in a different company (see **15.2.2**).

8.4.6 Specific devises

When taking instructions for a specific gift of a house or flat it is important to investigate the testator's intentions thoroughly and to draw his attention to the particular matters requiring consideration when leaving such property.

Tax

As seen in **8.3.2**, the general rule is that IHT on the property passing by will is payable from residue, and thus a specific devisee would receive the house free of tax. As the property may represent a substantial part of the estate, the testator may wish the beneficiary taking it to bear the burden of any tax due. In any event, express provision should be included for the sake of clarity on the face of the will. No such problem arises if the house is left to the testator's spouse, when the gift is exempt for IHT purposes.

Ademption

If the property is the testator's main residence, the fact that the gift will fail if the testator has moved house after the date of the will should be explained. The testator may wish to include a substitute provision to cover this possibility.

Mortgages

If the house is subject to a mortgage, AEA 1925, s 35 provides that the burden of the mortgage is borne by the property (see **27.7.1**). This means that the specific devisee would be liable to pay the mortgage debt. The testator may prefer to displace s 35 and place the burden of paying the mortage debt on residue. In any event the draftsman should ascertain whether the testator has any insurance arrangements to cover the mortgage debt in the event of his death. The terms of any such insurance should be investigated before drafting the will. The testator will usually wish to ensure that the benefit of the proceeds of the policy passes with the property, or into residue if the mortgage is to be paid from residue.

> SPECIMEN CLAUSE – GIFT OF HOUSE OR FLAT
>
> I give to [*full name*] [free of tax] [subject to tax] my [house] [flat] known as [*address*] [or such other property that at my death constitutes my principal private residence and if doubt exists as to which is my principal private residence the decision of my Trustees shall be final and binding] [and I direct that any charge on the house or flat shall be discharged out of my Residuary Estate].

8.5 PECUNIARY LEGACIES

Examples of typical pecuniary legacies with commentaries are found in Clause 4 of Mark King's will (see **4.2.2**) and Clause 5 of Julia Gold's will (see **4.3.2**).

Chapter 9

GIFTS OF RESIDUE

9.1 DRAFTING CONSIDERATIONS

In addition to the considerations listed in **8.3**, numerous other matters are relevant when drafting the gift of residue.

9.1.1 Purpose

The main purpose in drafting the gift of residue is to ensure that all the property which has not already been given away by the will passes to the testator's chosen beneficiaries on terms which the testator has selected. Any possibility of a partial intestacy should be avoided by means of substitutional provisions.

9.1.2 Is a trust required?

The form of the gift of residue will depend on whether or not an express trust is required. If there is no need for a trust, the drafting of the gift will be straightforward; if a trust is required, the drafting will be more complicated. (Examples of each may be found in Clause 5 of Mark King's will and Clause 6 of Julia Gold's will respectively in Chapter 4.) Thus, before beginning to draft, the draftsman must decide whether a trust is necessary. There are three common situations where, in a family will, a trust should be created.

Life interest

The testator may give express instructions for the residue of his estate to be held on trust. For example, he may wish to divide the beneficial interests by giving a life interest (the right to income for life) to one beneficiary and an interest in remainder (the right to receive the capital on the death of the life tenant) to another. This may only be achieved by giving the property to trustees to be held on the required terms.

Minority

More commonly, a trust may arise under a will because a beneficiary is under the age of 18 when the testator dies, and thus unable to give a valid receipt to his PRs. The PRs must hold that beneficiary's property for him until he is 18. An express trust should be created in the will so that the testator can select the terms on which the property is to be held. Thus, if there is any possibility that a beneficiary entitled to residue (or a share of residue) might be under the age of 18 when the testator dies, an express trust of residue should be created. Even if the primary beneficiaries are all adults when the will is made, the possible effect of a substitutional provision should be considered.

> *Example 1*
> Alan wishes to make a will leaving all his estate to his children, Ruth (now 20) and Martin (now 14), in equal shares. He intends to give vested interests to both children.
>
> If Alan dies while Martin is still under the age of 18, his PRs will have to hold Martin's share for him until he is 18. Until then, although Martin has a vested

Chapter 9 contents
Drafting considerations
Gift of residue: absolute interests
Gift of residue: life interest

interest, he cannot give a valid receipt. An express trust of residue should be created.

Example 2
At the time when Alan is making his will, Ruth is 30 and Martin 24. If Ruth and Martin both survive Alan, no trust will be necessary as they are both over 18. However, Alan wishes to provide that if either Ruth or Martin should die before him, leaving children, those children should take their deceased parent's share (ie a 'substitution of grandchildren' provision).

If, when Alan dies, the substitution takes effect (because, eg Ruth has died before him leaving children of her own) a minority may arise. Ruth's children, who will have a vested interest in half of Alan's estate, may be under the age of 18. An express trust of residue should be created.

Contingent interests
If a beneficiary has a contingent interest, the PRs must retain the property until his interest vests (or he dies). Again, an express trust should be included in the will so that the testator can choose the terms on which the property is held. In any will where the residue is given to beneficiaries contingently on attaining a specified age, an express trust should be included.

Example
Grace wishes to make a will leaving all her estate to her nephew Harry, now aged 18. Grace does not wish Harry to receive the gift until he is 25, and so she leaves her estate to him contingently on his attaining 25 years.

If Grace dies before Harry is 25, her PRs will continue to hold her estate until Harry is 25 (or dies under that age). An express trust of residue should be created.

9.1.3 What kind of trust should be created?

Before 1996, it was usual to impose an express trust for sale of residue because otherwise, if the residue included land, the Settled Land Act 1925 (SLA 1925) would apply to the land and a strict settlement would arise. Since 1 January 1996, no new strict settlements can be created. Under the Trusts of Land and Appointment of Trustees Act 1996 (TLATA 1996), all trusts which include land are 'trusts of land' and the trustees have wide powers to deal with the land.

This means that the main reason for creating an express trust for sale has gone. Trustees of land have power to sell or retain land at their discretion. However, there is some doubt about whether trustees who do not hold on express trust for sale have power to sell personalty. For this reason some draftsmen may continue to impose an express trust for sale. The alternative solution is to include a provision in the will giving trustees express power to sell personalty. (See **10.3.4**.)

9.1.4 Providing for payment of debts, funeral and testamentary expenses and legacies

Debts and funeral and testamentary expenses
It is usual practice to include an express direction in the will for the payment of debts and funeral and testamentary expenses from the residue of the estate. If no provision is included, these debts and liabilities are payable according to the

statutory order in AEA 1925 (see Chapter 27). Even if the testator does not wish to vary the effect of the statutory order, an express provision is usually included to ensure that his wishes are clear from the will itself.

Legacies

The rules governing the payment of pecuniary legacies are complex and may in some cases give rise to uncertainty (see Chapter 28). An express provision for payment of legacies from residue avoids any possible problems.

9.2 GIFT OF RESIDUE: ABSOLUTE INTERESTS

Example

Caroline wishes to make a will to provide for her husband, David, and children Luke aged 6 and Esther aged 4. She decides to leave the residue of her estate to David absolutely, with a provision that, if he dies before her, the residue should go to her children equally. As seen in **9.1.2**, an express trust should be created since there is a possibility that a minority may arise. Express provision should be made for the payment of debts, funeral and testamentary expenses and legacies, as seen in **9.1.4**. The additional matters listed below should also be considered when drafting the beneficial gifts.

9.2.1 Absolute gift to surviving spouse: survivorship

If the testator gives the residue of his estate unconditionally to an individual, such as the surviving spouse, he should be aware that the gift will vest immediately on his death. Once the gift has vested, his spouse will assume control over the ultimate destination of the property. The testator's overriding intention may be to give his spouse maximum freedom to enjoy the property during her lifetime, leaving his spouse free to dispose of the property in her lifetime or, on death, by will.

The draftsman should point out to the testator the possibility that his spouse might survive him for a very short period, or might be deemed to have survived him under LPA 1925, s 184 where their deaths occur apparently simultaneously in a common accident (see **15.3.2**). In such circumstances the testator may wish to ensure that his property will pass under the terms of his own will rather than that of his spouse. This may be achieved by means of a survivorship clause, which makes the gift to the spouse conditional upon the spouse surviving the testator for a specified period. In order to avoid a prolonged period of uncertainty, the specified period is usually 28 days. For IHT reasons, the specified period should not exceed 6 months. If the period is longer, an IHT 'settlement' will arise, with a possible charge to tax if the spouse dies before the period ends.

Example

Caroline's will may provide:

> Subject to the payment of my debts funeral and testamentary expenses and legacies I give all the rest of my estate to my husband David absolutely if he survives me for a period of 28 days.

9.2.2 Substitutional gift to children

Reasons for failure of primary gift
The gift to the spouse may fail because:

(1) the spouse dies before the testator; or
(2) the spouse dies after the testator but before the end of the survivorship period; or
(3) the spouse survives but the gift fails as a result of divorce (see **15.5**).

All these possibilities should be borne in mind when drafting the substitutional gift.

> *Example*
> The substitutional gift in Caroline's will may be introduced with the words:
> **If my husband dies before me or does not survive me by 28 days ...**

Gift by name or description
If the children are named in the will any children born after the date of the will are excluded. A testator who is unlikely to have further children may prefer to make gifts by name. The gift should be worded so as to avoid a partial intestacy if one of the children dies before the testator. For example, a gift to 'such of my children John and Mary as are living at my death and if both in equal shares' is preferable to a gift to 'my children John and Mary in equal shares'. In the first case, if Mary dies before the testator, John takes the whole residue. In the second, if Mary dies before the testator, half the residue passes on intestacy.

If the gift is made to 'such of my children as are living at my death and if more than one in equal shares', any children born after the date of the will are included. Unless the will shows a contrary intention the description includes adopted children (Adoption Act 1976), illegitimate children (Family Law Reform Act 1987) and children en ventre sa mère (ie conceived but not born) at the time of death.

Contingent gifts
If the gift to children is vested, a child will be entitled to receive his share of residue as soon as he is 18 (and can give a valid receipt). The testator may wish to postpone his children's enjoyment of the property until they are older. This may be achieved by making the gift to children contingent upon their attaining a specified age greater than 18 (eg 21 or 25). (It is important that the child should become entitled to the property, or an interest in the income from the property, at or before the age of 25; otherwise, adverse IHT consequences may follow.)

A contingent interest will also avoid the possibility that a share of residue might pass on the intestacy of a child who dies after the testator but before attaining the age of 18.

> *Example*
> Returning to Caroline's will, it is assumed that she wishes any future children to be included, and does not wish the children to receive their share until they are 21. Following the words of introduction, the substitution clause will continue:
>
> > **... I give all the rest of my estate to my trustees on trust to pay my debts funeral and testamentary expenses and legacies and to hold the residue for such of my children as are living at my death and**

attain the age of 21 years and if more than one in equal shares absolutely.

9.2.3 Substitution of grandchildren

A further substitutional provision may be included to take effect where a child of the testator dies before the testator leaving a child or children of his own. It is usual to provide that the deceased child's share should go to his own children equally 'per stirpes'. If the gift to the child is contingent, the substitution should be carefully drafted to ensure that it will take effect if the child dies after the testator but before the contingency occurs.

If no such express provision is made in the will, Wills Act 1837, s 33 introduces a statutory substitution provision for gifts to the testator's child or remoter issue (see **15.3.6**). It is, however, preferable to include an express provision in order to ensure that the matter is brought to the attention of the testator, and to avoid certain ambiguities in the application of s 33.

> *Example*
> Although Caroline's children are very young, a provision for substitution of grandchildren will probably be included. Her will might continue:
>> Provided that if any child of mine shall die without attaining a vested interest leaving a child or children him or her surviving such child or children shall take by substitution and if more than one in equal shares the share of my estate which his her or their parent would have taken had he or she attained a vested interest.

9.2.4 Specimen clauses

(1) RESIDUE TO AN ADULT BENEFICIARY WITH SUBSTITUTION OF ANOTHER ADULT BENEFICIARY

> I give all the rest of my estate subject to the payment of my debts funeral and testamentary expenses and legacies ('my residuary estate') to my mother Mary Robinson if she survives me by a period of 28 days. If my mother does not so survive me then I give my residuary estate to my brother Charles Robinson absolutely.

COMMENTARY

This will cannot give rise to a continuing trust as no minority or contingency can arise. The residue, after payment of debts funeral and testamentary expenses and legacies, is given directly to the beneficiaries. The survivorship clause ensures that the testator's will governs the destination of the testator's property if his mother should die shortly after the testator. A partial intestacy will arise only if both mother and brother die before the testator.

(2) RESIDUE TO SPOUSE WITH SUBSTITUTION OF VESTED GIFTS TO CHILDREN

(1) If my wife survives me by 28 days then I give all the rest of my estate (subject to the payment of my debts funeral and testamentary expenses and legacies) to her absolutely.

(2) If my wife does not so survive me I give all the rest of my estate to my trustees on trust to pay my debts funeral and testamentary expenses and legacies and to hold the residue on trust for such of my children as shall be living at my death and if more than one in equal shares absolutely provided that if any child of mine shall die in my lifetime leaving a child or children living at my death such child or children shall take by substitution and if more than one in equal shares the share of my estate which his her or their parent would have taken had he or she survived me.

COMMENTARY

No trust is necessary in the primary gift to the surviving spouse; this clause imposes a trust only in the substitutional gift to children. Alternatively, the trust may be imposed at the beginning of the clause before the gift to the spouse, as in specimen clause (3) below. Some draftsmen prefer the method in specimen clause (2) as it may seem clearer to the testator.

The trust is imposed with very simple words and there is no trust for sale. The trustee powers should include an express power to sell personalty. Specimen clause (3) below gives an example of a trust for sale using traditional wording. The duty of the trustees is to sell the property, but they are given an express power to postpone sale. The effect in relation to land is the same: a trust of land arises under TLATA 1996. There is no need to include a power to sell personalty.

Although a power to postpone sale is implied where land is held on trust for sale (TLATA 1996, s 4), an express power should be included in order to permit the trustees to retain personalty in the estate.

(3) RESIDUE TO SPOUSE (ALTERNATIVE FORM) WITH SUBSTITUTION OF CONTINGENT GIFTS TO CHILDREN

I give all the rest of my estate to my Trustees upon trust to sell call in and convert the same into money with power to postpone such sale calling in and conversion for so long as they in their absolute discretion think fit without being liable for loss and after payment thereout of my debts funeral and testamentary expenses [and legacies] to hold the residue ('my Residuary Estate') on the following trusts

(1) to pay my Residuary Estate to my husband if he survives me by 28 days but if he does not so survive me or if this gift fails for any other reason then

(2) to pay my Residuary Estate to such of my children as are living at my death who attain the age of 25 years and if more than one in equal shares provided that if any child of mine shall die before attaining a vested interest leaving children him or her surviving then such children shall take by substitution and if more than one in equal shares the share of my estate which his her or their parent would have taken if he or she had attained a vested interest.

COMMENTARY

The clause imposes a trust for sale before the gift to the spouse, even though the trust will be redundant if the spouse survives. Some draftsmen regard this as a neater method as it avoids the need to repeat the direction to pay debts. It may, however, be less readily understood by the testator.

The wording of the substitution of grandchildren provision is altered to allow for substitution where a child survives the testator but dies before his interest vests.

9.3 GIFT OF RESIDUE: LIFE INTEREST

Example

Simon, a wealthy man, wishes to provide in his will for his wife, Jenny, and his children, Adam 14 and Ben 12. He is particularly concerned to ensure that his estate will ultimately reach his sons, and so he decides to set up a trust in his will. His trustees will invest his estate and pay the income to Jenny during her life. When she dies, the capital will pass to the children.

Again, as seen in **9.1.2**, an express trust of residue should be created and provision included for the payment of debts, funeral and testamentary expenses and legacies, as seen in **9.1.4**. The additional matters listed below should also be considered when drafting the beneficial gifts.

9.3.1 Life interest to spouse

The residue should be given to the trustees on trust to pay debts, funeral and testamentary expenses and legacies. The trustees are directed to hold the residue on trust and to pay the income to the testator's spouse during her lifetime. The testator should consider whether further flexibility is needed in case the income should prove insufficient for the spouse's needs. The trustees' powers may be extended to allow the trustees to advance or lend capital to the spouse (see **10.3.6**). The testator may wish to separate the matrimonial home from the gift of residue, either by leaving it to the spouse absolutely or by giving the spouse a right of residence (see **8.4.6**).

9.3.2 Remainder to children

The matters to be considered in drafting an immediate gift to children (see **9.2.2**) are also relevant in drafting the interests in remainder. Thus the interests in remainder may be given to the children by name or by description, their interests may be vested or contingent and provision for substitution of grandchildren may be included.

The nature of the children's interests in remainder during the surviving spouse's lifetime should also be considered. Regardless of age, their interests may be made contingent on surviving both parents, with substitutional provisions to take effect where a child dies after the testator but before the surviving spouse, leaving children of his own living at the spouse's death.

SPECIMEN CLAUSE: LIFE INTEREST TO SPOUSE WITH REMAINDER TO CHILDREN

I give all the rest of my estate to my Trustees on trust to pay my debts funeral and testamentary expenses and legacies and to hold the residue ('my Residuary Estate') on the following trusts

(1) to pay the income to my husband Edward Watts during his lifetime and then
(2) to pay my Residuary Estate to such of my children Martin Watts Kenneth Watts and Janet Harvey as shall be living at the death of the survivor of myself and my husband and if more than one in equal shares provided that if any of my said children shall die before me or before attaining a vested interest leaving children living at the death of the survivor of myself and my husband then such children shall on attaining 18 take by substitution and if more than one in equal shares the share of my Residuary Estate which his her or their parent would have taken if he or she had attained a vested interest.

COMMENTARY

In this clause the children are named, probably because there is no question of further children being born. The children's interests do not vest until the death of the surviving spouse so that if a child dies before the life tenant that child's interest will devolve under the testatrix's will. Alternatively, the children could be given vested interests in remainder leaving them free to dispose of their interests in their lifetime or by will.

Chapter 10

ADMINISTRATIVE PROVISIONS

10.1 INTRODUCTION

10.1.1 Statutory powers of PRs and trustees

PRs have a wide range of powers which they may exercise in carrying out the administration of an estate. These powers are largely conferred on them by statute. The AEA 1925 gives some powers specifically to PRs. The Trustee Act 1925 (TA 1925) and the Trustee Investment Act 1961 (TIA 1961) confer powers on trustees for use in administering a trust. Since 'trustee' in the TA 1925 includes a 'personal representative', PRs have these powers as well. Details of other statutory powers not mentioned below may be found in Chapter 25.

10.1.2 Extending the statutory powers by will

The statutory powers of executors and trustees may be modified or extended by will. Extension of the executors' powers may make it easier for them to administer the estate efficiently and so should always be considered. If there is any possibility that the terms of the will might give rise to a continuing trust it is particularly important to consider extending the powers of the trustees, not only to make the administration of the trust easier but also to give greater flexibility to the trustees. The provisions discussed below are intended generally to widen the statutory powers of executors and trustees, rather than to replace them entirely. Thus it is usual to introduce a list of powers in a will in such a way as to make this clear.

SPECIMEN CLAUSE
> My trustees shall have the following powers in addition to their powers under the general law.

10.2 PROVISIONS CONCERNING THE ADMINISTRATION OF THE ESTATE

10.2.1 Introduction

The provisions which follow should be considered when drafting any will, as their inclusion in the will may simplify the administration of the estate. However, if the will is intended to be short and simple, the draftsman may decide not to extend the executors' statutory powers.

10.2.2 Power to appropriate assets without consent of beneficiary

The statutory provision
AEA 1925, s 41 gives PRs the power to appropriate any part of the estate in or towards satisfaction of any legacy or any other interest or share in the estate provided that the appropriation does not prejudice any specific beneficiary. Thus, if the will gives a pecuniary legacy to a beneficiary, the PRs may allow that beneficiary to take chattels or other assets in the estate up to the value of his legacy provided

---

Chapter 10 contents
Introduction
Provisions concerning the administration of the estate
Provisions concerning the administration of a trust
Trusts of land
The apportionment rules
Miscellaneous additional powers
Selecting the appropriate powers

that these assets have not been specifically bequeathed by the will. The section provides that the beneficiary (or his parent or guardian if he is a minor) must consent to the appropriation.

Extending the statutory power

SPECIMEN CLAUSE
> Power to exercise the power of appropriation conferred by section 41 of the Administration of Estates Act 1925 without obtaining any of the consents required by that section

COMMENTARY
This provision is commonly included in order to relieve the PRs of the duty to obtain formal consent. Nevertheless, the PRs should informally consult the beneficiaries concerned.

10.2.3 Power to insure

The statutory provision
TA 1925, s 19 gives PRs and trustees power to insure any building or other insurable property against loss or damage by fire for up to three-quarters of the value of the property, paying the premiums out of income.

Extending the statutory power
The PRs are likely to wish to insure property they are holding during the period of the administration against all risks and up to its full value, so the statutory power is commonly extended.

SPECIMEN CLAUSE
> Power to insure any asset of my estate on such terms as they think fit and to pay premiums at their discretion out of income or capital and to use any insurance money received either to restore the assets or as if it were the proceeds of sale

10.2.4 Power to accept receipts from or on behalf of minors

The statutory provision
Under the general law an unmarried minor cannot give a good receipt for capital or income. A married minor can give a good receipt for income only (LPA 1925, s 21). AEA 1925, s 42 gives PRs the power to appoint trustees to hold a legacy for a minor who is absolutely entitled under the will. The receipt of the appointed trustees (who could be the child's parents or guardians) discharges the PRs from further liability. This power does not apply where the child has a contingent interest (see **25.5.5**).

Extending the statutory power
Where a specific or pecuniary legacy is left to a minor it may be convenient to include a clause allowing the PRs to accept the receipt of the child's parent or guardian or of the child himself if over 16 years old. Such a provision avoids the need for a formal appointment of trustees under s 42. The provision may be incorporated into the legacy itself (as in Clause 4 of Mark King's will in **4.2.2**) or may be included in a list of powers (see **10.3.6**).

10.3 PROVISIONS CONCERNING THE ADMINISTRATION OF A TRUST

10.3.1 Introduction

At the end of the administration of an estate, the PRs may be able to distribute the residue to the beneficiaries, thus completing their task. However, in some cases distribution will be delayed and the PRs will hold the residue (or part of it) as trustees. This may happen:

(1) where the beneficiary is a minor, and so cannot give a valid receipt to the PRs;
(2) where the beneficiary has a contingent interest, and so cannot be given the property until the interest vests; or
(3) where the interests in the property are divided, for example between income and capital.

In any of these cases, as illustrated in the examples below, the draftsman should foresee the fact that a trust may or will arise under the terms of the will and should consider extending the statutory powers of the trustees. The provisions listed in **10.2** should be considered as well as those listed below the examples.

Example 1: Adam's trust
Adam dies leaving all his estate (£200,000) on trust for 'such of my children as are living at my death in equal shares'. He has two children: Vera (22) and Mary (16). The children have vested interests. When the administration is complete the executors will transfer half the residue to Vera.

Mary cannot give a valid receipt for her share and so the executors hold it as trustees for her. The trust ends when Mary is 18. The reason for the continuing trust is the minority of the beneficiary.

Example 2: Bella's trust
Bella dies leaving all her estate (£200,000) on trust for 'such of my children as attain 21 in equal shares'. Her children are Charles (19) and Dora (14). Both children have contingent interests and the trust will continue until their interests vest. The reason for the continuing trust is not only Dora's minority but also the contingency of the beneficiaries' interests.

Example 3: Christine's trust
Christine dies leaving all her estate (£200,000) on trust for 'my husband Henry for life with remainder to my children in equal shares'. Christine has one child, Stephen, aged 10. Stephen has a vested interest in remainder. The income from Christine's estate will be paid to Henry for the rest of his life and the estate will be distributed to Stephen when Henry dies (unless Stephen is still under 18). The reason for the continuing trust is Henry's life interest as well as Stephen's minority.

10.3.2 Power to invest trust funds

The statutory provisions
Under general law, trustees have a duty to invest trust money. Their choice of investments is governed by the TIA 1961, which gives trustees power to invest only in authorised investments. The Act also contains directions to trustees to obtain professional advice about their choice of investments.

Extending the statutory powers

SPECIMEN CLAUSE
> My trustees shall have power to invest trust money and to transpose investments with the same unrestricted freedom in their choice of investments as if they were an absolute beneficial owner

COMMENTARY
The powers given in the TIA 1961 are generally regarded as unduly restrictive and complicated to operate. It is usual to include a clause like this which gives the trustees complete discretion in their choice of investments. The trustees must still observe the normal standard of care by acting with the prudence of an ordinary person of business. Such a clause would normally be included in the wills of Adam, Bella and Christine.

10.3.3 Power to purchase land

The statutory provisions
Trustees have no power to purchase land under the TIA 1961. Even a wide power of investment in the will does not permit the trustees to buy a house for beneficiaries to live in since the term 'investment' means the purchase of an asset in order to produce income.

Trustees of land do have power to purchase land of any tenure as an investment or as a residence for a beneficiary or for any other reason (TLATA 1996, s 6(3)). Thus trustees have such powers if land is included as part of the original trust property, but an express power should be included in case there is no land in the residue of the estate.

Extending the statutory provisions

SPECIMEN CLAUSE
> My trustees may apply trust money in the purchase or improvement of any freehold or leasehold dwelling house and may permit any such dwelling house to be used as a residence by any person with an interest in my residuary estate upon such terms and conditions as my trustees may think fit

COMMENTARY
This clause gives trustees an express power to use trust money to buy or improve land for use as a residence by the beneficiaries. It leaves the question of responsibility for the burden of repairs and other outgoings to the discretion of the trustees.

10.3.4 Power to sell personalty

Until 1996, it was usual to draft the trust of residue as a trust for sale in order to avoid the accidental creation of a strict settlement (see **9.1.3**). Since the TLATA 1996, the draftsman may prefer to create an express trust of residue without imposing a duty to sell the trust property. If this is done, the trustees should be given an express power to sell personalty.

SPECIMEN CLASE
Power to sell mortgage or charge any asset of my estate as if they were an absolute beneficial owner.

10.3.5 Power of maintenance

The statutory provisions

When the trust funds in the three trusts in **10.3.1** have been invested, the investments will produce income. In Christine's trust, the income belongs to Henry, the adult life tenant, and the trustees will pay it to him. In the other two trusts, the trustees are holding the fund (or part of it) for a minor beneficiary. TA 1925, s 31 gives them power to use income they receive for the minor's maintenance, education or benefit.

TA 1925, s 31 states (inter alia):

'(1) Where any property is held by trustees in trust for any person for any interest whatsoever, whether vested or contingent, then, subject to any prior interests or charges affecting that property –

    (i) during the infancy of any such person, if his interest so long continues, the trustees may, at their sole discretion, pay to his parent or guardian, if any, or otherwise apply for or towards his maintenance, education, or benefit, the whole or such part, if any, of the income of that property as may, in all the circumstances, be reasonable, whether or not there is –

        (a) any other fund applicable to the same purpose; or
        (b) any person bound by law to provide for his maintenance or education; and

    (ii) if such person on attaining the age of eighteen years has not a vested interest in such income, the trustees shall thenceforth pay the income of that property and of any accretion thereto under subsection (2) of this section to him, until he either attains a vested interest therein or dies, or until failure of his interest:

Provided that, in deciding whether the whole or any part of the income of the property is during a minority to be paid or applied for the purposes aforesaid, the trustees shall have regard to the age of the infant and his requirements and generally to the circumstances of the case, and in particular to what other income, if any, is applicable for the same purposes; and where trustees have notice that the income of more than one fund is applicable for those purposes, then, so far as practicable, unless the entire income of the funds is paid or applied as aforesaid or the court otherwise directs, a proportionate part only of the income of each fund shall be so paid or applied.

(2) During the infancy of any such person, if his interest so long continues, the trustees shall accumulate all the residue of that income in the way of compound interest by investing the same and the resulting income thereof from time to time in authorised investments, and shall hold those accumulations ...

(3) This section applies in the case of a contingent interest only if the limitation or trust carries the intermediate income of the property.'

Application of s 31

Adam's trust

The trustees are holding £100,000 for Mary (16) who has a vested interest in the capital. Under s 31(1) the trustees have the power to pay all or part of the income to

Mary's parent or guardian or 'otherwise apply' it for Mary's maintenance, education or benefit. This could include paying bills (eg school fees) directly.

The power is limited to so much of the income as is 'reasonable'. The proviso directs the trustees to take into account various further points such as Mary's age and requirements and whether any other fund is available for her maintenance.

Section 31(2) directs the trustees to accumulate any income not used for maintenance and to invest it.

Bella's trust
The trustees are holding £100,000 for Dora (14) who has a contingent interest in the capital. They may pay or apply the income for Dora's maintenance, education or benefit in the same way as the trustees of Adam's trust.

The trustees are holding £100,000 for Charles (19) who also has a contingent interest in the capital. Section 31(1)(ii) directs them to pay all the income to Charles until his interest vests (ie until he is 21) when he will receive the capital, or his interest fails (ie if he dies before he is 21). The same will apply to the income from Dora's share from her eighteenth birthday onwards.

Christine's trust
The trustees are holding £200,000 for Henry for life with remainder to Stephen (10). They have no power to use the income for Stephen's benefit as Henry is entitled to it. If Henry dies while Stephen is still a minor, s 31 will apply to allow the trustees to apply income for Stephen's maintenance etc during the period from Henry's death until Stephen is 18 (when they will transfer the capital to Stephen).

Extending s 31

SPECIMEN CLAUSE
Section 31 of the Trustee Act 1925 shall apply to the income of my estate as if the words 'as the trustees shall in their absolute discretion think fit' were substituted for the words 'as may, in all the circumstances, be reasonable' in paragraph (i) of subsection (1) thereof and the proviso to sub-section (1) had been omitted and as if the age of 21 years were substituted for all references to the age of 18 wherever they occur in s 31 (references to 'infancy' being construed accordingly).

COMMENTARY
The clause begins by removing the 'reasonable' limitation in s 31. It gives the trustees complete discretion over whether to pay or apply income for minor beneficiaries and over how much income they pay or apply.

Secondly, it removes the right for a contingent beneficiary to receive all the income from the age of 18. The trustees' discretion under s 31 to pay or apply income for maintenance or to accumulate any surplus will continue until the beneficiary is 21. Thus, in Bella's trust, the trustees would have a discretion over the payment of income to Charles even though he is over 18.

Note that such a clause gives rise to IHT and CGT implications beyond the scope of this book.

10.3.6 Power to advance capital

The statutory provisions

TA 1925, s 32 allows trustees in certain circumstances to permit a beneficiary with an interest in capital to have the benefit of part of his capital entitlement sooner than he would receive it under the basic provisions of the trust.

Section 32 states:

> '(1) Trustees may at any time or times pay or apply any capital money subject to a trust for the advancement or benefit in such manner as they may, in their absolute discretion, think fit, of any person entitled to the capital of the trust property or of any share thereof, whether absolutely or contingently on his attaining any specified age or on the occurrence of any other event, ... and whether in possession or in remainder or reversion ...
>
> ... Provided that –
>
> (a) the money so paid or applied for the advancement or benefit of any person shall not exceed altogether in amount one-half of the presumptive or vested share or interest of that person in the trust property; and
>
> (b) if that person is or becomes absolutely and indefeasibly entitled to a share in the trust property the money so paid or applied shall be brought into account as part of such share; and
>
> (c) no such payment or application shall be made so as to prejudice any person entitled to any prior life or other interest, whether vested or contingent, in the money paid or applied unless such person is in existence and of full age and consents in writing to such payment or application'

Application of s 32

Adam's trust

Mary has a vested interest in the £100,000 capital. Section 32 allows the trustees to release some of the capital for Mary's benefit. 'Benefit' is widely construed: money could be used to pay educational or living expenses. The amount the trustees may advance is limited to half Mary's entitlement, ie £50,000.

Bella's trust

Charles and Dora have contingent interests in the capital, their presumptive shares being £100,000 each. Section 32 applies to allow the trustees to release up to £50,000 for the benefit of either beneficiary. The trustees could give money directly to Charles as he is old enough to give a valid receipt. The power applies even though the interests of Charles and Dora are contingent. If either beneficiary dies before the age of 21, there is no right to recover any advance even though that beneficiary's interest in capital has failed.

Section 32(1)(b) requires advances to be brought into account on final distribution. If the trustees give £50,000 to Charles now, he will receive £50,000 less than Dora when the fund is finally distributed to them.

Christine's trust

Henry has only an interest in income and s 32 does not permit the release of capital to him. The section does apply to Stephen's vested interest in remainder, and permits the trustees to apply up to £100,000 (half his interest) for Stephen's benefit.

Such an advance would prejudice Henry since his income would be substantially reduced. Section 32(1)(c) provides that no advance may be made without Henry's written consent.

Extending s 32

SPECIMEN CLAUSE 1

> Power to apply for the benefit of any beneficiary as my trustees think fit the whole or any part of the share of my residuary estate to which that beneficiary is absolutely or presumptively entitled and I leave it within the discretion of my trustees whether and to what extent the beneficiary shall bring into account any payments received under this clause

COMMENTARY

This clause extends the limit in s 32(1)(a) to the full amount of the beneficiary's share. Up to £100,000 could be advanced for Mary (in Adam's trust) or for Charles and Dora (in Bella's trust). In Christine's trust the whole fund could be advanced for Stephen provided that Henry consents.

The second part of the clause supersedes s 32(1)(b) and means that, if in Bella's trust £50,000 was advanced to Charles, the trustees could, on distribution, still divide the remaining fund equally between Charles and Dora.

SPECIMEN CLAUSE 2

> Power to pay or apply capital money from my residuary estate to any extent to or for the benefit of my husband

> Power to advance capital money from my residuary estate to my husband by way of loan to any extent upon such terms and conditions as my trustees may in their absolute discretion think fit

COMMENTARY

These provisions would permit the trustees in Christine's trust to give or lend capital from the fund to Henry even though he has only an interest in income, not capital. Such a clause may be included to give more flexibility in case the income proves insufficient for Henry's needs. Henry still remains dependent on the discretion of the trustees.

10.3.7 Power to accept receipts from and on behalf of minors

The statutory provisions

As seen in **10.3.4** and **10.3.5**, where a trust arises in favour of a beneficiary who is a minor, the trustees have statutory powers of maintenance and advancement under ss 31 and 32. Section 31 specifically allows the trustees to pay income to the child's parent or guardian or 'otherwise apply' it for the child's maintenance, education or benefit. Similarly, s 32 empowers the trustees to pay 'or apply' capital for the beneficiary's advancement or benefit. Thus the trustees will have no difficulty in obtaining a good receipt when exercising these powers.

Extending the statutory power

It may be thought unnecessary to include any further provisions in relation to receipts. However, if the testator wishes to give the trustees a wider power, a general provision may be included, which may even allow them to make payments to the child himself.

SPECIMEN CLAUSE

> Power in any case where my trustees have an obligation or discretion under the provisions of my will or under the general law to pay income or capital to or for the benefit of a minor to make payment either to a parent or guardian of the minor or to the minor personally if at least 16 years old so that their respective receipts shall be a full discharge to my trustees who shall not be required to see to the application of any income or capital so paid

COMMENTARY

This clause would apply to any specific or pecuniary legacies to minor beneficiaries as well as to the interest of any minor under a trust. It should be considered particularly if a provision replacing s 32 (rather than simply extending it) has been made.

10.3.8 Control of trustees by beneficiaries

TLATA 1996, s 19 provides that, where beneficiaries are sui juris and together entitled to the whole fund, they may direct the trustees to retire and appoint new trustees of the beneficiaries' choice. This means that in a case where the beneficiaries could by agreement end the trust under the rule in *Saunders v Vautier*, they now have the option of allowing the trust to continue with trustees of their own choice. The provision may be expressly excluded by the settlor. The draftsman should consider the terms of the trust to see whether the position could arise where all the beneficiaries are in existence and over 18 but the trust has not ended. If this is possible, the testator may wish to prevent the beneficiaries from choosing their own trustees.

SPECIMEN CLAUSE

> The provisions of section 19 of the Trusts of Land and Appointment of Trustees Act 1996 shall not apply to any trust created by this will so that no beneficiary shall have the right to require the appointment or retirement of any trustee or trustees.

10.4 TRUSTS OF LAND

10.4.1 Introduction

The TLATA 1996 gives special powers to a beneficiary under a trust of land who has an interest in possession. If, under the terms of the will, a trust with an interest in possession may arise the draftsman should consider whether to amend those powers. The Act does not define 'interest in possession', so it presumably has its usual meaning: a beneficiary has an interest in possession if he is entitled to claim the income of the fund as it arises (normally either because he has a life interest or because he is over 18 and entitled to claim income under TA 1925, s 31).

10.4.2 Duty to consult beneficiaries

Trustees exercising any function relating to the land must consult any beneficiary who is of full age and beneficially entitled to an interest in possession in the land and, so far as consistent with the 'general interest of the trust', give effect to the wishes of any such beneficiary (TLATA 1996, s 11). The duty to consult may be excluded by the trust instrument.

SPECIMEN CLAUSE
> The provisions of section 11 of the Trusts of Land and Appointment of Trustees Act 1996 shall not apply so that it shall not be necessary for my trustees to consult any beneficiaries before carrying out any function relating to land.

10.4.3 Beneficiary's right of occupation

A beneficiary with a beneficial interest in possession, even if not of full age, has the right to occupy land subject to the trust if the purposes of the trust include making the land available for occupation by him or if the trustees acquired the land in order to make it so available (TLATA 1996, s12). There is no power to exclude s 12, but a declaration that the purpose of the trust is not for the occupation of land could be made.

SPECIMEN CLAUSE
> The purposes of any trust created by this will do not include making land available for occupation of any beneficiary [although my trustees have power to do so if they wish].

10.5 THE APPORTIONMENT RULES

10.5.1 Introduction

One of the duties of trustees is to ensure that a fair balance is kept between the interests of the beneficiaries. This is particularly important where different beneficiaries are entitled to income and capital, for example where property is left on trust for X for life with remainder to Y as in Christine's trust above. The trustees must ensure that the investments they choose produce a reasonable income for X, the life tenant, and preserve the capital reasonably safely for Y, the remainderman.

10.5.2 *Howe v Dartmouth* and the duty to apportion income

The equitable rule in *Howe v Dartmouth* applies where a trust with successive interests (as above) arises by will in relation to residuary personalty. The rule imposes on trustees a duty to sell certain assets which by their nature are presumed to upset the balance between the life tenant and remainderman. The duty applies to 'wasting, hazardous and unauthorised' assets (such as the copyright to a book, which normally expires 50 years after the author's death). Such assets are presumed to produce income at the expense of capital. The rule also applies to assets of a 'reversionary' nature which produce no income for the life tenant (such as a life assurance policy where the life assured is still alive). The duty of sale in *Howe v Dartmouth* is superseded if the will imposes an express trust for sale.

Equity also imposes rules to maintain the balance between income and capital pending sale, by requiring apportionment. These rules apply where there is a duty to sell property, whether imposed impliedly under the rule in *Howe v Dartmouth* or expressly by a trust for sale in the will. They require income from wasting, hazardous or unauthorised investments to be apportioned so that the life tenant receives only a fixed percentage of the capital value of the asset, any surplus belonging to capital. Conversely when reversionary assets are sold or fall into possession, a proportion of the proceeds must be allocated to the life tenant to compensate for his loss of income.

Although this even-handed result may be desirable in theory, in practice the calculations required by the rules are complex and the time and expense involved is rarely justified. Thus it is usual to exclude the rules when drafting trusts to which they may apply (ie generally life interest trusts).

10.5.3 *Allhusen v Whittell*

The purpose of the equitable rule in *Allhusen v Whittell* is to preserve a fair balance between the life tenant and remainderman, this time in relation to the payment of the debts of the estate. It provides that the burden of the debts owed by the testator at the time of death, the expenses of administering the estate, any IHT payable from the residue and any legacies should be apportioned between income and capital according to a prescribed formula. Again, the time and expense of applying the rule is unlikely to be justified and it is usual to exclude its application when drafting life interest trusts.

10.5.4 Apportionment Act 1870

The Apportionment Act 1870, s 2 provides that income such as rent and dividends is to be treated as accruing from day to day and apportioned accordingly. Thus where assets in the estate produce income (such as dividends on shares) which is received after death but relates to a period partly before and partly after death, the income must be apportioned. The part accruing before death is capital, while that accruing after death is income. In addition, the Apportionment Act 1870 applies to any specific gift of an income producing asset, and to a contingent gift where the beneficiary is entitled to income but dies before the contingency is fulfilled.

> *Example 1*
> Mary dies leaving her estate on trust for Noel for life with remainder to Oliver. Mary's PRs receive income, such as rent and dividends, from the assets in her estate. The rent may relate to a period of occupation of Mary's property which fell, wholly or partly, before her death. Similarly, the dividends may represent profits for a period wholly or partly before Mary's death. The PRs must calculate how much of the income arose during Mary's lifetime: this amount forms part of the capital of her estate. Only the income arising after Mary's death is payable to Noel as life tenant.
>
> When Noel dies and his right to income ends, the trustees must make a similar apportionment of trust income received after Noel's death between Noel's estate and Oliver, the remainderman.
>
> *Example 2*
> Philip dies on 30 June 1995 leaving all his shares in ABC plc to Rose and the rest of his estate to his son Simon (now aged 20) if he attains the age of 25 years. In January 1996, Philip's executors receive £100, a dividend on the ABC shares for the year ended 31 December 1995. Rose is only entitled to £50, that part of the dividend which arose after Philip's death.
>
> Philip's trustees invest the residue of his estate and pay the income to Simon. Simon dies aged 24. The trustees must apportion the dividends they receive after Simon's death, and pay the part which arose during Simon's lifetime to his estate.

These apportionments can be very inconvenient where an estate or trust includes many shareholdings paying dividends in relation to different periods and so it is usual to exclude the Act, particularly in wills which create life interest trusts.

10.5.5 Excluding the apportionment rules

SPECIMEN CLAUSE

> Power to treat as income all the income from any part of my estate whatever the period in respect of which it may accrue and to disregard the Apportionment Act 1870 [and the rules of equity relating to apportionment including those known as the rules in *Howe v Dartmouth* and *Allhusen v Whittell* in all their branches]

COMMENTARY

This clause is appropriate in a will which creates a life interest trust such as Christine's trust in **10.3.1**. It is intended to exclude the application of all the apportionment rules described above. In a will containing a specific gift of an income producing asset or a contingent gift of residue, the clause could be included with the omission of the words in square brackets.

10.6 MISCELLANEOUS ADDITIONAL POWERS

10.6.1 Charging clause

Background law
The rule of equity that a trustee may not profit from his trust applies both to trustees and executors. Its effect is that an executor or trustee may claim only out-of-pocket expenses and may not charge for time spent in performing his office.

Extending the rule
In any case where a professional executor or trustee is appointed such as a bank, a firm of solicitors, an individual solicitor or an accountant, a power to charge should be included in the will. As discussed in **6.7.3**, such a power may be incorporated in the appointment clause or may be included in a list of powers at the end of the will.

SPECIMEN CLAUSE

> Any of my trustees being a solicitor or other person engaged in any profession or business may charge and be paid his usual professional charges for work done by him or his firm in the administration of my estate and the trusts arising under my will including acts which a trustee not engaged in any profession or business could have done personally

10.6.2 Power to appoint a trust corporation

SPECIMEN CLAUSE

> Power to appoint a trust corporation to be the sole trustee or one of the trustees of my will upon such terms and conditions in all respects as may be acceptable to the corporation so appointed

COMMENTARY

Provision of this kind is not commonly included in practice. Its purpose is to ensure that, if individual trustees wish to retire and no substitutes can readily be found, a bank (or other trust corporation) may be appointed even though there may be minor beneficiaries who are unable to give the required consent to the bank's usual terms and conditions, particularly in relation to charging.

10.6.3 Power to carry on business

Where an estate includes a business which was run by the deceased as a sole (unincorporated) trader, the powers of the PRs to run the business are limited. For example, they may only run the business with a view to selling it as a going concern and may only use those assets employed in the business at the date of death. These powers may be extended by will, although in practice PRs are unlikely to wish to involve themselves in the detailed running of a business. It may be preferable to bequeath the business by specific legacy. Details of this topic are beyond the scope of this book, but it is important to appreciate that there are special considerations to be taken into account when drafting a will for a sole trader.

10.7 SELECTING THE APPROPRIATE POWERS

10.7.1 Introduction

The role of the solicitor is to draw the testator's attention to the ways in which the powers of his PRs and trustees might usefully be extended in the circumstances of his particular will and to take his instructions. The draftsman should avoid the temptation to include a 'standard' package of administrative provisions without discussion with the client. In order to take instructions, the first step is to identify which provisions may be relevant to the client's will. The summary below (with references to this chapter) may be helpful.

10.7.2 Any will (whether or not trusts may arise)

Consider:

> appropriation (**10.2.2**);
> insurance (**10.2.3**);
> receipts for legacies to minors (**10.2.4**);
> charging clause, if appropriate (**10.6.1**);
> business, if appropriate (**10.6.3**);
> exclusion of Apportionment Act, if appropriate (**10.5.4**).

10.7.3 Any potential trust: minority, contingency or life interest

Consider in addition:

> investment (**10.3.2** and **10.3.3**);
> sale of personalty (**10.3.4**);
> maintenance (**10.3.5**);
> advancement (**10.3.6**);
> receipts (**10.3.7**);
> exclusion of beneficiaries' power to choose trustees (**10.3.8**);
> exclusion of beneficiaries' rights under a trust of land (**10.4**);
> exclusion of Apportionment Act (**10.5.4**).

10.7.4 Life interest trusts only

Certain provisions are only relevant when a life interest is created. Consider in addition:

> advancement – dispensing with the requirement for consent (**10.3.6**);
> advancement – power to loan or advance capital to the life tenant (**10.3.6**);
> exclusion of the equitable apportionment rules as well as the Apportionment Act (**10.5**).

Chapter 11

TAKING INSTRUCTIONS: GENERAL MATTERS

11.1 THE ROLE OF THE SOLICITOR

11.1.1 Taking the initiative

When taking instructions for a will, the solicitor's role is not merely to record his client's directions. The solicitor should also be prepared to draw his client's attention to legal provisions of which the client may be unaware, to explain the taxation and succession effects of the client's proposed dispositions and, where appropriate, to suggest alternatives which the client may not have considered.

11.1.2 Taking direct instructions

The solicitor should take instructions from the testator himself and, ideally, should interview the client personally. If the solicitor receives instructions from a third party, such as the testator's spouse or bank, The Law Society's conduct rules require him to write to the testator to confirm the instructions. The Law Society's Guide to the Professional Conduct of Solicitors states as follows:

> 'Where instructions are received not from a client but from a third party purporting to represent that client, a solicitor should obtain written instructions from the client that he wishes him to act, or in any case of doubt he should see the client or take other appropriate steps to confirm instructions.'

11.1.3 Conflict of interest

It is an established principle that a solicitor must not act where his own interests conflict with the interests of a client or a potential client.

Furthermore, The Law Society's Guide states that:

> 'Where a client intends to make a gift inter vivos or by will to his solicitor or to the solicitor's partner, or a member of staff or to the families of any of them and the gift is of a significant amount, either in itself or having regard to the size of the client's estate and the reasonable expectations of prospective beneficiaries, the solicitor must advise the client to be independently advised as to that gift and if the client declines, must refuse to act.'

If the client's instructions include a gift to the solicitor, or any of the connected persons listed in the above principle, the solicitor must decide whether the gift is 'significant'. If it is he must ensure that the client takes independent advice. The rule does not prohibit the solicitor from drafting the will provided that the client has been independently advised, although the solicitor may decide that it would be prudent not to draft it in order to avoid any possible allegations of suspicious circumstances which may affect the will's validity (see **13.3.2**).

Chapter 11 contents
The role of the solicitor
Is there an existing will?
The testator's property
Planning the will
Carrying out instructions

11.1.4 Furnishing proof of capacity

The solicitor should satisfy himself that his client has the capacity to make a will. If the solicitor is concerned that the client's capacity may be challenged, he should obtain a medical report and ensure that it is kept with the will (see **13.2.3**).

11.1.5 Methods of taking instructions

The solicitor must ensure that he takes accurate details of the testator's property, wishes and intended beneficiaries. Some solicitors find that time may be saved by asking the client to bring to the interview written details of his property and intended beneficiaries.

Some firms use a standard checklist which may be completed during the interview to ensure that no necessary information is overlooked.

11.1.6 Duty of care

The solicitor's duty of care when taking instructions for and drafting a will is not only owed to the testator. Under the principle in *Ross v Caunters* (see **13.5.4**), an intended beneficiary who, through the solicitor's negligence, fails to receive his gift may recover his loss in an action in tort against the solicitor.

In *Kecskemeti v Rubens Rabin & Co* (1992) *The Times*, 31 December, a solicitor failed to advise his client that certain land, owned jointly by the client and his wife, would pass on death by survivorship and not by will. The client's will contained a gift of half of the land to his son. The solicitor owed a duty of care to the son, as intended beneficiary, and was liable to compensate him for his loss.

11.2 IS THERE AN EXISTING WILL?

The solicitor should ascertain whether his client has previously made a will and, if so, where that will is kept and what it contains. If only minor changes are proposed, a codicil may be sufficient.

11.3 THE TESTATOR'S PROPERTY

11.3.1 Details required

The solicitor should take details of the property owned by the testator, not only to enable him to draft the will, but also so that he can give advice about the devolution of the property on death and about tax. Details of any joint property (whether held on a joint tenancy or as tenants in common), life assurance policies, lump sums payable under pension schemes and interests under trusts should be included.

11.3.2 Advice on succession

Some property may pass on death independently of the terms of the testator's will (see **2.4**). For example, an interest under a joint tenancy passes by survivorship to the surviving joint tenant; a life interest under a trust will end on the life tenant's death, and the capital of the trust fund will pass under the terms of the trust instrument to the remainderman. These matters should be explained to the client.

11.3.3 Advice on tax

The estate for IHT purposes may include property which passes independently of the terms of the will, such as the testator's share of property held on a joint tenancy and the capital of a trust fund in which the testator has a life interest. Other property of the testator may attract IHT reliefs, such as business property relief. For details on IHT, see Chapter 18.

The solicitor should explain these matters and should make a rough estimate of the potential charge to IHT on the testator's death. The testator may welcome advice on lifetime tax planning (see Chapter 12).

11.3.4 Foreign property

Special considerations apply where the client owns property abroad. The law of the relevant country may restrict the owner's freedom to dispose of land or other property on death. To the extent that such restrictions do not apply, a will disposing of foreign property should be prepared in the country concerned and the property should be excluded from the UK will.

Since foreign property owned by a person domiciled in a part of the UK is included in the estate for IHT purposes, double taxation questions may also arise.

Details of these matters are outside the scope of this book, but it is important to be aware of the need to take specialist advice.

11.4 PLANNING THE WILL

11.4.1 Choice of executors and trustees

The solicitor should explain the choices open to the client and should assist him to make an appropriate choice (see Chapter 6).

11.4.2 Legacies

The solicitor should ascertain the client's priorities: for example, if his main aim is to give a particular item of property to a beneficiary, a specific legacy is appropriate; but if the object is to benefit a particular individual, a pecuniary legacy may be preferable. Whatever the client's aims and priorities, the solicitor should obtain details of the property to be given and the names and addresses of the beneficiaries so that all can be identified. Such information will also enable the solicitor to deal with any particular drafting points, for example those relevant to a gift of shares or a gift to a minor or to a charity (see Chapter 8).

11.4.3 Residue

The solicitor should be prepared to suggest and explain the possible alternative dispositions (eg absolute gift or life interest) and why a survivorship clause might be advisable. Similarly, the client may not have considered the possibility that the primary beneficiary might die before him. The solicitor should raise this possibility and take instructions for substitutional provisions. Full details on gifts of residue and the matters to consider are to be found in Chapter 9.

11.4.4 Tax

The solicitor should explain the potential charge to IHT in the light of the client's proposed dispositions. Where appropriate, it may be possible to suggest alternative dispositions which would mitigate the burden of IHT. In family cases, account should be taken of the burden of tax not only on the testator's death but also on the death of the surviving spouse (see Chapter 12).

11.4.5 Family provision

If the testator's instructions are such that a claim for family provision might be made against the estate, the solicitor should explain the possibility to his client. The testator may have good reasons for failing to provide by will for a potential applicant. If so, an explanation of these reasons should be written by the testator and kept with the will. Should a claim arise, such an explanation will be admissible in evidence (see Chapter 17).

11.4.6 Review

Although the solicitor should attempt to prepare a will which provides for all reasonably foreseeable circumstances, he should draw to his client's attention the need to keep his will under review, particularly in the case of marriage or divorce.

11.5 CARRYING OUT INSTRUCTIONS

Having taken instructions to prepare a will, the solicitor must ensure that those instructions are carried out. The will must be prepared and arrangements made for its due execution (as described in Chapter 13) without delay. If a solicitor, in breach of his professional duty to a client, fails to carry out instructions to prepare a will then he may find himself liable to compensate intended beneficiaries. In *White and Another v Jones and Another* [1995] 2 AC 207, a testator executed a will disinheriting his two daughters as a result of a family argument. Following a reconciliation, he instructed his solicitor to draft a new will providing substantial legacies to each daughter. The solicitor negligently failed to draw up the will. The House of Lords held that the solicitor (and his firm) were liable to the daughters and had to compensate them for their lost legacies.

Chapter 12

TAKING INSTRUCTIONS: TAX CONSIDERATIONS

12.1 INTRODUCTION

Chapter 12 contents
Introduction
Estimating the potential tax bill
Lifetime gifts
Planning the will

Taking instructions for a will provides an opportunity to discuss with the client the potential burden of IHT on his estate and the ways in which that burden might be mitigated. It may be possible to reduce the burden of tax on death, either by making lifetime gifts to reduce the size of the estate or by adjusting the dispositions to be included in the will.

However, the practical implications of any tax-saving scheme must always be considered carefully. A client who requires the income from his shares in order to maintain his usual lifestyle is unlikely to want to give the shares away in order to save IHT on his death. In disposing of his estate by will a testator's main priority is usually to provide for his family, and he may be unconcerned about the ultimate effect of IHT.

12.2 ESTIMATING THE POTENTIAL TAX BILL

12.2.1 The estate for IHT purposes

The first step is to identify the property which constitutes the client's estate for IHT purposes and make a rough estimate of its value. For IHT purposes, the estate may include property which will not pass under the terms of the will, such as joint property and trust property where the client is entitled to the income (see **18.4**).

12.2.2 Exemptions and reliefs

Consider what exemptions and reliefs, if any, may be available on death.

Exemptions

Ascertain who will be entitled to the client's estate on his death (taking into account the proposed will). Any property passing to his spouse or to charity is exempt from IHT (see **18.6**). Spouse exemption applies to any property passing to the deceased's spouse, whether by will, by survivorship or otherwise. Thus, although the IHT estate includes the deceased's share of joint property, if the joint owners are husband and wife, the spouse exemption will apply.

Reliefs

Consider the nature of the property included in the IHT estate in order to see whether business or agricultural property reliefs may be available (see **18.7**).

12.2.3 Effect of lifetime transfers

Ascertain whether the client has made any immediately chargeable or potentially exempt transfers within the last 7 years (see **12.3.2**). Because of the principle of cumulation (see **18.8.2**), chargeable transfers made within 7 years of death erode, or may even exhaust, the nil rate band applicable to the estate, thus increasing the IHT bill on death.

12.2.4 The long view

In family cases it is important to consider not only the position immediately on death (when the spouse exemption may apply) but also the potential tax bill on, for example, the death of a surviving spouse. The client should also consider the possibility that his spouse might die first.

12.3 LIFETIME GIFTS

One obvious way to reduce the potential IHT bill on death is to reduce the size of the estate for IHT by making lifetime gifts.

The practical implications of any proposed lifetime gifts must be carefully considered. Can the client afford to make lifetime gifts? Consider the possibility that the client's financial circumstances may change. Tax planning by means of lifetime gifts is usually inadvisable unless the client is wealthy.

12.3.1 Use of exemptions

The simplest way to reduce the estate for IHT is to make gifts which fall within the lifetime exemptions, such as the annual exemption, small gifts exemption and marriage exemption (where appropriate). See **18.13.2** for further details.

Since gifts to the spouse are exempt whether made inter vivos or on death, there is, at first sight, no compelling reason to make use of the exemption by making lifetime gifts to the spouse. However, such gifts may enable the spouse to make use of her own lifetime exemptions and of her nil rate band on death (see **12.4.1**).

12.3.2 Potentially exempt transfers

A lifetime gift to an individual to which the lifetime exemptions do not apply is a potentially exempt transfer. Such a gift will become exempt if the transferor survives for 7 years. A wealthy client may wish to consider making potentially exempt transfers in the expectation that he will survive for 7 years. Careful consideration should be given to the effect of death within 7 years (see **18.13.3**). Not only will the gift itself become chargeable, so that the transferee may be called upon to pay IHT, but also the nil rate band applicable to the estate on death will be reduced or may even be used up completely.

If a client gives away property during his lifetime but continues to enjoy that property, the reservation of benefit provisions may apply to render the gift ineffective for IHT purposes. For an example, see **18.4.3**.

12.3.3 CGT

If the client makes a lifetime gift of a chargeable asset, the gift will be a disposal for CGT purposes which may give rise to an immediate charge to CGT. If a gift of cash is contemplated it may be necessary to sell assets (eg shares) in order to raise the cash. The sale may give rise to chargeable gain. The IHT advantages of lifetime gifts should be weighed against any possible CGT charge, bearing in mind that there will be no CGT if the asset is given away by will. The principles of CGT may be found in the LPC Resource Book *Pervasive Topics* (Jordans, 1997), Part I.

12.4 PLANNING THE WILL

12.4.1 Spouse exemption and nil rate band

Effect of spouse exemption
If the testator intends to leave his whole estate by will to his spouse, no IHT will be payable on his death as the gift is exempt. The same result will follow if the testator leaves all his estate on trust and gives his spouse a life interest (see **18.4.2**). However, on the subsequent death of the spouse, IHT will be charged on the combined estates of husband and wife (unless avoiding action is taken).

> *Example*
> John and his wife Mary each have property worth £250,000. John dies leaving all his estate to Mary. The whole estate is spouse exempt. Mary later dies leaving all her estate to the children. Her estate is now worth £500,000. Mary has made no lifetime gifts.
>
> Tax on Mary's death:
>
> | £215,000 | NIL |
> | £285,000 @ 40% | £114,000 |

Using each spouse's nil rate band
The effect in the above example could be mitigated if John were to use his own nil rate band to leave part of his estate to the children on his death.

> *Example*
> John leaves £215,000 to the children and the rest of his estate to his wife. No tax is payable on John's death as the gift to the children falls within John's nil rate band and the gift of residue is spouse exempt. When Mary dies leaving her estate to the children, it is worth £285,000 (Mary's £250,000 + £35,000, the residue of John's estate). Neither has made any lifetime gifts.
>
> Tax on Mary's death:
>
> | £215,000 | NIL |
> | £70,000 @ 40% | £28,000 |

Thus, in the long term, a tax saving of £86,000 has been achieved by making use of each spouse's nil rate band to leave property to the children.

Practical considerations
In family cases where no lifetime gifts have been made, it may be preferable for tax purposes to give a legacy equal to the testator's nil rate band to the children and the residue to the spouse. However, the testator must consider whether such an arrangement will leave the surviving spouse with sufficient money, particularly if the matrimonial home is a major part of the estate. Remember that if the house is held on a joint tenancy the testator's share will pass by survivorship regardless of the terms of the will.

Order of deaths
The client should consider the possibility that his spouse may die first. In such a case, the tax saving illustrated above can only be achieved if the spouse also leaves a sum equal to the nil rate band directly to the children by will and has sufficient funds to do so. Thus, if the tax saving effect is to be achieved, both husband and wife should make wills. If one spouse owns considerably more property than the other, lifetime gifts may be made (taking advantage of the spouse exemption) to ensure that each spouse's estate is at least equal to the nil rate band.

12.4.2 Use of reliefs

If a testator leaves property which qualifies for business or agricultural property relief to an exempt beneficiary, such as his spouse, the benefit of the relief has, in principle, been wasted. Again, practical considerations will prevail. The testator may particularly wish to give the business property to his spouse. However, if the testator intends to benefit, say, his spouse and children, the best arrangement for tax purposes is to give business property to the children.

> *Example*
> John's estate is worth £600,000. It includes a holding of shares in a private company. The shares are worth £300,000 and are eligible for business property relief at 100 per cent. He intends to give equal benefits to his wife and adult son.
>
> If John gives a specific legacy of the shares to his son and the residue of his estate to his wife, no IHT will be payable. The shares, after business property relief have no value for IHT purposes. The residue of £300,000 passing to John's wife is exempt.

12.4.3 Property outside the estate for IHT purposes

Life assurance policies written in trust
If a testator takes out a life assurance policy which is written in trust for a named beneficiary (eg his son), the benefit of the policy belongs to that beneficiary even during the testator's lifetime. On his death, the policy matures and the insurance company will pay the proceeds to the named beneficiary (or to trustees for him), regardless of the terms of the will. The policy proceeds do not form part of the testator's estate for IHT purposes because he was not beneficially entitled to the policy immediately before his death.

If the testator wishes to make provision for his family in a tax-efficient manner, a life policy written in trust for children might be considered. When the testator pays premiums on such a policy he is making lifetime gifts to the children. However, such payments will probably be exempt as part of normal expenditure out of income (see **18.13.2**).

Lump sum payments under pension schemes
A common provision in occupational pension schemes provides that if the employee dies while in the service of the employer, the trustees of the pension fund will, at their discretion, pay a lump sum to the employee's family. The amount of the lump sum is usually related to the employee's salary, and the employee is given an opportunity to indicate to the trustees how he would like them to distribute the lump sum. Again, the employee is not beneficially entitled to such a payment

immediately before his death, and so the money does not form part of his estate for IHT purposes. If he wishes to ensure that the maximum tax advantages are achieved, the employee should designate someone other than his spouse to receive the funds, such as his children. In this way provision may be made for a non-exempt beneficiary without payment of IHT.

Chapter 13

REQUIREMENTS FOR A VALID WILL

13.1 INTRODUCTION

When drafting a will, a solicitor must ensure that he creates a valid will, capable of taking effect when the testator dies. If a will is invalid for any reason, it cannot be admitted to probate and its provisions are of no effect.

There are three requirements which must be satisfied for a will to be valid:

(1) the testator's capacity;
(2) the testator's intention; and
(3) the formalities for execution.

A solicitor should consider from the outset whether the will that he is preparing for his client could be challenged in the future because of some problem connected with capacity, intention or formalities. He should take appropriate steps to safeguard his client and his client's estate from such risks.

This chapter is primarily concerned with practical matters. Further details of the background law may be found in Barlow, King and King, Mellows or Parry and Clark.

Chapter 13 contents
Introduction
Capacity
Intention
Formalities for execution
Choice of witnesses
Alterations

13.2 CAPACITY

The testator's capacity to make a valid will depends on his age and his state of mind (or 'testamentary capacity').

13.2.1 Age

The testator must be aged 18 or over when he executes his will (Wills Act 1837, s 7, as amended by the Family Law Reform Act 1969, s 3) unless he is entitled to make a 'privileged' will because he is a soldier or airman on actual military service or a sailor at sea. The details of privileged wills are outside the scope of this book.

13.2.2 Testamentary capacity

The basic rule

The testator must have the requisite mental capacity when he executes his will. This testamentary capacity was defined in *Banks v Goodfellow* (1870) LR 5 QB 549 as 'soundness of mind, memory and understanding'. This means that the testator must understand:

(1) the nature of his act and its broad effects;
(2) the extent of his property (although not necessarily recollecting every individual item); and
(3) the moral claims he ought to consider (even if he decides to reject such claims and dispose of his property to other beneficiaries).

If the testator lacked the requisite mental capacity when he executed his will, then generally the will is invalid.

Proof and presumptions

Initially, the burden of proving that the testator had testamentary capacity at the time he executed the will falls on the propounder of the will (ie the person who seeks to prove after the testator's death that the will is valid). However, there are two presumptions which may affect the burden of proof.

(1) If the will appears rational (ie reads sensibly) then the presumption is that the testator did have testamentary capacity. Consequently the propounder can shift the burden of proof. The will is admitted to probate by the registrar unless any person alleging that the will is invalid can provide enough evidence to rebut this presumption of capacity, in which case the propounder will actually have to prove testamentary capacity.

(2) Mental states are presumed to persist. If a person who does not ordinarily have testamentary capacity (eg through mental illness) makes a will, the presumption is that he still lacked testamentary capacity at the relevant time and the propounder of the will must actively prove that the testator had in fact recovered testamentary capacity (either temporarily or permanently) at the time he made the will.

13.2.3 Practical safeguards

If a solicitor has any doubts about whether his client has the testamentary capacity to make a will or believes that capacity may be challenged later on, he should take appropriate practical steps to forestall any possible future arguments.

In the case of *Kenward v Adams* (1975) *The Times*, 29 November, the court suggested guidelines for the will of an elderly and/or infirm testator. The solicitor should:

(1) arrange for a medical practitioner to examine the testator at the time the will is to be executed to verify his mental capacity and have that medical opinion recorded in writing; and
(2) ask that examining practitioner to witness the will.

Many hospitals, nursing homes etc have internal rules instructing their staff not to witness wills. It may be necessary therefore to have an external practitioner (such as the testator's own GP) examine the testator and, if possible, witness the will or, alternatively, for that practitioner to conduct and record the medical examination but to have non-medical witnesses for the will.

These arrangements will require great tact on the part of the solicitor. If a solicitor has had to consider potential capacity problems, it is prudent for him to make a detailed attendance note for the file.

13.3 INTENTION

In order to make a valid will, the testator must have both general and specific intention at the time he executes the will.

13.3.1 General intention

The testator must intend to make a will (as opposed to any other sort of document).

13.3.2 Specific intention

The testator must also have the intention to make the particular will now being executed (ie he must know and approve its contents). If he executes his will without knowing and approving its contents, the will is invalid and cannot be admitted to probate.

Proof and presumptions

As with testamentary capacity, the burden of proving the testator's knowledge and approval falls on the propounder of the will but there is one presumption which will usually assist.

A testator who has capacity and has executed his will is presumed to have the requisite knowledge and approval (particularly where he has previously read the text or had it read over to him). However, this presumption does not apply in the situations listed below.

TESTATOR BLIND/ILLITERATE/NOT SIGNING PERSONALLY

The presumption of the testator's knowledge and approval does not apply if the testator is blind or illiterate or another person signs the will on his behalf (eg because he has an injured hand).

In these cases the probate registrar will require evidence of the testator's actual knowledge and approval. The solicitor should therefore ensure that the will is read out to, and approved by, the testator in front of the witnesses and that the usual wording of the attestation clause is adapted to reflect this. One example of an appropriate form of words would be:

> This will having been read over
> to the above named testator in our
> joint presence and the testator
> appearing thoroughly to understand
> the same and to approve its contents
> was signed by (name of person signing)
> in his presence and by his direction
> as his last will in the presence of
> us present at the same time who at his
> request in his presence and in the
> presence of each other have hereunto
> subscribed our names as witnesses

Without such an attestation clause, the probate registrar will require affidavit evidence of the testator's knowledge and approval (see **20.7.2**) from a witness or someone else who was present at the execution. Providing such evidence involves time and expense.

SUSPICIOUS CIRCUMSTANCES

Similarly the presumption of the testator's knowledge and approval does not apply if there are suspicious circumstances surrounding the drafting and/or execution of the will (eg the will has been prepared by someone who is to be a major beneficiary under its terms or is the close relative of a major beneficiary).

In such cases, because the presumption does not apply, the propounder of the will must remove the suspicion by proving that the testator did actually know and approve the will's contents. Obviously the degree of suspicion arising will depend on the circumstances.

A solicitor who is drafting any will under which he will inherit as a beneficiary must be alert both to the risk of the will being challenged by an allegation of suspicious circumstances and also to his separate conduct obligation (see **11.1.3**) and take appropriate practical steps (see **13.3.3**). In the case of *Wintle v Nye* [1959] 1 WLR 284, the substantial gift to the solicitor draftsman was refused probate due to lack of the testator's knowledge and approval, but the rest of the will was duly admitted.

Proving absence of knowledge and approval

If the presumption of the testator's knowledge and approval applies, then any person who wishes to challenge this aspect of the will (or any part of it) must prove absence of knowledge and approval in order to prevent some or all of the document from being admitted to probate. This can be done by proving one or more of the following grounds:

FORCE, FEAR, FRAUD OR UNDUE INFLUENCE

The testator made his will (or part of it) as a result of force or fear (through actual or threatened injury); or fraud (eg after being misled by some pretence); or undue influence (where the testator's freedom of choice was overcome by intolerable pressure, even though his judgment remained unconvinced). The dividing line between vigorous persuasion and coercion amounting to undue influence is always difficult to identify but the character of the testator (eg any physical or mental weakness) is particularly relevant.

MISTAKE

All or part of the will was included by mistake. Any words included without the knowledge and approval of the testator will be omitted from probate. In this respect it is important to distinguish between actual mistake (ie absence of knowledge and approval) and misunderstanding as to the true legal meaning of words used in the will.

The probate court will not intervene over words which were badly selected and used by a testator (or draftsman) who was merely mistaken about their legal effect. Those words will still be admitted to probate unless a claim for rectification is possible (see **28.2.1**). The professional draftsman must therefore ensure that the legal effect of his clauses properly implements the testator's intentions.

13.3.3 Practical safeguards

The solicitor should take the following steps to help forestall any future claim that the will is invalid for lack of the testator's knowledge and approval:

(1) explain to the client the meaning and effect of all the clauses in his will;
(2) ask him to read the will before he executes it to ensure that it complies with his wishes; and
(3) comply with the conduct principle (see **11.1.3**) whenever the will is to contain a gift to the solicitor, his partner(s), staff or their respective families. (This will also help prevent the will being challenged in the future by an allegation of suspicious circumstances.)

13.4 FORMALITIES FOR EXECUTION

13.4.1 Wills Act 1837, s 9

The Wills Act 1837, s 9 (as substituted by Administration of Justice Act 1982, s 17) sets out the formalities required for execution of a will. Any will which does not comply with these requirements will be invalid and therefore cannot be admitted to probate.

A solicitor needs to know the detail of these formalities in order to:

(1) arrange for a client to execute his will in such a way that there is absolutely no doubt as to its compliance; and
(2) be able to examine an unfamiliar (and perhaps homemade) will and decide whether or not it complies with the statutory requirements and, in case of doubt, what further investigations to undertake.

Section 9 provides:

'No will shall be valid unless –

(a) it is in writing, and signed by the testator, or by some other person in his presence and by his direction; and
(b) it appears that the testator intended by his signature to give effect to the will; and
(c) the signature is made or acknowledged by the testator in the presence of two or more witnesses present at the same time; and
(d) each witness either –

(i) attests and signs the will; or
(ii) acknowledges his signature,

in the presence of the testator (but not necessarily in the presence of any other witness),

but no form of attestation shall be necessary.'

In writing

The will must be 'in writing', ie handwritten, typed or printed. It need not be in ink, but a mixture of ink and pencil raises the presumption that the pencil sections were not intended to be final and should therefore be omitted from probate. Professionally produced wills are typed, whereas many homemade wills are either entirely handwritten or on commercial will forms which contain many standard printed clauses with the remaining sections completed in handwriting.

Signed

The testator's usual signature is best in normal cases; but in unusual situations any words or marks which he intended to be his signature can suffice.

Another person (even a witness) can sign on the testator's behalf provided this is done in the testator's mental and physical presence and at his direction. For simplicity and certainty, it is preferable in such cases for that person to sign in his own name and for the wording of an adapted attestation clause to explain in full precisely what took place (see **13.3.2**).

Intention

The testator must intend the signature to give effect to the will. Originally s 9 required the testator's signature to appear at 'the foot or end' of the will and problems ensued over clauses which appeared below the signature. Under the amended s 9 the exact placing of the testator's signature is no longer crucial, provided it is apparent that the signature is intended to give effect to the entire will. However, to avoid unnecessary complications, it is preferable in practice to ask the testator to sign opposite the attestation clause at the end of the text.

Witnesses

The testator's signature must be made or acknowledged in the physical and mental presence of at least two witnesses. The testator can actually sign in front of the witnesses (who need not actually have seen the signature and need not necessarily know that the document being signed is a will). Alternatively, the testator can acknowledge in their presence, by words or conduct, a signature he made earlier.

For certainty and convenience, each witness should sign the will in the presence of the testator and preferably (but not necessarily) in the presence of the other witness/witnesses. Each witness should sign with the intention of validating the testator's signature. In practice the usual procedure (to reduce the possibility of future dispute) is for each witness to sign after the testator at the end of the text beside the attestation clause and below the testator's signature. The testator must be physically and mentally present, although he need not actually have seen the witnesses sign provided that he could have done so from his physical position had he decided to watch.

If a witness did not actually sign the will in the presence of the testator, this does not render the will invalid provided that this witness acknowledged his own signature (made earlier) in the testator's presence and with the requisite intention.

13.4.2 Summary of procedure

The simplest procedure to be certain of complying with the formalities is as follows:

(1) the testator and at least two suitable witnesses (see **13.5**) should remain together and stay alert throughout the process so that all are physically and mentally present;
(2) the witnesses watch the testator date and sign the will; and
(3) each witness then signs in turn while the testator looks on.

13.4.3 Attestation clause

Section 9 does not expressly require any attestation clause. However, the use of a conventionally worded clause, which recites that the s 9 formalities were observed, raises the presumption of due execution.

If there is no such attestation clause in the will the district judge (or registrar) must require an affidavit of due execution (see **20.7.2**) from a witness or any other person who was present during the execution or, failing that, an affidavit of handwriting evidence to identify the testator's signature, or refer the case to a judge (all of which involve time and expense).

Since codicils must also be executed in accordance with the same formalities, an appropriately worded attestation clause in a codicil (see **4.4.2**) is important to raise the same presumption of due execution.

13.5 CHOICE OF WITNESSES

13.5.1 Capacity

The testator's witnesses must be physically and mentally present when he executes the will and capable of attesting (ie intending to validate his signature by their own signature or acknowledgment).

A blind person is not capable of being a witness because he is not able to see the testator sign. Equally someone who is drunk or mentally unsound would not be capable.

Although there is no rule which prevents a minor from witnessing a will, the infant would need to understand the significance of his role in the process. It is better, if possible, to avoid a choice which might invite future dispute, and to choose an adult instead.

A witness may, in the event of any future dispute, be required to give evidence of due execution. When advising a client about his choice of witnesses, the solicitor should encourage him to avoid persons who are ill and/or old (as they may not outlive the testator) or passing acquaintances (who may be hard to trace in future if, for example, they move out of the area).

13.5.2 Wills Act 1837, s 15

The solicitor should ensure that he advises his client not to select as his witnesses anyone who is:

(1) a beneficiary under the will; or
(2) married to one of the beneficiaries at the time the will is executed.

This is because, under s 15, if a beneficiary, or the spouse of a beneficiary, witnesses the testator's will then, although the witness' signature is valid and therefore the will can be valid, the witness or spouse cannot take their gift in the will. If a witness later marries a beneficiary, the gift is unaffected. The aim of this rule is to ensure that wills are witnessed by independent people.

The rule also covers the benefit of a professional executor's charging clause (see **6.7.3**). Consequently a solicitor should not himself witness a will in which he as an individual, or the firm in which he is a partner, is appointed executor. If he does so, the charging clause will be void even though the appointment and the will remain effective. Similarly, none of the other partners in the firm should witness the will, or the benefit of the charging clause is lost.

If a client is executing his will in the solicitor's office, non-partners from the firm could be chosen instead. There is no rule against trainee solicitors and assistant solicitors acting as witnesses, even though they may in due course become partners and share in the profits of the charging clause. However, many firms prefer to recommend that the witnesses are selected from their non-legal support staff.

13.5.3 Wills Act 1968, s 1

Under the Wills Act 1968, s 1 there is an exception to the rule in s 15 above. The signature of a 'superfluous' witness/beneficiary, or witness/spouse of a beneficiary, can be disregarded (and hence the gift remain unaffected) provided that there are at least two other independent witnesses who are unaffected by s 15, so that the will is still duly executed.

If, for example, one of three witnesses is himself a beneficiary or married to a beneficiary, the beneficiary can still take the gift. If two out of three witnesses are themselves beneficiaries (or married to beneficiaries), neither of them (or their spouses) can take their gifts. In both instances the will remains valid.

13.5.4 Solicitor's duties

A solicitor must advise his client carefully and accurately on the choice of witnesses and how to execute the will, and should check that his advice has been effective, since he is under a contractual duty to the client and also owes a duty of care in tort to those beneficiaries whom the testator was intending to benefit.

In the case of *Ross v Caunters* [1980] Ch 297 the client executed his will at home following his solicitor's letter of instruction; but the solicitor had failed to warn him that the spouse of a beneficiary should not be a witness. The solicitor failed to check the executed will when it was returned to him, so he did not spot that one of the witnesses was married to a beneficiary and, consequently, did not take any remedial action. The legacy to the beneficiary failed and she sued the solicitor. It was held that the solicitor had been negligent and had to compensate the beneficiary for the loss of the legacy that she should have received.

Adoption of a standard office procedure can help reduce the risk of such mistakes.

13.5.5 Practical safeguards

Clients usually either execute their will in the solicitor's office or have the will sent to their home address for execution.

(1) If the execution takes place at the solicitor's office, the procedure below incorporates various safeguards to ensure that the will is valid:

   (a) ask the client to confirm that he has read the will, understood its provisions (previously explained to him) and that it accords with his wishes;
   (b) watched by at least two independent witnesses (ie not beneficiaries, spouses of beneficiaries or any partner/professional executor affected by a charging clause), the testator dates the original will and signs opposite the attestation clause;
   (c) watched by the testator, the witnesses each in turn sign below the attestation clause and write in their address and occupation (in case they have to be traced in future);
   (d) the solicitor makes an attendance note for his file.

(2) If a letter is to be sent to the client explaining how to execute his will, it should deal with the following points/instructions:

   (a) enclose the original will for execution plus a copy for the client's own records;
   (b) ask the client to re-read the will (the provisions of which should have been explained in detail at an earlier stage) to ensure that he understands it and that it accords with his wishes, and invite the client to contact the solicitor if he has any queries or wants to make any changes;
   (c) watched by at least two independent witnesses (ie not beneficiaries, spouses of beneficiaries or any partner/professional executor affected by a charging clause), the testator dates the original will and signs opposite the attestation clause;

(d) watched by the testator, the witnesses each in turn sign below the attestation clause and write in their address and occupation (in case they have to be traced in future);

(e) ask the client to return the original will for checking, but without clipping, pinning or stapling anything to the document (see **20.7.2** for an explanation of the reason for this request);

(f) suggest appropriate storage arrangements (eg in the firm's strongroom);

(g) invite the client to make contact if he is uncertain about any aspect of the procedure.

In either event, it is essential that the solicitor checks the executed will to ensure that all the requirements have been properly complied with, and keeps a copy of the validly executed will on file.

13.6 ALTERATIONS

It is possible that a testator may want to make some alterations to the text of his will at the time he executes it, or that a solicitor may be consulted after the testator's death about the validity and effect of a will which bears some manuscript alterations.

13.6.1 Basic rule

The basic rule (Wills Act 1837, s 21) is that any alteration made before execution of the will is valid, but any alteration made after execution is void unless:

(1) the alteration has been executed like a will (the initials of the testator and the witnesses in the margin opposite the alteration being sufficient); or
(2) the entire will including the alteration has been subsequently re-executed or confirmed by a codicil which refers to the alteration.

13.6.2 Presumptions

There are two presumptions which apply in the absence of any contrary extrinsic evidence (ie evidence outside the text of the will about the actual events):

(1) the completion of a blank space (eg the date) is presumed to have been done before execution (and is therefore valid and admissible to probate); but
(2) all other alterations are presumed to have been made after execution (and are therefore invalid and inadmissible to probate unless initialled, re-executed or confirmed by codicil as discussed in **13.6.1**).

13.6.3 Practical safeguard

In order to avoid any future requirement to prove whether alterations were made before or after execution, all alterations should be initialled by the testator and the witnesses.

13.6.4 Invalid alterations

Original wording apparent
Where an alteration is invalid but the original wording is apparent (ie it can be read by ordinary means including use of a magnifying glass or extra light) then the alteration is ignored and the original apparent wording is admitted to probate.

Example

'£250 to my brother Jonathan'

Despite being crossed out, the original wording of £250 will be admitted to probate.

Original wording not apparent

Where an alteration is invalid and the original wording is not apparent because it has been obliterated in some way, then the basic rule is that the will is admitted to probate with a blank space (because the original wording is held to have been revoked by destruction) unless there is evidence that the testator either did not intend to revoke the original wording or intended to revoke it only conditionally.

An example of conditional intention is where the testator has obliterated the original wording and then attempted to substitute words or figures, for example to increase a gift from £1,000 to £2,000.

In such a situation, the doctrine of dependent relative revocation can apply (see **14.3.1**) so that the testator is presumed to have intended that the original wording should be revoked only if the substitute wording is admissible to probate and can take effect. If it cannot, he is deemed to have intended not to revoke the original wording. This means that if the original wording can be ascertained by any extrinsic evidence (eg from copies of the will or drafts or infra-red photography), that original wording can be admitted to probate and take effect.

Chapter 14

REVOCATION

14.1 INTRODUCTION

A testator can always revoke his will during his lifetime provided he has testamentary capacity.

14.2 MUTUAL WILLS

In some situations the equitable doctrine of mutual wills may impose a trust on property to frustrate the effect of the revocation of a will.

The doctrine applies where two (or more) people make an agreement to dispose of their property on death in a particular way and, in accordance with that agreement, execute wills in similar terms. When either party dies leaving a will in the agreed terms, equity implies a trust over the property of the survivor. Although the survivor remains free to change his will, his property is bound by the trust, so that the beneficial interest will not pass under any new will.

These rules give rise to serious practical problems (eg how much of the survivor's property is bound by the agreement; does the survivor remain free to deal with his property during his lifetime?). Although married couples commonly make wills in similar terms (sometimes called 'mirror wills') they do not usually intend to impose a binding obligation upon one another. Mutual wills only arise where such an intention exists.

14.3 METHODS OF REVOCATION

14.3.1 By a later will or codicil

Under the Wills Act 1837, s 20 a will can be revoked in whole or in part by a later will or codicil.

Express revocation

If a later will is intended to revoke the whole of an earlier one, the new will should contain a suitable express revocation clause (see **5.2**). If a codicil is intended to revoke only certain parts of the earlier will, the codicil should be carefully worded to show clearly which parts of the will are revoked (together with any substitute provisions) and which sections are confirmed (see **4.4.2**).

Every will should include an express revocation clause (see **5.2**).

Implied revocation

Even if the new will or codicil does not contain an express revocation clause, the earlier will or codicil is impliedly revoked by the later one to the extent that the later document contains provisions which are inconsistent with, or repeat, the earlier one.

Chapter 14 contents
Introduction
Mutual wills
Methods of revocation

The doctrine of dependent relative revocation

If the express or implied revocation is held to be conditional in some way, and the condition has not been fulfilled, the doctrine of dependent relative revocation can apply to save a will (or part of it) from being revoked by a later will or codicil.

For example, if the revocation of the old will is construed as being conditional on the new will being effective, and the new will is not effective, then the doctrine can save the earlier will from being revoked.

The doctrine also applies to certain alterations in a will (see **13.6.4**).

14.3.2 By marriage

Basic rule

For wills executed after 31 December 1982 the basic rule is that, if the testator marries after executing a will, that marriage automatically revokes the will (Wills Act 1837, s 18, as substituted by the Administration of Justice Act 1982). The rule does not apply in certain cases where a testator makes a will prior to and in anticipation of his forthcoming marriage.

Will made in anticipation of marriage

Wills Act 1837, s 18(3) (as substituted) provides:

> 'Where it appears from a will that at the time it was made the testator was expecting to be married to a particular person and that he intended that the will should not be revoked by the marriage, the will shall not be revoked by his marriage to that person.'

A general plan to marry someone in the abstract is not sufficient and an express statement about the testator's particular expectation and intention should be included in the will as intrinsic evidence.

SPECIMEN CLAUSE
> **I make this will in expectation of my marriage to [full name] and I intend that this will shall not be revoked by that marriage.**

COMMENTARY
If, in the event, the testator marries someone else, then that marriage will revoke the will.

In addition, the Wills Act 1837, s 18(4) (as substituted) provides:

> 'Where it appears from a will that at the time it was made the testator was expecting to be married to a particular person and that he intended that a disposition in the will should not be revoked by his marriage to that person –
>
> (a) that disposition shall take effect notwithstanding the marriage; and
> (b) any other disposition in the will shall take effect also, unless it appears from the will that the testator intended the disposition to be revoked by the marriage.'

Note that extrinsic evidence of the testator's intention is not admissible.

Wills made in anticipation of marriage are relatively unusual and are primarily suitable as an interim measure, with the substantive will being drafted after the marriage has taken place. One of the main reasons for them is to provide for the partner even if the testator dies before the marriage takes place.

Will conditional on marriage

In order to cover a situation where the testator makes a will but the anticipated marriage does not take place for any reason (eg a broken engagement) and the testator does not make a new will, it is possible to make the will conditional on the marriage taking place within a specified period from the execution of the will. Then if the marriage does not take place, for whatever reason, the new will is void and does not revoke any earlier wills that the testator may have made.

SPECIMEN CLAUSE

> This will is conditional on my marriage with [full name] taking place within [state period] and if my marriage with [full name] takes place within [state period] all former wills and codicils made by me are revoked.

The effect of the testator's divorce

If the testator makes a will and is later divorced (or the marriage is annulled or declared void) then under the Wills Act 1837, s 18A (inserted by the Administration of Justice Act 1982 and applicable to deaths after 31 December 1982):

(1) the will takes effect as if any appointment of the former spouse as an executor or executor and trustee of the will were omitted (although other executors or executor/trustees are unaffected); and
(2) any devise or bequest to the former spouse lapses, except insofar as a contrary intention appears by the will.

Under s 3 of the Law Reform (Succession) Act 1995, s 18A of the Wills Act 1837 is amended with effect from 1 January 1996. From that date:

(1) provisions of the will appointing the former spouse as executor or trustee take effect as if the former spouse had died on the date on which the marriage is dissolved or annulled; and
(2) any property, or interest in property, which is devised or bequeathed to the former spouse passes as if the former spouse had died on that date.

This means that substitutional provisions in the will which are expressed to take effect if the testator's spouse predeceases him will also take effect if the marriage is dissolved or annulled. (See also **15.5**.)

As mentioned in **11.4.6**, the solicitor should advise a client to review his will in the event of matrimonial difficulties and should also explain the rights of a surviving spouse (including a former spouse) to apply for financial provision out of the testator's estate under the Inheritance (Provision for Family and Dependants) Act 1975 (see Chapter 17). A former spouse's rights under this Act are unaffected by the Wills Act, s 18A. The formal divorce settlement may, however. incorporate some agreement excluding any subsequent claim against the former spouse's estate.

14.3.3 By destruction

Physical destruction with intention

A will can be revoked by 'burning, tearing or otherwise destroying the same by the testator or by some person in his presence and by his direction with the intention of revoking the same' (Wills Act 1837, s 20). Physical destruction without the intention to revoke is insufficient; a will destroyed accidentally or by mistake is not revoked. If its contents can be reconstructed (eg from a copy) an order may be obtained allowing its admission to probate as a valid will.

Missing or damaged wills

If a will which was last known to have been in the testator's possession cannot be found at his death, it is presumed to have been destroyed with the necessary intention to revoke it. This presumption can be rebutted by contrary evidence (such as remarks by the testator shortly before his death about his will which suggest that he regarded it as valid and existing).

Similarly, if the will is found torn, burnt or in a similar state at his death, there is a presumption that the testator destroyed it with the intention of revoking it. This presumption can also be rebutted by contrary evidence.

Symbolic destruction

Physical destruction is required; symbolic destruction (eg simply crossing out wording or endorsing 'revoked' across the will) is not sufficient.

Destruction of part

Significant problems arise where the testator physically destroys only part of the will. If the part destroyed is a sufficiently vital part (eg his signature), this partial destruction may be held to revoke the entire will. If the part destroyed is less substantial or important, then the partial destruction may revoke only that part which was actually destroyed. The result depends on the testator's intention. In the absence of evidence as to the testator's actual intention the court will examine the physical condition of the document.

In *Re Everest* [1975] Fam 44 the testator physically severed certain parts of the will which contained trusts of residue. These were held to have been revoked but the rest of the will was valid. By contrast, in *Hobbs v Knight* (1838) 1 Curt 768 the testator cut out his signature and the entire will was held to have been revoked.

It is better for a testator who wants to revoke his will by destruction to destroy the entire will completely and, of course, an accurate revocation clause in any replacement will remove all doubt. Revocation of a will by destruction does not revoke any codicil to that will (although it may make the wording of the codicil difficult to implement) whereas a properly worded express revocation clause in a later will covers all previous testamentary dispositions.

Dependent relative revocation

The doctrine of dependent relative revocation (see **14.3.1**) can apply to revocation by destruction. If the court is satisfied that the testator intended the revocation by destruction to be conditional (as opposed to absolute) the revocation will only be effective if the condition is satisfied. External evidence is permitted to prove that the revocation was conditional (eg on making an effective new will, or on the intestacy rules having a certain effect on the estate when in fact their impact will be different from that anticipated by the testator when he destroyed his will).

When a solicitor has checked that a new will has been effectively executed and safely stored, he may suggest the physical destruction of earlier wills to avoid future confusion. Some practitioners prefer to store the original (dated) earlier wills with the new will in case the doctrine of dependent relative revocation is unexpectedly called on later.

PART II

LAW COMMON TO WILLS, PROBATE AND ADMINISTRATION

CONTENTS

Chapters 15 to 19 deal with the law which is relevant to both will drafting and post-death practice. Each chapter is designed to be a self-contained explanation of the relevant background law. Cross-references to these chapters appear in context in Part I and Part III.

TEXTBOOKS

Barlow, King and King, Mellows, and Parry and Clark are suitable reference books for Chapters 15, 16 and 17.

For Chapter 18 on Inheritance Tax, Barlow, King and King or Whitehouse are helpful textbooks. The relevant statutory material will be found in the Orange Tax Handbook.

For Chapter 19 on Financial Services: Probate Practice, reference should be made to the LPC Resource Book *Pervasive Topics* (Jordans, 1997), Part II and the textbooks mentioned in that section.

Chapter 15

FAILURE OF GIFTS BY WILL

15.1 INTRODUCTION

When a testator dies, it is the duty of the PRs (usually with the advice of a solicitor) to ascertain the beneficial entitlements under the will; that is, to decide the effect of the will in the light of the circumstances at the date of the testator's death. It is therefore important to understand and to be able to apply the legal rules which may cause a gift in a will to fail.

It is also necessary to have these rules in mind when taking instructions for and drafting a will. The possible failure of gifts in the will should be explained to the testator so that he can give express instructions for alternative provisions to be included in the will.

Chapter 15 contents
Introduction
Ademption
Lapse
Failure of contingency
Divorce
Uncertainty
Beneficiary witnesses will
Disclaimer
Abatement
Perpetuity and accumulations

15.2 ADEMPTION

15.2.1 The basic rule

A specific legacy or devise will fail if the subject matter of the gift does not form part of the estate at death: the gift is adeemed. Ademption usually occurs because the property has been sold, given away or destroyed during the testator's lifetime. The disappointed beneficiary has no right to compensation from the estate.

Example
In her will Ellen gives 'my diamond bracelet' to her sister Grace and the rest of her estate to her husband Harry. Ellen no longer owns the bracelet when she dies. Grace receives nothing: her legacy is adeemed. All Ellen's estate passes to Harry.

15.2.2 Changes in the nature of an asset

Problems may arise where, although the asset has been retained by the testator, it has changed its nature since the will was made. This happens most commonly with company shares. For example, a company may have been taken over since the will was made so that, on death, the testator owns shares in a different company; or the company may have altered its capital structure so that the old shares are represented by a different number of new ones. In each individual case it must be decided whether the asset has changed merely in name or form or whether it has changed in substance. Only if there has been a change in substance will the gift be adeemed. Many cases on this subject have reached the courts and it is preferable when drafting a specific legacy of shares to include an express provision to avoid the difficulty (see **8.4.5**).

15.2.3 Wills Act 1837, s 24

Wills Act 1837, s 24 provides that:

> 'Every will shall be construed, with reference to the real estate and personal estate comprised in it, to speak and take effect as if it had been executed immediately before the death of the testator, unless a contrary intention shall appear by the will.'

This provision is sometimes condensed into the maxim 'a will speaks from death with regard to property'. Its significance is not limited to specific gifts. A gift by will of 'all my estate' will, as a result of s 24, operate to pass all the property owned by the testator at the time of his death.

In the case of specific gifts, s 24 means that, for example, a gift of 'all my jewellery' is taken to include all jewellery owned at the date of death. Such a gift will only be adeemed if the testator owns no jewellery at all at that time.

It might be thought that s 24 would also apply to a gift of a single item of property such as 'my piano' or 'my car'. It has, however, been held in such a case that the use of the word 'my' indicates contrary intention to s 24 on the part of the testator, so that the property he intends to give away is taken to be the piano or the car which he owned at the date of the will. This means that if the piano or car is sold and replaced the gift will be adeemed. The beneficiary will not be entitled to the substitute piano or car owned at the date of death. It has been suggested that this construction may vary according to the circumstances, the relative values of the original and substituted assets being relevant. Such problems may be avoided by consulting the testator and expressing his wishes clearly in the will (see **8.4.1**).

15.3 LAPSE

15.3.1 The basic rule

If the beneficiary of a gift by will dies before the testator his gift will lapse, ie fail. If a legacy lapses, the property falls into residue. If a gift of residue lapses, the property passes under the intestacy rules, unless there is a substitutional gift in the will. A gift will not lapse if the beneficiary can be shown to have survived the testator, for however short a period.

15.3.2 LPA 1925, s 184

If the deaths of the testator and beneficiary occur close together in time it is important to establish the order in which those deaths took place. The law of succession does not accept the possibility that the testator and beneficiary might have died at the same instant. If two people die (eg in a car accident) in circumstances where the order of their deaths cannot be proved, s 184 provides that, for the purposes of succession to property, the younger is deemed to have survived the elder. Thus, in such circumstances, if the beneficiary is older than the testator his gift will lapse. If the beneficiary is younger than the testator the gift does not lapse but falls into the beneficiary's estate.

The presumption applies only for the purposes of succession to property. For IHT purposes, the testator and beneficiary are treated as having died at the same instant (see **18.4.5**).

15.3.3 Survivorship clauses

The testator may wish to prevent a gift in his will from taking effect where the beneficiary survives him for a short period only or is deemed to have survived under s 184. As described in **9.2.1**, this may be achieved by adding a survivorship clause which makes the gift conditional on the beneficiary surviving the testator for a specified period, usually 28 days. Such a gift will fail if the beneficiary survives the testator but dies within the specified period.

15.3.4 Substitutional gifts

The solicitor taking instructions for a will should point out the possibility of lapse to a testator so that he can decide who should take the property if the chosen beneficiary dies before him. A substitutional gift may be included in the will to take effect if the original beneficiary dies before the testator (or before the end of the survivorship period) (see **9.2.2**).

15.3.5 Lapse of gifts to more than one person

Joint tenants

If a gift is made to two or more beneficiaries as joint tenants, the gift will not lapse unless all the joint tenants predecease the testator. For example, if a gift is made 'to A and B jointly' and A dies before the testator, B will take the whole gift.

Tenants in common

If the gift includes words of severance, the beneficiaries take as tenants in common. The share of any beneficiary who dies before the testator will lapse. For example, if a gift is made 'to A and B in equal shares' and A dies before the testator, his gift lapses. B takes only his own share.

Class gifts

If the gift is a class gift (eg 'to my children in equal shares') the membership of the class is determined at the date of death. There is no lapse unless all the members of the class (eg all his children) predecease the testator.

A similar result may be achieved in a gift to named beneficiaries if the gift is made to 'such of A and B as are living at my death and if both in equal shares'.

15.3.6 Wills Act 1837, s 33

The Wills Act 1837, s 33 (as substituted by the Administration of Justice Act 1982) contains a statutory substitutional provision, which is implied into all gifts to the testator's children or remoter descendants unless the will shows a contrary intention. It provides that where a will contains a gift to the testator's child or remoter descendant who dies before the testator and leaves issue living at the testator's death, the gift takes effect as a gift to the issue. The issue take 'according to their stock, in equal shares' the gift their parent would have taken. The section applies both to vested and contingent gifts.

Example

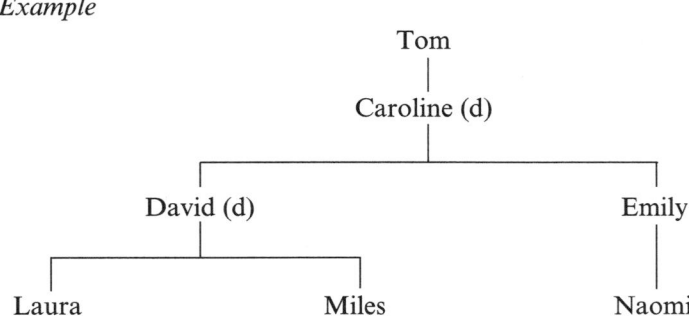

Tom dies leaving £40,000 to Caroline in his will. Both Caroline and David have predeceased him. The gift is saved from lapse by s 33 because Caroline was Tom's daughter and she left issue living at Tom's death. Under s 33, Emily receives half the gift (£20,000) while David's half passes to his children equally. Thus Laura and Miles take £10,000 each.

Note that s 33 only applies to gifts by will to the testator's child or other direct descendant. It does not apply to gifts to any other relatives. Contrast the substitutional provisions under the statutory trusts on intestacy (see **16.2.3**).

Class gifts

There is a similar provision in s 33(2) which applies to class gifts. Where a gift is made to a class of beneficiaries consisting of children or remoter descendants of the testator and a member of the class dies before the testator leaving issue living at the testator's death the share of the deceased beneficiary passes to the remoter issue 'per stirpes'.

Example

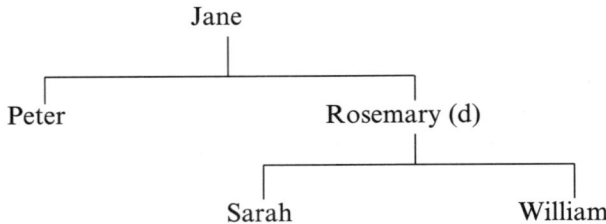

Jane leaves £100,000 'to my children equally'. Rosemary dies before Jane. Under s 33(2), Sarah and William take £25,000 each.

Reasons for including an express substitution clause

Section 33 operates only in the absence of contrary intention in the will. This is usually shown by including an express substitution provision (see **9.2.3**).

It is advisable to include an express provision in any will and not to rely on the effect of s 33, for the following reasons:

(1) the section applies only where the testator's child (or remoter descendant) dies before the testator; if the gift is contingent, express provision is required in case the child dies after the testator but before fulfilling the contingency;
(2) if the gift to the testator's child (or remoter descendant) is contingent it is not clear whether, under s 33, the issue take on a similar contingency;
(3) although s 33 refers specifically to class gifts, it is not clear whether it applies to the usual gift to children 'living at my death'; and
(4) an express provision ensures that the question of substitutional gifts is brought to the testator's attention and his express instructions are taken.

15.4 FAILURE OF CONTINGENCY

A contingent gift will both lapse if the beneficiary dies before the testator and fail if the beneficiary dies after the testator but before fulfilling the contingency. If a substitutional provision is included care should be taken to see that it applies in both situations (see specimen clause (3) at **9.2.3**).

15.5 DIVORCE

The Wills Act 1837, s 18A (inserted by the Administration of Justice Act 1982) provides that where, after the date of the will, the testator's marriage is dissolved or annulled or declared void 'any devise or bequest to the former spouse shall lapse, except in so far as a contrary intention appears by the will'.

In *Re Sinclair (Deceased)* [1985] Ch 446 the testator's will left a gift of residue to his wife if she survived him by one month; but if she predeceased him or failed to survive him by one month the residue was to go to a charity. The couple had divorced after this will was executed and the wife did survive the testator by one month. The wife was not entitled to the property, since her gift had lapsed, but the question was whether it would go to the charity (as if the wife had predeceased) or pass under the intestacy rules. The Court of Appeal examined the wording of the gift of residue in the light of s 18A and held that the statutory words 'shall lapse' simply mean 'shall fail' (as opposed to 'shall fail as if the former spouse had predeceased the testator'). The gift over to the charity was worded so that it could only take effect if the wife had predeceased the testator or failed to survive him by one month. In the absence of either of these situations, the gift to the charity could not take effect and so residue would pass under the intestacy rules.

Accordingly, the practice arose, when drafting a will for a married client, of wording all gifts to the spouse in such a way as to accommodate the testator's wishes in the event of subsequent marriage breakdown. If, in such circumstances, the client would want the property to go to an alternative beneficiary, the substitutional provision would be introduced using words such as the following:

> If [the spouse] predeceases me or does not survive me for [a specified period] or if the gift fails for any reason . . .

The Law Reform (Succession) Act 1995 substitutes a new s 18A which applies to deaths on or after 1 January 1996. From that date 'any property which, or an interest in which, is devised or bequeathed to the former spouse shall pass as if the former spouse had died' on the date of dissolution or annulment of the marriage. This new provision reverses the effect of *Re Sinclair*, so that the words 'or if the gift fails for any reason' are no longer necessary to ensure that a substitutional gift is effective if a spouse's gift fails on divorce.

15.6 UNCERTAINTY

15.6.1 Uncertainty of subject matter

A gift may fail for uncertainty if the property cannot be identified from the description in the will (see **8.4.1**). For example, a gift of 'my ring' where the testator owned many rings at the date of the will may fail; and a gift of 'the bulk of my estate' would fail.

15.6.2 Uncertainty of objects

A gift may fail for uncertainty if the beneficiary cannot be identified (see **8.3.3**). This principle applies both to individuals and to institutions (both charitable and non-charitable). A gift to charity may not fail for uncertainty of objects because it may be applied by means of a scheme prescribed by the Charity Commissioners.

15.7 BENEFICIARY WITNESSES WILL

Under the Wills Act 1837, s 15, a gift by will fails if the beneficiary or his spouse witnesses the will (see **13.5.2**).

15.8 DISCLAIMER

A beneficiary need not accept a gift given to him by will. He can disclaim the gift which will then fall into residue. If a gift of residue is disclaimed, it will pass on intestacy. Once the beneficiary has received a benefit from a gift (eg a payment of income) he is taken to have accepted the gift and may no longer disclaim. He may, however, give away his property; if he does so by variation then the gift may be treated for tax purposes as if it had been made by the testator (see Chapter 30).

15.9 ABATEMENT

If the estate is not large enough to pay all the debts and legacies, the legacies must be reduced, that is, they abate. The statutory order for payment of debts governs the order in which legacies abate. In general terms, once the residue is exhausted, remaining debts and expenses are paid from the general (usually pecuniary) legacies which are proportionately reduced. If the general legacies have abated to nothing and debts still remain, the specific gifts abate (see **27.7.2**).

15.10 PERPETUITY AND ACCUMULATIONS

A gift in a will may fail if it infringes the rules against perpetuity or accumulations. The rules are outside the scope of this book.

Chapter 16

INTESTACY

16.1 INTRODUCTION

This chapter explains how the intestacy rules apply to determine the devolution of property on death when the deceased has failed to dispose of it by will. The application of the rules is important primarily when administering the estate of a person who has died wholly or partially intestate. It is also relevant when advising a client on the desirability of making a will.

The intestacy rules are contained in the AEA 1925 and section numbers in this chapter refer to that Act unless otherwise stated.

16.1.1 Total intestacy

If a person dies without leaving a valid will he is said to die intestate. This may occur because the deceased never made a will at all, or because he revoked his will and did not make another, or because a purported will is invalid. Approximately two out of every three people who die in England and Wales each year die intestate.

16.1.2 Partial intestacy

A person dies partially intestate if he leaves a valid will but the will fails to dispose of all his estate. The intestacy rules apply to that part of the estate which has not been left by will.

If, as is usual, the will contains a valid residuary gift, a partial intestacy is avoided. Such a gift ensures that the will disposes of all the property owned by the testator at the time of his death, whether or not he owned it when he made his will. If any legacy in the will fails, the property falls into residue and passes under the residuary gift. A partial intestacy will therefore only arise if there is no residuary gift or if the residuary gift fails (wholly or in part) and there is no effective substitutional gift.

Example
Anna's will leaves £10,000 to her friend Barbara and the rest of her estate to her brother Charles. Charles dies before Anna.

On Anna's death, the £10,000 passes under her will to Barbara. The gift of residue lapses (see **15.3**) and the rest of Anna's estate passes under the intestacy rules. (This result would have been avoided if Anna's will had contained a substitutional gift of residue to take effect if Charles died before her.)

If the residue is given to more than one person and one of the beneficiaries dies before the testator, the result depends upon the wording of the gift. If residue is given to named beneficiaries in severed shares (creating a tenancy in common), one share may lapse and pass on intestacy. This result may be avoided if the residue is given to the beneficiaries as joint tenants or if there is a class gift (see **15.3.5**).

Chapter 16 contents
Introduction
Structure of the intestacy rules
Spouse and issue
Intestate survived by spouse and parents, brothers or sisters or their issue
Intestate survived by spouse and no other close relatives
Distribution where there is no surviving spouse
Intestacy and LPA 1925, s 184

Example 1
Dan's will leaves all his estate to Frank and Emma in equal shares. Frank dies before Dan. On Dan's death half his estate passes to Emma under the will. Frank's share lapses and passes under the intestacy rules.

Example 2
George's will leaves all his estate to Hannah and Claire jointly. Claire dies before George. The gift to Hannah and Claire contains no words of severance, so they take as joint tenants. On George's death, all his estate passes to Hannah and there is no partial intestacy.

Example 3
Janet's will leaves all her estate to 'such of my sisters as are living at my death in equal shares if more than one'. Janet has two sisters, Kirstie and Flora, but Flora dies before her.

On Janet's death all her estate passes to Kirstie. There is no lapse since membership of the class of beneficiaries is determined at the date of Janet's death.

16.1.3 Property passing on intestacy

The intestacy rules only apply to property which is capable of being left by will (see **2.4**).

Example
Laura dies intestate survived by her husband Michael and their two children. Laura and Michael own their house as beneficial joint tenants. Laura has taken out a life assurance policy for £100,000 which is written in trust for the children and she owns investments worth £150,000. The intestacy rules do not affect Laura's share of the house (which passes to Michael by survivorship) or the life policy (which passes to the children under the terms of the trust). Only the investments pass under the intestacy rules.

16.1.4 Hotchpot

The hotchpot rules required certain gifts made by the intestate during his lifetime or, in the case of a partial intestacy, by his will to be taken into account in calculating the entitlements of spouse and issue on intestacy.

These rules were abolished by the Law Reform (Succession) Act 1995 for deaths on or after 1 January 1996 and are not considered further in this book.

16.2 STRUCTURE OF THE INTESTACY RULES

16.2.1 Statutory trust for payment of debts etc

The intestacy rules impose a trust over all the property (real and personal) in respect of which a person dies intestate (s 33). This trust is similar to the usual express trust found in a will and includes a power of sale: it provides that the PRs must pay the funeral, testamentary and administration expenses and any debts of the deceased. The balance remaining (after setting aside a fund to meet any pecuniary legacies left by the deceased in the will) is the 'residuary estate' to be shared among the family under the rules of distribution set out in s 46. The PRs have power under s 41 to appropriate assets in or towards satisfaction of a beneficiary's share (with the beneficiary's consent).

16.2.2 Order of beneficial entitlement

The right of a person to benefit on intestacy depends on his relationship with the deceased and whether any closer relatives have survived. The various categories of beneficiary are listed in s 46 in order of priority. The general principle is that the estate is shared by the relatives in the highest category, to the exclusion of relatives in a later category. The division is more complicated if there is a surviving spouse. The spouse has priority over all other categories of beneficiary, but he or she may have to share the residuary estate with other beneficiaries (see **16.3**, **16.4** and **16.5**).

If the intestate has no surviving spouse, his estate passes to:

(1) his issue on the 'statutory trusts' (see **16.2.3**), but if none, to
(2) his parents, equally if both alive, but if none, to
(3) his brothers and sisters of the whole blood on the 'statutory trusts', but if none, to
(4) his brothers and sisters of the half blood on the 'statutory trusts', but if none, to
(5) his grandparents, equally if more than one, but if none, to
(6) his uncles and aunts of the whole blood on the 'statutory trusts', but if none, to
(7) his uncles and aunts of the half blood on the 'statutory trusts', but if none, to
(8) the Crown, Duchy of Lancaster, or Duke of Cornwall (bona vacantia).

Further details are given at **16.6**.

16.2.3 The statutory trusts

Apart from the spouse, parents and grandparents, each category of relatives takes 'on the statutory trusts'. The purpose of the statutory trusts is to determine membership of the class of beneficiaries and the terms on which they take, in much the same way as would normally be provided in a will (see **9.2.2** and **9.2.3**).

The statutory trusts are set out in s 47 and they contain three main provisions:

(a) The class of beneficiaries
The residuary estate is held on trust in equal shares for those of the relatives in the relevant category who are living at the intestate's death. The term 'living' includes a person en ventre sa mère, ie conceived but not born at the intestate's death.

(b) The contingency
The interests of the beneficiaries are contingent upon attaining 18 or earlier marriage.

(c) The substitution
If a member of the category has predeceased the intestate leaving issue, the issue take their deceased parent's share per stirpes and contingently upon attaining 18 or earlier marriage. This means that relatives not mentioned in s 46 (for example, nephews, nieces and cousins) may inherit on intestacy if their parent died before the intestate.

Examples of the application of the statutory trusts are included in context below.

16.3 SPOUSE AND ISSUE

16.3.1 Meaning of 'spouse'

Under the intestacy rules, a spouse is the person to whom the deceased was married at his death whether or not they were living together. A divorced spouse is excluded, as is a judicially separated spouse where the separation is continuing by virtue of Matrimonial Causes Act 1973, s 18(2).

16.3.2 Meaning of 'issue'

The term 'issue' includes all direct descendants of the deceased: ie children, grandchildren, great grandchildren etc. Adopted children (and remoter descendants) are included, as are those whose parents were not married at the time of their birth.

Example
Neville married Mary in 1980. Mary had a daughter, Petra, of her first marriage. Neville had not been married before, although he had a son, Robert, of an earlier relationship. Neville and Mary have a son, Oliver.

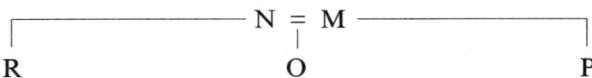

On Neville's death intestate, his issue are Robert and Oliver. His stepdaughter, Petra, is not included unless she was adopted by Neville.

16.3.3 Entitlement of spouse and issue

Where the intestate is survived by both spouse and issue, the 'residuary estate' (as defined in **16.2.1**) is distributed as follows:

(a) The spouse receives the personal chattels absolutely. 'Personal chattels' are defined in s 55(1)(x).

> '"Personal chattels" mean carriages, horses, stable furniture and effects (not used for business purposes), motor cars and accessories (not used for business purposes), garden effects, domestic animals, plate, plated articles, linen, china, glass, books, pictures, prints, furniture, jewellery, articles of household or personal use or ornament, musical and scientific instruments and apparatus, wines, liquors and consumable stores, but do not include any chattels used at the death of the intestate for business purposes nor money or securities for money.'

(b) In addition, the spouse receives a 'statutory legacy' of £125,000 free of tax and costs plus interest from death until payment. The rate of interest payable is determined from time to time by statutory instrument. If the residuary estate apart from the personal chattels is worth less than £125,000, the spouse receives it all (and the issue receive nothing).

(c) The rest of the residuary estate (if any) is divided into two equal funds. One fund is held on trust for the spouse for life with remainder to the issue on the statutory trusts. The other fund is held for the issue on the statutory trusts.

Example
George dies intestate survived by his wife, Helen, and his only child, Isobel, aged 21. His residuary estate is worth £230,000 including personal chattels worth £5,000.

Distribution:

£	
5,000	personal chattels to Helen
125,000	statutory legacy to Helen
50,000	on trust for Helen for life with remainder to Isobel
50,000	to Isobel absolutely
230,000	

George's PRs will invest the first £50,000 and pay the income to Helen. Isobel has a vested interest in remainder under the statutory trusts (see **16.3.4**) so she (or her estate if she is dead) will receive the capital when Helen dies. Isobel is the only person entitled to the remaining £50,000 under the statutory trusts, and she has a vested interest. Once the administration of George's estate is complete, George's PRs will pay the money to her.

For deaths after 1 January 1996, the entitlement of the intestate's spouse is conditional upon the spouse surviving the intestate for 28 days. Under the Law Reform (Succession) Act 1995, where the intestate's spouse dies within 28 days of the intestate, the estate is distributed as if the spouse had not survived the intestate. The effect in the example above is that if Helen dies within 28 days of George, the whole of George's estate passes under George's intestacy to Isobel.

16.3.4 Applying the statutory trusts for issue

(a) The class
Where property is held for 'issue' on the statutory trusts, the primary beneficiaries are the children of the intestate who are living at his death. Remoter issue are included only by substitution, where a child has died before the intestate.

(b) The contingency
The interests of the children are contingent upon attaining the age of 18 or marrying under that age. Any child who fulfils the contingency at the intestate's death takes a vested interest. If a child dies after the intestate but without attaining a vested interest, his interest fails and the estate is redistributed

(c) The substitution
Any children of the deceased child (grandchildren of the deceased) who are living at the intestate's death take their deceased parent's share equally between them, contingently upon attaining 18 or earlier marriage. Great grandchildren would be included only if their parent had also predeceased the intestate. This form of substitution and division is known as a 'per stirpes' distribution.

Example
Joanne dies intestate survived by her husband, Kenneth, and their children, Mark (who has a son, Quintin) and Nina. Their daughter, Lisa died last year. Her two children, Oliver and Paul, are living at Joanne's death.

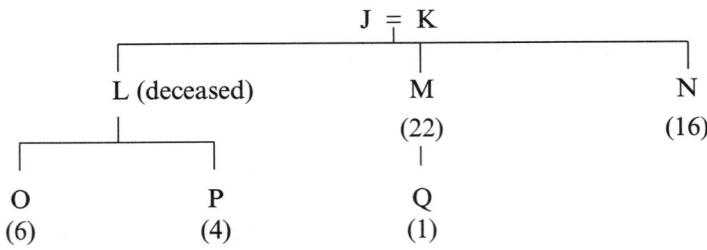

Joanne's estate consists of her share in the house, held as joint tenants with Kenneth, and other property worth £440,000 after payment of debts, funeral and testamentary expenses. This figure includes personal chattels worth £15,000.

DISTRIBUTION

Joanne's share in the house passes to Kenneth by survivorship. The rest of her estate passes on intestacy.

£	
15,000	personal chattels to Kenneth
125,000	statutory legacy to Kenneth
150,000	(Fund A) on trust for Kenneth for life remainder issue on the statutory trusts
150,000	(Fund B) for issue on the statutory trusts
440,000	

The statutory trusts apply to both funds of £150,000 to determine the distribution between Joanne's issue.

The primary beneficiaries under the statutory trusts are Mark and Nina, Joanne's children living at her death. However, Lisa's share is held for her children, Oliver and Paul in equal shares. The interests of Nina, Oliver and Paul are contingent upon attaining 18 or earlier marriage.

Thus, Mark has a vested interest in one-third of each fund. He is entitled to £50,000 on Joanne's death, and to one-third of Fund A when Kenneth dies. If Mark should die shortly after Joanne, his share in both funds would form part of Mark's estate on death. Quintin has no entitlement under Joanne's intestacy.

Nina has a contingent interest in one-third of each fund, which will vest when she is 18 or if she marries before 18. If Nina should die under the age of 18 and unmarried her interest would fail. One half of Nina's share would pass to Mark and the other half would be held for Oliver and Paul equally. This result would follow even if Nina had a child who survived her. The substitution of grandchildren only applies where a child of the intestate dies before him, whereas Nina was alive at the date of Joanne's death.

Oliver and Paul have contingent interests in one-sixth of each fund, which will vest at 18 or earlier marriage. If Oliver should die under the age of 18 and unmarried, his share would pass to Paul (and vice versa). If both Oliver and Paul were to die under the age of 18 and unmarried, their shares would be divided equally between Mark and Nina.

Intestacy

EFFECT FOR IHT

All property passing to the deceased's spouse on death is exempt from IHT. This principle applies to Joanne's share in the house, the personal chattels and the statutory legacy of £125,000. It also applies to the £150,000 in Fund A. Although Kenneth is only entitled to the income from this fund, the fund is treated for IHT purposes as if Kenneth were entitled to the capital (see **18.4.2** and **18.6.1**). On Kenneth's death, the capital of Fund A will be taxed as part of Kenneth's estate.

Only the £150,000 in Fund B is chargeable to IHT on Joanne's death. If Joanne has made no chargeable transfers in the 7 years before her death, there will be no tax to pay since the whole amount will fall within her nil rate band.

16.3.5 Spouse's right to redeem the life interest

Under s 47A, the surviving spouse may elect to take a lump sum in place of the life interest.

This means that the half of the residue which would, under the provisions outlined above, be held on trust for the spouse for life with remainder to issue will instead be divided between the spouse and issue. The spouse receives the capital value of the life interest immediately and the balance is held for the issue on the statutory trusts.

If all the issue entitled to share in the intestate's estate are sui juris (ie of full age and capacity), they can agree the capital value of the redemption with the surviving spouse. In the absence of agreement, or if any beneficiary is a minor, the amount which the surviving spouse receives is calculated in accordance with the Intestate Succession (Interest and Capitalisation Order) 1977. The effect is that the younger the spouse is the greater the lump sum will be, although it will never be the full capital value of the life interest.

The spouse must give written notice of his or her election to the PRs within 12 months of the grant of representation.

Example

Rosemary dies intestate survived by her husband, Simon, and her only child, Tessa, aged 30.

Out of Rosemary's residuary estate, Simon receives the personal chattels and the statutory legacy of £125,000. The residue is worth £360,000.

Distribution of residue:

£	
180,000	on trust for Simon for life with remainder to Tessa absolutely (under the statutory trusts)
180,000	to Tessa absolutely (as above)
360,000	

Simon elects to redeem his life interest for a lump sum, valued at £110,000.

Revised distribution of residue following Simon's election:

£	
110,000	to Simon absolutely
250,000	to Tessa absolutely (under the statutory trusts)
360,000	

EFFECT FOR IHT

When such an election is made, IHT is charged on the estate of the intestate as distributed following the election, and so must be recalculated. The effect of election will always be to reduce the value of the spouse exemption, and so additional IHT may be payable.

Example

In the example above (assuming that Rosemary had made no chargeable transfers within the seven years before her death), no tax was payable before Simon's election. The whole estate was spouse exempt except for the £180,000 passing immediately to Tessa, which fell within Rosemary's nil rate band.

Following Simon's election, only £110,000 of the 'life interest' fund attracts spouse exemption, and tax is payable as follows:

Chargeable estate: £250,000

	£	
Tax:	215,000	nil
	35,000	@ 40% = £14,000

16.3.6 Spouse's right to require appropriation of the matrimonial home

If the matrimonial home forms part of the estate passing on intestacy, the surviving spouse can require the PRs to appropriate the matrimonial home in full or partial satisfaction of the spouse's absolute interest in the estate (including the capitalised value of the life interest in residue) (Intestates' Estates Act 1952, s 5).

If the property is worth more than the spouse's entitlement, the spouse may still require appropriation provided he or she pays the difference, 'equality money', to the estate.

The election must be made in writing to the PRs within 12 months of the grant of representation.

The property is appropriated at its open market value at the date of the appropriation, not at its value at death. In times of rising house prices, a surviving spouse should exercise the right as soon as possible after the death.

Example

Len dies intestate survived by his wife, Mary, and their son. Len's residuary estate (in addition to personal chattels) is worth £155,000 and includes the house valued at £130,000.

Prima facie (and ignoring personal chattels) Mary receives:

(1) a statutory legacy of £125,000; and
(2) a life interest in one half of the residue, £15,000.

As the statutory legacy is less than the value of the matrimonial home, she may either:

(1) request the PRs to appropriate the matrimonial home to her leaving her to pay equality money to the estate; or
(2) redeem her life interest in half the residue for a capital sum, and request the PRs to appropriate the house to her in satisfaction of her entitlement to the statutory legacy and at least part of the capitalised sum (any balance being paid to her).

In view of the right of appropriation, the PRs should not sell or otherwise dispose of the matrimonial home during the 12 months from the date of the grant without the written consent of the surviving spouse, unless the debts and testamentary expenses of the intestate are such as to require its sale.

16.4 INTESTATE SURVIVED BY SPOUSE AND PARENTS, BROTHERS OR SISTERS OR THEIR ISSUE

Where the intestate leaves a surviving spouse but no issue, the distribution of the estate depends on whether any other close relatives survive. If the intestate is survived by either or both parents, by brothers or sisters of the whole blood or by issue of deceased brothers and sisters, the following rules apply.

16.4.1 Entitlement of spouse

From the 'residuary estate' (as defined in **16.2.1**) the spouse receives:

(a) the personal chattels absolutely (as in **16.3.3**);
(b) a statutory legacy of £200,000 free of tax and costs plus interest from the date of death until payment. If the residuary estate apart from the personal chattels is worth less than £200,000, the spouse receives it all (and the parents receive nothing);
(c) half the rest of the residuary estate absolutely (ie no life interest arises in this case).

For deaths on or after 1 January 1996, the spouse's entitlement is conditional upon surviving the intestate for 28 days. If the spouse dies within 28 days of the intestate, the intestate's estate is distributed as if the spouse had not survived him.

16.4.2 Distribution of remainder

If the intestate is survived by either parent, that parent receives the rest of the estate absolutely. If both parents survive, the rest of the estate is shared equally between them. If both parents have predeceased the intestate, the rest of the estate is divided between the intestate's brothers and sisters of the whole blood on the statutory trusts. The terms of the statutory trusts are the same as those for issue (see **16.3.4**). The substitution provision means that if a brother or sister of the intestate has predeceased him leaving issue, such issue (nephews and nieces of the intestate) take their parent's share.

> *Example 1*
> Andrew dies intestate survived by his wife, Wendy, and his parents, Mary and Frank. The matrimonial home, worth £100,000, is held by Andrew and Wendy as beneficial joint tenants. Andrew also owned personal chattels worth £10,000 and investments worth £300,000.
>
> The house passes to Wendy by survivorship. Wendy also receives the personal chattels, her statutory legacy of £200,000 and half the residue, £50,000 absolutely. The remaining £50,000 is divided equally between Mary and Frank (£25,000 each).
>
> If Andrew dies on or after 1 January 1996, Wendy's entitlement is conditional upon Wendy surviving Andrew for 28 days. If Wendy dies during that period, Andrew's whole estate passes on his intestacy to Mary and Frank. The

matrimonial home still passes to Wendy by survivorship immediately upon Andrew's death, and will form part of Wendy's estate on her death.

Example 2

Irene dies intestate. Her estate passing on intestacy is worth £350,000 (including personal chattels of £10,000). She is survived by her husband, Henry, and brother Brian and sister Susan. She has no issue and both her parents are dead.

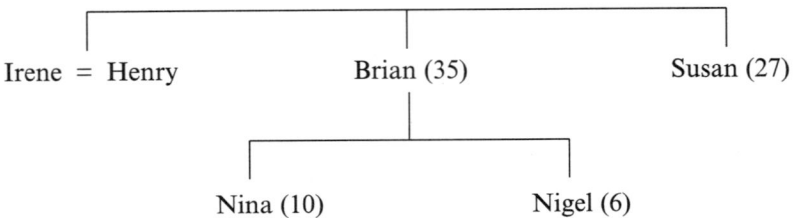

Henry receives: £
    10,000   personal chattels
    200,000   statutory legacy
    70,000   one half of the residue absolutely

(Again, if Irene dies on or after 1 January 1996, Henry will only be entitled as above if he survives Irene for 28 days.)

The remaining £70,000 is held for the brothers and sisters on statutory trusts. This means that it is divided equally between Brian and Susan, who both have vested interests because they are over 18.

If Brian had predeceased Irene, his share (£35,000) would be held for his children, Nina and Nigel, equally, contingently upon attaining the age of 18 or earlier marriage.

16.4.3 Right of spouse to require appropriation of the matrimonial home

As described in **16.3.6**, the surviving spouse may elect to take the matrimonial home in full or partial satisfaction of his interest in the estate.

Example

On the facts in Example 2 above, assume that Irene's estate includes the matrimonial home (held in Irene's name alone) worth £240,000. Henry may elect to take the house as part of his entitlement. In addition he will receive £30,000 (the balance of his total entitlement of £270,000) and the personal chattels.

If the house is worth more than Henry's total entitlement (say £290,000) he may still elect to appropriate it provided that he pays equality money (£20,000) to the estate. The entitlement of Brian and Susan is thus unaffected.

16.5 INTESTATE SURVIVED BY SPOUSE AND NO OTHER CLOSE RELATIVES

Where the intestate leaves a surviving spouse but no issue, parent, brother or sister of the whole blood or issue of a deceased brother or sister, the whole estate, however large, passes to the spouse absolutely. More distant relatives, such as half brothers and sisters, grandparents and cousins are not entitled.

If the intestate dies on or after 1 January 1996, the spouse's entitlement is conditional upon surviving the intestate for 28 days. If the spouse dies within that period, the estate is distributed as if the spouse had not survived the intestate.

16.6 DISTRIBUTION WHERE THERE IS NO SURVIVING SPOUSE

As seen at **16.2.2**, where there is no surviving spouse (or, for deaths after 1 January 1996, where the spouse dies within 28 days of the intestate), the 'residuary estate' is divided between the relatives in the highest category in the list, however large the estate.

16.6.1 The statutory trusts

Each category other than parents and grandparents takes 'on the statutory trusts'. This means that children under 18 take their interest contingently upon attaining 18 or marrying earlier, and that issue of a deceased relative may take that relative's share.

Example 1
Tom dies intestate. He was not married to his partner, Penny, although the couple have a son, Simon, aged 13, Tom's only child. Tom's parents predeceased him but he is survived by his only sibling, his brother Bob, aged 40.

Tom's estate is held on trust for Simon, contingently upon attaining 18 or marrying earlier. If Simon dies before the contingency is fulfilled, Tom's estate passes to Bob absolutely.

Example 2
Vera, a widow aged 80, is cared for by her step-daughter Carol (the child of her deceased husband's first marriage). Her only living blood relatives are cousins, the children of her mother's brothers and sisters. Vera dies intestate. Her estate is divided 'per stirpes' between her cousins (and the children of any cousins who predeceased her). Carol receives nothing from Vera's estate.

16.6.2 Adopted and illegitimate children

Adopted children are treated for intestacy purposes as the children of their adoptive parents and not of their natural parents. If a person who was adopted dies intestate without spouse or issue, his estate will be distributed between the closest relatives in the adoptive family. An adopted child may also inherit on the intestacy of any member of his adoptive family.

Similarly, the intestacy rules are applied regardless of whether or not a particular individual's parents were married to each other. However, on the intestacy of an individual whose parents were not married to each other, it is presumed that the individual has not been survived by his father or by any person related to him through his father unless the contrary is shown (Family Law Reform Act 1987, s 18(2)). This presumption avoids any necessity for the PRs to make awkward enquiries where the identity or whereabouts of the father is unknown.

Example
Jessica, whose parents did not marry, dies intestate. Her only known relative is a half brother, the child of her mother's later marriage. Nothing is known of Jessica's father or any other children he may have had. Jessica's PRs may distribute her estate to her half brother, relying on the presumption in s 18(2).

16.6.3 Bona vacantia

Where an estate passes bona vacantia, the Crown, Duchy of Lancaster or Duke of Cornwall has a discretion to provide for dependants of the intestate or for other persons for whom the intestate might reasonably have been expected to make provision.

16.7 INTESTACY AND LPA 1925, SECTION 184

The Law of Property Act 1925, s 184 provides that, where two or more people die in circumstances where the order of deaths cannot be ascertained, for succession purposes the younger is deemed to have survived the elder. The section applies to determine the succession to property whether the deceased left a will or died intestate (see **15.3.2**).

For deaths on or after 1 January 1996, a spouse is only entitled on intestacy if he or she survives the intestate for 28 days. Thus, s 184 is no longer applicable.

Example 1
Mary (a widow) and her elder daughter, Emma, are killed in a plane crash in July 1996. There is no evidence of the order of their deaths. They both die intestate. Their only living relatives are Mary's younger daughter, Yvonne, and Emma's husband Harry.

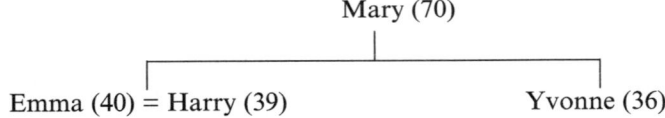

Under s 184 Emma is deemed to have survived her mother. Mary's estate will pass in equal shares to Emma and Yvonne under the intestacy rules. Emma's share will pass, along with her own estate, to Harry provided that he survives her by 28 days (and part to Yvonne if the total value of Emma's estate excluding chattels exceeds £200,000; see **16.4.1**).

Example 2
On the same facts, suppose that Harry also dies intestate in the same accident. Again, there is no evidence of the order of the three deaths. Harry has not survived Emma by 28 days and so he is not entitled to Emma's estate on her intestacy. Emma's estate (including her half of Mary's property) passes on her intestacy to her sister, Yvonne.

Similarly, Harry's estate does not pass to his wife, Emma, as she did not survive him for 28 days. His estate will pass to his nearest relative(s) under the intestacy rules.

Chapter 17

THE INHERITANCE (PROVISION FOR FAMILY AND DEPENDANTS) ACT 1975

17.1 INTRODUCTION

17.1.1 Purpose of the Act

It is a principle of English law that a person may give his property during his lifetime or on his death to any person of his choice. The Inheritance (Provision for Family and Dependants) Act 1975 (I(PFD)A) does not alter this principle. It allows persons who are aggrieved because they have been left out of the will, or are not inheriting on an intestacy, to apply for a benefit from the estate following the testator's or intestate's death. The Act can also be used by a person who has received some benefit under the will or intestacy but is dissatisfied as to the amount of the inheritance.

17.1.2 Advising clients

Although a person cannot bring a claim until the death has occurred, solicitors need to be aware of the provisions of I(PFD)A in two distinct sets of circumstances.

When advising a client on the making of a will
At this stage, the solicitor should ascertain the identity of the testator's family and his wishes. The testator should be made aware of the I(PFD)A if he is deliberately proposing to exclude a person from his will or leave somebody less than they might reasonably expect.

Where a solicitor believes that the testator's intentions could expose his estate to a successful claim under the I(PFD)A following his death, he should discuss the possibility of avoiding this by including a suitable gift in the will. Where a client is reluctant to do this he should be encouraged to leave a letter with the will explaining why the person has been ignored or left a relatively small gift. A claim cannot be prevented, but the letter can be presented to the court by the PRs as evidence which will be taken into account when determining the merits of any claim.

When advising the PRs in the administration of an estate
PRs need to consider the possibility of a claim and should not distribute the estate until the time-limit given by the I(PFD)A has expired (see **17.2.1**). If a claim is brought, as a matter of conduct the solicitor acting for the PRs must not also represent the claimant as there is a clear conflict of interest between them.

17.1.3 Reaching a settlement

If all the beneficiaries under the will or intestacy are sui juris when a claim is brought against an estate, there is nothing to prevent them from trying to reach agreement with the claimant as to the level of entitlement of each of them. Out of court settlements are to be encouraged, because litigation is costly and usually acrimonious, but there are very few reported cases and this makes it difficult to advise clients on the current levels of successful claims.

Chapter 17 contents
Introduction
The right to bring a claim
Application by the surviving spouse
Application by a former spouse
Application by a child of the deceased
Application by a person treated as a child of the family
Application by a person being maintained by the deceased immediately before his death
Application by a cohabitee
Orders and their effect
Anti-avoidance provisions
Summary of points to bear in mind in the office
Standing search

17.2 THE RIGHT TO BRING A CLAIM

The relevant law is contained in the I(PFD)A and section numbers refer to that Act unless otherwise stated.

17.2.1 Time-limit for application

An application must be brought within six months of the date of issue of the grant of representation to the deceased's estate (s 4). The court has a discretion to extend this time-limit.

17.2.2 Applicants who can make a claim

The following persons can make a claim (s 1(1)):

(1) the spouse of the deceased;
(2) a former spouse of the deceased who has not remarried;
(3) a child of the deceased;
(4) any person (not being a child of the deceased) who, as a result of the deceased's marriage, the deceased treated as a child of the family;
(5) any person who, immediately before the death of the deceased, was being maintained by him either wholly or in part.

For applicants in the fifth category, a person is 'maintained' if 'the deceased, otherwise than for full valuable consideration, was making a substantial contribution in money or money's worth towards the reasonable needs of that person' (s 1(3)).

Under the Law Reform (Succession) Act 1995, a sixth category of applicant was added for deaths on or after 1 January 1996.

(6) any person who, during the whole of the period of two years ending immediately before the date when the deceased died, was living:
   (a) in the same household as the deceased, and
   (b) as the husband or wife of the deceased.

17.2.3 Grounds for claim

The only ground for a claim is that 'the disposition of the deceased's estate effected by his will or the law relating to intestacy, or a combination of his will and that law, is not such as to make reasonable financial provision for the applicant'. Section 1(2) sets out two standards for judging 'reasonable financial provision':

(1) 'the surviving spouse standard' which allows a surviving spouse such financial provision as is reasonable in all the circumstances 'whether or not that provision is required for his or her maintenance' (s 1(2)(a)); and
(2) 'the ordinary standard' which applies to all other categories of applicant and allows 'such financial provision as it would be reasonable in all the circumstances ... for the applicant to receive for his maintenance' (s 1(2)(b)).

17.2.4 The common guidelines

Section 3 contains guidelines to assist the court in determining whether the will and/or intestacy does make reasonable financial provision for the applicant. Some matters should be considered for every claimant (ie the common guidelines). There are also special guidelines for each category of applicant, which are discussed in context below.

The common guidelines in s 3(1) are:

(1) the financial resources and needs of the applicant, other applicants and beneficiaries of the estate now and in the foreseeable future;
(2) the deceased's moral obligations towards any applicant or beneficiary;
(3) the size and nature of the estate;
(4) the physical or mental disability of any applicant or beneficiary;
(5) anything else which may be relevant, such as the conduct of the applicant.

When considering these matters, and the special guidelines, the court takes into account:

(1) the facts at the date of the hearing (s 3(5)); and
(2) with regard to the financial resources and needs of the applicant:

   (a) his earning capacity; and
   (b) his financial obligations and responsibilities (s 3(6)).

17.3 APPLICATION BY THE SURVIVING SPOUSE

The claimant must have been married to the deceased at the date of his death. If the claimant remarries between the deceased's death and the date the application is actually heard, this is a factor which will be taken into account by the court in deciding whether an order should be made.

17.3.1 Reasonable financial provision

In determining whether the deceased's will and/or intestacy has made reasonable financial provision for the spouse, the court considers what financial provision would be reasonable in the circumstances for that spouse, whether or not that provision is required for his maintenance.

Example
The husband dies leaving his estate to charity. The wife owns the matrimonial home, has savings of her own and an annual income of £20,000. She is therefore able to maintain herself. However, as a wife might quite reasonably expect to receive something from her husband's estate, a claim by her would probably succeed.

17.3.2 Guidelines

In helping it to decide the merits of an application, and any order, the court considers:

(1) the common guidelines in s 3(1) (see **17.2.4**); and
(2) the special guidelines.

The special guidelines are:

(1) the age of the applicant and duration of the marriage (the older the applicant and the longer the marriage, the stronger the claim);
(2) the contribution made by the applicant to the welfare of the family including looking after the home;
(3) what the applicant might have received if the marriage had ended in divorce rather than being terminated by death.

17.4 APPLICATION BY A FORMER SPOUSE

A former spouse is a person who has been married to the deceased but whose marriage was annulled or terminated by a decree absolute before the death occurred. The category is limited to a former spouse who has not remarried at the time of the hearing.

Before an application is made by a former spouse, the terms of the decree of divorce should be checked. Either party to the marriage can ask the court in divorce proceedings to ban the other party to the marriage from bringing a claim in the event of a death. If such an order was made, the court may not entertain an application under s 1 by the former spouse.

17.4.1 Reasonable financial provision

'Reasonable financial provision' means such financial provision as it would be reasonable in all the circumstances for the applicant to receive for his maintenance (ie 'the ordinary standard' stated in **17.2.3**). What constitutes reasonable maintenance is difficult to define. It is more than mere subsistence but is unlikely to extend to a level covering everything that a person might want.

17.4.2 Guidelines

The court considers:

(1) the common guidelines in s 3(1) (see **17.2.4**); and
(2) the special guidelines.

The special guidelines are:

(1) the age of the applicant and the duration of the marriage; and
(2) the contribution made by the applicant to the welfare of the family including looking after the home.

Where a successful application is made and the court orders the making of periodical payments from the deceased's estate (**17.9**), these will cease if the applicant remarries.

Because of the wide powers of the courts to make financial settlements on divorce, relatively few former spouses apply under the I(PFD)A. Claims are only likely to be entertained where either there has been a material improvement in the deceased's financial position since the divorce or the deceased was paying maintenance by way of periodic payments immediately prior to his death.

17.5 APPLICATION BY A CHILD OF THE DECEASED

Any child of the deceased whether legitimate, legitimated, adopted or of a non-marital relationship may make an application, as may a child who was en ventre sa mère (ie conceived but not born) at the date of a parent's death.

There is no age restriction and, of itself, marriage is not a bar to a claim.

17.5.1 Reasonable financial provision

Where an application is brought by a child of the deceased, the 'ordinary standard' is applied to determine whether reasonable financial provision has been made by the deceased (see **17.2.3**).

The courts have shown a reluctance to award financial provision to adult able-bodied sons, for example in *Re Coventry (Deceased)* [1980] Ch 461 it was said 'applications ... for maintenance by able-bodied and comparatively young men in employment and able to maintain themselves ... need to be approached ... with a degree of circumspection'.

Although *Re Coventry* was an application by a son, it must be assumed that a court would take a similar approach to an application by a daughter in the absence of special circumstances. An able-bodied adult child might succeed where, for example, he had given up work to look after an old or sick parent.

17.5.2 Guidelines

The court considers:

(1) the common guidelines in s 3(1) (see **17.2.4**); and
(2) the special guideline, which in this case is the manner in which the applicant was being or might expect to be educated or trained.

> *Example*
> James is 16 years old and at a private boarding school. He is intelligent and hopes to go to university. His wealthy father, Alfred, has just died leaving his entire estate to his wife, Camille, who is James' stepmother. Camille thinks James should leave school and find a job.
>
> A claim by James against his father's estate for 2 years' school fees and maintenance during a degree course would probably succeed.

17.6 APPLICATION BY A PERSON TREATED AS A CHILD OF THE FAMILY

This category includes any person whom the deceased has treated as his child in relation to any marriage of the deceased (eg a stepchild). The applicant must show that the deceased took on a parental role, which is more than showing affection and kindness. An adult may apply, even if, for example, he was over 18 when the deceased married his parent.

17.6.1 Reasonable financial provision

Where an applicant brings a claim it is for 'the ordinary standard' of reasonable financial provision (see **17.2.3**). As with an application by a child of the deceased, an able-bodied adult applicant is unlikely to succeed unless there are special circumstances.

17.6.2 Guidelines

The court considers:

(1) the common guidelines in s 3(1) (see **17.2.4**); and
(2) the special guidelines.

The special guidelines are:

(1) the manner in which the applicant was being or might expect to be educated or trained;
(2) the extent of responsibility assumed by the deceased towards the applicant;
(3) whether the deceased knew the child was not his own; and

(4) whether anyone else is legally responsible for the applicant's maintenance, for example whether the natural father pays maintenance under a court order.

17.7 APPLICATION BY A PERSON BEING MAINTAINED BY THE DECEASED IMMEDIATELY BEFORE HIS DEATH

An application may be made by a person who is being maintained by the deceased immediately before his death. Applicants under this category will include the elderly or infirm parent of the deceased and a cohabitee.

Note the definition of 'maintenance' in s 1(3) as stated in **17.2.2**.

> *Example 1*
> The deceased provided his niece, who is a qualified nurse, with free board and lodging in return for nursing care at home. She does not benefit under his will. The provision of free accommodation is prima facie maintenance by the deceased, but the care may be construed as consideration. If it is consideration then a claim by the niece will fail or the amount awarded will be reduced.

> *Example 2*
> Frank has died intestate. For the 12 months before his death he lived with Joan. During the week they lived in Joan's London flat, spending the weekends at Frank's country cottage. They shared the cost of household bills and holidays. Joan earns £20,000 pa.
>
> Joan cannot claim against Frank's estate unless she can show 'maintenance' by Frank. (Contrast a claim by a surviving spouse at **17.3.1** or by a two-year cohabitee at **17.8**.)

As a general rule it is a condition of eligibility that the maintenance continued until, and only ceased because of, the death. Where illness has supervened to prevent the deceased continuing a settled maintenance arrangement right up until his death, it will be presumed that the arrangement did so continue.

> *Example*
> Doris lives with Elsie in Elsie's house, Elsie paying all the bills. Elsie falls ill and, after one month in hospital, dies. Doris is still regarded as having been maintained up to Elsie's death.

17.7.1 Reasonable financial provision

The court applies 'the ordinary standard' of reasonable financial provision (see **17.2.3**). This can make it difficult for a relatively wealthy applicant to succeed, and the level of provision awarded to an unmarried partner will usually be less than that awarded to a surviving spouse.

17.7.2 Guidelines

The court considers:

(1) the common guidelines in s 3(1) (see **17.2.4**); and
(2) special guidelines.

The special guidelines are:

(1) the extent to which, and basis upon which, the deceased assumed responsibility for the maintenance of the applicant; and
(2) for how many years the maintenance had been assumed.

17.8 APPLICATION BY A COHABITEE

This category applies only where the death occurred on or after 1 January 1996. It includes any person who lived as the husband or wife of the deceased and in the same household as the deceased during the whole period of two years immediately before the death. This means that a cohabitee may bring a claim without having to prove that he or she was being maintained by the deceased.

17.8.1 Reasonable financial provision

Although the cohabitee may bring a claim without having to prove maintenance by the deceased, the 'ordinary standard' of reasonable financial provision still applies. This means that the court must decide whether the disposition of the deceased's estate makes such financial provision as it would be reasonable in all the circumstances for the cohabitee to receive for his or her maintenance.

17.8.2 Guidelines

In addition to the common guidelines (see **17.2.4**) the following special guidelines apply to a claim by a cohabitee:

(1) the age of the applicant and the length of the period during which the applicant lived as the husband or wife of the deceased and in the same household as the deceased; and
(2) the contribution made by the applicant to the welfare of the family of the deceased, including any contribution made by looking after the home or caring for the family.

17.9 ORDERS AND THEIR EFFECT

17.9.1 Orders which a court can make (s 2)

The court can make orders for:

(1) periodical payments for any period;
(2) a lump sum payment;
(3) the transfer of property;
(4) the settlement of property;
(5) the acquisition of property for transfer; or
(6) variation of a marriage settlement for either party or children of marriage/family.

17.9.2 Orders made against the net estate of the deceased

(1) The 'net estate' against which an order can be made includes:

    (a) property which the deceased has, or could have, disposed of by will (subject to the deduction of funeral, testamentary and administration expenses, debts and liabilities) (s 25); and

    (b) any asset passing on death by virtue of a nomination.

(2) In addition the court can make an order against the deceased's share of any property to which he was beneficially entitled as a joint tenant immediately before his death provided that the application for an order under s 2 is brought within 6 months of the issue of the grant of representation.

17.9.3 General effect of an order

The most common order is a lump sum either of cash or through the transfer of a specific asset. An order has two direct effects on an estate:

(1) the original beneficiary(ies) under the will or intestacy now receive less; and
(2) it may involve recalculating the IHT payable on the estate.

17.9.4 Burden of an order

The burden of an order can be thrown onto any part of the estate. It must not be assumed that the order will be satisfied out of the residue.

Example

Kerry's will leaves:

(1) my house (worth £14,000) to Len;
(2) £5,000 to Matt;
(3) residue (£10,000) to Nora.

Olive brings a successful claim.

If the court awards Olive £2,000 out of residue, Len and Matt remain unaffected but Nora's inheritance is reduced.

If the court awards Olive the house, prima facie this means Len receives nothing under the will, but Matt and Nora are unaffected. However, the court has the power to include in its order a direction that, for example, Matt's £5,000 be divided between Matt and Len, or part of the residue be given to Len to compensate him.

17.9.5 IHT consequences of an order

For IHT purposes, when an order is made it is treated as if the deceased's will or intestacy had contained that order. The IHT payable on the estate may have to be adjusted. If the order increases or decreases the size of the chargeable IHT estate there will be respectively more or less IHT to pay.

Example 1
Peter by will leaves all his estate (£350,000) to his son, Roger.

Executors pay IHT as follows:

£215,000 @ 0% = nil

£135,000 @ 40% = £54,000

IHT   = £54,000

The court subsequently orders a lump sum of £100,000 to Peter's wife, Sian.

The effect is as if Peter had left in his will a legacy of £100,000 to his wife Sian, and the residue (£250,000) to Roger.

IHT will be recalculated and the IHT bill will be smaller because the £100,000 is covered by the spouse exemption.

	£
Estate	350,000
deduct spouse exempt property	100,000
chargeable	250,000

£215,000 @ 0% = nil

£35,000 @ 40% = £14,000

IHT   = £14,000

As £54,000 has actually been paid, a refund of £40,000 is due to the estate.

Example 2
Tessa dies leaving all her estate (valued at £500,000) to her husband, Unwin.

Initially there will be no IHT to pay because the estate passes to the spouse with the benefit of the spouse exemption. Subsequently, the court orders half the estate to be given to the children. IHT will be recalculated because half the estate is now chargeable.

	£
Estate	500,000
deduct ½ passing to spouse (exempt)	250,000
chargeable	250,000

£215,000 @ 0% = nil

£35,000 @ 40% = £14,000

IHT   = £14,000

IHT payable as a result of the court order is £14,000.

17.10 ANTI-AVOIDANCE PROVISIONS

The provisions contained in ss 10 and 11 are designed to prevent the provisions of I(PFD)A being defeated by the deceased giving away his property during his lifetime. As a result of the provisions, the court can make an order under s 2 in favour of a claimant against, for example, any property the deceased has given away within 6 years of his death with the intention of defeating a claim.

17.11 SUMMARY OF POINTS TO BEAR IN MIND IN THE OFFICE

17.11.1 Advising a client on making a will

When taking instructions, the solicitor should mention the I(PFD)A to ascertain whether there are any potential claimants. If the I(PFD)A is likely to be relevant, the solicitor should point out the problems that may arise if a claim is brought.

Where appropriate, the solicitor may suggest a suitable legacy or share of residue, or a lifetime gift, or a life insurance policy written in trust for the potential claimant. Details of the provision and motive should be recorded by the client as evidence of his belief that he has made reasonable financial provision for that person.

Where a testator does not wish to make provision for a person, he should be encouraged to make a signed statement explaining his motives. This often takes the form of a letter to the PRs and is kept with the will. If a claim is brought after the testator's death, the statement is admissible in evidence and will be considered by the court. It is inadvisable to include the statement in the will itself as, following the issue of the grant of representation, the will becomes a document of public record available to any person who wishes to read it.

An unmarried client should make a will if he wishes to guarantee that on his death any of his property passes to his partner. A cohabitee or unmarried partner has no right to share in an estate on an intestacy (see Chapter 16). To claim under the I(PFD)A, he or she will have to show that he or she lived in the same household, and as the husband or wife of the deceased, for the whole of the two years immediately before death. Even so, the cohabitee may claim only such financial provision as is reasonable for his or her maintenance.

It is essential that the solicitor makes a file note of any advice given and anything said by the client as this may be used in evidence in the event of a claim.

Having acted for the testator in the preparation of his will, a solicitor must not subsequently act for a person claiming against the estate.

17.11.2 Acting for the PRs

PRs should be advised not to distribute the estate until 6 months have elapsed from the issue of the grant. In any event they must not distribute once they have notice of a possible claim. If PRs do distribute within the 6-month period and an applicant subsequently brings a successful claim, the PRs will be personally liable to satisfy the claim if insufficient assets remain in the estate. Where a court permits an application out of time, the PRs will not be liable personally if they have distributed the estate, but the claimant may be able to recover property from the beneficiaries.

Once instructions have been accepted from the PRs to act for them in the administration of the estate, the firm must not then accept instructions to act for a claimant against the estate as there would be a conflict of interest.

17.11.3 Acting for a claimant

When a firm is instructed by a client to bring a claim under the I(PFD)A against an estate, the matter will normally be handled by its litigation department, especially if the claim cannot be settled out of court.

Consider carefully the professional conduct position: a solicitor cannot act for a claimant if he or his firm is already acting for the PRs (see **17.11.2**), or if he advised the testator in connection with the will (see **17.1.2**).

Any claim must be brought within 6 months of the issue of the grant of representation. The court has a discretion to extend this period, but it is unwise to delay unnecessarily as the court will agree to extend the limit only in exceptional circumstances. If the claimant's solicitor failed to lodge the I(PFD)A claim in time, the court might refuse to extend the time-limit, since the claimant would have grounds for a negligence claim against the solicitor. Even if permission is given for a late application, the court has no power to include the jointly owned property of the deceased in any order.

In agreeing the amount of an award the burden of IHT should be taken into account. In many situations the amount actually received by a claimant (and possibly the beneficiaries of the will/intestacy) will be affected by whether the award is 'free of tax' or 'subject to tax'. Except where the court makes an order in favour of the deceased's spouse an award expressed to be 'free of tax' may be substantially more generous to the claimant than an order for a similar amount 'subject to tax'. Conversely, if the original residuary gift was IHT exempt, any 'free of tax' legacy ordered by the court will cost the estate not only the amount of the order but also the tax attributable to it and grossing up will apply (see **18.6.3**).

17.12 STANDING SEARCH

To ensure that a potential claimant brings his claim in time, a solicitor can make a standing search at a probate registry. A standing search will:

(1) reveal the issue of any grant of representation to the estate in question during the preceding 12 months; and
(2) ensure the claimant is notified if a grant is issued in the following 6 months.

A standing search can be renewed. If a standing search is made and reveals that a grant has already been issued, or a grant is issued within the following 6 months, the probate registry will supply a copy of the grant to the searcher. This enables a potential claimant to discover the names and addresses of the PRs and of any solicitor acting for them, and also ensures that the claimant knows the date by which he has to bring his claim.

Chapter 18

INHERITANCE TAX

18.1 INTRODUCTION

This chapter explains the stages in the process of calculating and paying IHT on death. Details of the charge on lifetime transfers are included where relevant for the calculation of tax on death and also for lifetime tax planning.

An introduction to inheritance tax (IHT) is contained in the LPC Resource Book *Pervasive Topics* (Jordans, 1997), Part I. The basic principles in that book provide the foundations for this chapter.

IHT is governed principally by the Inheritance Tax Act 1984 (IHTA) and section numbers refer to that Act unless otherwise stated. The Act may be found in the Orange Tax Handbook and further explanation in Barlow, King and King, and Whitehouse.

18.2 WHEN IS IHT CHARGEABLE?

IHT is charged on 'the value transferred by a chargeable transfer'. The term 'chargeable transfer' means 'a transfer of value made by an individual which is not exempt' (IHTA, ss 1, 2).

This charge may apply both to lifetime transfers and to transfers on death.

18.2.1 Lifetime transfers

'transfer of value'
The term 'transfer of value' is defined to mean any lifetime disposition made by a person ('the transferor') which reduces the value of his estate. Thus any lifetime gift falls within the definition.

'which is not exempt'
LIFETIME EXEMPTIONS APPLYING AT THE TIME OF TRANSFER
Certain lifetime transfers are exempt, either wholly or in part, at the time when they are made. There will never be any IHT to pay on a gift, or part of a gift, which is covered by an exemption.

> *Example*
> On 1 June 1992 Anne gives £3,000 to her son Ben. The transfer falls within Anne's lifetime annual exemption for IHT and is exempt.
>
> On 1 June 1993 Anne gives £9,000 to Ben. £3,000 of the transfer is exempt.

POTENTIALLY EXEMPT TRANSFERS
Any lifetime transfer which would otherwise be chargeable is 'potentially exempt' if it is made to another individual. A potentially exempt transfer (PET) becomes chargeable if the transferor dies within 7 years of the date of the transfer. If the transferor survives for 7 years, the PET becomes exempt (s 3A).

Chapter 18 contents
Introduction
When is IHT chargeable?
How to calculate IHT on death: a summary
Step 1: identify the estate
Step 2: value the estate
Step 3: apply any relevant exemptions
Step 4: apply business and agricultural property reliefs (if relevant)
Step 5: calculate tax at the appropriate rate
Liability for IHT on death
Time for payment of IHT on death
Burden of IHT on death
Example of the application of IHT to an estate on death
Lifetime transfers

Example

On 1 March 1992 Sarah gives £250,000 to Tim. Assume no lifetime exemptions apply. The gift is a PET: no IHT is chargeable at the date of the gift.

If Sarah dies before 1 March 1999, the PET becomes chargeable. Tim is then liable to pay IHT. If Sarah survives until 1 March 1999, the PET becomes exempt. There will never be any IHT payable on it and it has no further significance for IHT purposes.

18.2.2 Death

When a person dies, he is treated for IHT purposes as having made a transfer of value immediately before his death, ie there is a deemed transfer of value. The value transferred is the value of the deceased's 'estate' immediately before his death. The effect of this deemed transfer of value is that IHT is chargeable on an individual's 'estate' on death unless an exemption applies (s 4). 'Estate' has a particular meaning in this context (see **18.4.1**).

18.3 HOW TO CALCULATE IHT ON DEATH: A SUMMARY

This paragraph summarises the five steps involved in the calculation. Each of these steps is examined in greater detail in **18.4–18.8** as indicated.

18.3.1 Step 1: identify the estate

The estate is defined for IHT purposes to mean all the property to which the deceased was beneficially entitled (see **18.4**).

18.3.2 Step 2: value the estate

The basic rule is that assets in the estate are valued for IHT at their open market value immediately before the death. There are special valuation rules for certain types of property. Debts owed at the time of death and funeral expenses may be deducted (see **18.5**).

18.3.3 Step 3: apply any relevant exemptions

The main exemptions available on death depend on the identity of the beneficiary. Property which passes on death to the deceased's spouse or to charity is exempt (see **18.6**).

18.3.4 Step 4: apply business and agricultural property reliefs (if relevant)

If any of the assets in the estate are eligible for business or agricultural property relief, their value may be reduced by 100 per cent or 50 per cent (see **18.7**).

18.3.5 Step 5: calculate tax at the appropriate rate

If the deceased has made no chargeable transfers in the 7 years before death, the rate of tax on the first £215,000 of his estate is 0 per cent. This is known as the 'nil rate band'. It is not an exemption; tax is chargeable but at a nil rate. If his estate exceeds £215,000, IHT is charged on the excess at 40 per cent.

Example

Arshad dies on 1 June 1997. The value of his estate for IHT purposes, after deduction of exemptions and reliefs is £250,000. He has made no chargeable transfers since 1 June 1990.

Tax on Arshad's estate: on £215,000 @ 0% = nil
on £35,000 @ 40% = £14,000

If the deceased has made chargeable transfers in the 7 years before death, such transfers must be cumulated in order to find the rate of tax applicable to his estate on death. This means that chargeable transfers made within 7 years of death reduce the nil rate band applicable to the estate, and may use it up altogether. This cumulation principle applies not only to immediately chargeable transfers made within 7 years of death (which are relatively unusual): it also applies to PETs which have become chargeable because the transferor has died within 7 years.

Example

In 1995, Nayna gave £90,000 to her sister, Hemini. No lifetime exemptions were available. The gift was a PET.

In June 1997, Nayna dies. The value of her estate for IHT (after deduction of exemptions and reliefs) is £135,000. The PET made in 1995 has become chargeable because Nayna has died within 7 years. The chargeable transfer made within 7 years of Nayna's death must be cumulated: it uses up £90,000 of Nayna's nil rate band, and only £125,000 remains for the estate.

Tax on Nayna's estate: on £125,000 @ 0% = nil
on £10,000 @ 40% = £4,000

For further examples of cumulation and the calculation of IHT on death, see **18.8**.

The steps summarised above are now examined in detail.

18.4 STEP 1: IDENTIFY THE ESTATE

18.4.1 Definition of 'estate'

A person's estate is the aggregate of all the property (other than 'excluded property') to which he is beneficially entitled immediately before his death (s 5(1)).

Property included within this definition falls into three categories as set out below.

(1) Property which passes under the deceased's will or on intestacy. The deceased was 'beneficially entitled' to all such property immediately before he died.

(2) Property to which the deceased was 'beneficially entitled' immediately before his death but which does not pass under his will or intestacy. This category consists of:

   (a) the deceased's interest in any joint property passing on his death by survivorship to the surviving joint tenant; and
   (b) nominated property, ie money deposited in an account with a friendly society or an industrial and provident society which does not pass under the will or intestacy because the deceased has nominated a particular individual to receive it on his death. (This may include National Savings

Bank accounts or National Savings Certificates nominated before 1 May 1981.)

(3) Property included because of special statutory provisions. By statute, the deceased is treated as having been 'beneficially entitled' to certain types of property which would otherwise fall outside the definition. These rules apply to certain trust property (see **18.4.2**) and to property given away by the deceased in his lifetime but which is 'subject to a reservation' at the time of death (see **18.4.3**).

18.4.2 Trust property included in the estate for IHT purposes

Section 49(1) provides as follows:

> 'A person beneficially entitled to an interest in possession in settled property shall be treated ... as beneficially entitled to the property in which the interest subsists.'

A person has an interest in possession in settled (trust) property if he is entitled to claim the income, or part of the income, as it arises, ie the trustees have no power to withhold it from him. The most common example of a trust with an interest in possession is a life interest trust.

> *Example*
> In her will, Gina left all her estate to her executors/trustees, Tom and Tessa, on trust to pay the income to Gina's son, Simon, for life with remainder to Rose absolutely. Both Simon and Rose are over 18 years old.
>
> Tom and Tessa must invest the property to produce income. Simon is entitled to the income during his life. Tom and Tessa must pay it to him. Thus Simon, the life tenant, has an interest in possession.
>
> When Simon dies, his rights under the trust cease. Under the terms of the trust instrument (Gina's will), Rose is now entitled to the trust fund, and Tom and Tessa must transfer all the trust property to her.
>
> For IHT purposes, Simon has an interest in possession. Although he was only entitled to the income from the trust property and had no control over the disposition of the fund on his death, he is treated for tax purposes as 'beneficially entitled' to the whole trust fund. The fund is taxed on his death as part of his estate. The tax on the trust property will be paid from the trust fund.

A person who is entitled to part of the income under a trust is treated for IHT purposes as 'beneficially entitled' to a proportionate part of the capital.

> *Example*
> A fund worth £300,000 is held on trust to pay the income to Lisa, May and Nora in equal shares. On Lisa's death, one-third of the fund (£100,000) is treated as part of her estate for IHT purposes.

18.4.3 Property subject to a reservation

The Finance Act 1986 contains provisions designed to prevent people from avoiding tax by giving property away more than 7 years before death but continuing to enjoy the benefit of the property. The rule applies where the deceased gave away property during his lifetime, but did not transfer 'possession and enjoyment' of the property to the donee or was not entirely excluded from enjoying the property.

If property is subject to a reservation at the time of the donor's death, the donor is treated as being 'beneficially entitled' to the property.

Example
In 1990, Diana gave her jewellery, worth £100,000, to her daughter Emma, but retained possession of it. Diana dies in 1998, when the jewellery (still in her possession) is worth £120,000. Although the jewellery belongs to Emma, tax is charged on Diana's death as if she were still beneficially entitled to it. The jewellery, valued at £120,000, is taxed as part of Diana's estate. The tax on the jewellery will be borne by Emma.

18.4.4 Property outside the estate for IHT purposes

Property to which the deceased was not 'beneficially entitled' immediately before his death falls outside the definition. Thus if the deceased took out a life assurance policy written in trust for a named beneficiary the proceeds are not part of his estate for IHT purposes. Similarly, a discretionary lump sum payment made from a pension fund to the deceased's family is not part of the estate for IHT purposes.

18.4.5 Excluded property

Certain property which would otherwise be included in the estate for IHT purposes is defined in the IHTA as 'excluded property'. Excluded property is not part of the estate for IHT purposes. One example of excluded property is a 'reversionary interest'. For IHT purposes this means any future interest under a settlement.

Example
In the first example in **18.4.2** (the trust set up by Gina), Simon has a life interest (an 'interest in possession' for IHT purposes) while Rose has a vested interest in remainder (a future or 'reversionary' interest for IHT purposes because Rose will receive nothing until Simon's death). If Rose dies before Simon, her reversionary interest, since it is vested, passes under Rose's will or intestacy and Rose's beneficiary will receive the trust fund on Simon's death. However, the value of Rose's 'reversionary interest' is not part of her estate for IHT purposes as it is excluded property. It will not affect the calculation of IHT on her estate at her death.

18.4.6 LPA 1925, s 184

Section 184 provides that where two (or more) persons die in circumstances where the order of their deaths cannot be proved, the younger is deemed for succession purposes to survive the elder (see **15.3.2**). This rule does not apply for the purposes of IHT payable on death. In circumstances where s 184 would apply for succession purposes then, for IHT purposes, the deaths are presumed to occur at the same instant (s 4(2)).

Example
Andrew (aged 28) and his friend Mary (aged 26) are killed outright in a plane crash. Andrew's will leaves all his property to Mary. Mary's will leaves all her property to her sister, Sally.

Succession: by virtue of s 184, Mary is deemed to have survived Andrew. His will operates to pass his estate to Mary. Her property (combined with Andrew's) passes to Sally.

IHT: when Andrew's property passes to Mary, it is charged to IHT in the normal way. When calculating the tax on her estate passing to Sally, the property which Mary received from Andrew is not included.

If Andrew and Mary were husband and wife, there would be no IHT on Andrew's death because the spouse exemption would apply. On Mary's death only her estate would be charged to IHT, and Andrew's estate would escape any charge.

18.5 STEP 2: VALUE THE ESTATE

18.5.1 Basic valuation principle

Assets in the estate are valued for IHT purposes at 'the price which the property might reasonably be expected to fetch if sold in the open market' immediately before the death (s 160).

This means that the value immediately before death of every asset forming part of the estate for IHT purposes must be assessed and reported to the Inland Revenue in the Inland Revenue account (unless the estate is excepted from this requirement: see **21.2**). Some assets, such as bank and building society accounts and quoted shares, are easy to value. Others, such as land, may be more difficult. Negotiations may be required (in the case of land, with the district valuer) in order to reach an agreed valuation.

The value of an asset agreed for IHT purposes is known as the 'probate value'.

18.5.2 Modification of the basic valuation principle: s 171

Section 171 provides that, where the death causes the value of an asset in the estate to increase or decrease, that change in value should be taken into account.

> *Example*
> Brian has insured his life for £50,000. The benefit of the policy belongs to him (ie the policy is not written in trust). Immediately before Brian's death, the value of the policy (surrender value) is considerably less than its maturity value of £50,000. Under s 171, the effect of Brian's death on the value of the policy is taken into account: its value for IHT purposes is £50,000.

18.5.3 Application of valuation principles to particular assets

Bank and building society accounts
Their value for IHT purposes is the balance on the account including interest up to the date of death.

Quoted shares
The value of quoted shares is taken from the Stock Exchange Daily Official List for the date of death (or the nearest trading day). The list quotes two prices. To value the shares for IHT, take one-quarter of the difference between the lower and higher price and add it to the lower price.

> *Example*
> John died owning 200 shares in ABC plc. On the date of John's death the quoted price per share is 102p/106p. The value of each share for IHT is 103p, and so the value of John's holding is £206.

Unquoted shares

The value of unquoted shares is more difficult to ascertain, although the basic principle of open market value still applies. Information about the company and its record will be required.

Land

If the deceased owned an interest in land, whether as tenant in common or joint tenant, that share is part of his estate for IHT purposes and must be valued. The usual method is to take the value of the whole property and divide it by the number of shares, but a discount is normally allowed (of between 10 and 15 per cent).

Debts owed to the deceased

If a debt is owed to the deceased, its value is part of his estate for IHT purposes. One of the PRs' duties is to ensure that the deceased's lifetime income tax position has been settled (see **29.5.1**). If the deceased has paid too much income tax during his lifetime, the overpayment will be reclaimed from the Inland Revenue. Thus, when he died this amount was owed to the deceased and should be included as part of his estate for IHT purposes.

18.5.4 Debts and expenses

Liabilities owed by the deceased at the time of death are deductible for IHT purposes providing that they were incurred for money or money's worth (s 505). Thus debts such as gas and telephone bills may be deducted. In addition, the deceased may not have paid enough income tax on the income he received before he died; this amount may also be deducted.

Reasonable funeral expenses are also deductible (s 162).

18.5.5 Related property

The related property rules also modify the basic valuation principle. The rules apply to property owned by spouses where the items of property owned by husband and wife are worth more valued together than separately. Each spouse's property must be valued not in isolation, but as a proportion of the whole.

> *Example*
> Vivien owns 30 per cent of the shares in a private company. Her husband, Jack, owns 30 per cent of the shares in the same company. Vivien dies. Her shares will be valued as one half of a 60 per cent shareholding (to reflect the fact that a 60 per cent shareholding is worth more than twice a 30 per cent shareholding because it gives control of the company).

18.6 STEP 3: APPLY ANY RELEVANT EXEMPTIONS

The main exemptions applicable on death depend on the identity of the beneficiary. Thus it is important to see who is entitled to the property on death.

18.6.1 Spouse exemption

Basic rule

Section 18 provides as follows:

> 'A transfer of value is an exempt transfer to the extent that the value transferred is attributable to property which becomes comprised in the estate of the transferor's spouse.'

Any property included in the estate for IHT purposes is exempt if it passes to the deceased's spouse under the deceased's will or intestacy or, in the case of joint property, by survivorship.

Trust property

The rule applicable to 'interest in possession' trusts is that IHT is charged as if the person with the right to income owned the capital (see **18.4.2**). This rule applies for the purpose of spouse exemption, both on creation of the trust and on the death of a life tenant.

CREATION OF TRUST

If, in his will, the deceased leaves his estate to trustees on trust to pay the income to his wife for life with remainder to the children, the spouse exemption applies to the whole estate. Although the wife has only been given the right to income, the IHT rules are applied as if she had been given the capital.

DEATH OF LIFE TENANT

If, on the death of a life tenant the trust property passes under the terms of the trust to the life tenant's spouse, the spouse exemption applies and no tax is payable on the trust property.

Survivorship clauses

Normally, the spouse exemption applies only where the gift to the transferor's spouse takes effect immediately. However, the spouse exemption still applies where property is given to the testator's spouse conditionally upon surviving for a specified period which, for this purpose, must not exceed 12 months. (The survivorship period should not exceed 6 months to avoid the creation of a settlement for IHT purposes. See **9.2.1**.)

> *Example*
>
> Karen leaves all her estate to her husband, Len, if he survives her by 28 days. If he does not, the property is to pass to the children.
>
> If Len is living at Karen's death, the gift to him does not take effect immediately. Len's interest vests 28 days from Karen's death, if he is still alive. Spouse exemption applies. If Len dies during the 28-day period, the spouse exemption does not apply. IHT is charged as if Karen had left her estate directly to the children (s 92).

18.6.2 Charity exemption

Section 23(1) provides as follows:

> 'Transfers of value are exempt to the extent that the values transferred by them are attributable to property which is given to charities.'

Any property forming part of the deceased's estate for IHT purposes which passes on death to charity is exempt. The exemption most commonly applies to property which passes to charity under the deceased's will. However, if the deceased had a life interest in trust property which passes under the terms of the trust to charity, the charity exemption applies.

A similar exemption applies to gifts to certain national bodies and bodies providing a public benefit, such as museums and art galleries, and to political parties.

18.6.3 Partially exempt transfers

Sometimes only a part of an estate on death is exempt for IHT purposes and the other part is not exempt. Difficulties may arise in determining how much tax is payable. Any tax relating to the non-exempt part of the estate can affect the calculation of the size of the exempt beneficiary's inheritance. Provisions designed to resolve these difficulties are contained in s 38. In general these provisions apply relatively rarely and give rise to complicated calculations. It is, however, important to understand their effect where there are legacies on which tax is chargeable combined with a gift of residue to an exempt beneficiary.

Example

In her will Pippa gives £221,000 to her son Roger and the rest of her estate to her husband Hugh. Pippa has made no lifetime gifts in the 7 years preceding her death. Her estate is worth £300,000. The legacy to Roger exceeds Pippa's nil rate band, and there will be tax to pay. Residue is exempt. The amount of tax payable depends on who is liable to pay the tax.

(i) If Pippa's will gives the legacy to Roger 'subject to tax', simply calculate tax on the legacy in the usual way.

		£
Calculate tax on £221,000		
£215,000 @ 0%		nil
£6,000 @ 40%		2,400
Distribution: Tax bill		2,400
Roger receives legacy (less tax)		218,600
Hugh receives residue		79,000
		300,000

(ii) If Pippa's will gives the legacy to Roger 'free of tax', the calculation is more complicated. Section 38(3) provides that the value transferred is the aggregate of the value of the gift and the 'tax which would be chargeable if the value transferred equalled that aggregate'. This means that the benefit given to Roger is £221,000 net, ie tax paid, the tax being paid from the residue. In order to find the value transferred, it is necessary to calculate what sum would, after deduction of tax at the appropriate rate, leave £221,000: ie the legacy must be grossed up.

Gross up Roger's legacy:		£
£215,000 (grossed up @ 0%)		215,000
£ 6,000 (grossed up @ 40%) 6,000 × $\frac{100}{60}$		10,000
Gross gift		225,000

		£
Calculate tax on £225,000		
£215,000 @ 0%		nil
£10,000 @ 40%		4,000
Distribution:	Roger receives legacy	221,000
	Tax bill	4,000
	Residue to Hugh (after payment of tax)	75,000
		300,000

Will drafting

It is particularly important to be aware of these provisions when drafting a will. If a legacy is given 'free of tax', the tax bill may be considerably higher than if the legacy were given 'subject to tax'. Compare the tax paid in the example above. If the will is silent, tax on the legacy is payable from residue under the AEA 1925, s 34. The alternatives should be explained to the testator so that clear instructions can be taken and express provision included as to whether the legacy is to be free of tax or subject to tax.

18.7 STEP 4: APPLY BUSINESS AND AGRICULTURAL PROPERTY RELIEFS (IF RELEVANT)

Business and agricultural property reliefs operate to reduce the value transferred by a transfer of the property to which they apply. It is important to check whether they apply to any of the property included in the estate for IHT purposes, whether passing by will or intestacy, by survivorship or under the terms of a trust in which the deceased had a life interest. Both reliefs apply not only on death but to lifetime transfers as well (see **18.13.1**).

18.7.1 Business property relief (s 105)

Business property relief operates to reduce the value transferred by a transfer of 'relevant business property' by either 100 per cent or 50 per cent. Generally, the transferor must have owned the property for the period of two years before the transfer.

100 per cent relief
Available for:

(1) a business or partnership share; and
(2) unquoted shares.

Example 1
James owns a newsagent's shop. His estate on death includes the assets and debts of the business. After deducting the debts the value of the business is £100,000. For IHT purposes, this value is reduced to nil.

Example 2
Kate owns 10 per cent of the shares in a private company. The shares are worth £100,000. The value of the shares in her estate on death for IHT is reduced to nil.

50 per cent relief
Available for:

(1) quoted shares provided the transferor had control of the company immediately before the transfer; and
(2) land, buildings, machinery or plant which immediately before the transfer were used wholly or mainly for a business of which the transferor was a partner or used for a company's business where the transferor controlled the company.

Example
Len owns factory premises occupied by Len Ltd, a private company which he controls. On Len's death the premises are valued for probate at £250,000. The value is reduced for IHT purposes by 50 per cent to £125,000.

18.7.2 Agricultural property relief (s 116)

Agricultural property relief applies to property which was either:

(1) occupied by the transferor for agriculture throughout the 2 years immediately before the transfer; or
(2) owned by the transferor throughout the 7 years immediately before the transfer (provided it was occupied by someone for agriculture throughout the 7-year period).

100 per cent relief
Available where the transferor:

(1) had the right to vacant possession immediately before the transfer; or
(2) let the land and either (a) the tenancy commenced on or after 1 September 1995 or (b) the current tenant succeeded to the tenancy on the death of the previous tenant on or after 1 September 1995.

Example
Michael farms his own land and has done so for many years. The agricultural value of his farm is £250,000. The agricultural value of the farm in his estate on death is reduced to nil.

50 per cent relief
Available on any other qualifying agricultural property.

Example
Naomi owns a farm which has been let to a tenant farmer for the last 10 years. The agricultural value of the farm subject to the tenancy is £200,000. On Naomi's death, this value is reduced to £100,000 for IHT purposes.

18.8 STEP 5: CALCULATE TAX AT THE APPROPRIATE RATE

18.8.1 Rate of tax

The rates of tax applicable on death are:

    0% on the first £215,000 (the nil rate band)
    40% on the balance of the estate on death.

However, lifetime chargeable transfers made in the 7 years before death reduce the nil rate band available on death: such transfers must be 'cumulated' with the estate.

18.8.2 Cumulation

The deceased's cumulative total is calculated by taking 'the aggregate of ... the values transferred by previous chargeable transfers made by him' in the 7 years ending with the date of death (s 7(1)). The PRs must ascertain whether the deceased made any transfers of value in the 7 years before he died.

These may include:

(1) immediately chargeable transfers made during the 7-year period, such as gifts into discretionary trusts; and, more commonly,
(2) potentially exempt transfers which have become chargeable as a result of the transferor's death within 7 years.

The 'values transferred' by such transfers must be aggregated. This means that any lifetime exemptions or reliefs which operate to reduce the value transferred are taken into account. Note that tapering relief reduces tax on lifetime gifts made more than 3 years before the death, but it does not reduce the value transferred by such gifts. It therefore does not reduce the deceased's cumulative total of chargeable transfers.

Example 1
David makes the following gifts:

> in 1994, £50,000 to his wife
> in 1996, £85,000 to his son

In August 1997, David dies leaving his estate, valued at £150,000, to his son.

The 1994 transfer was exempt as a transfer to a spouse, and does not affect David's cumulative total.

The 1996 transfer was a PET which has now become chargeable. The value transferred is £85,000 less £6,000 (David's annual exemption for the tax year of the transfer and the preceding tax year). David's cumulative total is £79,000.

	£
The nil rate band applicable to David's estate on death is	215,000
less cumulative total	79,000
	136,000

Tax on David's estate:

£136,000 @ 0% =	nil
£14,000 @ 40% =	£5,600

Example 2
Felicity makes the following gifts:

> on 1 May 1993, £66,000 to her nephew
> on 1 June 1994, £168,000 to her niece

Felicity dies on 5 August 1997. Her estate is worth £200,000. Both gifts are PETs which have now become chargeable. Their values must be cumulated.

Cumulative total:

	£	£
transfer on 1 May 1993	66,000	
less 2 annual exemptions	6,000	60,000
transfer on 1 June 1994	168,000	
less 1 annual exemption	3,000	165,000
		225,000

Tax on Felicity's death:

Felicity's nil rate band is exhausted. Tax on her estate of £200,000 @ 40% = £80,000.

(Note that in this example Felicity's niece will be liable for tax on the transfer made on 1 June 1994. Since more than 3 years have elapsed between the transfer and Felicity's death, the tax payable will be reduced by tapering relief, but this does not affect Felicity's cumulative total. See **18.13.4**, where the tax payable by Felicity's niece is calculated.)

18.8.3 The estate rate

The term 'estate rate' means the average rate of tax applicable to each item of property in the estate for IHT. When tax on the estate has been calculated, it may be necessary for various reasons to work out how much of the tax is attributable to a particular item of property in the estate. For example:

(1) since tax on certain types of property, such as land, may be paid in instalments, the PRs must calculate how much of the tax relates to that property;
(2) the PRs may not be liable to pay all the tax on the estate. If the estate for IHT purposes includes trust property, the trustees are liable to pay the tax attributable to that property;
(3) the will may give a legacy 'subject to tax'.

The principle is that tax is divided between the various assets in the estate proportionately, according to their value. This may be applied by calculating the average rate of tax on the estate as a percentage, ie the 'estate rate'. For example, if the deceased's nil rate band was completely used up by lifetime transfers, the 'estate rate' would be 40 per cent. However, it is not strictly necessary to calculate the estate rate as a percentage; instead, the amount of tax on a particular item of property in the estate may be calculated by applying to the value of that property the proportion which the total tax bill bears to the total chargeable estate.

Example 1

Graham, who has made no lifetime transfers, leaves a house, valued at £225,000, to Henry, subject to payment of IHT, and the rest of his estate, valued at £75,000 net to Ian.

| Tax on Graham's estate: | £215,000 @ 0% | nil |
| | £85,000 @ 40% | £34,000 |

The 'estate rate' is: $\dfrac{£34,000}{£300,000}$ (total tax bill) / (total chargeable estate)

Henry pays tax on the house: £225,000 × $\dfrac{£34,000}{£300,000}$ = £25,500

Ian pays tax on the residue: £75,000 × $\dfrac{£34,000}{£300,000}$ = £8,500

Example 2

Trustees are holding property worth £280,000 on trust for Janet for life with remainder to Kate. Janet dies leaving property worth £120,000 net to her son. She had made no lifetime transfers.

For IHT purposes Janet had an interest in possession in the trust fund, and tax is charged as if she owned the capital (see **18.4.2**). Her estate, including the trust fund, for IHT is worth £400,000.

| Tax on Janet's death: | £215,000 @ 0% | nil |
| | £185,000 @ 40% | £74,000 |

Janet's PRs are only liable to pay tax on the £120,000 which vests in them. The trustees must pay the tax on the trust property.

Tax payable by PRs: £120,000 × $\dfrac{£74,000}{£400,000}$ = £22,200

Tax payable by trustees: £280,000 × $\dfrac{£74,000}{£400,000}$ = £51,800

18.8.4 Quick succession relief

This relief reduces the amount of tax payable on a deceased person's estate if the deceased received property under a chargeable transfer made to him within the 5 years before he died. The amount of the reduction is a percentage of the tax paid on the first transfer. The percentage reduction varies according to the length of time between the transfer and the death, for example, 80 per cent if the previous transfer was 1–2 years before death; 20 per cent if the previous transfer was 4–5 years before death.

The relief only applies where:

(1) tax was paid on the transfer to the deceased; and
(2) tax is payable on the deceased's estate.

It is not necessary to show that the deceased still owned the property given to him by the chargeable transfer.

Example

Linda dies leaving her estate, worth £250,000 to her son Mark. Two years later, Mark dies leaving his estate, worth £400,000 to his friend Naomi. Tax on

Mark's death is calculated in the usual way, and is then reduced by a percentage of the tax paid on Linda's death.

18.9 LIABILITY FOR IHT ON DEATH

18.9.1 Meaning of 'liability'

The rules which follow concern the question of who is liable to account to the Revenue for the payment of the tax due as a result of death. The Inland Revenue are concerned with obtaining payment of the tax, and not with the question of who bears the burden of the payment. Payment will usually be obtained from people who are not beneficially entitled to the property but who hold property in a representative capacity, ie PRs and trustees. Those who ultimately receive the property are concurrently liable with such representatives, but in most cases tax will have been paid before the beneficiaries receive the property. The question of the burden of IHT is considered in **18.11**.

18.9.2 The PRs: tax on the non-settled estate

The PRs are liable to pay the IHT attributable to any property which 'was not immediately before the death comprised in a settlement' (s 200). This includes:

(1) the property which vests in the PRs (ie the property which passes under the deceased's will or intestacy); and
(2) property (other than trust property) which does not pass to the PRs but is included in the estate for IHT because the deceased was beneficially entitled to it immediately before death (ie property which passes by survivorship (the deceased's interest in property held on a beneficial joint tenancy) or by nomination (certain accounts with friendly societies or industrial and provident societies for which the deceased completed a nomination form)).

Thus the PRs are liable to pay the IHT on joint and nominated property even though that property does not vest in them. Their liability is, however, limited to the value of the assets they received, or would have received but for their own neglect or default.

Concurrently liable with the PRs is 'any person in whom property is vested ... at any time after the death or who at any such time is beneficially entitled to an interest in possession in the property' (s 200(1)(c)). This means that tax on property passing by will or intestacy may in principle be claimed by the Inland Revenue from a beneficiary who has received that property. Similarly, the Inland Revenue may claim tax on joint or nominated property from the surviving joint tenant or nominee. Such tax is normally paid by the PRs and it is relatively unusual for the Revenue to claim tax from the recipient of the property.

> *Example*
> Oliver dies intestate. His estate for IHT purposes consists of property worth £80,000 which passes on Oliver's intestacy to his sister and an interest in a house held by Oliver and his friend Penny as beneficial joint tenants. Oliver's interest in the house is valued for IHT purposes at £160,000.
>
> Tax on Oliver's death:
> on   £215,000 @ 0%   nil
>   £25,000 @ 40%   £10,000

Oliver's PRs are liable to pay the £10,000 to the Revenue. Penny is concurrently liable for that part of the £10,000 attributable to the joint property as the property is vested in her. If the property worth £80,000 (or any part of it) becomes vested in Oliver's sister before tax on it has been paid, she will become liable for the tax on that property.

18.9.3 The trustees: tax on settled property

If the estate for IHT purposes includes any property which was 'comprised in a settlement' immediately before the death, the trustees of the settlement are liable for IHT attributable to that property. This principle is relevant where the deceased had an interest in possession under a trust. Again, any person in whom the trust property subsequently vests or for whose benefit the trust property is subsequently applied is concurrently liable with the trustees.

Example
Property worth £300,000 is held on trust for Ruth for life with remainder to Arthur. Ruth dies leaving property worth £200,000 which passes under her will to Tessa. The trust fund is taxed as part of Ruth's estate as she had an interest in possession for IHT purposes (see **18.4.2**). She had made no lifetime transfers.

Tax on Ruth's death:
$$\text{on} \quad £215,000 \ @ \ 0\% \qquad \text{nil}$$
$$£285,000 \ @ \ 40\% \qquad £114,000$$

The trustees are liable to pay the tax on the trust fund (calculated according to the estate rate):

$$£300,000 \times \frac{£114,000}{£500,000} = £68,400$$

Arthur, the remainderman, is concurrently liable if any of the trust property is transferred to him before the tax has been paid.

Ruth's PRs are liable to pay the tax on Ruth's free estate:

$$£200,000 \times \frac{£114,000}{£500,000} = £45,600$$

18.9.4 Additional liability of PRs

Gifts with reservation of benefit
As seen in **18.4.3**, property which the deceased gave away during his lifetime is treated as part of his estate on death if the donor reserved a benefit in the property which he continued to enjoy immediately before death. The donee of the gift is primarily liable to pay tax attributable to the property. However, if the tax remains unpaid 12 months after the end of the month of death, the PRs become liable for the tax.

PETs
Where a person dies within 7 years of making a PET, the transfer becomes chargeable and IHT may be payable. The transferee is primarily liable, but again, the PRs become liable if the tax remains unpaid 12 months after the end of the month of death.

Protection of PRs

In each of the above cases the liability of the PRs is limited to the extent of the assets they actually received, or would have received but for their neglect or default. However, PRs cannot escape liability on the grounds that they have distributed the estate and so they should ideally delay distribution until IHT on any such lifetime gifts has been paid (see **29.2.3**).

18.10 TIME FOR PAYMENT OF IHT ON DEATH

Some types of property attract the right to pay the IHT on them by instalments and some do not. The time for payment will depend on this distinction.

18.10.1 Non-instalment option property

The 'due date'
The IHT payable on the property in the estate which does not attract the instalment option is due for payment 6 months after the end of the month of death. Interest is payable on tax which remains outstanding after that date.

Delivery of Inland Revenue account
PRs must, on delivery of the Inland Revenue account, pay all the IHT for which they are liable (other than IHT on property which attracts the instalment option). Since the grant of representation cannot be obtained before delivery of the Inland Revenue account, PRs will normally pay their IHT before the 'due date'. PRs must in any event deliver an Inland Revenue account within 12 months of the end of the month of death. If they fail to do so, they become liable for penalties.

18.10.2 Instalment option property

General effect
Where property in the estate qualifies for the instalment option the PRs may elect to pay the tax on that property in 10 equal yearly instalments, the first instalment being payable 6 months after the end of the month of death. Thus, on delivery of the Inland Revenue account before the expiry of the 6-month period, the PRs need not pay any IHT on instalment option property.

Qualifying property
The instalment option applies to:

(1) land of any description;
(2) a business or an interest in a business;
(3) shares (quoted or unquoted) which immediately before death gave control of the company to the deceased;
(4) unquoted shares which do not give control if either:

   (a) the holding is sufficiently large (a holding of at least 10 per cent of the nominal value of the company's shares and worth more than £20,000); or
   (b) the Inland Revenue is satisfied that the tax cannot be paid in one sum without undue hardship; or
   (c) the IHT attributable to the shares and any other instalment option property in the estate amounts to at least 20 per cent of the IHT payable on the estate.

Interest

Where the instalment option is exercised in relation to tax on shares or any other business property or agricultural land, instalments carry interest only from the date when each instalment is payable. Thus, no interest is due on the outstanding tax provided that each instalment is paid on the due date.

In the case of other land, however, interest is payable with each instalment (apart from the first) on the amount of IHT which was outstanding for the previous year.

Example

Ursula dies on 8 May 1997 having made no lifetime transfers. Her estate for IHT consists of her house worth £150,000 and other property worth £100,000.

Tax on Ursula's estate: £215,000 @ 0%   nil
                         £35,000 @ 40%   £14,000

Ursula's PRs deliver an Inland Revenue account on 1 July 1997, exercising the instalment option. They must pay IHT on the £100,000 non-instalment option property. The amount of IHT is ascertained by applying the estate rate:

$$£100,000 \times \frac{£14,000}{£250,000} = £5,600$$

Tax on the house is payable by instalments. Apply the estate rate:

$$£150,000 \times \frac{£14,000}{£250,000} = £8,400$$

The first instalment of £840 is due on 30 November 1997 (6 months after the end of the month of death). No interest is payable unless the instalment is late. Tax of £7,560 remains outstanding.

The second instalment is due on 30 November 1998, together with interest for the last year on the balance of £7,560. The outstanding balance is now reduced to £6,720.

Sale

If the instalment option property is sold, all outstanding tax and interest becomes payable.

18.11 BURDEN OF IHT ON DEATH

18.11.1 Meaning of 'burden'

The PRs are liable to pay the IHT on the non-settled estate to the Inland Revenue (see **18.9**). The question of burden concerns how that IHT is to be borne as between those who become entitled to the property, whether under the will or by intestacy or survivorship.

18.11.2 Property which vests in the PRs

Subject to contrary intention in the will, IHT on the property which vests in the PRs is treated as part of the general testamentary and administration expenses of the estate (s 211). Thus in order to decide where the burden of tax lies, it is necessary first to look at the will (if any).

Commonly, pecuniary and specific legacies are expressed to be made 'free of tax', and the gift of residue is expressed to be made subject to administrative and testamentary expenses. The effect is that all the IHT on the property passing by will is borne by residue. Sometimes, however, a legacy may be given 'subject to tax' so that the beneficiary must bear the tax on the property which has been left to him (calculated according to the estate rate).

If the will is silent, or if the deceased died intestate, tax is payable, like other testamentary expenses, according to the statutory order set out in AEA 1925. This normally means that tax is borne by residue. (Further details of the statutory order are found in **27.5**.)

18.11.3 Property which does not vest in the PRs

Where PRs are liable to pay IHT on property which does not vest in them, they are entitled (subject to contrary intention in the will) to recover the tax from the person in whom the property is vested (s 211(3)). This provision is required because the PRs are liable to pay IHT on the deceased's non-settled estate, which includes property passing outside the will such as the deceased's interest in joint property passing by survivorship. It entitles the PRs to recover the tax they have paid from the person entitled to the property, ie the surviving joint tenant.

Note that where the deceased was entitled to a life interest under a trust so that the trust fund is treated for IHT as part of the estate, the PRs are not concerned with liability for IHT or burden of IHT. The trustees are liable to pay the tax (see **18.9.3**) and the burden falls on the trust fund.

18.12 EXAMPLE OF THE APPLICATION OF IHT TO AN ESTATE ON DEATH

Facts

Veronica dies intestate on 3 August 1997 survived by her partner William (to whom she was not married) and their children Brian (19) and Carla (22). She holds the following property:

	£
House (in joint names with William): full value	200,000
Bank a/c (in joint names with William): full value	10,000
Life assurance policies:	
(1) payable to PRs: maturity value	35,000
(2) written in trust for William: maturity value	30,000
Unquoted shares: 15% holding	15,000
Building society account	19,000
Car and chattels	15,000
Life interest under her father's will: value of trust fund	80,000
(the fund passes to the children on Veronica's death)	

There are various debts, including funeral expenses, which total £4,000.

Two years before her death, Veronica made a gift of £131,000 in cash to William.

Step 1: identify the estate *(see* **18.4***)*
Property to which Veronica was beneficially entitled immediately before death:

Passing on intestacy (to children):	life assurance policy (1) unquoted shares building society account car and chattels
Passing by survivorship:	interest in house interest in bank account
Included by special statutory provision:	capital of trust fund (Veronica had an interest in possession)

(Life assurance policy (2) is not included in the estate for IHT purposes.)

Step 2: value the estate *(see* **18.5***)*

	£	£
Passing on intestacy:		
life assurance policy (1) (full maturity value)	35,000	
unquoted shares (market value)	15,000	
building society account		
(including interest to date of death)	19,000	
car and chattels	15,000	
		84,000
Joint property:		
interest in the house		
(£100,000 less discount of, say, 10%)	90,000	
interest in the bank account	5,000	
		95,000
Trust property:		
value of capital in which life tenant's interest subsisted		80,000
		259,000
Less debts (including funeral expenses)		4,000
Value of estate (before reliefs)		255,000

Step 3: apply exemptions *(see* **18.6***)*
No exemptions apply to Veronica's estate as she had no spouse and left no property to charity.

Step 4: apply reliefs *(see* **18.7***)*
The unquoted shares qualify for business property relief at 100 per cent:

100% of £15,000	£15,000
Value of estate for IHT	£240,000

Step 5: calculate tax at the appropriate rate *(see* **18.8***)*
Cumulate the value transferred by chargeable transfers made in the 7 years before death. The gift to William was a PET which has now become chargeable.

	£
Value of gift	131,000
Less 2 annual exemptions	6,000
Value transferred	125,000

Only £90,000 of Veronica's nil rate band remains available on her death.

Calculate tax on the estate of £240,000:

> on £90,000 @ 0%   nil
> on £150,000 @ 40%   £60,000

Liability (see 18.9)

The PRs are liable for tax on the 'free estate', ie the property passing on intestacy and the joint property.

	£	£	£
Property passing on intestacy		84,000	
Less: debts	4,000		
business property relief	15,000	19,000	65,000
Joint property			95,000
			160,000

Calculate tax on £160,000 by applying the estate rate:

$$£160,000 \times \frac{£60,000}{£240,000} = £40,000$$

The trustees are liable for tax on the trust property (£80,000).

Calculate tax on £80,000 by applying the estate rate:

$$£80,000 \times \frac{£60,000}{£240,000} = £20,000$$

Time for payment of IHT (see 18.10)

Assuming that the PRs deliver the Inland Revenue account before 28 February 1998 (6 months after the end of the month of death), they must, on delivery of the account, pay the tax on that part of the free estate which does not attract the instalment option.

	£
Free estate	160,000
Less instalment option property:	
share of house	90,000
Tax payable on delivery of account on	70,000

Calculate tax on £70,000 by applying the estate rate:

$$£70,000 \times \frac{£60,000}{£240,000} = £17,500$$

The PRs must pay £17,500 on delivery of the Inland Revenue account.

Tax on the house is payable in 10 equal annual instalments.

Tax on the house, £90,000:

$$£90,000 \times \frac{£60,000}{£240,000} = £22,500$$

The first instalment is payable on 28 February 1998 (6 months after the end of the month of death).

Subsequent instalments are payable on each succeeding 28 February with interest on the amount outstanding during the previous year.

Burden of IHT (see 18.11)

IHT on the property passing on intestacy is a testamentary expense, payable from the property before division between the children.

IHT on the joint property (the house and joint bank account) is borne by William, the surviving joint tenant.

IHT on the trust property is borne by the trust fund.

18.13 LIFETIME TRANSFERS

When giving lifetime tax planning advice, it is important to be aware of those IHT exemptions and reliefs which relate to lifetime gifts, and to understand the effect of the death of the transferor on potentially exempt transfers made within 7 years before the death.

18.13.1 Exemptions and reliefs which apply to lifetime transfers and on death

Certain exemptions and reliefs considered above apply to lifetime transfers as well as to the deemed transfer on death. They are:

(1) spouse and charity exemptions (see **18.6**); and
(2) business and agricultural property reliefs (see **18.7**). Some additional points arise in the application of business and agricultural property reliefs to lifetime gifts.

Example
Catherine owns 40% of the shares in a private company. The shares are worth £50,000 and Catherine has owned them since May 1990.

In June 1997, Catherine transfers half of her shares (a 20% holding) to her son David.

Catherine dies in December 1997.

The gift in June 1997 was a PET, which would have become exempt if Catherine had survived for 7 years.

On Catherine's death, the PET becomes chargeable. The following principles apply.

(1) At the time of the transfer the shares were 'relevant business property' being unquoted shares which Catherine had owned for the last 2 years.

(2) The appropriate rate of business property relief is 100%.

(3) Relief is available only if David still owns the shares and they are still 'relevant business property' at the date of Catherine's death (s 113A). The fact that David has not owned the shares for 2 years is ignored for this purpose.

(4) If David has sold the shares and used the proceeds to buy more 'relevant business property' the relief may still be available (s 113B).

18.13.2 Exemptions and reliefs which apply only to lifetime transfers

The annual exemption
The annual exemption applies to the first £3,000 transferred by lifetime transfers in each tax year. Unused annual exemption may be carried forward for one year only, so that a maximum exemption of £6,000 may be available. It is important to remember that this exemption does not apply on death, even though the exemption for the last tax year may be unused.

Small gifts
In addition to the annual exemption, lifetime gifts in any one tax year of less than £250 to any one person are exempt.

Normal expenditure out of income
A lifetime transfer is exempt if it can be shown that:

(1) it was made as part of the transferor's normal expenditure (ie there must be regular payments); and
(2) it was made out of the transferor's income; and
(3) after allowing for all such payments the transferor was left with sufficient income to maintain his usual standard of living.

Gifts in consideration of marriage
Lifetime gifts on marriage are exempt up to:

(1) £5,000 by a parent of a party to the marriage;
(2) £2,500 by a remoter ancestor of a party to the marriage; and
(3) £1,000 in any other case.

Tapering relief
Tapering relief reduces the amount of tax payable on a PET which has become chargeable if the transferor dies more than 3 years after the transfer. The tax is reduced to the following percentages:

    transfers 3–4 years before death: 80% of death charge;
    transfers 4–5 years before death: 60% of death charge;
    transfers 5–6 years before death: 40% of death charge;
    transfers 6–7 years before death: 20% of death charge.

Since the relief reduces the amount of tax payable on the chargeable transfer, no relief is available if the transfer falls within the transferor's nil rate band. Similarly, the relief does not alter the value transferred and so the transferor's cumulative total of chargeable transfers is not affected by it.

18.13.3 Applying exemptions and reliefs to lifetime transfers

Where a lifetime transfer is eligible for business or agricultural property relief at the rate of 50 per cent and the annual exemption is also available, the order in which the relief and the exemption are applied becomes important. Since business and agricultural property reliefs reduce the value transferred, the relief should be applied first before deducting the annual exemption.

Example
John bought Manor Farm in 1985 and let it to Tony. In May 1994 John gave the farm (subject to the tenancy) to his son Simon. The loss to John's estate

was £200,000. John died in June 1997. Simon still owns Manor Farm and Tony is still his tenant. John made no other lifetime gifts.

John died within 7 years of the PET to Simon so it has become a chargeable transfer. Agricultural property relief is available at the rate of 50% as the farm was subject to a tenancy created before 1 September 1995.

	£
Loss to John's estate	200,000
Less APR @ 50%	100,000
Value transferred	100,000
Less annual exemptions for 1993/4 and 1994/5	6,000
Chargeable transfer	94,000

No tax is payable by Simon as the transfer falls within John's nil rate band. Since no tax is payable, tapering relief does not apply, even though John died more than 3 years after making the transfer.

John's cumulative total of chargeable transfers made within 7 years of his death is £94,000 and so the nil rate band applicable to his estate is reduced to £121,000.

18.13.4 Effect of death within 7 years of a PET

Any lifetime gift to an individual which falls outside the lifetime exemptions is a potentially exempt transfer. If the transferor dies within 7 years, the PET becomes chargeable. This is relevant from two points of view:

(1) *Tax on the transfer*

The transferee may be liable to pay IHT on the chargeable transfer.

(2) *Tax on the estate*

The principle of cumulation means that the nil rate band applicable on death is reduced.

In **18.8.2** the effect of cumulation was considered. It is important to distinguish the effect of death from the point of view of the transferee.

Example
The facts are as in **18.8.2**, *Example 2*.

Felicity makes the following gifts:

on 1 May 1993, £66,000 to her nephew
on 1 June 1994, £168,000 to her niece

Felicity dies on 5 August 1997. As seen above, both gifts have become chargeable transfers because Felicity died within 7 years of making them. The effect of this on Felicity's estate is considered at **18.8.2**, *Example 2*. The effect of her death on the transfers is as follows:

Transfer on 1 May 1993 (assuming that no previous transfers have been made):

	£
Value transferred	66,000
Less 2 annual exemptions	6,000
Chargeable transfer	60,000

The transfer falls within Felicity's nil rate band, so no IHT is payable by Felicity's nephew.

Transfer on 1 June 1994:

	£
Value transferred	168,000
Less 1 annual exemption	3,000
Chargeable transfer	165,000

Cumulate the value transferred by any chargeable transfers made in the previous 7 years, ie £60,000. Only £155,000 of Felicity's nil rate band remains.

Tax on £155,000 @ 0%   nil
    £10,000 @ 40%   4,000

Felicity died between 3 and 4 years after the transfer. Tapering relief applies, reducing the tax payable to 80% of the normal death rate.

80% of £4,000 = £3,200

Felicity's niece is liable to pay IHT of £3,200. If the tax remains outstanding 12 months after the end of the month of Felicity's death, Felicity's PRs will become liable (see **18.9.4**).

Chapter 19

FINANCIAL SERVICES: PROBATE PRACTICE

19.1 INTRODUCTION

The law on financial services and their regulation is described in the LPC Resource Book *Pervasive Topics* (Jordans, 1997), Part II. Reference should be made to that book before considering the aspects relevant to probate practice.

The general principle introduced by the Financial Services Act 1986 ('the Act') is that a person carrying on investment business must be authorised to do so. A solicitor will normally seek authorisation from The Law Society, which requires compliance with the Solicitors' Investment Business Rules 1995 ('SIBR'). If the solicitor carries on discrete investment business, the rules are more stringent than if only non-discrete investment business is conducted.

Thus, a solicitor must be able to identify those areas where investment business may be involved and to decide whether an activity amounts to discrete investment business. This chapter is concerned primarily with the identification of investment business.

Estate administration within the probate department of a firm is one of the areas of professional practice where investment business is most likely to arise. It may do so:

(1) in relation to sales of assets within the deceased person's estate to raise money to pay the funeral and testamentary expenses (including IHT) and debts; and
(2) when advising beneficiaries as to the investment of their inheritance.

19.2 ESTATE ADMINISTRATION

The sale of assets by the PRs to raise money to pay debts, funeral and testamentary expenses is inevitable in most estates, because there is normally insufficient cash in the deceased's bank or building society account or in assets such as life policies which mature on death.

Normal administration work also includes receiving income, such as dividends, from assets retained in the estate, taking up any bonus or rights issues in relation to shares in the estate and preparing estate accounts.

Not all such work will necessarily fall within the provisions of the Act. In order to decide whether a particular activity amounts to investment business, three questions should be considered:

(1) Is the asset an 'investment'?
(2) Is the solicitor carrying on a listed activity?
(3) Does an exclusion apply?

Chapter 19 contents
Introduction
Estate administration
Discrete investment business?
Advising the beneficiaries

19.2.1 Is the asset an 'investment'?

The term 'investment' has a particular meaning for the purposes of the Act. Assets such as company shares, government stock, unit trusts and life assurance policies are 'investments'. Land, chattels, bank and building society deposit accounts, building society share accounts, National Savings Certificates and Premium Bonds are all excluded from the definition. A solicitor may arrange the sale of such assets or receive their income in the course of the administration of an estate without concern as to the application of the Act.

19.2.2 Is the solicitor carrying on a listed activity?

The concept of investment activity within the Act includes dealing and arranging deals in investments, managing investments and giving investment advice. A solicitor may be dealing or (more probably) arranging deals in investments when assets are sold in the course of the administration of an estate. For example, a solicitor who instructs a broker to sell shares in the estate is 'arranging'. Helping PRs to decide which assets to sell and which to retain may amount to investment advice. However, the normal work of controlling assets – administrative management – will probably not amount to managing within the terms of the Act. This is because 'managing' is interpreted as 'discretionary management', ie the solicitor can make decisions to buy or sell investments in the estate. He will be able to do this where he is PR on his own or is PR jointly with others in the firm. If he is PR jointly with 'lay' PRs or acts for PRs all of whom are lay people, he will not have discretion to buy or sell investments without consulting the other PRs.

19.2.3 Does an exclusion apply?

Excluded activities are listed in Sch 1, Pt III of the Act and include the following.

Private company shares
Arrangements made or advice given in relation to acquisitions and disposals of shares can be excluded from the Act but generally only if 75 per cent or more of the voting rights are involved. Thus, if shares held in the family company are to be sold to raise money, the transaction may not be an investment activity within the Act.

It is probable that this exclusion will seldom be of assistance because, even if the estate contains shares carrying 75 per cent of the voting rights, often the family will not wish the shares in their family company to be sold to raise money to pay the debts, taxes etc; only in the last resort will the shares be placed on the market and even then it may be difficult to find a suitable buyer.

Trustees and PRs
Two separate exclusions may be relevant where a solicitor is acting as PR.

The 'dealing as principal' exclusion will apply if, for example, a solicitor PR sells unit trusts during the administration. However, this exclusion applies only to dealing, and the PRs will probably be involved in other activity such as arranging deals, advising or managing.

The specific exclusion for trustees and PRs would seem of particular value as it applies not only to dealing but also to the activities of making arrangements, advising and managing. However, once again, it may be of only limited application for a number of reasons:

(1) It will only be available in relation to the activities of a solicitor who is a PR. Thus, if it is the solicitor PR who arranges the sale of an investment to raise the desired amount of money, this will be an excluded activity. However, if it is the solicitor's firm, rather than the individual solicitor, which carries out an investment activity there will be no exclusion. For example, if the 'financial services department' of the solicitor PR's own firm does the investment activity, the exclusion cannot be relied on.

(2) The exclusion will be unavailable to the solicitor PR where he receives remuneration for the investment activity in addition to any remuneration received for discharging the normal duties as a PR. Thus, even if the solicitor PR does the investment activity, the exclusion will be unavailable if a professional fee is received in addition to the fee for usual estate administration work.

Advice given and arrangements made in the course of carrying on a profession

This exclusion applies to giving advice or making arrangements where it is necessary to do so in the course of carrying on a profession.

At first it would appear that this exclusion is of particular value to the legal profession. Once again there are difficulties associated with the exclusion, although it is possible that they can be overcome in some instances. If so, the particular activity of giving advice or making arrangements will fall outside the terms of the Act.

The difficulties are:

(1) It must be shown that the activity is a necessary part of the services provided by the solicitor. However, 'necessary' is given a limited meaning. A useful test is 'could the solicitor only provide the legal services if he also provides the investment activity?' If another person could equally well provide the investment activity for the PRs, it is not 'necessary' that the solicitor provides it. In the context of estate administration, it may be possible to say that the solicitor's investment activity is a 'necessary' part of the estate administration, for example when he advises or makes the arrangements to sell investments to raise money to repay a loan used to pay IHT due before the grant of probate can be obtained.

(2) It must also be clear that the solicitor does not receive any 'separate remuneration' for the particular investment activity. Normally this presents no problem in practice, because this restriction can be avoided by making no separately itemised charge for the investment activity on the bill of costs in relation to the administration of the estate.

19.2.4 Conclusion

If none of the above exclusions apply, the investment activity carried on by a solicitor in relation to 'investments' (as defined) may amount to investment business by the solicitor. Although the giving of advice and making of arrangements may fall outside the Act on the basis that these are activities which are a necessary part of estate administration, the extent of this exclusion is uncertain. Advice and arrangements which exceed what is 'necessary' will give rise to an activity within the Act. Even if this exclusion applies, discretionary management may arise within the probate department but only where the solicitor is the PR or is PR jointly with others within the firm.

If the solicitor is involved in investment business because of management of assets, or for any other reason, he must have authorisation to conduct the investment business, and must keep certain records in relation to the investment business in accordance with the SIBR. However, in most cases the solicitor will not need to comply with many of the other provisions of the SIBR, providing the investment business is not 'discrete investment business' ('DIB').

19.3 DISCRETE INVESTMENT BUSINESS?

Investment business within estate administration can normally be conducted as non-DIB should the firm so wish.

Activity as PR
SIBR, r 10(1) provides 'no activity carried out by the firm or a partner, employee, or officer of the firm ... as a personal representative of any deceased's estate shall be discrete investment business'.

Thus, provided the solicitor is acting as PR, then discretionary management, arrangements or advice will not amount to DIB.

Incidental activity
If someone in the solicitors' firm (eg an assistant solicitor) carries out the investment activity for lay PRs who are clients of the firm, SIBR, r 10(1) will not apply. However, even in these cases DIB may be avoided, because it will normally be possible to bring the activity within the incidental exception to DIB (ie the activity will be incidental to the administration of the estate). In the case of PRs, the incidental exception is available even if the investment is a unit trust and certain other investments (known in the SIBR as 'packaged products'). Generally, 'packaged products' cannot benefit from the exclusion for incidental activity.

Permitted third parties (PTP)
When the firm acts as disclosed agent for a named client and the investment activity is carried out by a PTP this will also ensure that DIB is avoided by the solicitor. For this exception to apply it is necessary that procedural formality when appointing the PTP is followed (see LPC Resource Book *Pervasive Topics* (Jordans, 1997), Financial Services).

19.4 ADVISING THE BENEFICIARIES

The solicitor who is either a PR personally, or who is acting for the PRs, may be asked by one or more of the beneficiaries for advice in connection with the investments and other assets inherited from the deceased client. If so, any advice which the solicitor may give and any arrangements he may make for the beneficiary will be independent of the administration of the estate. There will be a new solicitor/client relationship established between the solicitor and the beneficiary to which the Act and the SIBR may apply.

The extent to which the Act and the SIBR apply will depend on the degree of involvement of the solicitor. For example, if he personally provides advice and makes arrangements in relation to the beneficiary's investments, and none of the exclusions in the Act is available, he must be authorised to conduct the investment business; further, he will generally need to comply with the whole of the SIBR, because DIB will be involved.

To avoid the obligation to comply with the greater part of the SIBR, the solicitor should obtain investment advice for the beneficiary from another person, such as a stockbroker, who is a PTP. If the advice is accepted, the stockbroker should be instructed to implement it on behalf of the beneficiary. By involving a stockbroker in this way, provided he is properly instructed, the solicitor will avoid DIB, and many of the obligations of the SIBR.

PART III

PROBATE AND ADMINISTRATION

CONTENTS

The following chapters deal, in chronological order, with the practice and procedure to be followed after the death of a client in order to obtain the grant of representation and to administer the estate. Chapter 30 deals with the separate, though related, topic of post-death variations and disclaimers.

Appendices 1–3 contain case studies which illustrate the use of forms of oath and Inland Revenue accounts. Appendix 4 contains an example of an estate account, and Appendix 5 contains selected non-contentious probate rules. Appendix 6 sets out a practice direction concerning oaths.

TEXTBOOKS

Tristram and Coote is the recognised practitioner text on probate practice and procedure.

Butterworths WPA Service may also be useful for reference.

The best student text for this area is probably Barlow, King and King.

Chapter 20

PROBATE PRACTICE AND PROCEDURE

20.1 INTRODUCTION

This chapter considers the events immediately following the death of a person. That person may have been the client of the solicitor. Whether or not that is the case, the solicitor's clients at this stage are the deceased's PRs. The solicitor himself (or his firm) may be acting as PR (or one of several PRs). In either case the practice and procedure will be substantially the same.

20.2 THE SOLICITOR'S CLIENTS AND DUTIES

20.2.1 Identification of clients

If the deceased's PRs instruct a solicitor to act then, clearly, they are the solicitor's clients and it is to them that the solicitor will owe professional duties. Although not his clients, the solicitor must consider the deceased's family and/or beneficiaries with whom he may have contact or dealings during the administration of the estate. If any dispute arises during probate and administration, the solicitor must be careful to avoid any conflict of interest which might arise from advising the family and/or beneficiaries.

Often the PRs, family and beneficiaries will be the same individual(s) but it must be remembered that PRs have particular duties and responsibilities towards the estate (see Chapter 24).

If the solicitor is appointed as executor, he will owe the duties of a PR to the estate as a whole.

20.2.2 Who are the PRs?

The PRs will be either the deceased's executors or intended administrators.

The executors

If the will is valid and contains an effective appointment of executors of whom one or more is willing and able to prove the deceased's will, a grant of probate will be issued to him or to them (see **22.2**).

Administrators with the will annexed

If there is a valid will but there are no persons willing or able to act as executors, then the next persons entitled to act are administrators with the will annexed who should be appointed in accordance with r 20 of the Non-Contentious Probate Rules 1987 ('NCPR') (see **22.3.2**).

Administrators (simple administration)

If a deceased left no will, or no valid will, the estate will be administered in accordance with the law of intestacy by administrators appointed by the application of NCPR, r 22 (see **22.4**).

Number of PRs required

One executor may obtain a grant and act alone. This is so even if the estate contains land which may be sold during the administration, because a receipt for the proceeds of sale from one executor is sufficient for the purchaser. This is in contrast to the position of trustees where, if a good receipt for the proceeds of sale of land is to be given to a purchaser, it must be given by at least two trustees (or a trust corporation).

In the case of administrators (with or without the will), it will often be sufficient for one to act in the administration of the estate. However, where the will or intestacy creates a life or minority interest, two administrators are normally required (see **22.3.4** and **22.4.5**).

Authority of PRs before the grant

An executor derives his authority to act in the administration of an estate from the will. The grant of probate confirms that authority. Although he has full power to act from the time of the deceased's death, the executor will be unable to undertake certain transactions (eg sale of land) without producing the grant as proof of authority.

An administrator (with or without the will) has very limited powers before a grant is made, because his authority stems from the grant which is not retrospective to the date of death.

20.2.3 The solicitor's duties

The duties of a solicitor instructed by the PRs include:

(1) giving advice in relation to the relevant succession and revenue law;
(2) taking practical steps on the PRs' behalf during the administration, such as:
    (a) proving the testator's will;
    (b) preparing the appropriate oath and Inland Revenue account forms;
    (c) administering the estate; and
    (d) preparing estate accounts showing the distribution of the estate among the beneficiaries.

20.3 FIRST STEPS AFTER RECEIVING INSTRUCTIONS

Following a person's death, a number of matters will require the immediate attention of the solicitor who is to act for the PRs. These may include one or more of the following matters listed in **20.3.1–20.3.6**.

20.3.1 The deceased's will

Ascertain whether the deceased made a will. If so, the original will should be obtained. It may be held for safe custody in the deceased's bank or the solicitor's own safe or strongroom, or it may be in the possession of the deceased's family.

If the deceased left a will, ensure the executors named in the will receive copies of the will.

20.3.2 Directions as to cremation etc

Give immediate consideration to the terms of the will to ascertain any special directions by the deceased as to cremation or the use of his body for medical research or other purposes. This requires careful discussion with the deceased's family and PRs.

20.3.3 Funeral arrangements

Assist the deceased's family with making arrangements for the funeral, if requested.

20.3.4 The deceased's property

Ensure that appropriate steps are taken to secure the deceased's property; for example, important and valuable assets and documents should be removed to a place of safe-keeping if they would otherwise remain in an empty house.

20.3.5 Financial arrangements

Advise on and, if appropriate, make arrangements for temporary loan facilities from a bank where members of the deceased's immediate family (or other beneficiaries) may otherwise have no money available to them until after the deceased's estate has been administered.

20.3.6 Death certificate

Obtain a copy (or copies) of the deceased's death certificate from the Registrar General.

20.4 PREPARING TO OBTAIN A GRANT OF REPRESENTATION

20.4.1 Details of assets and liabilities

The solicitor should obtain details of the deceased's property and of any debts outstanding at the date of death by asking the PRs for building society passbooks, share certificates and details of bank accounts etc. These documents are unlikely to produce precise values and the solicitor must ascertain exact valuations by writing to the various institutions holding the deceased's assets, producing the death certificate as evidence of death, if so required.

Enquiries should be made of the deceased's bank manager as to whether the bank hold in safe custody any share certificates or other property owned by the deceased. (The bank manager will require sight of the death certificate before giving such information.)

From these details the solicitor will be able to begin to evaluate the size of the deceased's estate, and the amount of any liability to IHT (as discussed in Chapter 18).

At the same time as providing the details of the assets, the institutions should be asked to send withdrawal or transfer forms for signature by the PRs. These can be signed immediately so that they are ready for use once the grant is obtained and the administration of the estate begins.

20.4.2 Details of the beneficiaries

From the deceased's will (if any), the solicitor must establish the identity of the beneficiaries, and the nature and extent of their entitlement (eg whether as legatee or as residuary beneficiary). If specific legacies have been given, it is important to ascertain whether the property given by those specific gifts is part of the estate (if not the gift(s) will have adeemed). If the deceased has died intestate, it is necessary to establish which members of the family have survived so that the basis of distribution of the estate may be established in accordance with the rules discussed in Chapter 16.

20.4.3 Missing and/or unknown creditors and beneficiaries

The position as PR carries with it responsibility to administer the deceased's estate correctly and failure by a PR to carry out his duties can give rise to personal liability. PRs may be faced with the problem that persons entitled under the will or intestacy rules have disappeared or are unknown to them (eg because they were children born outside the deceased's marriage but whose identity he did not disclose). In addition, the PRs may not be sure that they have identified all the deceased's debts and creditors.

The solicitor must ensure that the PRs are protected against personal liability so far as possible should any adverse claims arise: see **24.2** and **27.4** for details.

20.4.4 The probate papers

The solicitor should prepare the appropriate oath and Inland Revenue account (if necessary) in readiness for the application for the grant of representation (ie the grant of probate or letters of administration to the estate).

Oath for executors or administrators
The entitlement to apply for the grant and the completion of the appropriate oath form are discussed in Chapters 22 and 23. The oath must be sworn (or affirmed) by the PRs before the application for the grant can proceed.

Inland Revenue account
All assets must be valued in accordance with the IHT valuation principles described in Chapter 18. Often the solicitor will need to instruct stockbrokers or other valuers to prepare valuations of the deceased's assets. These values, and the amounts of any debts and liabilities due at death, will be inserted into the appropriate Inland Revenue account (if one is required) as discussed in Chapter 21. The amount of IHT payable before the application for the grant is made can now be ascertained. The solicitor will normally have to make arrangements for loan facilities at a bank so that this amount can be borrowed since, generally, the deceased's assets will not be available to the PRs until the grant has been obtained.

20.5 PROBATE BUSINESS

20.5.1 Conducting non-contentious business

Non-contentious probate business is conducted by the district judges of the Principal Registry of the Family Division in London or by the district probate registrars in one of the district probate registries or sub-registries. It is conducted in accordance with the NCPR, which give the district judge (or registrar) wide powers in relation to the issue of grants and many other matters. Some of these are referred to in the following chapters. There is no particular registry in which the executor or administrator must apply for a grant of representation. It is convenient and usual to apply in the registry for the locality where the PRs' solicitor practices. However, some solicitors prefer to apply to a district registry outside their locality in order to prevent publication of details of the deceased's will and estate in the local press.

20.5.2 Meaning of non-contentious business

Under Supreme Court Act 1981, s 28, non-contentious or common form probate business is:

> '... the business of obtaining probate and administration where there is no contention as to the right thereto ... and all business of a non-contentious nature in matters of testacy and intestacy not being proceedings in any action, and ... the business of lodging caveats ...'

20.5.3 Assistance of the court

Beyond application to the court for the issue of the grant, generally the court is not involved further in non-contentious probate business. If problems do arise, for example as to entitlement to the grant or as to the meaning of the will, the court can be asked to resolve the matter.

20.6 NECESSITY FOR A GRANT OF REPRESENTATION

A grant enables the PRs to prove their authority to deal with the deceased's property which passes under the will or the intestacy rules. However, it should not be presumed that it is always necessary to obtain a grant of representation. The ability to realise assets without the production of a grant is particularly useful where the deceased's family needs funds immediately for IHT or other purposes.

A grant may not be required where:

(1) the assets in the estate passing to the PRs are of such a type that they may be realised without production of a grant; and/or
(2) the assets in the estate that are to be realised do not pass through the hands of the PRs; and/or
(3) the assets to be realised do not form part of the deceased's estate.

These three possibilities are considered in more detail below.

20.6.1 Assets which may pass to the PRs without grant

Administration of Estates (Small Payments) Act 1965
Orders made under this Act permit payments to be made under various statutes and statutory instruments to persons appearing to be beneficially entitled to the assets without formal proof of title. This facility is restricted in that it is not available if the value of the asset exceeds £5,000; in addition, the payments are made at the discretion of the institutions concerned, that is, it is not possible for executors to insist that payments should be made. Subject to these points, payments can be made in respect of, for example:

(1) money in the National Savings Bank and Trustee Savings Bank (but not in other bank accounts);
(2) National Savings Certificates and Premium Bonds; and
(3) money in building societies and friendly societies.

Chattels

Items of movable personal property such as furniture, clothing, jewellery, and cars can normally be sold without the PRs having to prove to the buyer that they are entitled to sell such items. Occasionally, a grant will be required to prove entitlement, for example if the deceased's jewellery is deposited at a bank.

Cash

Normally the PRs do not require a grant before taking custody of any cash found in the deceased's possession (ie found in the home of the deceased as opposed to deposited in a bank or other account).

20.6.2 Assets not passing through the PRs' hands

Joint property

On death, any interest in property held by the deceased as joint tenant in equity with another (whether it is an interest in land or personalty, eg a bank account) passes by survivorship to the surviving joint tenant. As it does not pass via the PRs, any grant is irrelevant. The survivor has access to the property and can prove title to the whole of it merely by producing the deceased's death certificate. Since it is common for married couples to own property jointly, there are many occasions where a grant is not required for this reason.

(Conversely, if the property is held by persons as beneficial tenants in common, the share of each tenant in common passes on his death to his PRs for distribution.)

Nominated property

Such property was described in **2.4.2**. Nominated property passes directly to the chosen nominee who need only produce the deceased's death certificate to prove title to the property.

20.6.3 Property not forming part of the estate

Life policies held in trust

The deceased may have insured his own life but in such a way that the policy and its proceeds are held in trust for others. As mentioned in **2.4.3**, a trust may be established by writing the policy under the Married Women's Property Act 1882, s 11 ('a Married Women's Property Act policy') for the spouse or children of the deceased, or by making a separate declaration of trust for other beneficiaries. On death the policy money is payable to the trustees of the policy on production of the death certificate. A grant is not required since the money does not form part of the estate. As the deceased had no beneficial interest in the policy or its proceeds (because of the trust) no IHT will be payable on the proceeds. Such a policy is particularly advantageous as the proceeds make tax-free provision for dependants of the deceased and can be collected in immediately following the death.

Pension benefits

If the deceased has entered a discretionary scheme of the type described in **2.4.4**, then any payments made by the pension fund trustees are made to the beneficiaries on production of the death certificate. Once again, a grant is not required since the pension benefits do not form part of the deceased's estate. It is another method of making tax-free provision for dependants, and such provision can be collected in immediately following the death.

20.7 APPLICATION FOR GRANT

Where a grant is required, it is necessary to apply to the Principal Registry of the Family Division or a district probate registry. The application will be dealt with by a district judge in the Principal Registry or a district probate registrar in the district probate registry. This chapter, and following chapters, assume that application is made to a district probate registry and is dealt with by a registrar. The application is made by lodging such of the following documents as are appropriate to the particular case:

(1) unless the estate is an 'excepted estate' (see **21.2.1**), an Inland Revenue account Form 202 or 200 receipted with payment of any IHT (see Chapter 21);
(2) the deceased's will and codicil, if any, marked by the executors (or administrators if there are no proving executors) and the solicitor before whom the supporting oath is sworn or affirmed (see Chapter 23);
(3) oath, sworn or affirmed by the executors or administrators (see Chapters 22 and 23);
(4) any affidavit evidence which may be required (see **20.7.2**);
(5) probate court fees (an administration fee based on the value of the net estate passing under the grant);
(6) a copy of any post-death variation or disclaimer (see **20.8**) made prior to the application for the grant, together with a written notice of election (see **30.3.2**) if the Inland Revenue account is assessed to take into account the effect of the variation.

20.7.1 Admissibility of will to probate

In view of the necessity to lodge the deceased's will with the application, the solicitor must ascertain at an early stage that it is admissible to probate. If it is not, application will be made instead for a grant of simple administration.

To ensure that the will is admissible, the solicitor should check the following:

(1) that the will is the last will of the testator;
(2) that it has not been validly revoked (see Chapter 14);
(3) that it is executed in accordance with the Wills Act 1837, s 9 (see **13.4.1**); and
(4) that it contains an attestation clause which indicates that the will was executed in accordance with the requirements of the Wills Act 1837 and raises a presumption of 'due execution' (see **13.4.3**).

20.7.2 The registrar's additional requirements

If the application is in order the registrar will issue the original grant, sealed with the court seal and signed by him. However, before issuing the grant the registrar may require further evidence. The solicitor should endeavour to anticipate any requirements of the registrar for further evidence. This will avoid any delay in obtaining the grant if, for example, affidavit evidence is required. Extracts from relevant NCPR are set out in Appendix 5.

Affidavit of due execution
If there is no attestation clause, if the clause is in some respect defective or if there are doubtful circumstances about the execution of the will, the registrar will require affidavit evidence to establish that the will has been properly executed. The evidence

is provided by means of an affidavit of due execution. If an affidavit is required, it will usually be given by an attesting witness.

If there is doubt about the mental capacity of the testator to make a will, the affidavit of a doctor may be necessary. In such cases, the doctor should have been asked to examine the testator to ascertain whether he had sufficient capacity at the time the will was made and, if so, to make a written statement to this effect. He should also have been asked to be one of the witnesses to the testator's signature (see **13.2**).

Affidavit as to knowledge and approval

It may appear to the registrar that there is doubt as to whether the testator was aware of the contents of the will when he executed it. This may arise through the blindness, illiteracy or frailty of the testator, or because of suspicious circumstances, for example where the person who prepared the will for the testator benefits substantially by its terms.

As discussed in **13.3.2**, in any of these circumstances the attestation clause should be suitably adapted, ideally by indicating that the will was read over to the testator or was independently explained to him. In the absence of this, the registrar will require to be satisfied that the testator had knowledge and approval of the contents of the will. The evidence is provided by means of an affidavit of knowledge and approval of contents made by someone who can speak as to the facts. Normally this will be one of the attesting witnesses, but it could be an independent person who explained the provisions of the will to the testator.

Affidavit of plight and condition

If the state of the will suggests that it has been interfered with in some way since execution, the registrar will require further evidence by way of explanation. This may arise:

(1) where the will has been altered since its execution;
(2) where there is some obvious mark on it indicating a document may have been attached to it (eg the marks of a paperclip raising a suggestion that some other testamentary document may have been attached); or
(3) where it gives the appearance of attempted revocation.

Generally, the explanation required will take the form of an affidavit of plight and condition made by some person having knowledge of the facts.

Lost will

A will which was known to have been in the testator's possession but which cannot be found following the death is presumed to have been destroyed by the testator with the intention of revoking it.

However, if the will has been lost or accidently destroyed, probate may be obtained of a copy of the will, such as a copy kept in the solicitor's file, or a reconstruction. A court order will first be required.

In such a case, application should be made to the registrar, supported by affidavit evidence from the applicant for the grant of probate as to:

(1) the existence of the will following the death; or, failing this,
(2) the facts which rebut the presumption referred to above that the will was revoked by destruction; and
(3) the accuracy of the reconstruction or copy as appropriate.

The registrar may also require an affidavit of due execution of the original will.

20.7.3 Office copy grant

Because the grant is used by the PRs as evidence of their title to collect in the deceased's assets, it is common practice to request office copies when applying for the grant. These are photocopies of the original grant which are sealed with the court seal and signed by the registrar but, unlike the original grant, there is no copy of the will (if any) attached to the office copy. Except in the case of title to land, office copies are generally as acceptable, as evidence of title, as the original grant.

20.7.4 Death certificate

It will be noticed that the deceased's death certificate is not lodged with the application for the grant. Confirmation of the death is contained in the oath for executors or administrators. However, copies of the death certificate will be made available by the Registrar General for the PRs to use when obtaining particulars of the deceased's assets and their values (see **20.4.1**).

20.8 POST-DEATH VARIATION OR DISCLAIMER

One of the most difficult aspects of probate practice is to know whether and when to raise the possibility of formal variation of the terms of the deceased's will or of the intestacy rules applicable on the death. However, at some point when taking instructions from the PRs it will be appropriate to raise this matter.

It is possible by post-death variation, or by disclaimer of benefit, to change the succession and taxation effects of the dispositions of the deceased's will or the intestacy rules and, in consequence, the IHT position on the death. The conditions that must be satisfied to make an effective post-death variation or disclaimer are complex; they are considered in Chapter 30.

If such action is to be taken it must be taken within 2 years of the death. However, it may be prudent to consider the possibility of a variation or disclaimer at a much earlier stage, choosing to do so when the opportunity most naturally arises. If a variation or disclaimer is made before application for the grant, it is possible to pay IHT on the basis of the variation or disclaimer being incorporated into the testator's will or the intestacy rules. In this case, a copy of the variation and election and/or disclaimer must be lodged when making the application for the grant. This may result in paying less IHT to obtain the grant.

20.9 CONCLUSION

To a practitioner, 'probate practice' implies two separate and distinct stages:

(1) obtaining the grant of representation; and
(2) administering the deceased's estate.

An outline of the procedure for obtaining the grant has been covered in this chapter together with an explanation of the preparatory steps to be taken before lodging the necessary documentation at the probate registry. The documentation (ie oath and Inland Revenue account) is covered in detail in Chapters 21, 22 and 23.

Administration of the deceased's estate is considered in Chapter 24 onwards.

Chapter 21

COMPLETING THE INLAND REVENUE ACCOUNT

21.1 INTRODUCTION

As mentioned in Chapter 20, one of the first steps towards obtaining the grant of representation is the preparation of the appropriate Inland Revenue account and the calculation of any IHT payable.

If the estate is an 'excepted estate', the PRs do not need to complete and submit an Inland Revenue account (see **21.2.1**). Where an estate is not excepted, the PRs will prepare, normally, one of two accounts: Form IHT 200 or Form IHT 202 (see **21.3–21.5**).

In theory, every application for a grant of representation could be accompanied by a Form IHT 200, or, if the deceased died domiciled outside the UK, Form IHT 201. However, Form IHT 200 is time-consuming to complete, and complicated to explain to lay clients. It should only be used where no alternative procedure is available. Information about Form IHT 201 is not included in this book as it is beyond the scope of the course.

21.1.1 Purpose of an Inland Revenue account

Reference should be made to Chapter 18 before attempting to complete an Inland Revenue account.

The Inland Revenue account is an inventory of the assets to which the deceased was beneficially entitled and of his liabilities, and a form for claiming reliefs and exemptions and calculating the IHT payable. It should usually be delivered within 12 months of the end of the month in which the death occurred, although it may be delivered later in certain circumstances. Usually PRs aim to deliver the account within 6 months to comply with IHT time-limits (see **18.10.1**). Until the account is submitted no grant of representation can be issued.

IHT is payable on all property to which the deceased was beneficially entitled immediately before his death whether or not such property vests in his PRs. There are a number of valuation rules to assist in calculating such property for tax purposes. In addition, certain types of property qualify for tax relief, for example business or agricultural property, or an exemption may apply because of the identity of the beneficiary (ie the surviving spouse or a charity) (see **18.6** and **18.7**).

The two Inland Revenue accounts divide the deceased's assets into property without and property with the instalment option. IHT on property without the right to pay by instalments must be paid within 6 months of the end of the month in which the death occurred (ie if a person dies on 10 January, IHT is due on 31 July or on delivery of the Inland Revenue account, if earlier). Until this tax has been paid, no grant can issue to the deceased's estate. Where there is property which qualifies for the right to pay the tax on it by instalments, the tax on that property is not due until the expiry of the 6-month period. If the option is exercised, only the first instalment of one-tenth must then be paid. In an estate where it is not possible to deliver the Inland Revenue account within that period, then all tax on non-instalment option

Chapter 21 contents
Introduction
The requirement for an Inland Revenue account
Points common to the completion of Forms IHT 202 and IHT 200
Form IHT 202
Form IHT 200
Action following completion of account

property plus the appropriate number of instalments on property with the option and interest must be paid on delivery of the account. Interest runs on all tax not paid on the due date.

21.1.2 Valuations

General principles

Assets and liabilities should be valued in accordance with the principles discussed in Chapter 18. For example, quoted shares are valued at '¼ up' on the lower of the two prices quoted for the date of death; unquoted shares are usually valued initially by the company's accountants before the value is ultimately negotiated with the Shares Valuation Division of the Inland Revenue; liquid assets such as bank accounts are valued as the amount standing to the credit of the deceased at the date of death, plus accrued but uncredited interest; life policies are shown at their maturity value.

In addition, land is valued at its open market value at the date of death. This is usually ascertained from a local estate agent but, before the administration of the estate can be completed, the valuation must be agreed with the local district valuer, probably after negotiation.

Jointly owned assets

There is a special valuation rule where the deceased was the co-owner, rather than the sole owner, of land at his death. The rule applies equally whether the land is held by the deceased with others as tenants in common or as beneficial joint tenants.

Where there is joint ownership of land, the market value at the date of death may be discounted to reflect the virtual impossibility of selling a part interest in property. The probate value of the deceased's interest is the discounted market value at the date of death divided proportionately between the co-owners. A discount of 10–15 per cent is normally considered reasonable.

> *Example 1*
> Mary and Nellie owned a house as joint tenants. The value of the house at Mary's death was £100,000. Apply a 10 per cent discount.
>
> The discount is £100,000 × 10% = £10,000
> and her half share is £100,000 − £10,000 = £90,000 ÷ 2 = £45,000.
>
> The probate value of Mary's share is £45,000.

The discount is not available where the co-owners are husband and wife because of the related property rules (see **18.5.5**).

There is no such discount where the co-ownership is of an asset other than land. For assets such as bank and building society accounts, the probate value is the account balance as at the date of death plus interest, and for quoted shares or personal chattels the probate value is the total value of those shares or chattels, in each case divided proportionately between the joint owners.

> *Example 2*
> Mary and Nellie were joint owners of an account with Midshire Building Society and some personal chattels. At Mary's death their building society account balance was £200 with uncredited interest of £10 and the chattels had a market value of £1,000. Mary's interest in the building society account is £100 + £5, and in the chattels is £500.

21.1.3 Funding the IHT

Where there is IHT to pay on delivery of an Inland Revenue account, the PRs must arrange for the appropriate amount of money to be sent to the Inland Revenue with the account. Until this tax is paid the grant cannot issue. Funding the tax bill may be problematic as all the deceased's assets vesting in the PRs are 'frozen', and therefore untouchable, until the grant issues giving the proof of title to the PRs.

The five options which may be available to raise the IHT are set out below.

The deceased's building society account or life assurance

If there is sufficient cash in a building society account or policy of insurance on the deceased's life, the institution holding the funds may be willing to release funds to pay the IHT. If so, the funds will generally be paid directly to the Inland Revenue and not to the PRs or their solicitors.

Assets realisable without production of the grant

By applying the Administration of Estates (Small Payments) Act 1965 (see **20.6.1**) assets may be realised without production of the grant. The maximum value of any one asset that may be realised is £5,000. This Act gives discretion to the institution to allow assets to be realised. Where an estate is reasonably large or complex, this discretion will often not be exercised. In such cases, the grant must be produced to release the asset concerned.

Loans from beneficiaries

Wealthy beneficiaries may be prepared to fund the IHT from their own resources, on condition that they will be repaid from the deceased's estate once the grant issues. Alternatively, beneficiaries may already have received assets as a result of the death which they are prepared to use to pay the tax, such as money from a jointly held bank account or the proceeds of a life policy vested in them under the Married Women's Property Act 1882. However, it is likely that the deceased arranged for such assets to provide financial assistance for that beneficiary while his estate was being administered and the beneficiary may not be able to afford to make a loan.

Bank borrowing

Banks will usually lend against an undertaking by the PRs. A bank may also require an undertaking from the solicitor to repay the loan from the proceeds of the estate. Where the solicitor is not a PR, any undertaking should be limited to 'such proceeds as come into the solicitor's control'.

While it is often the only viable option, bank borrowing is expensive, because the bank will charge an arrangement fee and interest on the amount borrowed. Money borrowed should be repaid at the earliest opportunity so as to honour any undertaking and to stop interest running. Income tax relief is available on interest paid on a separate loan account in respect of IHT payable on personalty vesting in the PRs (see **29.5.3**).

National Savings

Payment of tax may also be made from National Savings Bank accounts or from the proceeds of National Savings Certificates, any Government stock held on the National Savings register or any other National Savings investment. Full details of the investments and the procedure are given in the Inland Revenue leaflet IHT 11. However, this may involve a delay of up to 4 weeks before the monies are available for payment of tax (see **21.6**).

21.2 THE REQUIREMENT FOR AN INLAND REVENUE ACCOUNT

21.2.1 Excepted estates

If the estate is an excepted estate there is no need for an account to be submitted although the Inland Revenue can demand an account to be completed. The demand must be made within 35 days of the date of issue of the grant of representation. If an estate which initially appears to be excepted is subsequently found not to be so, the PRs must submit the appropriate account within 6 months of the discovery.

To qualify as an excepted estate, the estate must fulfil six criteria. If any criterion is not satisfied, an account will be required. The criteria for deaths on or after 6 April 1996 are as follows:

(1) the deceased must have died domiciled in the UK; and
(2) the deceased must not have made any chargeable transfers within 7 years of his death other than transfers consisting only of cash, quoted shares or quoted securities with a total gross value not exceeding £50,000 (PETs made more than 7 years before the death are not chargeable); and
(3) the total value of any foreign assets owned by the deceased must not exceed £30,000; and
(4) the deceased must not have been entitled to any type of interest in a trust immediately before his death; and
(5) the only assets owned by the deceased immediately before his death pass as a result of the death by will/intestacy and/or survivorship and/or nomination; and
(6) the combined value of the gross IHT estate and the value transferred as in para (2) above must not exceed £180,000.

Example

Adam has just died. His will leaves his estate to his wife Brenda and daughter Clare in equal shares. He is UK domiciled and has made no lifetime transfers.

His estate consists of:

House owned jointly with Brenda (half share)	£50,000
Building society a/c (sole name)	£10,000
Personal chattels	£2,000
Debts (funeral bill and Access a/c)	£1,800

Adam's estate satisfies the first five criteria and it has an IHT value of £62,000 gross. (Note that IHT exemptions and reliefs are ignored when ascertaining the gross IHT estate.)

This is an excepted estate and no Inland Revenue account is required. This fact will also be noted on the oath (see Chapter 23).

21.2.2 Form IHT 202

A specimen Form IHT 202 can be found in Appendix 2. It should be used whenever an estate is not excepted but does not require the longer Form IHT 200. An estate (which is not excepted) must satisfy all of the following six criteria if Form IHT 202 is to be used:

(1) the deceased must have died domiciled in the UK;
(2) the deceased must not have made any chargeable transfers in the 7 years prior to his death (see Chapter 18);
(3) the deceased had no interest in any settled property at his death or in the 7 years prior to his death;
(4) the estate must consist only of UK property which vests in the PRs as a result of the death and/or joint property and/or property which passes by nomination;
(5) the total chargeable (taxable) estate after claiming reliefs and exemptions does not exceed the nil rate band (ie currently £215,000); and
(6) the gross value of the IHT estate before deducting exemptions and reliefs does not exceed twice the IHT threshold.

If the deceased owned any foreign property, Form IHT 202 cannot be used. Indeed, if any criterion above is not satisfied, Form IHT 200 or IHT 201 must be used. Form IHT 201 is used where the deceased was domiciled somewhere other than in the UK and is beyond the scope of this book.

21.2.3 Form IHT 200

A specimen Form IHT 200 can be found in Appendix 3. It must be used whenever the deceased dies domiciled in the UK, his estate is not 'excepted' and the conditions for Form IHT 202 are not satisfied.

It is therefore required in the following circumstances:

(1) if the total chargeable estate exceeds £215,000; or
(2) the gross IHT estate exceeds twice the IHT threshold; or
(3) the deceased had an interest in any settlement at his death or in the 7 years prior to his death; or
(4) the deceased made chargeable transfers in the 7 years prior to his death; or
(5) the estate includes foreign property and is not an excepted estate.

Commonly, but not invariably, therefore, there will be IHT to pay on an estate requiring the completion of Form IHT 200.

The remainder of this chapter describes how to complete Forms IHT 202 and IHT 200.

21.3 POINTS COMMON TO THE COMPLETION OF FORMS IHT 202 AND IHT 200

An Inland Revenue account (ie Form IHT 202 or IHT 200) is a detailed financial report of the deceased's affairs at the date of his death. Each form contains marginal notes designed to help a person fill it in quickly and correctly. The Inland Revenue have also produced Guidance Notes (IHT 210) which contain much of the information given in Chapter 18 (rates of IHT, exemptions and reliefs, etc); to avoid unnecessary repetition, the Guidance Notes are not included in this book.

21.3.1 Personal details

The first page of each form is designed to give general information to the Inland Revenue about the deceased and his personal representatives.

21.3.2 Layout of the forms

Both forms are divided into 'sections' distinguishing between property which vests in the PRs and that which does not but which is still within the IHT estate, for example joint property. The sections are sub-divided, separating property without the instalment option from property with that option (see **18.10.2**). The question of whether or not property is capable of having the instalment option determines in which sub-division it is disclosed. The fact that the PRs may choose not to take the option in any given case is irrelevant when selecting the appropriate sub-division.

Property without the instalment option
Such property includes bank and building society accounts, arrears of salary, quoted shares, National Savings Certificates and Premium Bonds and personal chattels. Generally non-instalment property comprises cash and/or assets that are easily converted into cash.

Property with the instalment option
Assets to which the instalment option applies include:

(1) land;
(2) business interests (sole trader and partnership);
(3) any shares giving control of a company;
(4) unquoted shares if:
   (a) they form a sufficiently large holding (10 per cent and exceed £20,000 in value); or
   (b) the Revenue is satisfied that all the IHT cannot be paid at once without undue hardship; or
   (c) the IHT attributable to the shares or otherwise payable by instalments amounts to at least 20 per cent of the total IHT payable on the deceased's estate.

The instalment option is generally available to assist with spreading the burden of IHT over a number of years on property which may be difficult to sell, on the assumption that the money to pay the tax is not readily available without such a sale.

21.3.3 Meaning of 'free estate'

In both forms (ie on page 2 of Form IHT 202 and pages 3 and 4 of Form IHT 200), the Inland Revenue distinguish between joint/nominated property and 'free estate' which is defined as 'All the property of the deceased in respect of which the grant is required'.

For the purposes of the forms only, 'free estate' has a particular meaning convenient to the Inland Revenue. In general, the term 'free estate' is accepted as including all the property which vests in the PRs and other property (except trust property) which does not pass to the PRs but which is included in the estate for IHT because the deceased was beneficially entitled to it immediately before death (eg joint property passing by survivorship and nominated property) (see **18.9.2**). However, the Inland Revenue subdivide free estate on the forms as follows:

Nominated and Joint Property	Free estate, ie the other 'free' property which vests in the PRs and in respect of which a grant is required

In the sections on each form headed 'All the property of the deceased in respect of which the grant is required' the PRs must declare the value of property vesting in them even if they do not actually require a grant in order to realise it, for example, property covered by the Administration of Estates (Small Payments) Act 1965, and personal effects (see **20.6.1**).

21.3.4 Debts

Debts are recorded at the end of each section containing the assets out of which such a debt would generally be paid. For example, general debts should be set against property without the instalment option and secured debts should be set against the property over which they are charged.

21.3.5 Presentation of figures

When entering the values of assets or debts, omit pence: for example a bank account balance at the date of death of £236.72 is shown on the account as £236; a gas bill of £73.24 owed by deceased is shown on the account as £73.

21.3.6 Schedules

The Inland Revenue produce two schedule forms: IHT 37 and IHT 40. These schedules should be completed and annexed to the account where the estate includes land and shares respectively.

If the deceased held a number of shareholdings in quoted companies it is usual to have the shareholdings valued by a stockbroker. In such a case, the stockbrokers' formal valuation report may be annexed in place of Form IHT 40, and the account will merely show the total value of all the holdings. If no brokers' report is obtained, valuation details of the shares must be set out on Form IHT 40.

Similarly, details and values of unquoted shares may either be given in a written report from the company's accountant or set out on Form IHT 40.

Form IHT 37 should be completed and annexed if the estate contains any land, whether in the deceased's sole name or held jointly with others. Alternatively the Inland Revenue may be given a formal written valuation prepared by an estate agent.

For other assets, if there is more than one entry under a particular heading on the form, it is good practice to annex a schedule detailing the various sources so that only the total figure appears on the account. This keeps the account uncluttered and is less likely to cause arithmetical errors.

Example

Thora has just died. Her estate includes accounts with two building societies.

The Inland Revenue account will show:

'[Cash in] [Money with]
a building society: see schedule annexed   £3,052'

The schedule will show:

'X Building Society	£500	
interest accrued	£52	£552
Y Building Society	£2,490	
interest accrued	£10	£2,500
Total carried to Inland Revenue account		£3,052'

21.3.7 Totals

At the end of each sub-section there is a 'Total' box in which the total amount of assets and/or liabilities for that part of the form should be recorded. These totals must be carried forward as instructed on the form (ultimately to the probate summary and tax calculation).

21.3.8 Probate summary

The purpose of this calculation is to discover the gross and net values of the property vesting in the PRs as these figures must also appear on the oath (see **23.2**).

21.3.9 Declaration

The declaration is found at the end of each form, that is page 4 of IHT 202 and page 12 of IHT 200.

The account must be signed and dated by the PRs but it does not need to be sworn. The signatures should appear below the declaration.

The PRs will be personally liable to prosecution and fine if the content of the form is false. Where the form has been completed by a solicitor or other person, the PRs should check the completed form carefully before signing the declaration.

The declaration must be completed as directed on the form.

In many estates, the value of some of the assets, particularly personal chattels, will be estimated by the PRs. It is also common for the value of a known debt to be estimated, for example underpaid income tax. Provided that it is made clear within the body of the form which figures are estimates there is no need to exhibit further information to the declaration. This is generally only necessary where an application is being made for an expedited grant (ie one required urgently) before any assets or liabilities have been properly valued.

Example
Henry, a widower, died on holiday. His will leaves his estate to his two teenage children who were financially dependent on him and have no assets of their own.

If the exact values of all assets and liabilities are ascertained before an application for a grant is made, several months will elapse during which time the children may be penniless. The PRs should estimate the estate from information immediately available and complete the Inland Revenue account accordingly with an explanation annexed to the declaration, so that the grant can be applied for at the earliest date.

21.4 FORM IHT 202

This section should be read in conjunction with **21.2.2** and **21.3**. The contents of Form IHT 202 may be summarised in the following diagram:

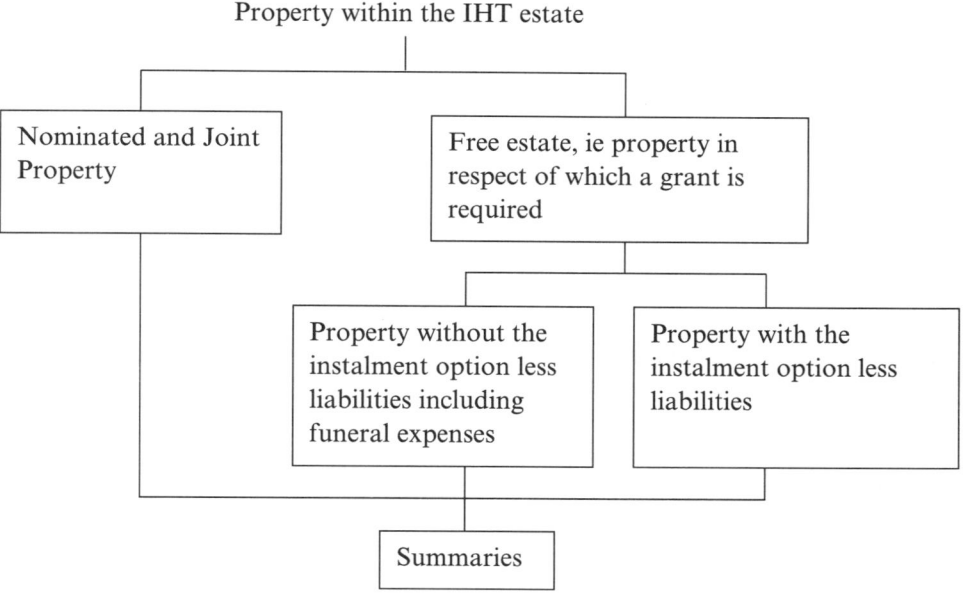

21.4.1 Page 1

See **21.3.1**.

21.4.2 Nominated and joint property: questions

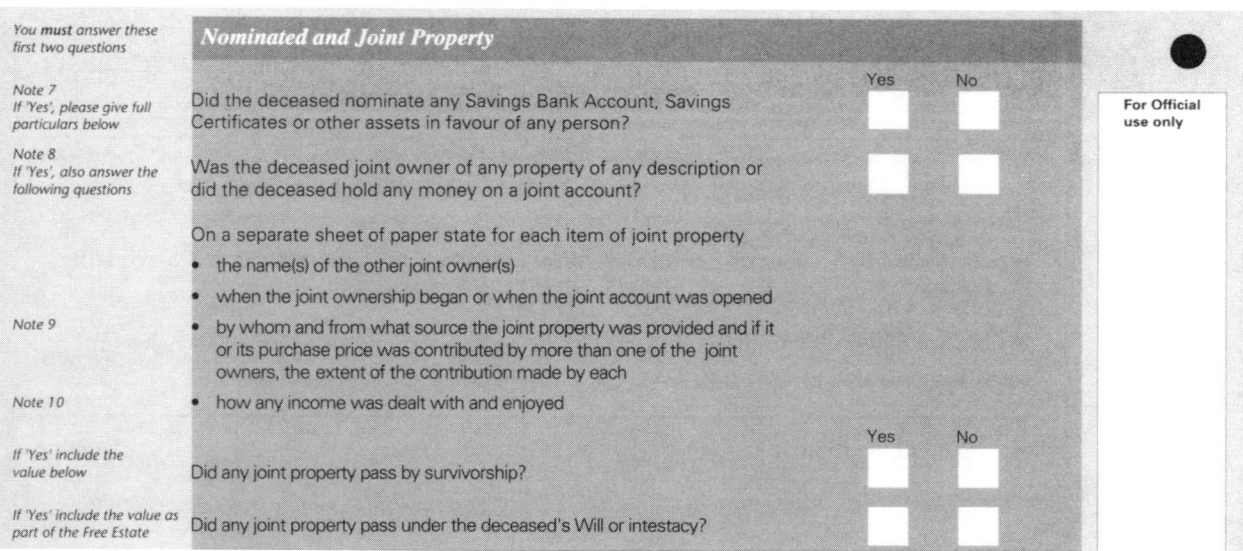

The form asks whether the deceased had nominated any asset in favour of any person or whether he held any jointly owned property at his death. If the deceased was the joint owner of any property, further information concerning that joint property must be given on a separate sheet of paper.

However, where jointly owned assets pass to the deceased's spouse alone, further information on the history of the joint ownership need not be given.

Consider the last two questions in particular:

DID ANY JOINT PROPERTY PASS BY SURVIVORSHIP?
This covers any property held as joint tenants in equity. The value of the deceased's share in such property must then be entered in the box headed 'Particulars of the property'.

DID ANY JOINT PROPERTY PASS UNDER THE DECEASED'S WILL OR INTESTACY?
This covers any property held as tenants in common in equity. The value of the deceased's share in such property must be included as part of the free estate. (Usually, such property would comprise a house or flat, in which case its value would be included with 'Property with the Instalment Option'.)

21.4.3 Nominated and joint property

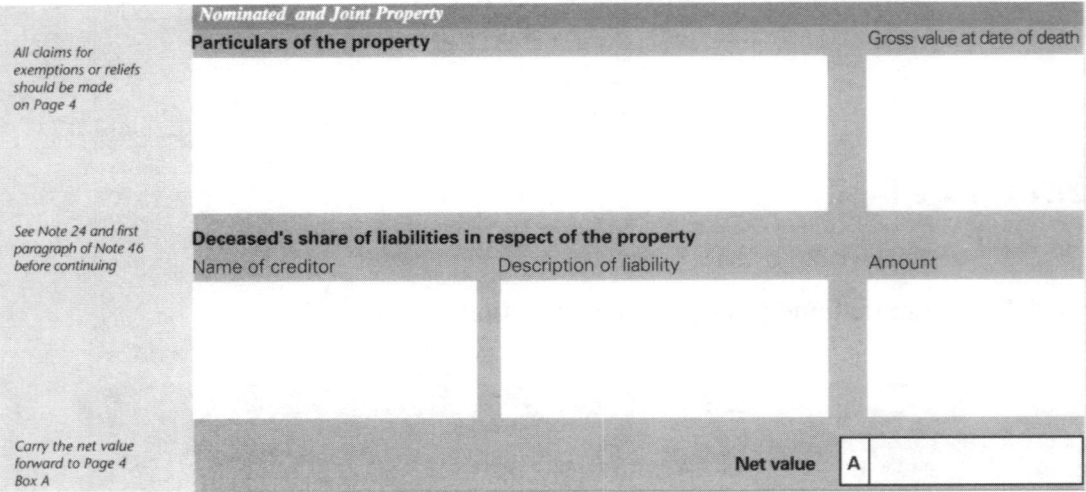

Recorded in this account are all assets owned by the deceased before his death which pass either by nomination following his death or by survivorship.

Where an asset was jointly owned it is the value of the deceased's share, not the total value, which is shown.

Any debts payable out of the nominated or joint property should be shown and the total of such debts deducted to give the net value of joint and nominated property at 'A'.

21.4.4 Free estate

An explanation of the meaning of this section and what it covers is given in **21.3.3**.

Property without the instalment option

Free Estate

All the property of the deceased in respect of which the grant is required

Property without the Instalment Option

Note	Item	Gross value at date of death
Note 13 — All claims for exemptions or reliefs should be made on Page 4		
Notes 14, 15 and 16	Stocks, shares, debentures and other securities, as set out on IHT 40 quoted or listed in the Stock Exchange Daily Official List and others, except those qualifying for the instalment option	
Note 17	Premium Savings Bonds and National Savings Certificates (including interest)	
	Cash and cash at Bank or Savings Bank, a building society, a co-operative or friendly society, including interest to the date of death, as statement attached	
Note 20	Policies of insurance and bonuses thereon (if any) on the life of the deceased, as statement attached	
	Saleable value of policies of insurance and bonuses (if any) on the life of any other person, as statement attached	
	Income Tax repayable	
	Carried forward	

Property without the Instalment Option - continued

	Brought forward	
Note 21 — Please attach a valuation if one has been obtained	Household and personal goods, including pictures, china, clothes, books, jewellery, stamp, coin and other collections, motor cars, boats etc	
	Sold, realised gross	
	Unsold, estimated	
Note 22 — Please state the name and date of death of the testator or intestate	Interest in an unadministered estate	
	Other assets not included above or as instalment option property	
Carry the total forward to Page 4 Box B	**Total** B	

For Official use only

Listed within this part of the form are assets which were in the deceased's sole name (or which he held as a beneficial tenant in common) and on which tax would be immediately payable had the estate been above the IHT threshold. Included are quoted shares, bank and building society accounts, National Savings Certificates and Premium Bonds, life policies not written in trust and personal chattels. Each asset should be detailed and its probate value shown. If there is insufficient space on the form, use schedules (see **21.3.6**).

Liabilities

Notes 24, 25 and 26	Liabilities at the date of death and funeral expenses		
	Name of creditor	Description of liability	Amount
Note 27 Carry the total forward to Page 4 Box E			Total E

The names of the deceased's creditors (eg 'British Gas') and the nature of the debt (eg 'gas bill') are recorded in the next part of the form together with the funeral expenses.

Property with the instalment option

	Property with the Instalment Option	Gross value at date of death
Note 28	Land and buildings as described on IHT 37 attached	
Note 29	Business interests (state nature of business)	
	• Net value of deceased's interest in business, as statement or balance sheet attached	
Note 30 Please give the name of the firm	• Net value of deceased's interest as a partner in the firm of	
	as statement or balance sheet attached	
Note 31	Stocks, shares, debentures and other securities as set out on form IHT 40	
	• which gave the deceased control of the company	
	• other unquoted shares or securities.	
Carry the total forward to Page 4 Box C		Total C
Note 32	Liabilities	
	Name of creditor	Description of liability (and property on which charged)	Amount
Carry the total forward to Page 4 Box F		Total F

This section records assets in the deceased's sole name which would qualify for the right to pay the tax attributable to them by instalments were tax to be due. Also recorded here is the deceased's share of any land which he held with others as beneficial tenants in common because that property passes under his will or intestacy, not automatically to the surviving co-owners.

The final part of this section requires details of any debts secured on assets in the immediately preceding part, for example the mortgage debt on a house owned by the deceased.

21.4.5 Probate summary

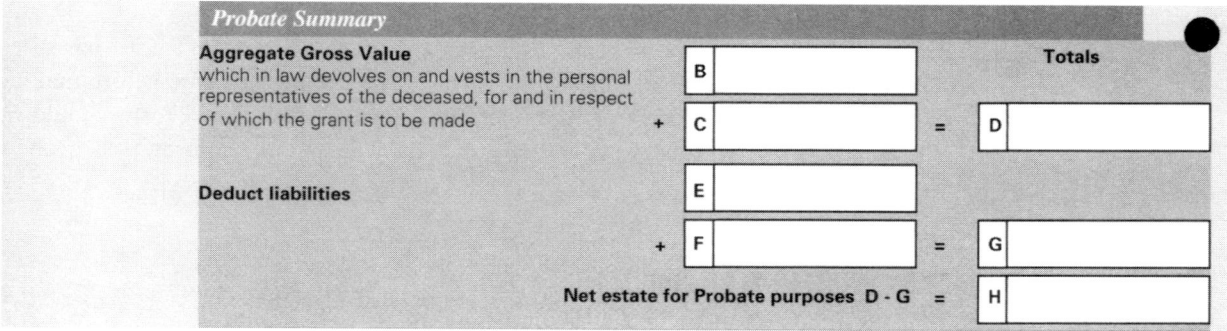

This calculates the value of property vesting in the PRs. Normally a grant of representation will be required before the PRs can deal with such assets. Probate court fees are calculated on the basis of the net estate.

The totals at 'D' and 'H' should also appear on the oath sworn by the PRs as follows: 'the gross estate amounts to £ [Total D] and the net estate amounts to £ [Total H]' (see **23.2**).

21.4.6 Tax summary

This takes the value of the estate for probate purposes and adds to it the joint and nominated property which do not vest in the PRs (and which are not part of the estate for probate purposes).

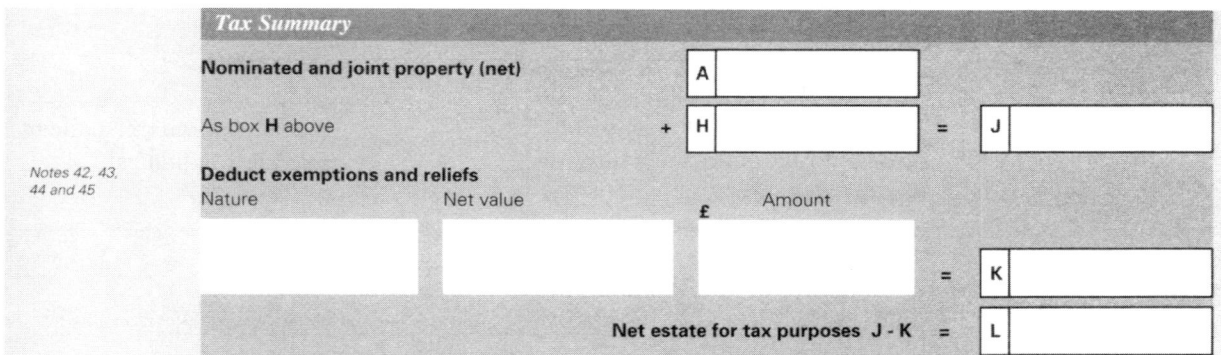

The final stage of the form is the calculation of the IHT estate.

Total 'J' represents the net IHT estate before exemptions and reliefs. This figure is achieved by adding together the deceased's net joint and nominated property (Total 'A') and the net value of the property vesting in the PRs (Total 'H').

In order to calculate the net IHT estate, all available reliefs and exemptions must be deducted. Each relief or exemption claimed is stated separately and their total (at 'K') is deducted from Total 'J'. The result is the total chargeable estate called on the form 'net estate for tax purposes' (ie Total 'L'). This figure may be anything from nil to £215,000.

21.4.7 Declaration

See **21.3.9**.

Because there is no tax to pay on an estate where Form IHT 202 has been completed, there is no need to send the form to the Inland Revenue before making an application for the grant of representation. Instead, the signed form should be sent to the probate registry with the oath, any will and the appropriate probate court fees.

21.5 FORM IHT 200

This section should be read in conjunction with **21.2.2** and **21.3**. The contents of Form IHT 200 can be summarised as shown below.

The main sections at a glance are:

Section 1 – Questions about lifetime gifts (because of effect on cumulative total)

Section 2 – Questions about nominated and joint property, then subdivision:

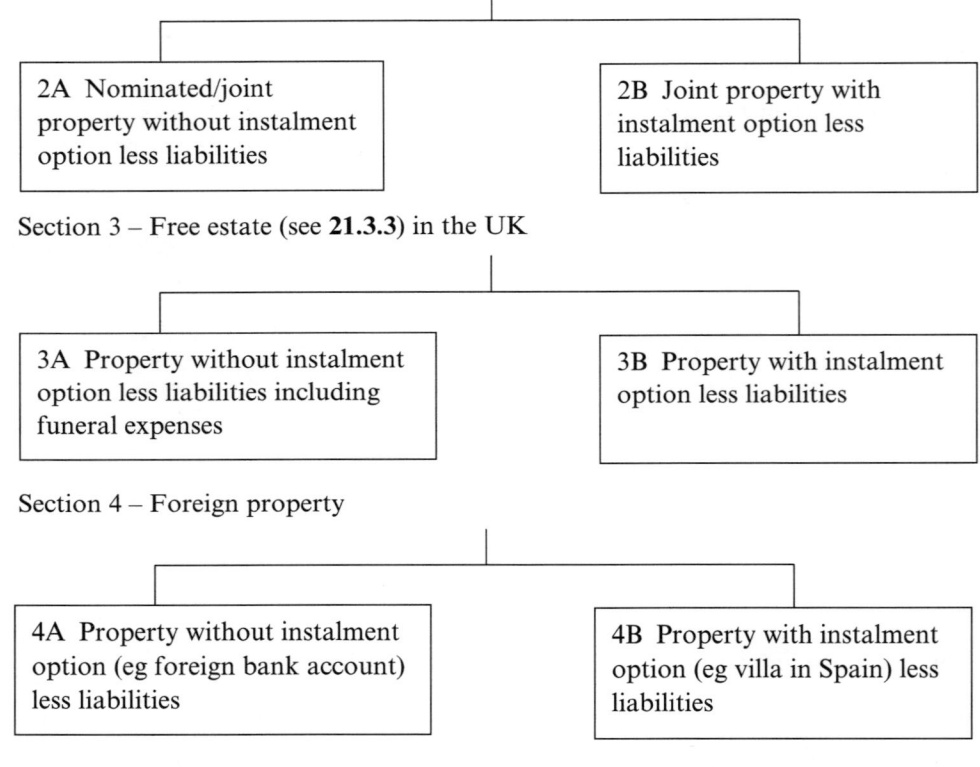

Section 3 – Free estate (see **21.3.3**) in the UK

Section 4 – Foreign property

Section 5 – Settled property and gifts with reservation (because although the PRs are unlikely to be liable for IHT on such property, it may affect the total IHT payable)

Section 6 – Exemptions ... and reliefs on property in the earlier sections

21.5.1 Page 1

See **21.3.1**.

21.5.2 Section 1 – Lifetime gifts

This section (on page 2 of the form) contains a number of questions about gifts and transfers of value made by the deceased during his lifetime and each question must be answered by ticking the appropriate Yes/No box. Where a question is answered in the affirmative, full particulars must be set out on the form. All information must be given, even though it may have already been supplied to the Inland Revenue during the deceased's lifetime. The information is sought because such gifts or transfers of value will affect the deceased's cumulative total and, ultimately, the amount of IHT payable as a result of the death.

The information sought is explained below each extract.

Actions of deceased within 7 years of death

You must answer all the questions in this section	Section 1 - Lifetime gifts or transfers of value	Yes	No	For Official use only
	Did the deceased within 7 years of death			
Note 1	make any gift, settlement, or other transfer of value? (See Note 1 as to the transfers you should not include)	☐	☐	
Note 2	pay any premium on a policy of life assurance not included on Page 4 Section 3A of this form?	☐	☐	
Note 3	cease to be entitled to any beneficial interest in possession in settled property?	☐	☐	

These questions seek disclosure of all inter vivos transfers and PETs made within 7 years of the death, including an interest in possession in any settlement which the deceased gave up (for whatever reason) within 7 years of his death. Gifts between spouses and those covered by the £3,000 pa and £250 pa small gift exemptions can be ignored.

The second question covers any premiums paid by the deceased on an insurance policy written in trust for the benefit of another person (other than the deceased or the deceased's spouse). It would also include a Married Woman's Property Act 1882 policy taken out for the benefit of the deceased's children. All such insurance policies must be declared at this point but there are unlikely to be any IHT consequences, as the proceeds will fall outside the deceased's estate and the premiums will generally be exempt as normal expenditure out of income.

If the deceased paid any such premium, a copy of the 1882 Act policy (or, if the policy was held on trust, a copy of the trust documentation) should be enclosed with Form IHT 200.

Gifts made on or after 18 March 1986

Note 4 — Did the deceased at any time on or after 18 March 1986 dispose of any property by way of gift where

- possession and enjoyment of the property was not bona fide assumed by the donee? ☐ Yes ☐ No
- the property was not enjoyed to the entire exclusion of the deceased? ☐ Yes ☐ No
- any benefit was retained by contract or otherwise? ☐ Yes ☐ No

These questions are designed to discover if any property was given away by the deceased but in which he reserved a benefit to himself or which he continued to enjoy after making the gift (see **18.4.3**). The value of any such property must be included in section 5 of the form (see **21.5.6**).

Details of lifetime gifts or transfers of value

Details of lifetime gifts or transfers of value

Please enter in chronological order details of each lifetime gift or transfer of value. You should deduct any exemptions or reliefs due (See Note 5). Enter the chargeable value showing how you have calculated this

Date of disposition	To whom given (name and address)	Description of asset(s) at date of transfer	Value

Carry the total chargeable value of lifetime transfers to Page 10 Box A unless the property given was subject to a reservation retained by the deceased at the date of death, in which case it should be included in Section 5 on Page 8

Total chargeable value of gifts made within 7 years of death ☐

Show on a schedule details of all gifts made within 7 years of the earliest transfer but do not carry the value of these gifts to Page 10 (See Note 54).

All non-exempt transfers of value made by the deceased during his lifetime should be entered in chronological order. Any available exemptions (eg £3,000 annual exemption, or the exempt amount of a gift in consideration of marriage) and reliefs (eg business property relief) should be shown as having been deducted.

Superannuation benefits

> **Note 6**
>
> **Superannuation benefits**
> Was any provision, apart from State Pension, made by the deceased, the deceased's employers or otherwise for retirement, pension, or other superannuation benefits? Yes ☐ No ☐
>
> If 'Yes' were any benefits payable, or dispositions made as described in Note 6? Yes ☐ No ☐

Here the Inland Revenue seeks disclosure of any lump sum benefit payable under a pension policy as a result of the death.

The first question relates to any pension provisions arising as a result of the deceased's death. If payment is made out of a discretionary scheme (such as that described in **2.4.4**) then the answer to the second question is 'No'. This is the most likely situation to arise.

The benefits described in Note 6 (and requiring the 'Yes' box to be ticked) include a lump sum paid to the deceased's PRs as of right (which must be included in section 3A on page 5 under 'Other personal property') or the disposal by the deceased of such a benefit, for example by a declaration of trust, within 2 years of his death (which would be included in Section 1).

21.5.3 Section 2 – Nominated and joint property

The section begins with a series of questions to establish whether the deceased owned any joint property (whether as beneficial joint tenant or tenant in common) or property subject to a nomination immediately before his death. Where there was jointly owned property, further information must be given. However, where jointly owned assets pass to the deceased's spouse alone, information on the history of the joint ownership need not be given.

> **You must answer the first two questions in this Section**
>
> **Section 2 - Nominated and Joint Property**
>
> Note 7
> If 'Yes', please give full particulars in Section 2A
>
> **Did the deceased nominate** any Savings Bank Account, Savings Certificates or other assets in favour of any person? Yes ☐ No ☐
>
> Note 8
>
> **Was the deceased joint owner** of any property of any description or did the deceased hold any money on a joint account? Yes ☐ No ☐
>
> On a separate sheet of paper state for each item of joint property
> - the name(s) of the other joint owner(s)
> - when the joint ownership began or when the joint account was opened
>
> Note 9
> - by whom and from what source the joint property was provided and, if it or its purchase price was contributed by more than one of the joint owners, the extent of the contribution made by each
>
> Note 10
> - how any income was dealt with and enjoyed.
>
> If 'Yes' include the value in Section 4A or 4B
> Was any joint property situated outside the UK? Yes ☐ No ☐
>
> If 'Yes' include the value in Section 2A or 2B if the property was situated in the UK
> Did any joint property pass by survivorship? Yes ☐ No ☐
>
> If 'Yes' include the value in Section 3A or 3B if the property was situated in the UK
> Did any joint property pass under the deceased's Will or intestacy? Yes ☐ No ☐
>
> For Official use only

The value of any property declared as a result of the questions must be entered in one of the sections of the form as follows:

(1) nominated property – 2A

(2) UK non-instalment option property (eg a bank account) held as beneficial joint tenant – 2A
(3) UK instalment option property (eg a house or flat) held as beneficial joint tenant – 2B
(4) UK non-instalment option property held as beneficial tenant in common – 3A
(5) UK instalment option property held as beneficial tenant in common – 3B
(6) foreign property – 4A or 4B if the PRs are liable to pay the IHT on it, otherwise 5.

After the questions, the section subdivides as shown below.

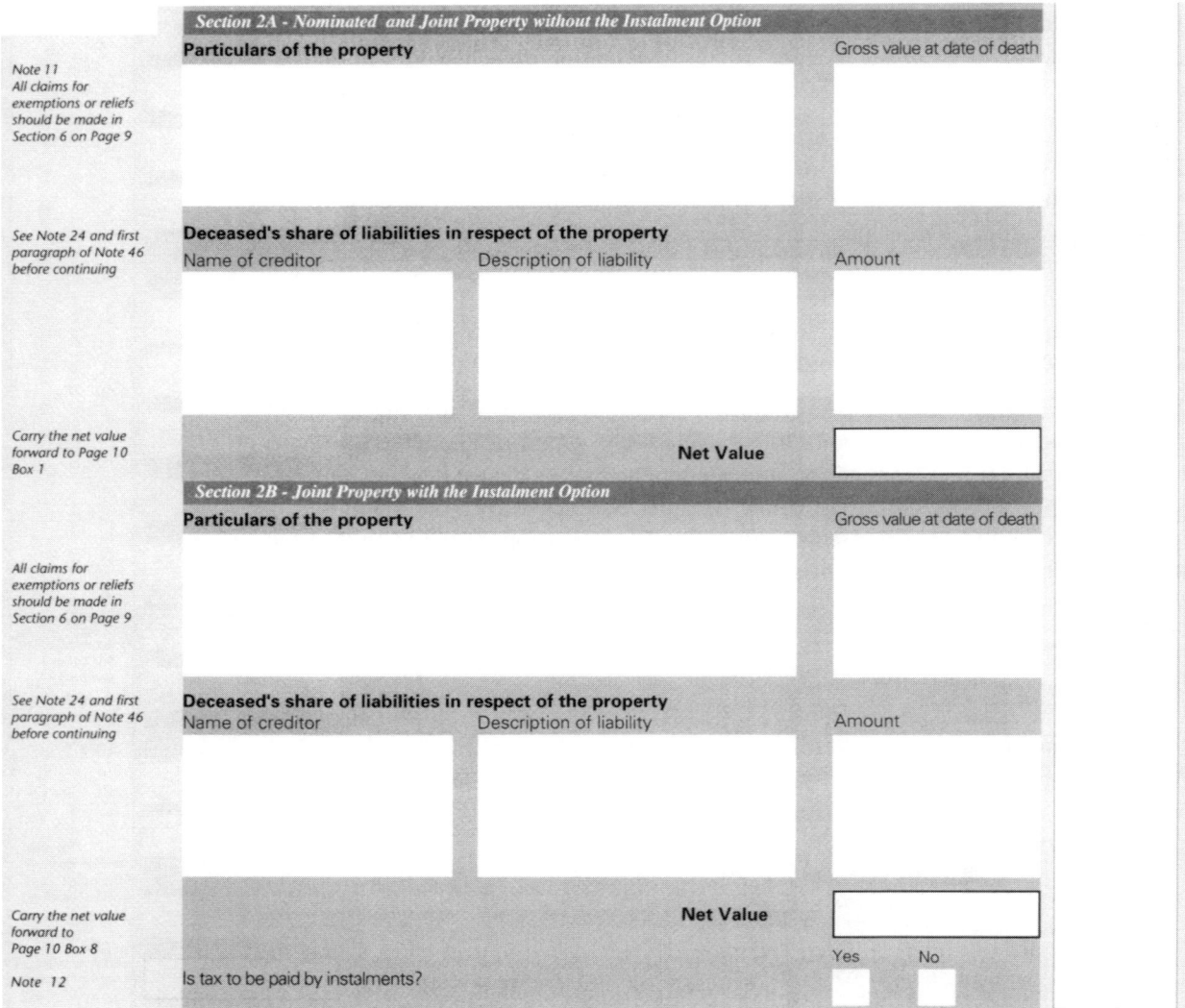

Any liabilities attaching to section 2A or 2B property are deducted from the respective gross totals.

The question relating to the payment of tax by instalments should not be overlooked. If the PRs wish to pay IHT by instalments on any property qualifying for the instalment option, they must answer the question 'Yes'.

If the right to pay by instalments is adopted, the instalments are paid in the way described in **18.10.2**.

21.5.4 Section 3 – Free estate in the UK

Section 3A – Property without the instalment option

	Section 3 - Free Estate in the UK	
Note 13 All claims for exemptions or reliefs should be made in Section 6 on Page 9	**All the property of the deceased in respect of which the grant is required**	For Official use only
	Section 3A - Property without the Instalment Option	
Notes 14, 15 and 16	Stocks, shares, debentures and other securities as set out on IHT 40:	Value at date of death
	quoted or listed in the Stock Exchange Daily Official List except so far as included in Section 3B	
	others, except so far as included in Section 3B	
	Uncashed dividends and interest received, dividends declared, and interest accrued due to the date of death in respect of the above investments, as statement attached	
	Premium Savings Bonds	
Note 17	National Savings Certificates including interest to the date of death	
	Bank accounts including interest to the date of death, as statement attached	
	Money with the National Savings Bank, a building society, a co-operative or friendly society, including interest to the date of death, as statement attached	
	Cash (other than cash at banks, etc)	
	Money out on mortgage including interest to the date of death, as statement attached	
Note 18	Debts due to the deceased including interest to the date of death (except book debts included in section 3B) as statement attached	
	Rents including apportionment of rents of the deceased's own real and leasehold property to the date of death	
Note 19	Income arising, but not received before the death, from real and personal property in which the deceased had a life or other limited interest	
Please state the source	Accrued	
	Apportioned	
	Any other income, apportioned where necessary, to which the deceased was entitled at the date of death (for example pensions, annuities, director's fees, etc), as statement attached	
Note 20	Policies of insurance and bonuses thereon (if any) on the life of the deceased, as statement attached	
	Saleable value of policies of insurance and bonuses (if any) on the life of any other person, as statement attached	
	Amounts payable under private health insurance schemes	
	Income Tax repayable	
Note 21 Please attach a valuation if one has been obtained	Household and personal goods, including pictures, china, clothes, books, jewellery, stamp, coin and other collections, motor cars, boats etc	
	Sold, realised gross	
	Unsold, estimated	
Note 22 Please state the name and date of death of the testator or intestate	Interest in an unadministered estate	
	Carried forward	

continued over

	Section 3A - Property without the Instalment Option - continued	
	Brought forward	For Official use only
Note 23 Please state how the deceased acquired the interest and the estimated value at the date of the deceased's death	Interest in expectancy	
	Other personal property as listed below or as statement attached	
Carry the total forward to the Probate Summary on Page 11 Box L	**Gross value of property without the Instalment Option**	

An explanation of the meaning of this section and what it covers is given in **21.3.3**. Most of the entries required on pages 4 and 5 of the form should be self-explanatory, but some may require further explanation.

QUOTED STOCKS AND SHARES
These are valued on the '¼ up' principle (see **18.5.3**).

Dividends declared but not paid and any interest accrued to the date of death are recorded separately. Note any markings in the official list (or as shown in any valuation) which may affect the value of the shares. For example, if the share value is ex-dividend, the PRs must account separately (as uncashed dividends etc) for the relevant net dividend.

Where an estate includes several holdings of stocks and shares a schedule should be used (see **21.3.6**).

'INCOME ARISING, BUT NOT RECEIVED BEFORE THE DEATH . . .'
If the deceased had an interest in possession (ie a right to the income) in any settlement immediately prior to his death, it will be necessary to look at the trust instrument to see whether or not the provisions of the Apportionment Act 1870 have been excluded (see **10.4**). If excluded, then any dividend or interest declared on trust assets, but not actually paid over to the deceased by the trustees at the date of death, belongs to the deceased's estate and should be recorded on Form IHT 200 as income 'Accrued'. Any dividends declared or interest arising after the date of death belong to the remainderman irrespective of the period to which they relate. If the apportionment rules have not been excluded, income from the trust must be apportioned, on a daily basis, between the deceased's estate and the trust. Such apportioned income is an asset of the deceased's estate and recorded at 'Apportioned'.

'POLICIES OF INSURANCE . . .'
The figure required is the maturity value of any policy of insurance on the deceased's life to which he was beneficially entitled immediately before his death. A copy letter from the insurance company stating the value of the policy and any bonus should be enclosed with the Form IHT 200. The value of any insurance

policy written in trust for a third person should not be included, because such policies do not form part of the deceased's IHT estate (although a copy of such a policy and the trust documentation will have been supplied in answer to the second question on page 2 of the account: see **21.5.2**).

'INTEREST IN EXPECTANCY'
This entry refers to the value of the deceased's interest in remainder under any trust where a prior interest is still subsisting.

Example
Tom set up a trust for Ada for life remainder to Brenda.

Brenda has just died. Ada is still alive.

Brenda's interest in the trust is vested although not in possession.

Such an interest does pass under Brenda's will or intestacy and therefore must be included in section 3A. Any relief by virtue of it being 'excluded property' should be claimed on page 9 of the account.

(For further discussion of the tax treatment of interests in remainder, see **18.4.4**.)

Section 3A – Liabilities at the date of death and funeral expenses

Name of creditor	Description of liability	Amount

See Note 24 and first paragraph of Note 46 before continuing
Note 25

Funeral expenses

Note 26

Note 27
Carry the total forward to the Probate Summary on Page 11 Box Q

Total liabilities

Carry the net total forward to Page 10 Box 2

Value of property without the Instalment Option less liabilities

On page 5, all general liabilities of the deceased should be listed, for example any gas bill, credit card bills, outstanding income tax and 'reasonable' funeral expenses.

Section 3B – Property with the instalment option

	Section 3B - Property with the Instalment Option	Value at date of death	
All claims for exemptions or reliefs should be made in Section 6 on Page 9 **Note 28**	Land etc owned by the deceased in the UK (not being settled land) as described on IHT 37 attached		For Official use only
Note 29	Business interests Net value of deceased's interest in the business(es), as statement or balance sheet attached		
Note 30 Please give the name of the firm	Net value of deceased's interest as partner in the firm of as statement or balance sheet attached		
Note 31	Stocks, shares, debentures and other securities, as set out on IHT 40 Shares or securities which gave the deceased control of the company immediately before the death (*Section 228(1)(a) Inheritance Tax Act 1984*)		
	Unquoted shares or securities within Section 228(1) (b), (c) or (d) Inheritance Tax Act 1984. (All other unquoted shares or securities should be included in Section 3A)		
Carry the total forward to the Probate Summary on Page 11 Box M	**Gross value of property with the Instalment Option**		

This section (on page 6) details all items excluding foreign property, which vest in the PRs and attract the instalment option, whether or not that option is exercised.

The following types of assets are included in this section:

(1) Land, both freehold and leasehold, of which the deceased was the absolute sole owner or a tenant in common. Where land was held as tenants in common only the value of the deceased's share (discounted as per **21.1.2**) should be included. A formal valuation or Form IHT 37 should be annexed (see **21.3.6**).

(2) Business interests, ie the net value of the business in which the deceased was the sole proprietor and/or the net value of the deceased's interest in a business in which he was a partner. The principal activity of the business or partnership should be indicated and, preferably, a copy of the partnership agreement or a statement of the terms on which it carried out its activities should be attached to the Form IHT 200.

The net value of the business (or interest in a business) is ascertained from the balance sheet and accounts, preferably those prepared to the date of death. Failing this, a statement of the assets and liabilities of the business or partnership at that date should be attached. The Inland Revenue may, after the grant has issued, ask for the previous 3 years' business balance sheets. The balance sheets are normally prepared by the person who, or firm which, has acted as accountant to the business in the preceding period.

(3) Certain holdings of shares, namely:

   (a) quoted or unquoted shares if they gave the deceased control of the company; and
   (b) qualifying unquoted shares (see **21.3.2**).

   A formal valuation or Form IHT 40 should be annexed (see **21.3.6**).

(4) Woodlands.

	Liabilities charged at the date of the deceased's death on the property included above other than those already reflected in the net value of Business Interests		
See Notes 24, 32 and the first paragraph of Note 46 before continuing	Name of creditor	Description of liability and property on which charged	Amount
Carry this total forward to the Probate Summary on Page 11 Box R		**Total liabilities**	
Carry the net total forward to Page 10 Box 9	**Value of property with the Instalment Option less liabilities**		
Note 33	Is tax to be paid by instalments?		Yes ☐ No ☐

Liabilities charged on section 3B property at the date of death (eg a mortgage) are deducted from the total value of section 3B property. If these liabilities exceed the value of section 3B assets, the excess can be set against section 3A assets.

The final part of the section asks whether the tax attributable to the section 3B property is to be paid by instalments.

If the right to pay by instalments is adopted, the instalments are paid in the way described in **18.10.2**.

21.5.5 Section 4 – Foreign property

Section 4 - Foreign Property

Note 34

Section 4A - Property without the Instalment Option

Note 35

All claims for exemptions or reliefs should be made in Section 6 on Page 9

Particulars of the property — Value at date of death

Gross Value

Note 36

Liabilities in respect of the property above or due outside the UK

Name and address of creditor | Description of liability | Amount

Total liabilities

Carry the net total forward to Page 10 Box 3

Value of property without the Instalment Option less liabilities

Section 4B - Property with the Instalment Option

Note 35

All claims for exemptions or reliefs should be made in Section 6 on Page 9

Particulars of the property — Value at date of death

Gross Value

Liabilities in respect of the property above or due outside the UK

Name and address of creditor | Description of liability | Amount

Total liabilities

Carry the net total forward to Page 10 Box 10

Value of property with the Instalment Option less liabilities

Note 37

Is tax to be paid by instalments?   Yes ☐   No ☐

For Official use only

Included in this section is any property owned by the deceased but situated outside the UK on which the PRs are liable to pay tax, for example a holiday cottage in France. Again the section divides into property without and property with the instalment option.

21.5.6 Section 5 – Settled property and gifts with reservation

> **Note 38**
>
> **Section 5 - Settled Property and Gifts with Reservation**
>
> **All other property** to which the deceased was beneficially entitled or was treated as beneficially entitled.
>
> *You must answer the question opposite*
>
> Was the deceased, at the date of death, entitled to a life interest, annuity or other interest in possession in settled property whether as beneficiary under a settlement or otherwise? See Note 39.   Yes ☐   No ☐
>
> **Note 39**
>
> If so, please state below the name(s) of the settlement(s), the trustees and their solicitors.
>
> *For Official use only*

Settled property

If the deceased had any interest in settled property, the question at the start of the section must be answered 'Yes'.

Appropriate details must be given including the names of the trustees of the settlement/trust and the names and addresses of their solicitors or other agents.

Included in this section will be details of any trust fund in which the deceased had an interest in possession (eg a right to the income) immediately before his death.

> *Example*
> £100,000 is held in trust with a direction to pay the income to Celia for life, with remainder to David. On Celia's death the £100,000 is recorded in section 5 of her Inland Revenue account.
>
> The PRs are unlikely to be liable for the IHT due on property within this section (because the trustees are liable for tax on trust property). Nevertheless, the value of trust property must be included here so that both the total value of the estate for IHT purposes and the amount of IHT payable on delivery of the account can be correctly calculated.

Note that an interest in possession is not restricted to the situation where a beneficiary has the right to income from the trust property. An interest in possession also arises where a beneficiary is allowed to reside in the trust property rent free or is given the right to use and enjoy chattels.

Gifts with reservation

This includes property which was given away by the deceased during his lifetime but in which he reserved a benefit which subsisted until his death.

> *Example*
> Justin transferred the legal title to his house to his son but continued living there until his death. On Justin's death the value of the house is part of his taxable estate.
>
> Where the deceased made a gift but reserved a benefit to himself, this fact must be disclosed in the answers to the questions in section 1 of the form (see **21.5.2**). The question at the start of section 5 is answered 'No' (provided there is no settled property as described above).

Details of any such property and its value must be included in this section. In addition, the name(s) and address(es) of the legal owner(s) of the property must be given.

Again, the PRs are unlikely to be liable for the IHT due on any property with reservation (because the beneficiary of the property is primarily liable for the tax). However, the value must be included so that the total value of the estate for IHT purposes and the amount of IHT payable on delivery of the account can be correctly calculated.

Note 40
Please note that the value of any property within Section 5 must be included on Page 10 even if you are not liable for the tax on that property.
Enter the value in Box 15 and/or Box 16 unless you are paying tax on delivery, in which case enter it in Box 4 and/or Box 11.

All claims for exemptions or reliefs should be made in Section 6 on Page 9

Section 5A - Property without the Instalment Option

Particulars of the property	Value at date of death
Liabilities in respect of the property above	**Amount**

Carry the net value forward to Page 10 Box 4
Property on which tax is being paid now on delivery of this Account — Net value

Carry the net value forward to Page 10 Box 15
Property on which tax is not being paid now — Net value

Section 5B - Property with the Instalment Option

All claims for exemptions or reliefs should be made in Section 6 on Page 9

Particulars of the property	Value at date of death
Liabilities in respect of the property above	**Amount**

Carry the net value forward to Page 10 Box 11
Property on which tax is being paid now on delivery of this Account — Net value

Carry the net value forward to Page 10 Box 16
Property on which tax is not being paid now — Net value

Note 41
Is tax to be paid by instalments? Yes ☐ No ☐

The section is again subdivided into property without and with the instalment option. If any property carries the option, the question at the bottom of page 8 (ie 'Is tax to be paid by instalments?') must be answered.

> *Example*
> Kevin had a life interest in a trust. The trust fund consisted of quoted shares and a house. On Kevin's death the shares will be section 5A property and the house section 5B property.

Sections 5A and 5B are further subdivided, so separate totals must be shown for property on which tax is being paid on delivery of this account and property on which tax is not being paid now.

Property on which tax is being paid . . .
This is the property on which the IHT will be paid on delivery of the account, ie by the PRs. Entries under this heading are likely to be rare, because the principal liability for IHT on property which falls within section 5 is on the trustee or donee and not on the PRs. (For discussion of the burden of IHT see Chapter 18.)

Tax may be paid on trust property where, for example, the beneficiaries under the trust and will are the same, the trustees and the PRs are the same and it is administratively easier for the PRs to pay all the tax, or where the trustees and PRs are different people and the PRs have been given the money by the separate trustees to pay the tax on their behalf.

Property on which tax is not being paid now
Most section 5 entries will fall into this category. Although the tax attributable to section 5 property is not paid by the PRs, the property does form part of the deceased's tax estate. The total IHT payable as a result of the death is then apportioned between the sections; the PRs pay the IHT on sections 3 and 4 and the trustees or donees on section 5 (see Chapter 18).

21.5.7 Section 6 – Exemptions, exclusions and reliefs against capital

On page 9, PRs claim any exemptions or reliefs from IHT on property taxable as a result of the deceased's death.

Any part of the estate passing to a surviving spouse or to a charity is exempt from IHT and the exemption should be claimed in respect of the full net value of that property. If claiming charity exemption then, unless the charity is a household name, the registered number should be given. In addition, assets qualifying for business property relief or agricultural property relief should have 100 per cent or 50 per cent relief claimed against their value as appropriate. (See Chapter 18 for a detailed discussion of reliefs and exemptions.)

The exemptions and reliefs are claimed against the section of the form in which the qualifying asset is recorded, as illustrated below.

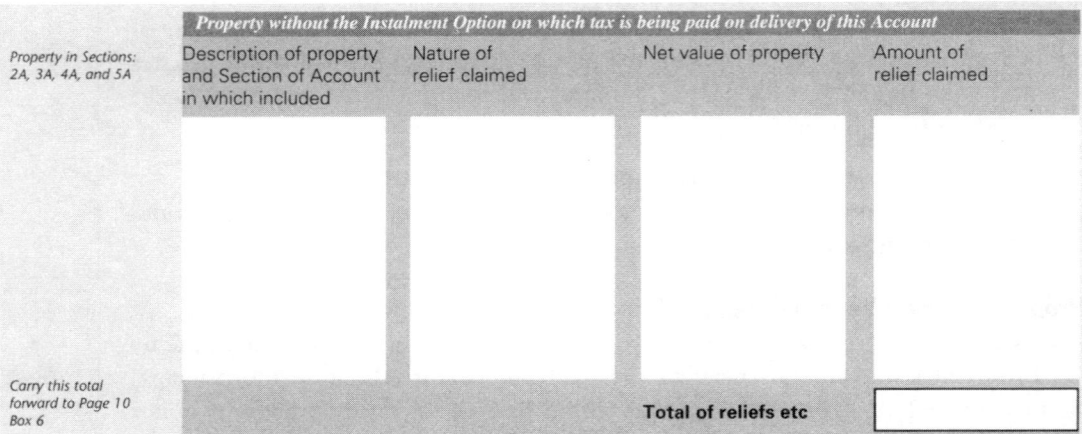

This part is for exemptions and reliefs against any property which does not carry the instalment option and is particularly likely to relate to property disclosed in sections 2A and 3A.

Example

Derek has recently died leaving a one half share (worth £5,000) of a bank account owned jointly with his wife, £15,000 in his own building society account and personal chattels worth £10,000. By his will, he left all his property to his wife.

The first part of page 9 will read as follows:

Description of property and Section of Account in which included	Nature of relief claimed	Net value of property	Amount of relief claimed
2A: Bank account	Spouse exemption	£5,000	£5,000
3A: All	Spouse exemption	£25,000	£25,000
		Total of reliefs etc	£30,000

Property with the Instalment Option on which tax is being paid on delivery of this Account

Property in Sections: 2B, 3B, 4B, and 5B

Description of property and Section of Account in which included	Nature of relief claimed	Net value of property	Amount of relief claimed

Total of reliefs etc

Carry this total forward to Page 10 Box 13

The second part is for exemptions and reliefs relating to all the instalment option property on which the PRs are liable to pay IHT, whether or not they are claiming the instalment option. It is most likely to relate to property in sections 2B and 3B.

Example

Derek (from the example above) also left a house (worth £300,000 and owned by him alone) to his wife and a 22% holding in Derek's Diner Ltd (worth £30,000) to his son.

The second part of page 9 would be completed as follows:

Property with the Instalment Option on which tax is being paid on delivery of this Account

Property in Sections: 2B, 3B, 4B, and 5B

Description of property and Section of Account in which included	Nature of relief claimed	Net value of property	Amount of relief claimed
3B: House	Spouse exemption	£300,000	£300,000
22% Derek's Diner Ltd	BPR @ 100%	£30,000	£30,000

Total of reliefs etc £330,000

Carry this total forward to Page 10 Box 13

The third part of page 9 is generally for property on which the PRs are not liable to pay IHT.

Property on which tax is not being paid on delivery of this Account

Property in Sections: 2B, 3B, 4B, 5A and 5B

Description of property and Section of Account in which included	Nature of relief claimed	Net value of property	Amount of relief claimed

Total of reliefs etc

Carry this total forward to Page 10 Box 18

Example

Lily was the life tenant of a trust fund worth £200,000. On her death, the property passes under the terms of the trust to a named charity absolutely. If there were any tax to pay on the trust fund as a result of Lily's death, it would have been the trustees' responsibility. Lily's interest would have been declared by her PRs in section 5A.

Page 9 of Lily's account would read as follows:

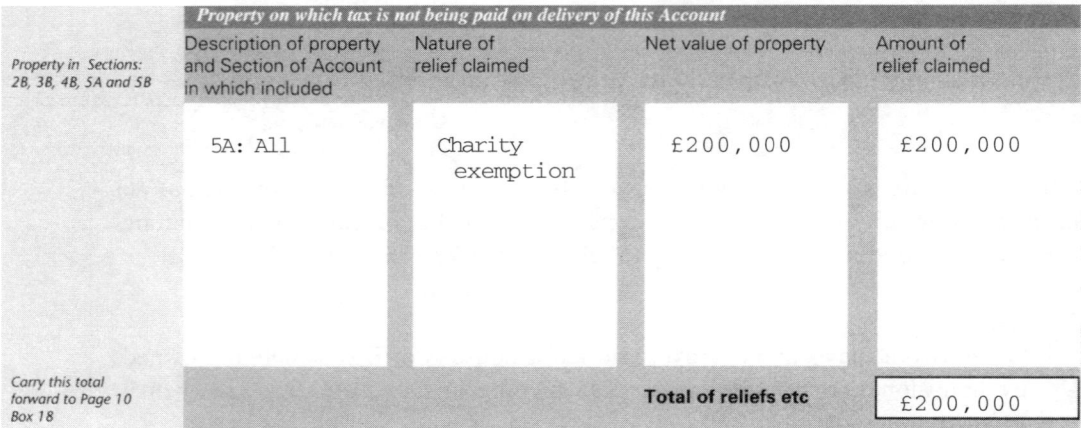

21.5.8 Section 7 – Liabilities within the Finance Act 1986, s 103

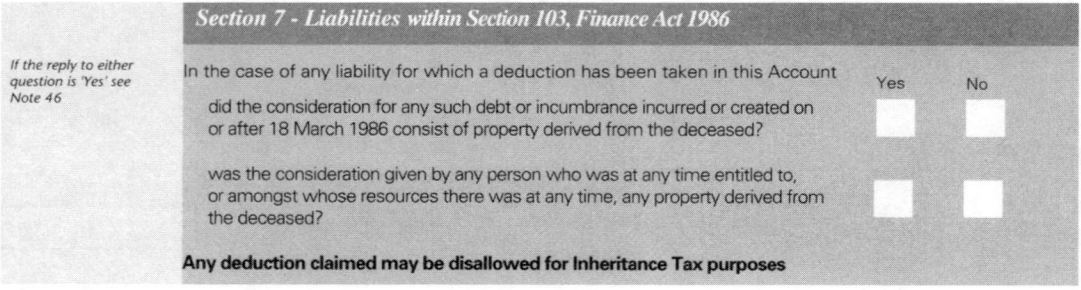

Section 103 of the Finance Act 1986 prevents the deduction of certain debts from the value of the estate. It applies to debts artificially created under tax avoidance schemes. This section requires the PRs to declare that the statutory provisions do not apply to the debts in this form. A 'yes' entry is rare and beyond the scope of this book.

21.5.9 Calculation of IHT

The purpose of pages 10 and 11 is to calculate the total IHT payable as a result of the death and, if appropriate, to apportion the tax between property without the instalment option and property with the instalment option, and between the PRs and others. The calculations of both tax and interest must show pence; a full illustration will be found in Appendix 3.

Step 1: Summary for determining the chargeable estate

Note 47

Calculation of Inheritance Tax

The tax calculated to be due is payable prior to lodging the application for the grant. The Account will be fully examined after the grant has been issued.

You may use the reliefs box to show against which property a particular exemption, exclusion or relief has been taken

Summary for determining the chargeable estate

Section 1	Total of chargeable transfers from Page 2	A
Part 1.	Property without the Instalment Option	

Bring forward the totals from Sections 2A, 3A, 4A, 5A and 6

Section	Net Total	Reliefs	Value after Reliefs
2A	1		
3A	2		
4A	3		
5A	4		
Sub-total	5	6	7

Part 2. Property with the Instalment Option

Bring forward the totals from Sections 2B, 3B, 4B, 5B and 6

Section	Net Total	Reliefs	Value after Reliefs
2B	8		
3B	9		
4B	10		
5B	11		
Sub-total	12	13	14

Part 3. Other Property on which tax is not being paid on this Account

Bring forward the totals from Sections 5A, 5B and 6

Section	Net Total	Reliefs	Value after Reliefs
5A	15		
5B	16		
Sub-total	17	18	19

	Box 5 + 12 + 17	Box 6 + 13 + 18	Box 7 + 14 + 19
Totals			B

Aggregate chargeable transfers A + B = C

The purpose of this part of page 10 is to calculate the total chargeable estate and the rate(s) of IHT.

The first entry is the total of chargeable transfers in section 1, followed by the totals taken from the other sections (except section 7). All figures are carried to this summary as per the instructions in the marginal notes.

Figures carried to the 'summary for determining the chargeable estate' go into the left-hand column. The totals from sections 2A, 3A, 4A and 5A (property on which tax is being paid now) are then added together. The totals from sections 2B, 3B, 4B and 5B (property on which tax is being paid now) are also added together.

These two totals are then added to the value of any property in sections 5A and 5B on which tax is not being paid on delivery of the account.

The middle column is headed 'reliefs' and the right-hand column also refers to reliefs. The term includes exemptions and exclusions. Any reliefs, exemptions and/or exclusions claimed on page 9 should be shown.

Working across the line, 'Net Total' minus 'Reliefs' equals 'Value [of property] after Reliefs', for example Sub-total '5' minus Sub-total '6' equals '7'.

All sub-totals in each vertical column must also be added together to give the 'Totals'.

The combined total of entries under the heading 'Value after Reliefs' is labelled 'B' on the form. This is the total chargeable estate. To establish the rate(s) of IHT applicable to the total chargeable estate, it is added to the cumulative total of all chargeable transfers made by deceased (ie Total 'A').

Step 2: Calculation of tax

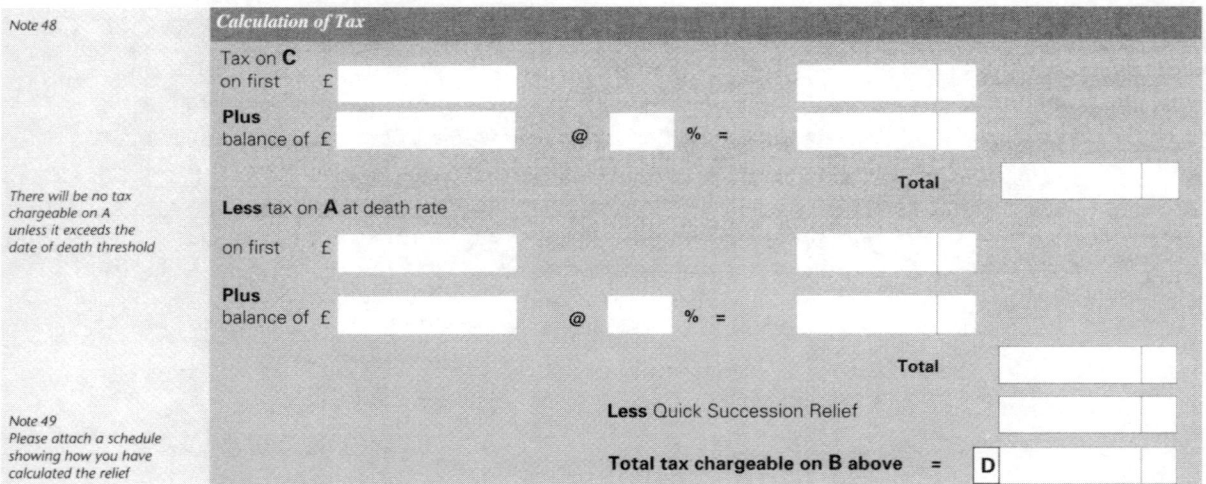

This part of page 10 is designed to provide the mechanics for the calculation of IHT payable on the total chargeable estate.

Example 1
Assume that the deceased had no cumulative total and that the total at 'B' and therefore also at 'C' is £215,000. The calculation would be:

Calculation of Tax

Note 48

Tax on **C**
on first £ 215,000
Plus balance of £ 6,000 @ 40 % = 2,400 00

Total 2,400 00

There will be no tax chargeable on A unless it exceeds the date of death threshold

Less tax on **A** at death rate
on first £

Plus balance of £ @ % =

Total

Less Quick Succession Relief

Note 49
Please attach a schedule showing how you have calculated the relief

Total tax chargeable on B above = **D** 2,400 00

If the deceased made any lifetime chargeable transfers (including PETs which have become chargeable as a result of his death), the calculation must show how much tax is now payable on those transfers (for a full discussion of cumulation see Chapter 18).

Example 2
The facts are as in the previous example but the deceased had made inter vivos transfers totalling £40,000.

		£
Total of chargeable transfers	A	40,000
Total value after reliefs	B	221,000
Aggregate chargeable transfers	C	261,000

Calculation of Tax

Note 48

Tax on **C**
on first £ 215,000
Plus balance of £ 46,000 @ 40 % = 18,400 00

Total 18,400 00

There will be no tax chargeable on A unless it exceeds the date of death threshold

Less tax on **A** at death rate
on first £ 40,000   NIL

Plus balance of £ @ % =

Total NIL

Less Quick Succession Relief

Note 49
Please attach a schedule showing how you have calculated the relief

Total tax chargeable on B above = **D** 18,400 00

Where quick succession relief is claimed, the amount of that relief should also be deducted.

Step 3: Apportionment of tax payable on this account

Apportionment of tax payable on this Account

Note 50 — Any capital figure multiplied by $\frac{D}{B}$ gives the proportion of tax assessable on the capital

From Box 7 opposite — **Property without the Instalment Option** £ ____ × $\frac{D}{B}$ = ____

Note 51
Please attach a schedule showing how you have calculated the relief

Less reliefs against tax other than Quick Succession Relief ____

Net tax **E** ____

Note 52
Tax becomes due 6 months after the end of the month during which the death occurred. Unpaid tax including tax being paid by instalments carries interest from and including the day after the due date irrespective of the reason for the late payment

Carry this total forward to Box F below

Add interest on net tax from 19__ to 19__ , ____ years ____ days @ ____ % = ____

Total tax and interest on property without the Instalment Option **F** ____

That part of Box 14 opposite on which tax is to be paid now either in full or by instalments

Property with the Instalment Option £ ____ × $\frac{D}{B}$ = ____

Less reliefs against tax other than Quick Succession Relief ____

Net tax **G** ____

Add interest on net tax from 19__ to 19__ , ____ years ____ days @ ____ % = ____

Note 33

Instalments ____ tenths of net tax **H** ____

Include the date the last instalment became due

Add interest on instalments now assessed from: 19__ to 19__ , ____ days @ ____ % = ____

If the due date for the second or subsequent instalment has now passed and interest relief is not appropriate, add here interest on the whole of the net tax on property with the Instalment Option up to the due date of the last instalment

Add interest on whole of net tax on instalment property from 19__ to 19__ , ____ years ____ days @ ____ % = ____

Carry this total forward to Box J below

Total tax and interest on property with the Instalment Option **J** ____

Having calculated the total IHT payable, it is necessary to determine how much of that tax is to be paid on delivery of the account. It should be recalled that:

(1) all IHT is due 6 months from the end of the month in which the death occurred; but

(2) IHT on non-instalment option property has to be paid on delivery if the account is delivered within that 6-month period; and

(3) the PRs can elect to pay some or all of the IHT on instalment option property on delivery of the account and must pay the first instalment and any other instalment which has fallen due if the account is delivered later than 6 months from the end of the month in which the death occurred.

Example

Robin died 3 months ago, leaving his estate to his son Peter. Robin's assets are cash and quoted shares valued at £100,000 net and a house valued at £200,000 net.

	£
Step 1 – Chargeable estate	
Property without the instalment option	100,000
Property with the instalment option	200,000
	B = 300,000
Step 2 – Calculation of tax	
On first £215,000 @ 0%	nil
On balance of £85,000 @ 40%	34,000
Total tax	D = 34,000

Step 3 – Apportionment

Property without option £100,000 × $\frac{D}{B}$ ie $\frac{£34,000}{£300,000}$

$$E \text{ and } F = £11,333$$

There is no need to calculate the tax payable on the house as it is not yet due. If the PRs had decided to pay the tax on the house on delivery of the account, the next part of the 'Apportionment' section would be completed as follows:

Property with the instalment option £200,000 × $\frac{D}{B}$ ie $\frac{£34,000}{£300,000}$ = £22,667

$$G = £22,667$$

If the first instalment was due, this would also be calculated:

Instalment ¹⁄₁₀ of net tax   H = £2,267

The reference to 'reliefs against tax other than Quick Succession Relief' is to double taxation relief and is beyond the scope of this book. Reliefs and exemptions such as business property relief and the spouse exemption have already been claimed on page 9 and in Step 1 above, and must not be claimed again.

Although the account only has to be delivered within 12 months from the end of the month in which the death occurred, interest is payable on tax outstanding 6 months from the end of the month of death. Where the account is delivered later than the 6 months, interest calculated on a daily basis must be paid in addition to the tax payable on delivery.

The amount of tax and interest (if any) now payable is carried to the Tax Summary on page 11.

Tax Summary

For official use only

EDP

Financial Services Office

Total tax and interest - Property without the Instalment Option   F

Total tax and interest - Property with the Instalment Option   J

Total tax and interest payable now on this Account   K

Signature of Solicitor(s) or agent(s) for the applicant(s)   Date

If tax is payable, send the Account for receipting to Inland Revenue Financial Services Office **by post** at Barrington Road Worthing West Sussex BN12 4XH or by DX 90950 Worthing 3 or take it **by hand** to Room G21 West Wing Somerset House Strand London WC2

The Tax Summary ends with instructions on what to do if IHT is payable. The account, together with a cheque, for the amount shown at 'Total ... K', should be sent or taken to the Financial Services Office (IHT Cashiers) at the address shown on the form.

21.5.10 Probate summary

Aggregate Gross Value which in law devolves on and vests in the personal representatives of the deceased, for and in respect of which the grant is to be made.	Section 3A	L
	Section 3B	M
	Section 5	N
Total to be carried to the Probate papers		P
Deduct Section 3A, total of liabilities and funeral expenses		Q
Section 3B, total of liabilities		R
Net estate for Probate purposes		S

Only include at N general power property

This summary sets out the gross and net values of the property vesting in the PRs as a result of the death. The two figures at P (gross) and S (net) are also inserted on the oath which will accompany the application for the grant.

21.5.11 Declaration

Page 12 contains the PRs' declaration as to the accuracy of the details recorded in the account (see **21.3.9**).

21.6 ACTION FOLLOWING COMPLETION OF ACCOUNT

If IHT is payable, Form IHT 200 and a cheque for the appropriate amount of tax are sent (or taken) to the Financial Services Office, which is a branch of the Inland Revenue (address shown on page 11 of the account). The Financial Services Office will carry out preliminary checks on the account and, if all appears satisfactory, the office will receipt page 11 and return the whole account, which then accompanies the other papers sent to the probate registry on an application for a grant of representation.

After the grant has been issued, the Capital Taxes Office (CTO), another branch of the Inland Revenue, will carry out a detailed examination of the account. This may lead to queries being raised with the PRs or corrections being made.

There is no need to send the account to the CTO before it goes to the probate registry unless advice is required in calculating the IHT due or it falls within a 'special case' (eg IHT is to be paid from a National Savings Bank deposit account, the proceeds of National Savings Certificates or any other National Savings investment: see **21.1.3**). Other special cases are set out in the explanatory notes in booklet IHT 210 but are beyond the scope of this book.

It is advisable to keep a copy of the completed account on file and, in particular, a note of the date on which it was signed. This information is required by the CTO before they will issue a clearance certificate at the end of the administration (see **29.4**).

Chapter 22

OATHS: THE BACKGROUND LAW

22.1 INTRODUCTION

Every application for a grant of representation must be supported by the appropriate form of oath. This chapter considers the purpose of oaths, the selection of the persons entitled to act as PRs and the correct form of oath that those PRs should complete. It also considers what happens if a proving PR dies without completing the administration, if the person entitled to the grant refuses to act and to what extent objections can be raised against the appointment of a person as PR. Chapter 23 provides a detailed analysis of how to complete each of the three types of oath most commonly needed in practice.

Chapter 22 contents
Introduction
Oath for executors
Oath for administrators with will annexed
Oath for administrators
Effect of grant
Limited grants
The chain of representation and grant de bonis non administratis
Caveats and citations

22.1.1 Types of oath

The three most common types of oath are as follows:

(1) oath for executors (see **22.2**);
(2) oath for administrators with will annexed (see **22.3**);
(3) oath for administrators (see **22.4**).

22.1.2 Purpose of oath

The oaths differ from each other in detail but they have a common purpose, namely:

(1) to give details of the deceased;
(2) to set out the basis of the applicant's claim to take the grant;
(3) to require the applicant to swear that he will administer the estate correctly;
(4) in the case of oaths for executors and oaths for administrators with the will annexed, to identify and exhibit the will and any codicils.

Unless the appropriate oath is accurately completed and submitted to the probate registry by, or on behalf of, those PRs who may properly make an application, no grant of representation will be issued.

22.1.3 Swearing or affirming the oath

Before the oath is submitted to the probate registry, the PRs must swear or affirm the truth of its contents. This must be done before a commissioner for oaths or a solicitor holding a current practising certificate, neither of whom is connected with the firm of solicitors acting for the PRs. PRs who prefer to affirm say: 'I do solemnly sincerely and truly declare and affirm that . . .'. A PR who swears the oath will be required to hold the New Testament or Bible while saying: 'I swear by Almighty God that . . .'.

Once the oath has been sworn or affirmed it should be sent to the probate registry with any will, Inland Revenue account and the appropriate probate court fees.

22.2 OATH FOR EXECUTORS

22.2.1 Entitlement to act

The oath for executors will lead to a grant of probate. The executors are entitled to a grant of probate where they have been appointed by a valid will (see Chapter 6). One executor may obtain a grant and act alone.

> *Example 1*
> Alex by his will appoints Brian and Colin to be his executors and leaves his entire estate to a named charity.
>
> Brian and/or Colin can apply for a grant of probate by lodging an oath for executors, and the will, with the probate registry.
>
> The appointment is not affected by the fact that the will may fail to dispose of some or all of the deceased's estate.
>
> *Example 2*
> Diana has just died. Her will appoints Eric as her executor and leaves her entire estate to Freda. Freda died before Diana whose estate will therefore be distributed according to the intestacy rules. Eric is alive and prepared to act as executor. Eric will apply for a grant of probate by swearing an oath for executors.

22.2.2 Capacity to act

Capacity to act as executor is judged at the time of the application for the grant.

Mental incapacity

A person appointed as an executor by the will but who, at the testator's death, is suffering from mental incapacity may not act as executor or apply for the grant.

Minors

There is no prohibition on a testator naming a minor as his executor. However, if the executor is still a minor at the testator's death he cannot act as an executor nor obtain a grant of probate until he attains majority.

Where one of several executors is a minor, the other(s) being adult, probate can be granted to the adult executor(s) with power reserved to the minor. (For an explanation of 'power reserved' see **22.2.4**.) If the administration of the estate has not been completed by the time the minor attains the age of 18, he can then apply for a grant of double probate to enable him to act as executor alongside the other proving executor(s).

Example
George dies appointing his wife Ingrid and his son Harry (aged 16) as his executors.

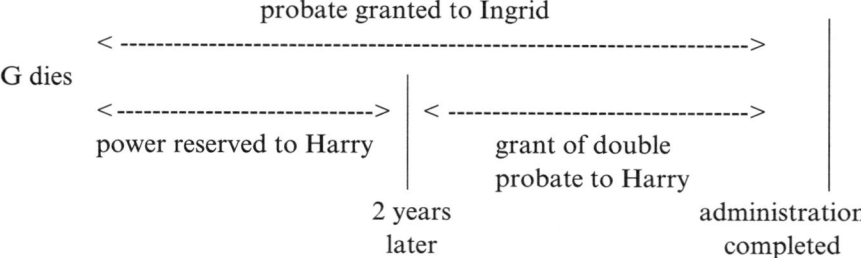

Where the minor is the only executor appointed by the will (or the adult executors are not able or willing to act), the testator's estate cannot be left unadministered until the executor reaches the age of 18. A grant of letters of administration with will annexed for the use and benefit of the minor will be made, usually to the parent(s) or guardian(s) of the minor, until the minor attains 18 years. On obtaining his majority the executor may apply for a cessate grant of probate (see **22.6.4**).

The former spouse

If the testator appointed his spouse as his executor and the marriage subsequently ended in divorce, that appointment will fail unless the testator has shown a contrary intention in the will (Wills Act 1837, s 18A: see **15.5**).

If the spouse was one of several executors, the others may apply for the grant of probate without her. If she was the sole executrix, application should be made for a grant of letters of administration with will annexed (see **22.3**). In either case, the oath to lead to the appropriate grant should cite the fact and date of the divorce.

22.2.3 Renunciation

Any person appointed as an executor may renounce his right to take the grant provided that he has not intermeddled in the estate. A person has intermeddled when he has done tasks a PR might do, for example notifying the deceased's bank of the death. Acts of common humanity, such as arranging the funeral, do not amount to intermeddling. Once an executor has intermeddled, he must take the grant.

Provided there has been no intermeddling, the executor who does not wish to act can renounce his right. His rights as executor then cease and the administration of the estate proceeds as if he had never been appointed.

The renunciation must be made in writing, signed by the person renouncing and that signature must be witnessed.

The renunciation must be filed at the probate registry. This is normally done by the PRs who are applying for a grant when they lodge their application at the probate registry. On an application for a grant of probate by the other executors, they do not have to refer specifically to the renunciation in their oath.

22.2.4 Power reserved

Whilst there is no limit on how many executors can be appointed by the will, probate will only be granted to a maximum of four executors. Power may be reserved to the other(s) to take out a grant in the future if a vacancy arises.

Example 1

Alan's will appoints B, C, D, E and F to be his executors. All are willing and able to act. Probate is granted to C, D, E and F. 'Power is reserved' to B. If F dies before the administration is complete, B can then apply for a grant. It is not automatic.

If there is a dispute between the executors as to which of them should apply for a grant, this may be resolved by summons before a registrar (NCPR, r 27(6)).

There is no need for every executor to act. A person appointed as one of several executors may not wish to act initially, but he may not want to take the irrevocable step of renouncing his right to a grant of probate.

Example 2

Alan appoints Ben and Charles as his executors. When Alan dies, Ben is working in Germany, but is due to return to England in 12 months. Ben does not feel that he should act as executor while he is abroad and is happy to leave everything to Charles, but he does want to help in the administration if it has not been completed by the time he returns to England.

Charles should apply for the grant 'with power reserved to Ben'.

22.3 OATH FOR ADMINISTRATORS WITH WILL ANNEXED

22.3.1 Entitlement to act

As the title of this oath suggests, it is used in an estate where there is a valid will but no executor willing and able to apply for a grant of probate.

There may be no executor because:

(1) the will fails to appoint executors;
(2) the appointment was of the testator's spouse and has failed as a result of the testator's divorce (Wills Act 1837, s 18A: see **22.2.2**);
(3) the executor has predeceased the testator;
(4) the executor has died after the testator but before taking the grant; or
(5) the executor has renounced.

22.3.2 NCPR, r 20

The order of priority of the person(s) entitled to a grant of letters of administration with will annexed is governed by NCPR, r 20. The rule states as follows:

'Where the deceased died on or after 1 January 1926 the person or persons entitled to a grant in respect of a will shall be determined in accordance with the following order of priority, namely –

(a) the executor . . . ;
(b) any residuary legatee or devisee holding in trust for any other person;
(c) any other residuary legatee or devisee (including one for life) or where the residue is not wholly disposed of by the will, any person entitled to share in the undisposed of residue (including the Treasury Solicitor when claiming bona vacantia on behalf of the Crown), provided that –
   (i) unless a registrar otherwise directs, a residuary legatee or devisee whose legacy or devise is vested in interest shall be preferred to one entitled on the happening of a contingency, and
   (ii) where the residue is not in terms wholly disposed of, the registrar may, if he is satisfied that the testator has nevertheless disposed of the whole or

substantially the whole of the known estate, allow a grant to be made to any legatee or devisee entitled to, or to share in, the estate so disposed of, without regard to the persons entitled to share in any residue not disposed of by the will;
- (d) the personal representative of any residuary legatee or devisee (but not one for life, or one holding in trust for any other person), or of any person entitled to share in any residue not disposed of by the will;
- (e) any other legatee or devisee (including one for life or one holding in trust for any other person) or any creditor of the deceased, provided that, unless a registrar otherwise directs, a legatee or devisee whose legacy or devise is vested in interest shall be preferred to one entitled on the happening of a contingency;
- (f) the personal representative of any other legatee or devisee (but not one for life or one holding in trust for any other person) or of any creditor of the deceased.'

Each applicant is listed in priority. When applying for the grant, any person falling in category (b) or below must explain on the oath why there is no applicant from a higher ranked category. This is called 'clearing off'. A person in a lower ranked category may only apply if there is nobody in a higher category willing and able to take the grant.

The categories will now be considered in detail with examples of clearing off.

'(a) the executor . . .'

NCPR, r 20 in fact provides the 'order of priority for grant where deceased left a will'. This covers both grants of probate and letters of administration with the will annexed. If an executor has been appointed in the will and is able and willing to act then he has first right to a grant (and will apply for probate).

The remaining categories assume that, for whatever reason, no executor is available: see **22.3.1**.

'(b) any residuary legatee or devisee holding in trust . . .'

Example
Arthur has died leaving a will. Although he failed to appoint executors, he left his residue to Brian and Claire on trust for Debbie. Brian and Claire are the residuary legatees (or devisees, depending on the type of trust property) and so they have first right to a grant. Clearly, Arthur was happy for them to deal with his property otherwise he would not have appointed them as trustees. They will have to state that 'no executor was appointed in the will'.

'(c) any other residuary legatee or devisee . . .'

Example 1
Amanda has died leaving a will appointing Boris as her executor and giving the residuary estate to Carol, ie Carol is the residuary legatee and devisee.

Carol can apply for a grant only if Boris is unable or unwilling to act. She must 'clear off' Boris by saying, 'the executor named in the will has [renounced probate] [predeceased the deceased]' or as the case may be.

Note that strictly it is also necessary to clear off trustees of residue (ie 'any residuary legatee or devisee holding on trust for any other person'). However, unless such trustees were specifically appointed in the will this is often not done. Such practice is acceptable to the probate registrars.

Example 2
The facts are the same as in Example 1, but Boris was appointed 'executor and trustee' and the residue was given to Carol for life.

Carol must clear off Boris in both capacities by saying, 'the executor and trustee named in the will has [renounced probate] etc . . .'.

'. . . or . . . any person entitled to share in the undisposed of residue'

If a partial intestacy arises because the will fails to dispose of all or part of the residuary estate, those people entitled to the residue by virtue of the intestacy rules (see Chapter 16) may apply for a grant under NCPR, r 20, but they must show why they are entitled to the grant and clear off all persons in higher ranked categories.

Example
Damien's will appoints Errol to be his sole executor and residuary beneficiary. Errol died last month and Damien has just died. Damien's closest living relative is his mother, Florence.

As the sole residuary beneficiary has predeceased the deceased (and the gift is not saved by any substitutional gift), the residue is undisposed of and will be distributed according to the intestacy rules: see Chapter 16. Damien has left no spouse, nor issue but is survived by his mother, Florence, who is next entitled to the property.

Florence will apply for a grant of letters of administration with will annexed by clearing off the executor. She must also establish her entitlement to the undisposed of property and, therefore, to the grant. She will say 'the executor and residuary legatee and devisee has predeceased the deceased [and the deceased died a bachelor without issue] . . .'

(d) the PR of a deceased residuary legatee or devisee . . .

Where there is no proving executor and, for example, the residuary beneficiary survives the testator to take a vested interest in the estate, but then dies without having taken the grant, that beneficiary's PR may apply for the grant. This is because the gift under the will forms part of the beneficiary's estate and needs to be collected by his PR.

Example
Gloria died last week leaving a will appointing Honor as executrix and giving the residuary estate to Ian absolutely. Honor has predeceased Gloria and Ian died yesterday. Ian's will appoints Janice as his sole executrix and beneficiary.

Janice may apply for a grant of letters of administration with annexed to Gloria's estate. To do so the oath must clear off Honor and Ian by saying, 'the sole executrix predeceased the deceased and the sole residuary legatee and devisee named in the said will survived the deceased and has since died without having proved the said will'.

'(e) any other legatee or devisee . . . or any creditor of the deceased . . .'

This category covers any other beneficiary under the will, for example, a specific devisee who has been left the deceased's house or a general legatee who has been left £5,000 by the deceased. It also covers creditors of the deceased.

(f) the PR of any other legatee or devisee . . . or of any creditor . . .
This category works on the same principles as category (d) above.

Beneficiary with vested interest preferred
Where there is more than one person of equal rank but one has a vested and one a contingent interest in the estate, the court generally prefers an application by the beneficiary with the vested interest.

> *Example*
>
> Keri's will leaves her residuary estate to her two children, Lisa and Matthew, contingent on their attaining 25 years of age. There is no executor appointed in the will. At Keri's death Lisa is 30 years old and Matthew 23 years old.
>
> Lisa and Matthew can make a joint application, but if they were to apply separately the court would prefer Lisa because Matthew's interest is still contingent.

22.3.3 Minors

A minor cannot act as administrator with will annexed nor can he apply for a grant. His parent(s) or guardian(s) may apply for a grant 'for his use and benefit' on his behalf. The grant is limited until he attains the age of 18 (see **22.6.4**).

If there is a person not under a disability who is entitled in the same degree as the minor then that person will be preferred to the guardian of the minor (NCPR, r 27(5)).

22.3.4 The number of administrators

Maximum number
If there are several people entitled to act as administrators the grant will not issue to more than four of them (Supreme Court Act 1981, s 114). It is not possible for an administrator to have power reserved to him.

If a person is entitled to act as administrator but does not obtain a grant (eg because there are four other applicants), this does not affect that person's beneficial entitlement to the estate.

Number in the same category
Subject to the provisions of s 114 of the Supreme Court Act 1981 (see below), where two or more people are entitled in the same degree, a grant can be made on the application of any one of them without notice to the other or others (NCPR, r 27(4)).

> *Example*
>
> Jane dies leaving her residuary estate by will to her two adult brothers Ken and Larry. Jane's will does not appoint an executor. Larry does not wish to act.
>
> Ken can apply for a grant alone. This does not affect Larry's beneficial entitlement to half the estate.

Need for two administrators
If there is a valid will but no executor and the will does not dispose of all the estate, the appropriate grant is still letters of administration with will annexed. The

property undisposed of by the will is distributed according to the intestacy rules (see Chapter 16).

Where the will or intestacy rules create a life interest or pass property to an infant (whether the interest is vested or contingent), the court normally requires a minimum of two administrators to apply for the grant (Supreme Court Act 1981, s 114). The court may dispense with this and allow a single administrator in special limited circumstances.

Example 1
Max has just died leaving a valid will which:

(1) appoints Nora his executor;
(2) gives £1,000 to Olive (aged 6);
(3) gives the residue of his estate to Peter and Paul.

Nora renounces probate.

Both Peter and Paul must apply for the grant because there is a minority interest, ie the legacy to Olive.

Example 2
Quentin's will fails to appoint an executor. He leaves his estate to his wife Rose for life with remainder to his adult son Sam.

Both Rose and Sam must apply for the grant because of Rose's life interest.

Example 3
Tim's will leaves his residuary estate to his friend Una, whom he has also appointed executrix. Una has predeceased Tim. Tim is divorced and has three children: Victor (21), Wendy (19) and Zena (15).

Tim, therefore, dies partially intestate. By virtue of the intestacy rules his children take the residuary estate on the statutory trusts.

Victor and Wendy must both apply for the grant because part of the estate goes to Zena who is a minor.

22.3.5 Renunciation

Any person entitled to apply for a grant of letters of administration with will annexed can renounce in the same way as an executor, except that an administrator does not lose the right to renounce by intermeddling (see **22.2.3**). Renunciation does not affect his beneficial entitlement.

22.4 OATH FOR ADMINISTRATORS

22.4.1 Entitlement to act

This oath is required if the deceased has died totally intestate.

The person or persons entitled to the grant are listed in NCPR, r 22 as follows:

'(1) Where the deceased died on or after 1 January 1926, wholly intestate, the person or persons having a beneficial interest in the estate shall be entitled to a grant of administration in the following classes in order of priority, namely –

(a) the surviving husband or wife;
(b) the children of the deceased and the issue of any deceased child who died before the deceased;
(c) the father and mother of the deceased;
(d) brothers and sisters of the whole blood and the issue of any deceased brother or sister of the whole blood who died before the deceased;
(e) brothers and sisters of the half blood and the issue of any deceased brother or sister of the half blood who died before the deceased;
(f) grandparents;
(g) uncles and aunts of the whole blood and the issue of any deceased uncle or aunt of the whole blood who died before the deceased;
(h) uncles and aunts of the half blood and the issue of any deceased uncle or aunt of the half blood who died before the deceased.

(2) In default of any person having a beneficial interest in the estate, the Treasury Solicitor shall be entitled to a grant if he claims bona vacantia on behalf of the Crown.

(3) If all persons entitled to a grant under the foregoing provisions of this rule have been cleared off, a grant may be made to a creditor of the deceased or to any person who, notwithstanding that he has no immediate beneficial interest in the estate, may have a beneficial interest in the event of an accretion thereto.'

Some of the descriptions of relations may require further explanation as follows.

'children'

On an intestacy no distinction is drawn between those who have been born legitimate, those who have been adopted and those whose parents were not married.

The one exception is where a child whose parents were not married dies intestate. In such circumstances it is presumed that his natural father and all relatives of his natural father predeceased him (Family Law Reform Act 1987, s 18(2)). This presumption can be rebutted (eg where both parents are living together or the father maintains contact with his child).

Equally entitled with the deceased's children are the children or grandchildren of any child who predeceased the deceased.

'brothers and sisters'

Brothers and sisters of the deceased are also known as 'siblings'. A sibling is of the 'whole blood' where they share both parents in common with the deceased, and of the 'half blood' where they have only one common parent.

Example

Susan has been married twice. By Tom she had two children, Una and Victoria, and by Tony she had a daughter, Wendy.

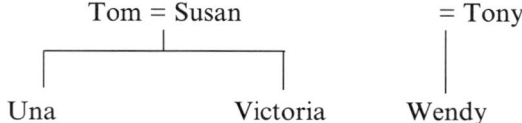

Una and Victoria are sisters of the whole blood.

Wendy is their sister of the half blood.

'uncles and aunts'

Uncles and aunts of 'the whole blood' are the children of both grandparents of the intestate. Aunts and uncles of the 'half blood' are the children of only one of the deceased's grandparents.

Example

David has died recently and his closest living relations are his uncles, Ben and Charles. Ben and David's mother, Ann, were children of the same parents; Charles was the son of David's grandfather, Fred, and Fred's mistress, Joan.

```
        Martha (d) = Fred (d) ---------- Joan (d)
                    |                      |
            ┌───────┴───────┐              |
          Ann (d)          Ben          Charles
            |
          David
```

Ben is David's uncle of the whole blood.

Charles is David's uncle of the half blood.

22.4.2 Clearing off

Each category is listed in priority in NCPR, r 22. Like the applicant under NCPR, r 20 (**22.3.2**), an applicant under r 22 must explain on the oath why nobody in a higher category is able to apply for the grant (again this is called 'clearing off'). Examples of clearing off are given in **23.4**.

22.4.3 The need for a beneficial interest in the estate

Unless the applicant is the Treasury Solicitor or a creditor, he must have a beneficial interest in the estate (or would have such an interest if there was an accretion to the estate) by virtue of the intestacy rules (see Chapter 16); hence there is a similarity between NCPR, r 22 and AEA 1925, s 46 (see **16.2.2**).

Example 1

Clara dies intestate survived by her mother and one brother.

Only the mother can apply for the grant because she is solely and absolutely entitled to Clara's estate under the intestacy rules.

Example 2

David dies intestate survived by his wife Eve and father Fred. David's estate is valued at £300,000.

As Eve and Fred share the estate by virtue of the intestacy rules, Fred can apply for the grant if Eve does not, although Eve ranks in priority and must be cleared off if Fred applies for the grant.

Example 3

The facts are the same as in Example 2 but David's estate is worth £90,000. Prima facie, Fred would seem to have no interest and would therefore be unable to apply for a grant if Eve failed to do so. But Fred can apply in these circumstances on the basis that if additional assets were found in David's estate Fred would then share the estate with Eve. It is irrelevant that David's estate never actually increases above £90,000. Again, Eve ranks in priority.

22.4.4 Minors

A minor cannot act as administrator nor can he apply for a grant. The same rule as that discussed in **22.3.3** above should be applied.

22.4.5 Renunciation

A person entitled to a grant under NCPR, r 22 can renounce his right to the grant in the same way as an administrator with the will annexed. If he is the only relative of the deceased with a beneficial entitlement, the grant will be made to a creditor of the deceased. Renunciation does not affect the beneficial entitlement.

> *Example*
> Graeme dies intestate survived by one brother, Henry, and an uncle, Jack. Graeme owes Kirsty £100.
>
> Henry has priority over Jack under r 22. As Jack has no beneficial interest in the estate under the intestacy rules he cannot apply for the grant if Henry fails to do so. In that event, Kirsty should apply for the grant of letters of administration.

It is common for a creditor to take the grant if the estate is insolvent.

22.4.6 The number of administrators

Reference should be made to **22.3.4** above as the rules applying to the number of administrators with will annexed apply equally to administrators of a totally intestate estate.

Maximum number
The grant will issue to a maximum of four administrators. If there are more than four people with an equal entitlement, it is not possible to have 'power reserved' to a non-proving administrator.

Number in the same category
Where two or more people are entitled in the same degree, a grant can be made on the application of any one of them without notice to the other(s).

Need for two administrators
A minimum of two administrators is generally required where the intestacy creates a life interest in favour of the surviving spouse and/or minority interests through property being held for minors on the 'statutory trusts'. The court may dispense with the need for two administrators in special circumstances.

> *Example 1*
> Grace dies intestate with an estate with a net value for probate purposes of £250,000. She is survived by her husband, Henry, and her adult daughter, Ingrid.
>
> The grant must be taken by Henry and Ingrid because the intestacy rules give Henry a life interest in part of the estate.
>
> *Example 2*
> John dies intestate with a net estate for probate purposes of £300,000 and is survived by his wife, Karen, and children, Laura (20) and Mike (16).
>
> Karen and Laura must take the grant. Two administrators are needed because the intestacy creates a life interest and a minority interest. Mike cannot be an administrator because he is a minor.

Example 3
Nigel dies intestate, a bachelor without issue. Both his parents are dead.

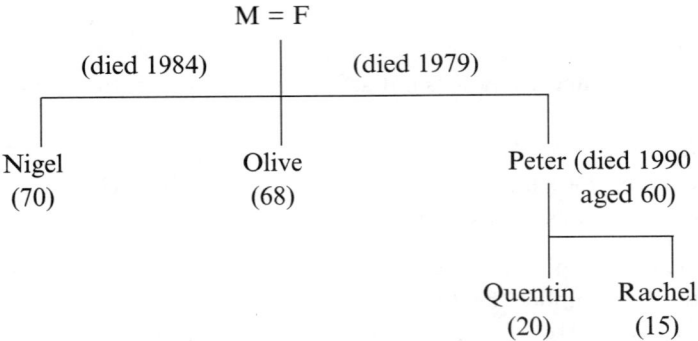

His sister and the issue of his deceased brother are equally entitled to apply for the grant as they share the estate under the intestacy rules. Both Olive and Quentin must apply because Rachel is a minor.

22.5 EFFECT OF GRANT

The three most common grants of representation are as follows:

(1) grant of probate (obtained by submitting oath for executors);
(2) grant of letters of administration with the will annexed (obtained by submitting oath for administrators with will annexed);
(3) grant of letters of administration (obtained by submitting oath for administrators).

22.5.1 Grant of probate

A grant of probate confirms the authority of the executor(s) which stems from the will and arises from the time of the testate's death (see **20.2.2**).

The grant provides conclusive evidence of the title of the executor(s) and of the validity and contents of the will.

22.5.2 Grant of administration (with or without will)

A grant of administration (with or without will annexed) confers authority on the administrator and vests the deceased's property in the administrator. Until the grant is issued, the administrator has no authority to act (see **20.2.2**) and the deceased's property is vested in the President of the Family Division.

The grant provides conclusive evidence of the administrator's title and of the validity and contents of any will (or intestacy). Normally the grant is not retrospective to the date of the deceased's death.

22.6 LIMITED GRANTS

22.6.1 Introduction

A grant of representation is normally general, ie it is expressed to relate to 'all the estate which by law devolves to and vests in the PRs of the deceased'.

When necessary a grant may be limited; for example, it may be:

(1) limited as to a specified part of the deceased's property;
(2) limited to settled land (any settled land vested in the deceased is usually excepted from a general grant if the land remains settled after his death);
(3) limited to a special purpose, for example for the use and benefit of a minor.

22.6.2 Grant limited to property

In **6.4** it was noted that a testator might wish to limit the appointment of executors to certain property only. For example, a novelist might appoint literary executors to administer his literary estate; general executors would be responsible for his general estate.

In the above example, when the novelist dies, his literary executors may apply for a grant of probate limited to his literary works; in such a case the other executors will apply for a grant of probate 'save and except' the literary works. The oath forms must be adapted to meet the needs of any such case.

22.6.3 Grant limited to settled land

Example

A settlement of land was created under the SLA 1925 for Caitlin for life, then to Derek for life, remainder to Ernest. Caitlin has just died. The settlement continues after her death and the settled land devolves on the settlement trustees (Tom and Tony). Caitlin left a will appointing Frank as the executor of her estate.

Frank will apply for a grant of probate 'save and except' the settled land. (See the effect of this on the oath for executors in **23.2** at **I**.)

Tom and Tony will submit an oath of special executors for probate limited to settled land. The oath is similar to the usual oath for executors (**23.2**), but reference is made to the grant to Frank save and except the settled land, and to the settlement itself. Tom and Tony will be granted probate limited to settled land.

If the general executor(s) and the trustees of the settlement are the same persons then separate grants are not necessary (see **23.2** at **I**).

22.6.4 Grant for the use of a minor

A minor cannot take out a grant of representation (see **22.2.2**, **22.3.3** and **22.4.4**).

If the person entitled to apply for a grant is a minor, then application should be made by his parent(s) or guardian(s) for a grant for his use and benefit. The practice in making such grants is governed by NCPR, r 2.

The parent(s)/guardian(s) will submit an oath for administrators (with or without the will as appropriate) for the use of the minor. The facts surrounding the application must be recited on the oath form, but in other respects the oath will follow the usual format.

The grant confers on the parent(s)/guardian(s) authority to act until the child attains 18 and usually expires automatically on his eighteenth birthday. The minor is entitled to apply for a 'cessate grant' of probate or administration (with or without the will) depending on the circumstances. The cessate grant enables the applicant to complete administration of the estate.

Note there is a different rule where the minor is one of several executors and the other(s) are able and willing to act (see **22.2.2**).

22.7 THE CHAIN OF REPRESENTATION AND GRANT DE BONIS NON ADMINISTRATIS

22.7.1 Introduction

If there are several proving PRs administering an estate and one dies after taking the grant but before the administration has been completed, the surviving PRs continue to act. The continuing PRs' powers remain unaffected. Where the death leaves a sole surviving PR, the court may exercise its powers to appoint an additional PR. This might happen, for example, where there is a life or minority interest and the court prefers a minimum of two PRs (Supreme Court Act 1981, s 114).

If a person entitled to be a PR (either as the executor under a will or by virtue of NCPR, r 20 or r 22) survives the deceased but then dies himself without taking out a grant of representation, AEA 1925, s 5 provides that his rights concerning the grant die with him (unless it is an exceptional case where his PR may apply for a grant under NCPR, r 20: see **22.3.2**).

> *Example 1*
> David dies appointing Elizabeth as his executrix and leaving his estate to Richard. Elizabeth dies a few days after David and without having proved his will. Richard should apply for a grant of letters of administration with will annexed to David's estate.

The position is more complicated on the death of a sole or sole surviving PR if the administration is incomplete.

> *Example 2*
> Anthony died 6 months ago appointing Edward as his sole executor.
>
> Edward obtained a grant of probate to Anthony's estate and had begun to deal with the assets when he died. The house is on the market but unsold and the final IHT assessment cannot be agreed because tax is being paid on the house by instalments. The administration is therefore incomplete. What happens?

22.7.2 Chain of representation

The office of executor is personal to the executor appointed by the testator in his will. Because it is an office of personal trust, an executor cannot assign that office, although he can appoint an attorney (see **25.5.2**). However, AEA 1925, s 7 provides for the automatic transmission of that office on the death of a proving executor: 'an executor of a sole or last surviving executor of a testator is the executor of that testator'.

Unbroken chain
The chain of representation is applicable only where there is an unbroken sequence of proving executors.

Example

Colin died leaving a will appointing Diane as his executrix.

Diane proved the will and obtained a grant of probate.

Diane died before she had completed the administration of Colin's estate.

Diane's will appointed Eric to be her executor. If Eric applies for probate of Diane's will, he automatically becomes executor of Colin's estate.

It is not possible to accept the office of executor to Diane's estate and refuse to be executor by representation of Colin's estate.

AEA 1925, s 7

Section 7 provides that an executor by representation:

(1) has the same rights in respect of the testator's estate as if he was the original executor; and
(2) is, to the extent to which the testator's estate has come into his hands, answerable as if he was the original executor.

Broken chain

If for any reason there are not successive executors the chain of representation will be broken.

Example 1

Fiona appointed Graham to be her executor. Graham obtained probate to Fiona's estate. Graham then died intestate. Graham's PR under NCPR, r 22 is Ian, who obtains a grant of letters of administration to Graham's estate. Ian will not become the executor of Fiona's estate.

Example 2

John died intestate and Kelly obtained a grant of letters of administration to his estate. Kelly died leaving a will appointing Louise to be her executrix. Louise proved Kelly's will and obtained probate. Louise does not become the executrix of John's estate.

22.7.3 Grant de bonis non administratis

In situations where the chain of representation cannot apply because there are not successive proving executors, a grant de bonis non administratis must be obtained to the original estate (usually known as a 'grant de bonis non'). The grant de bonis non may be one of administration with the will or one of simple administration, depending on the circumstances (see the examples below).

It is issued in estates where the sole, or sole surviving, PR has died after obtaining the grant but without having completed the administration and it relates only to the unadministered part of the estate. Two requirements apply:

(1) there must have been a prior grant of probate or letters of administration to a PR who has now died; and
(2) the chain of representation must not apply.

The grant de bonis non will issue to the person who would have been entitled had the original PR never taken the grant. The order of priority will depend on NCPR, r 20 or r 22 as appropriate.

Example 1
Martin dies leaving a will appointing Nigel as his executor and leaving the residuary estate to Oliver.

If Nigel had predeceased Martin or renounced probate, Oliver would have been entitled to a grant of letters of administration with will annexed under r 20 (see **22.3.2**).

If Nigel proved Martin's will and then died, the grant of letters of administration with will annexed de bonis non would issue to Oliver.

Example 2
Paul died intestate survived by his two adult sisters, Rachel and Susan. Rachel obtained a grant of letters of administration, but died before completing the administration.

Both Rachel and Susan were entitled to apply for that grant under r 22 (see **22.4.1**) and so Susan should now apply for a grant of letters of administration de bonis non to Paul's estate.

22.8 CAVEATS AND CITATIONS

Caveats and citations are available under NCPR to assist in the event of a dispute over the right to take out a grant of representation to an estate. They are designed to resolve disputes without the expense and delay of contentious proceedings.

22.8.1 Caveats (NCPR, r 44)

The effect of a caveat is to prevent the issue of a grant of representation. The person lodging or entering a caveat is called a 'caveator'. A caveat might be used, for example, where a beneficiary believes the executor named in the will lacks the mental capacity to act or where the validity of the will is questioned.

Example 1
The will appoints Eric as executor, gives a legacy to Ann and the residue to Ben.

Eric wants to act as executor but Ann challenges his capability. Ann should enter a caveat before a grant of representation is issued so that the court can decide who should act as PR.

Example 2
On Dan's death, a homemade will is found appointing Edward as executor and sole beneficiary. Freda would be entitled to Dan's estate under the intestacy rules and Freda believes the will is invalid. She should enter a caveat to prevent any grant of representation issuing until the court has decided the validity or otherwise of the will.

A caveat is entered by completing and sending a standard form, together with a small fee, to any probate registry. The probate registry acknowledges receipt by issuing a formal receipt.

Once issued the caveat is effective for 6 months. If no application for a grant of representation is made within that period the caveat can be renewed. A caveator can withdraw his caveat at any time (so long as he has not entered an appearance to a warning) on production to the probate registry of the official receipt.

When the intending executor or administrator applies for a grant of representation, the probate registry will notify him of the existence of the caveat and that his application cannot proceed.

At this point the intending PR has a choice of action:

(1) if he does not think that he and the caveator can resolve their differences, he should issue a writ to commence a probate action – the matter then becomes contentious probate business;
(2) alternatively, he can enter a warning requiring the caveator to explain why he has entered a caveat.

If the intending PR takes this latter course of action, then the caveator has 8 days from the service on him of the warning to respond. If at the end of that period the caveator does not respond, the caveat will be removed by the probate registry and the application for the grant of representation can proceed.

If the caveator has no entitlement to take a grant in place of the intending PR but nevertheless wishes to prevent the PR taking a grant (as in Example 1 above) he must, within those 8 days, issue and serve a summons for directions. The probate registrar will then take evidence from the PR and the caveator before deciding whether the PR's application for the grant can proceed.

If the caveator claims a contrary right to take the grant (as in Example 2 above) he should enter an appearance to the warning. Usually the entry of an appearance will lead to the commencement of a probate action.

22.8.2 Citations (NCPR, r 46)

Only executors or persons specified under NCPR, r 20 or r 22 can take a grant of representation. If the person initially entitled to take the grant refuses to do so and also refuses to renounce, the estate remains unadministered and the beneficiaries are left waiting indefinitely for their inheritance. In such circumstances a citation provides a remedy.

There are several types of citation which can be issued by the probate registry at the request of a beneficiary ('the citor').

Citation to take probate
A citation to take probate may be used where an executor has lost his right to renounce probate by intermeddling in the estate (eg by advising the deceased's bank of his death, see **22.2.3**) but has not applied for a grant of probate within 6 months of the testator's death and shows no signs of so doing. Once cited, the executor must proceed with an application for a grant of probate. If he does not (without good reason), the citor can apply to the court for an order allowing the executor to be passed over and a grant of letters of administration with will annexed to issue to the person(s) entitled under NCPR, r 20.

Citation to accept or refuse a grant
A citation to accept or refuse a grant is the standard method of clearing off a person with a prior right to any type of grant who has not applied, and shows no intention of applying, for a grant. If the person cited does not take steps to take out the grant, a grant may be issued to the citor.

Example
Adam's will appoints Bert his executor and Clare the residuary beneficiary. Bert takes no steps towards administering the estate or proving the will. Clare may cite Bert to act and, if Bert does nothing, Clare may apply by virtue of NCPR, r 20 for a grant of letters of administration with will annexed.

Chapter 23

COMPLETING THE OATH

23.1 INTRODUCTION

This chapter describes how to complete an oath for executors and the two principal oaths for administrators and should be read in conjunction with the background detail and law for each oath set out in Chapter 22.

Much of the content of an oath is standard to all three types. Consequently, the oath for executors is considered in full at **23.2** but, to avoid repetition, the paragraphs on oaths for administrators (**23.3** and **23.4**) concentrate on the points unique to those forms. The approach is to follow the chronology of the form. The forms are reproduced for teaching purposes only by kind permission of The Solicitors' Law Stationery Society Ltd.

Blank forms of each oath appear in the text. In each case there are capital letters marked in the right-hand margin. These capital letters correspond with the letter in the text explaining how to complete that part of the form. The left-hand margin of every commercially produced oath form contains notes to assist in filling in the blank spaces on the oath form. Those notes should be read carefully and followed as appropriate.

Appendices 1, 2 and 3 contain examples of completed oaths as part of simple probate case studies.

Chapter 23 contents
Introduction
Oath for executors
Oath for administrators with will annexed
Oath for administrators
Conclusion

23.2 OATH FOR EXECUTORS

The paragraph letters in the text below refer to the correspondingly marked parts of the blank oath set out below.

A

Where a solicitor is applying for the grant on behalf of the executors it is usual to put his name (or his firm's name), address and reference at the top of the form. This information will appear on the grant of probate. This is useful for:

(1) correspondence by the probate registry; and
(2) for third parties wishing to make contact with the solicitor acting for the PRs. For example a person with a potential family provision claim under the I (PFD)A 1975 will be sent an office copy of the grant of probate by the probate registry if he has lodged a standing search (see **17.12**). The appearance of the solicitor's name and address on the grant will enable the possible claimant to notify the executor's solicitors of his claim.

B

The probate registry is part of the High Court. The Principal Registry is at Somerset House in London. There are also a number of district registries. An application can be made in any registry. It does not have to be the one in the geographical area where the deceased died, although this is usually administratively convenient (see **20.5.1**).

C

One of the functions of the oath is to identify the deceased. His full true name should be set out in the oath. If the deceased held assets in any other name, for whatever reason, that other name must also be given. Failure to do this will mean that the executors have no proof of title to assets in the deceased's other name(s).

Example 1

The deceased's true name as shown on his will was Charles Reginald Smith. The deceased usually called himself, and had a bank account in the name of, Reg Smith. The executor's oath will read:

> in the Estate of Charles Reginald Smith deceased otherwise known as Reg Smith.

Whenever the deceased is referred to on the oath it must show his alternative names. In addition, at the foot of the oath the reason why the deceased is described with various names must be given.

Example 2

The facts are the same as the example above. At the foot of the oath it will be stated:

> The deceased's true name was Charles Reginald Smith however he was also known as Reg Smith and held an account in that name with X Bank at the date of his death

If the deceased was always known by an alias but only held assets in the name appearing on the will it is not necessary to give the alias.

Example 3

Throughout her life the deceased was known as Betty Jones. Her will and all her assets are in her name of Margaret Jones. Only the name 'Margaret Jones' will appear on the oath.

D

The full names and addresses of the proving executors should be set out. There is no need for the executors' names to appear in the same order as in the will. It is quite common for the professional executor's name to appear last on the will but first on the oath. In the absence of a solicitor's name and address on the oath, the probate registry will address all correspondence to the first named executor on the oath.

E

The form continues 'make OATH and say that'. Where a PR prefers to affirm the contents of the oath the words 'make OATH and say' should be deleted and the words 'do solemnly and sincerely affirm' should be substituted.

F

An oath for executors is being completed because there is a valid will. The executors must swear (or affirm) that they believe the will to be the valid last will of the deceased. If there are any codicils to the will this fact must be disclosed. When the oath is sworn or affirmed the will (and codicils) must be 'marked up' as exhibits (see **N** and **23.2.1** below).

Completing the Oath 227

Oath for Executors

IN THE HIGH COURT OF JUSTICE   Extracting Solicitor..   A

Family Division   Address ....

† "Principal" or "District Probate". If "District Probate" add "at...................".   The†   Registry   B

* If necessary to include alias of deceased in grant add "otherwise (alias name)" and state below which is true name and reason for requiring alias.

(1) "I" or "We". Insert the full name, place of residence and occupation, or, if none, description of the deponent(s). adding "Mrs", "Miss", as appropriate, for a female deponent.   IN the Estate of*   deceased.   C

(¹)   D

(2) *Or "do solemnly and sincerely affirm"*.   make Oath and say (²)   that   E

(3) Each testamentary paper must be marked by each deponent, and by the person administering the oath.   (¹)   believe the paper writing now produced to and marked by (³)   F
to contain the true and original last Will and Testament (⁴)

(4) "with one, two (or more) Codicils", as the case may be.   of*   C
of

formerly of   G

deceased

(5) If exact age is unknown, give best estimate.   who died on the   day of   19 ,   H
aged   years (⁵) domiciled in (⁶)
(6) Where there are separate legal divisions in one country, the state, province, etc., should be specified.   and that to the best of   knowledge, information and belief there was (⁷) [no]
land vested in the said deceased which was settled previously to h   death (and
(7) Delete "no", if there was land vested in deceased which remained settled land notwithstanding his or her death.   not by h   Will (⁴)   )   I
and which remained settled land notwithstanding h   death (⁸)

(8) Settled land may be included in the scope of the grant provided the executors are also the special executors as to the settled land; in that case the settlement must be identified.   And (¹)   further make oath and say (²)
that notice of this application has been given to   J

(9) Delete or amend as appropriate. Notice of this application must be served on all executors to whom power is to be reserved unless dispensed with by a Registrar under Rule 27 (3).   the executor(s) to whom power is to be reserved, [save
]. (⁹)
And (¹)   further make Oath and say (²)
that (¹⁰) (¹¹)

(10) "I am" or "we are". Insert relationship of the executors to the deceased only if necessary to establish title or identification.   Execut   K

(11) "The sole", or "the surviving", *or* "one of the", *or* "are the", *or* "two of the", etc.   named in the said

(12) If there was settled land and the grant is to include it, insert "including settled land" but, if the grant is to exclude the settled land, insert "save and except settled land"

and that (^{1})   will (i) collect, get in and administer according to the law the real and personal estate (^{12})   of the said deceased; (ii) when required to do so by the Court, exhibit on oath in the Court a full inventory of the said estate (^{12})
and when so required render an account of the administration of the said estate to the Court; and (iii) when required to do so by the High Court, deliver up the grant of probate to that Court; and that to the best of   knowledge, information and belief

L

(13) Complete this paragraph only if the deceased died on or after 1 April 1981 and an Inland Revenue Account is not required; the next paragraph should be deleted.

(14) The amount to be inserted here should be in accordance with the relevant figure shown in paragraph 1 of the PEP List.

(15) The amount to be inserted here should be in accordance with the relevant figure shown in paragraph 2 of the PEP List.

(16) Complete this paragraph only if an Inland Revenue Account is required and delete the previous paragraph.

N.B. The names of all executors to whom power is to be reserved must be included in the Oath.

(^{13}) [the gross estate passing under the grant does not exceed (^{14}) £   , and the net estate does not exceed (^{15}) £   , and that this is not a case in which an Inland Revenue Account is required to be delivered]

M

(^{16}) [the gross estate passing under the grant amounts to £
and the net estate amounts to £   ].
*

SWORN by   the above-named
Deponent
at
this   day of   19   ,

Before me,

A Commissioner for Oaths/Solicitor.

N

Probate 4

G

The last usual residential address of the deceased should be given. Where the last residential address of the deceased differs from that on the will the address on the will should also be inserted following the words 'formerly of'.

Example

When Beverley made her will she was living at 5 York Road, Chester. This address appears on the will. Beverley moved house several times after making her will and was living at 17 Lancaster Street, Guildford at her death. The oath should read:

> Of 17 Lancaster Street, Guildford
> (her only and permanent address)
> (formerly of 5 York Road, Chester)

H

The date on which the deceased died must be inserted as must the deceased's age and domicile, eg England and Wales.

I

It is uncommon for an estate to include land settled under the SLA 1925 and which continues to be settled following the deceased's death. No new Settled Land Act settlements can be created after 1 January 1997 (TLATA 1996, s 2). Assuming that there is no such settled land, the statement should be left as printed. In an estate where there is settled land the word '(no)' must be deleted. The example below was considered in **22.6.3** ('limited grants').

Example

A settlement was created under the SLA 1925 to Caitlin for life then to Derek for life with remainder to Ernest. Caitlin has just died. The settlement continues after her death and following the death the settled land devolves on the settlement trustees. Tom and Tony are the settlement trustees.

How the oath is worded depends on whether or not Caitlin's general executors and the trustees of the settlement are the same persons.

(1) Caitlin dies appointing Frank as her executor.

Tom and Tony will take out a special grant limited to the settled land. The oath sworn by Frank will read:

> There was ~~no~~ land vested . . .
>
> (a) Collect, get in and administer . . . estate SAVE AND EXCEPT SETTLED LAND of the said deceased
> (b) . . . inventory of the said estate SAVE AND EXCEPT SETTLED LAND and when so required etc

(2) Caitlin appoints Tony and Tom as her executors. There is no need for them to take out a separate grant. Instead the oath will read:

> There was ~~no~~ land vested . . .
>
> (a) Collect, get in and administer . . . estate INCLUDING SETTLED LAND of the said deceased
> (b) . . . inventory of the said estate INCLUDING SETTLED LAND and so when required etc

J

Notice of the intention to make an application for a grant of probate must be given by the proving executor(s) to all non-proving executors to whom power is being reserved. Confirmation that this notice has been given must appear on the oath by completion of this paragraph. Occasionally one of several executors cannot be found following the testator's death. In such circumstances, power should be reserved to the missing executor and consent should be sought from the probate registrar to dispense with the need to give notice to that missing executor. Application for such dispensation is made by letter. In an estate where power is not being reserved to any other executor these last three lines should be deleted.

K

The executors must explain their right to apply for the grant.

> *Example*
> A will appoints Alexis and Bernard as executors.
>
> (1) If both are applying for the grant, they should say:
>
> > That we are the two executors named in the said will . . .
>
> (2) If only Alexis is applying, she should say:
>
> > That I am one of the executors named in the said will . . .
>
> This indicates that either:
>
> > (a) Bernard has power reserved to himself and the oath should be completed accordingly (see **N** below); or
> >
> > (b) Bernard has renounced, in which case his notice of renunciation should accompany the application for the grant but no reference needs to be made to this on the oath.
>
> (3) If only Alexis is applying because Bernard is dead, she should say:
>
> > That I am the surviving executrix named in the will
>
> This indicates that Bernard has died. (There is no need to produce additional evidence of his death.)

L

The three sub-paragraphs (i), (ii) and (iii) set out the duties of a personal representative. These duties are found in AEA 1925, s 25 (see **24.2.1**). No alteration should be made to this paragraph unless there is settled land (see **I** above).

M

The PRs must swear or affirm in the oath as to the gross and net values of the property of the deceased vesting in them. This does not include joint property passing by survivorship, nominated property or property in which the deceased had a life interest.

Paragraph **M** is in the alternative:

> (1) The Gross estate passing under grant does not exceed £   and the Net estate does not exceed £   and this is not a case in which an Inland Revenue Account is required to be delivered.
>
> or

(2) The Gross estate . . . passing under the grant amounts to £ . . . and the Net estate . . . amounts to £ . . .

Either (1) or (2) must be completed and the other paragraph deleted. The key to which paragraph to complete lies in the words 'and this is not a case in which an Inland Revenue Account is required to be delivered'. An Inland Revenue account is not required in an excepted estate (see **21.2.1**). Therefore, whenever an application is being made for a grant in an estate which is 'excepted' for IHT purposes, paragraph (2) should be deleted and paragraph (1) completed. When completing paragraph (1) it is not necessary to swear to the exact value of the gross and net estates. Instead the oath requires the value of the estate to be stated by reference to bands. The gross estate should be sworn to as not exceeding £180,000 (deaths on or after 6 April 1996), and the net estate should be sworn to as not exceeding £200,000, £100,000, £70,000, £40,000, £25,000 or £10,000 (as appropriate). The net estate is used to calculate the level of probate court fees. All of these figures are published in the probate estate provisions (PEP) list.

Example 1
Deceased's estate

House in joint names	£60,000
Money in bank account	£10,000
Personal chattels	£2,000
Debts	£3,500

Swear that the gross estate does not exceed £180,000 and the net estate does not exceed £10,000.

Example 2
Deceased's estate

Quoted shares	£30,000
Money in bank account	£10,000
House	£80,000
Mortgage debt	£15,000

Swear that the gross estate does not exceed £180,000 and the net estate does not exceed £200,000.

Unless the estate is 'excepted', an Inland Revenue account is required (see Chapter 21). Whenever an Inland Revenue account is required to be completed, paragraph (1) should be deleted and paragraph (2) completed. This requires the values of the actual gross and net estates vesting in the PRs to be stated.

Example 1
Deceased's assets

Money in bank account	£25,000
Shares	£50,000
House	£150,000

Deceased's debts

| Access card | £2,000 |
| Mortgage | £30,000 |

Swear (or affirm) that the gross estate passing under the grant amounts to £225,000 and the net estate amounts to £193,000.

Example 2
Deceased's assets

Money in bank account	£8,000
Personal chattels	£2,000
House in joint names of deceased and sister (deceased's ½ share)	£200,000
Deceased's debts	
HP agreement	£1,000

Swear (or affirm) that the gross estate passing under the grant amounts to £10,000 and the net estate amounts to £9,000.

An Inland Revenue account is required because the deceased's taxable estate amounts to £210,000 gross. However, the grant is only required to enable the administration of property vesting in the PRs (ie the money in the deceased's bank account and personal chattels in this case).

N – THE JURAT

The oath must be sworn or affirmed by all proving executors, in each case in the presence of an independent solicitor or commissioner for oaths (ie a solicitor from a firm different from that acting for the executors). The full address of the independent solicitor, together with the date of swearing/affirmation, should be inserted on the oath by this solicitor. Where there are two or more executors, the name of each executor should be added between the words 'sworn by' and 'the above named deponent'. 'Sworn' should be deleted and the word 'affirmed' substituted if the deponent is to affirm rather than swear to the truth of the oath.

23.2.1 'Marking' the will

The will and any codicils must also be produced by the proving executor to the independent solicitor. The will (and codicils) are exhibited to (ie incorporated into) the oath. Each executor should sign the will (usually along the top or in the margin) and the independent solicitor likewise signs the will. This procedure is normally called 'marking the will'.

23.3 OATH FOR ADMINISTRATORS WITH WILL ANNEXED

Much of the oath for administrators with will annexed is identical to the oath for executors. Reference in the text is made only to differences between this oath and an oath for executors. The paragraph letters in the text refer to the correspondingly marked parts of the blank oath set out below. As the jurats (contained on the back of the forms) are identical, the jurat on this, and the later oath form at **23.4**, have been omitted.

There are two significant differences between this oath and that for executors.

A

If the will (or partial intestacy) creates a life or minority interest in any part of the deceased's property which vests in his personal representatives, it is normally necessary for there to be two administrators (see **22.3.4** and **22.4.6**). Accordingly, it is necessary to state on the oath whether a minority and/or life interest arises in the estate.

Example 1
Alan's will leaves his entire estate to his wife for life, remainder to his two children absolutely. The executor has pre-deceased Alan. His children are aged 19 and 15. The oath will read:

> That a minority and a life interest . . .

Example 2
Brenda's will leaves a legacy to her infant godson and the residue of her estate to charity. The executor has renounced probate. The oath will read:

> That a minority ~~and~~ but no life interest . . .

Example 3
Chloe's will fails to appoint an executor. She leaves her estate to her two children, Damien and Ella, contingent on them attaining 25 years of age. Damien is 26 and Ella 23. The oath will read:

> That no minority and no life interest . . .

B
At this point on the form the administrators must clear off all persons in a higher category of entitlement to the grant and then establish their own right to the grant. Priority is governed by NCPR, r 20 (see **22.3.2**).

Clearing off
The first step is to explain why there are no executors. This can be done by stating that the will did not appoint any executors, that the appointed executor has renounced or predeceased the deceased or as the case may be.

If the residuary beneficiary is not applying for the grant, the reason why must be stated; this must be continued until all higher ranked categories have been accounted for (see **22.3.2** for further examples and discussion).

Example 1
Agnes has just died. Her will appointed Bernard as executor and left the residuary estate to Kathy. Bernard died last year. Kathy will swear:

> that Bernard the executor appointed in the will predeceased the deceased.

Example 2
Donald had just died leaving a will appointing his friend Eva as sole executrix and residuary beneficiary. Eva died two days before Donald whose closest living relative is his widowed mother Freda.

Freda will swear:

> that Eva the sole executrix and residuary beneficiary named in the will predeceased the deceased and that the deceased died a bachelor without issue.

Oath for Administrators with the Will

IN THE HIGH COURT OF JUSTICE

Family Division

Extracting Solicitor ....

Address ....

* "Principal" or "District Probate". If "District Probate" add "at _____".

† If necessary to include alias of deceased in grant, add "otherwise (alias name)" and state below which is true name and reason for requiring alias.

(1) "I" or "We". Insert the full name, place of residence and occupation or, if none, description of the deponent(s).

The*   Registry

IN the Estate of†

                                                                                                                  deceased.

(^{1})

(2) Or "do solemnly and sincerely affirm".

(3) Each testamentary paper must be marked by each deponent, and by the person administering the oath.

(4) "With one, two (or more) Codicils", as the case may be.

(5) If exact age is unknown, give best estimate.

(6) Where there are separate legal divisions in one country, the state, province, etc., should be stated.

(7) Complete both blanks. When either such interest arises, two grantees may be required unless a trust corporation is applying.

(8) Delete "no", if there was settled land vested in deceased which remained settled land notwithstanding his death.

(9) If there was settled land such land may be included in the scope of the grant, but the settlement must be identified and all the applicants must show that they are also entitled to a grant in respect of the settled land.

(10) Here state manner in which all prior rights are satisfied, e.g., residuary legatees/devisees must show that no executors were appointed, or that those appointed either died before deceased or survived him and have since died without taking probate, or that they have renounced probate, or have failed to take a grant after being cited so to do *(the order authorising a grant to citor being quoted)*.

(11) "I am" or "we are" and state title of applicants to the grant, including their relationship to the deceased only if necessary to establish title or identification.

(12) If there was settled land and the grant is to include it, insert "including settled land", but, if the grant is to exclude the settled land, insert "save and except settled land".

(13) Complete this paragraph only if the deceased died on or after 1 April 1981 and an Inland Revenue Account is not required; the next paragraph should be deleted.

(14) The amount to be inserted here should be in accordance with the relevant figure shown in paragraph 1 of the PEP list.

(15) The amount to be inserted here should be in accordance with the relevant figure shown in paragraph 2 of the PEP list.

(16) Complete this paragraph only if an Inland Revenue Account is required and delete the previous paragraph.

make Oath and say (^{2})   that
(^{1})   believe the paper writing   now produced to and marked by (^{3})
to contain the true and original last Will and Testament (^{4})

of†

of

formerly of

                                                               deceased,   **A**
who died on the   day of   19 ,

aged   years (^{5}) domiciled in (^{6})

and that there is (^{7})   minority and (^{7})   life interest in the estate of the said deceased; and that to the best of   knowledge, information and belief there was (^{8}) [no] land vested in the deceased which was settled previously to h   death (and not by h   Will (^{4})   ) and which remained settled land notwithstanding h   death (^{9})

and (^{1})   further make Oath and say (^{2})
                    that (^{10})

that (^{11})   **B**

                                              ; and that
(^{1})   will (i) collect, get in and administer according to the law the real and personal Estate (^{12})   of the said deceased; (ii) when required to do so by the Court, exhibit on oath in the Court a full inventory of the said Estate, (^{12})   and when so required render an account of the administration of the said Estate to the Court; and (iii) when required to do so by the High Court, deliver up the grant of letters of administration with Will annexed to that Court; and that to the best of   knowledge, information and belief.

(^{13}) [the gross estate passing under the grant does not exceed (^{14}) £   , and the net estate does not exceed (^{15}) £   , and that this is not a case in which an Inland Revenue Account is required to be delivered]

(^{16}) [the gross estate passing under the grant amounts to £
and the net estate amounts to £   ].
*

Establishing a right to the grant

Having cleared off all persons with better entitlement the applicant needs to state his right to take the grant of letters of administration with will annexed.

Example 1

George's will appoints Harry as executor and leaves his residuary estate to Ivy and Joan in equal shares. Harry renounces his right to probate. The oath will read (depending on whether both Ivy and Joan apply or just one of them) either:

> that Harry the sole executor named in the will has renounced probate and that I am one of the residuary beneficiaries named in the said will; or
>
> that Harry the sole executor named in the will has renounced probate and that we are the two residuary beneficiaries named in the will

Example 2

Karen has just died never having married. Her will appoints Laura as executrix and after a number of small legacies gives the residue to her widowed father Martin. Martin died last month and Laura renounces probate. Karen is survived by her adult sisters Nora and Olive. Nora would make oath and say:

> That Laura the sole executrix named in the will has renounced probate and that Martin the residuary beneficiary named in the will has predeceased the deceased and that the deceased died a spinster without issue or parent or any other persons entitled to share in the estate by virtue of any enactment; that I am a sister of the whole blood of the deceased and one of the persons entitled to share in the undisposed of estate of the said deceased

The reason for the reference to 'any other persons entitled . . . by virtue of any enactment' is given in **23.4** at **B**.

23.4 OATH FOR ADMINISTRATORS

The format of the oath for administrators, which is set out below, is similar to that for executors and administrators with will annexed. The points which are unique to the oath for administrators are marked by capital letter on the oath and discussed below.

A

At this point the intending administrator must clear off all categories of person with a higher priority to take the grant under NCPR, r 22 (see **22.4.2**).

Where there is a surviving spouse and he or she is applying for the grant either alone or with others, there is nobody with a higher priority to clear off and therefore there is no need to add anything after the word 'intestate'.

Where there is no surviving spouse, this fact must be stated by saying that the deceased died intestate, 'a bachelor', or 'a spinster', or 'a widower', or 'a widow', as the case may be.

Oath for Administrators

IN THE HIGH COURT OF JUSTICE

Extracting Solicitor..

Address ....

Family Division

* "Principal" or "District Probate". If "District Probate" add "at.....................
† If necessary to include alias of deceased in grant, add "otherwise (alias name)" and state below which is true name and reason for requiring alias.

(1) "I" or "We". Insert the full name, place of residence and occupation or, if none, description of the deponent(s).

(2) or "do so solemnly and sincerely affirm".

(3) If exact age is unknown, give best estimate.

(4) Where there are separate legal divisions in one country, the state, province, etc., should be stated.

(5) Here give the status of deceased – "a spinster", "a widower", etc., and where necessary clear off the classes entitled in order of priority to applicant, e.g., "without issue or parent".

(6) The words which follow clear illegitimate, legitimated and adopted children and should be deleted if application made by surviving spouse (unless in the special circumstances it is necessary to clear issue) or a child. If appropriate substitute "without" for "or".

(7) Complete both blanks. When either such interest arises two grantees may be required unless a trust corporation is applying.

(8) Delete "no", if there was land vested in deceased which remained settled land notwithstanding his or her death.

(9) If there was settled land such land may be included in the scope of the grant, but the settlement must be identified and all the applicants must show that they are also entitled to a grant in respect of the settled land.

(10) "I am" or "we are".

(11) Show applicant's title, e.g., "brother of the whole blood and one of the persons entitled to share in the estate".

(12) If there was settled land and the grant is to include it, insert "including settled land", but, if the grant is to exclude the settled land, insert "save and except settled land".

(13) Complete this paragraph only if the deceased died on or after 1 April 1981 and an Inland Revenue Account is not required; the next paragraph should be deleted.

(14) The amount to be inserted here should be in accordance with the relevant figure shown in paragraph 1 of the PEP List.

(15) The amount to be inserted here should be in accordance with the relevant figure shown in paragraph 2 of the PEP List.

(16) Complete this paragraph only if an Inland Revenue Account is required and delete the previous paragraph.

The*   Registry

IN the Estate of†   deceased.

(^{1})

make Oath and say (^{2})
that*
of
                                                                            deceased
died on the   day of   19 ,
aged   years (^{3}) domiciled in (^{4})
Intestate (^{5})

(^{6}) or any other
person entitled in priority to share in h   estate by virtue of any enactment and that
(^{7})   minority (^{7})   life interest arises under the intestacy; and that
to the best of   knowledge, information and belief there was (^{8}) [no] land vested
in the said deceased which was settled previously to h   death and which remained settled
land notwithstanding h   death (^{9})

And (^{1})   further make Oath and say (^{2})
         that (^{10})   the (^{11})

                                                                of the said Intestate,
and that (^{1})   will (i) collect, get in and administer according to the law the real and
personal Estate (^{12})   of the said
deceased; (ii) when required to do so by the Court, exhibit on oath in the Court a full inventory
of the said Estate (^{12})
and when so required render an account of the administration of the said Estate to the Court;
and (iii) when required to do so by the High Court, deliver up the grant of letters of administration
to that Court; and that to the best of   knowledge, information and belief

(^{13}) [the gross estate passing under the grant does not exceed (^{14}) £   , and the
net estate does not exceed (^{15}) £   , and that this is not a case in which an
Inland Revenue Account is required to be delivered]

(^{16}) [the gross estate passing under the grant amounts to £
and the net estate amounts to £   ].
*

A
B
C

D

Where the applicant needs to clear off categories of relation in addition to the spouse he will do so by stating that the deceased died intestate 'without issue' or 'parents' or 'brothers and sisters of the whole blood' or 'their issue' etc.

A guide to the appropriate words to use can be found in the Family Division Practice Direction in Appendix 6.

Example 1
Alice has died intestate survived by her son. Her husband died 5 years ago.

The oath will read:

> INTESTATE a widow

Example 2
Brian who never married has just died intestate aged 92 years. He is survived by his two brothers.

The oath will read:

> INTESTATE a bachelor without issue or parents

B
These words indicate that there are no adopted or legitimated relatives or relatives whose parents were not married surviving the deceased. They must always be deleted where there is a surviving spouse and also where there are surviving issue (whether or not there is also a surviving spouse) because such persons would not rank in priority to the applicant. In all other cases the line remains on the oath as typed.

Example 1
Clive died intestate survived by his wife and four children.

The oath will read:

> INTESTATE ~~or any other person entitled in priority to share the said estate by virtue of any enactment~~

Example 2
Doreen has died intestate. She was widowed last year and has three children including a daughter who is adopted.

The oath will read:

> INTESTATE a widow ~~or any other person entitled in priority to share the said estate by virtue of any enactment~~

Example 3
Edward has died intestate. His wife died last year and his only surviving relative is a nephew.

The oath will read:

> INTESTATE a widower without issue or parents or brother or sister of the whole blood or any other person entitled in priority to share the said estate by virtue of any enactment

C

As with an oath for administrators with will annexed, it is necessary to state whether there is a minority and/or a life interest in the estate. On this oath such an interest can only arise as a result of the intestacy rules (see Chapter 16). For examples see also **22.4.6**.

D

Here the applicant must show his precise relationship to the deceased and also indicate whether he is solely entitled to the intestate estate or one of several people entitled to share in it.

The surviving spouse should be described as 'the lawful husband', or 'the lawful widow', as appropriate. The word 'lawful' is not required to describe any other relationship other than that of an adopted child who should be described as 'the lawful adopted . . .'

Example 1
Frances has just died intestate survived by her husband Greg and two children. Her estate is valued at £50,000.

Greg will make oath and say:

> . . . I am the lawful husband of the deceased and the only person entitled to share in the estate of the said intestate

Example 2
Harvey has died intestate, a widower, survived by his three sisters, two of whom apply for the grant.

Their oath will read:

> we the sisters of the whole blood and two of the persons entitled to share in the estate of the said intestate

23.5 CONCLUSION

It is essential not only to select the appropriate form of oath but also to ensure the oath is completed correctly.

A mistake on the face of an oath sent to the probate registry, whether a mistake of law or a typographical error, will result in the probate registry issuing a 'stop notice'. This prevents the application for the grant proceeding until the error is rectified. Often the only way of dealing with this is to have the oath resworn by the PRs, which delays the administration and causes the solicitor to appear inefficient, and possibly negligent, in the eyes of the client.

Having lodged the oath, any will, the Inland Revenue account (if appropriate) and probate court fee with the probate registry, the grant will normally issue within 5 to 15 working days.

Chapter 24

ADMINISTRATION OF AN ESTATE

24.1 INTRODUCTION

Having obtained the grant of representation, the PRs have full power to undertake the administration of the estate. The work involved in administering an estate is broadly the same whether the deceased left a will or died intestate. However, in the latter case the beneficiaries will be ascertained by application of the law of intestacy rather than from construction of the will.

Chapter 24 contents
Introduction
Duties of the PRs
Record keeping and estate accounts
File management and time organisation

24.1.1 The main elements of an administration

The administration of an estate may be divided into five elements or stages as follows:

(1) considering the duties of and powers available to the PRs in carrying out their task;
(2) collecting the deceased's assets;
(3) paying the deceased's funeral and testamentary expenses and debts;
(4) distributing the legacies; and
(5) completing the administration and distributing the residuary estate.

The following five chapters consider each of these elements in detail.

24.1.2 The administration period

All five of the above elements in the administration occur within the 'administration period'. This is the period which commences at the moment immediately following the death and ends when the PRs are in a position to vest the residue of the estate in the beneficiaries, or the trustees if a trust arises under the will or the intestacy law.

24.2 DUTIES OF THE PRS

24.2.1 What are the PRs' duties?

AEA 1925, s 25 (as substituted by AEA 1971, s 9) states that the PRs of a deceased person are under a duty to 'collect and get in the real and personal estate of the deceased and administer it according to law'.

Case-law has established that this duty includes paying the deceased's debts with due diligence and taking reasonable care in preserving the deceased's estate.

24.2.2 Breach of duty

The duties to be undertaken by a PR are generally said to be onerous. A PR who accepts office by taking a grant of representation, or acting as executor, is personally liable for loss to the estate resulting from any breach of duty he commits as PR. A breach of duty, known as a 'devastavit' or a wasting of assets, can occur in a number of ways including:

(1) omission to safeguard assets, for example failure to take appropriate steps to preserve the value of assets and, in consequence, the estate;
(2) maladministration, for example using assets to pay creditors or legatees other than in accordance with the order provided by statute or by the deceased's will (see Chapters 27 and 28);
(3) misappropriating assets, for example using estate assets for the PRs' own purposes and not for the benefit of the deceased's beneficiaries.

24.2.3 Personal liability

The general rule is that although a PR is liable for his own acts and omissions, a PR is not vicariously liable for a devastavit committed by a co-representative (whether an executor or administrator). He may, however, be liable if he fails to prevent a co-representative from committing a breach of duty since, if he knew of it or should reasonably have known of it, he may then be in breach of his own duty of due administration of the estate.

24.2.4 Relief from liability

TA 1925, s 61 gives the court power at its discretion to relieve a PR from liability for breach of duty if satisfied that the PR 'has acted honestly and reasonably and ought fairly to be excused for the breach'. Alternatively, an executor may be able to rely on a clause in the deceased's will providing protection from liability for mistakes made in good faith.

24.2.5 Protection against liability

Failure to pay an unknown creditor or beneficiary is a breach of duty by the PR. As a positive step, a PR should be advised to obtain protection against personal liability to creditors or beneficiaries of whom he is unaware. This can be achieved by complying with the statutory advertisement provisions of the TA 1925, s 27, discussed in **27.4**.

24.2.6 Missing beneficiaries

Breach of duty will also arise if PRs, being aware of the existence of a beneficiary, fail to take him into account when distributing the estate. TA 1925, s 27 (mentioned in **24.2.5**) will not provide protection for the PRs in these circumstances.

PRs should be advised to obtain protection by application to the court for a Benjamin Order (*Re Benjamin* [1902] 1 Ch 723) permitting them to distribute the deceased's estate on a given basis. This will normally permit distribution on the assumption that the missing beneficiary predeceased the testator leaving no issue. If the person concerned is later proved to have survived the deceased he, or his PRs, may recover his share of the estate from the other beneficiaries; however, the PRs are protected from personal liability on the basis of the order.

Before making an order, the court will require evidence that the fullest possible enquiries were made to trace the missing person. If the court considers the advertisements made in addition to the TA 1925, s 27 are insufficient it will direct that further enquiry be made.

24.3 RECORD KEEPING AND ESTATE ACCOUNTS

24.3.1 Accounting requirement

Accounts showing the deceased's real and personal estate which devolves on the PRs, its administration and ultimate distribution to the beneficiaries must be produced at the end of the administration period. To facilitate the production of accounts it is important that adequate records are maintained by the PRs from the start of the administration period.

24.3.2 Accounting records

There are no particular systems to adopt when keeping accounting records. However, any system devised should distinguish the folowing.

Cash

Normally an adequate record of cash will follow closely, or may even be, the bank statements showing the debit and credit entries in the PRs' bank account. A note of explanation made against each entry on the statement as soon as it is received from the bank is generally sufficient.

Non-cash assets

Normally the record of non-cash assets will be closely based on the assets as disclosed in the Inland Revenue account. In simple cases, notes of transactions made in relation to assets entered on the Inland Revenue account will suffice. In more complex cases, separate records will be necessary.

24.3.3 Entries in the accounting records

In order to comply with their accounting obligations, at all stages during an administration the PRs should make the appropriate entries in their accounting records, for example, when shares are sold to raise money to pay IHT, debts or the legacies, the shares should be clearly identified in the records as having been sold, together with the sale price.

24.3.4 Preparation of estate accounts

Estate accounts, and their preparation, are considered further in **29.7** as part of the distribution of the residuary estate.

24.4 FILE MANAGEMENT AND TIME ORGANISATION

Probate and estate administration work is one of the largest areas of complaint against solicitors. Occasionally, it is because of a solicitor's dishonesty in handling clients' money. Commonly, the complaint is of delay in the administration of the estate and poor provision of information to PRs and beneficiaries. The majority of complaints can be avoided by efficient file management and time organisation.

24.4.1 File management

Probate work generates large amounts of paper and consequently the files tend to be bulky. It can also take months, and sometimes years, to complete the administration of a complicated estate. It is impossible for a busy solicitor to keep all the details of every file in his head and yet it is time-consuming and inefficient to have to read through the file every time action is required or there is a request for information from a client. Good file management should:

(1) Ensure that every letter is filed in date order as soon as it is received; copies of letters sent out, or notes made of meetings or telephone calls, should similarly be filed. If any action needs to be taken at a future date, this date should be entered into the diary or file-prompt system (which should be checked every day).

(2) Require checklists kept at the top of the file to be completed regularly to give an immediate overview of progress to date in the administration. Commercial packs of such checklists are available for practitioners who do not want to design their own. The checklists should, as a minimum, list the assets and liabilities, the steps needed to be taken in the administration and all relevant names and addresses (eg the deceased's bank, stockbroker, executors and beneficiaries).

Example

1.	Assets	Notified of death	Probate value	Collected
			£	
	Lloyds Bank current a/c	28/6	575.63	
	Leeds Building Society	28/6	2,246.00	
	etc			

2.		
	Date of death	25 June
	Inland Revenue a/c signed	3 September
	Probate application made	10 September
	Probate issued	
	s 27 Trustee Act 1925 Notice expires	8 September
	1st instalment of IHT due	31 December
	etc	

Such lists must be updated regularly. In addition, they should be updated every time action is taken on the file.

24.4.2 Time organisation

Peaks and troughs of activity
A probate and administration matter can easily develop unwelcome peaks and troughs of activity. For example, immediately after the initial instructions to act are received, activity is at a peak, because all debtors and creditors of the deceased must be notified of the death, valuations of assets must be obtained and beneficiaries contacted. The danger then is to ignore the file for several weeks, while replies are

received, until activity resumes with several hours being set aside to complete the Inland Revenue account and the oath.

Assets and liabilities should be recorded on the Inland Revenue account Form IHT 200 or IHT 202 as soon as the details are received. A draft estate account should also be set up and assets and liabilities recorded at their probate value. Then, as soon as the checklist shows that the values of all known assets and liabilities have been recorded, the IHT liability of the estate can be estimated quickly.

Preliminary meeting with the PRs

It is normally possible to anticipate at the outset of an administration whether any IHT will be payable on the delivery of the Inland Revenue account. This must be paid before the grant can be obtained. Therefore, at an early meeting with the PRs, it is sensible to discuss how this IHT is to be funded (see **27.1**). Arrangements should be made to obtain the funds so that there are no delays in raising the money once the Inland Revenue account has been signed by the PRs.

Preparation of the oath at same time as the Inland Revenue account ensures that this can be sworn by the PRs at the same time as they sign the account. Also, in order to avoid delays in collecting the deceased's assets once the grant is obtained, the PRs should be asked at the same meeting to sign any necessary withdrawal or closure forms, for example those closing the deceased's bank or building society accounts.

This meeting also facilitates discussion of other funding aspects of the administration with the PRs. The Inland Revenue account will indicate the liquidity of the estate, and show whether there is sufficient cash in the deceased's various bank and building society accounts and life policies to cover all known debts and administration expenses. If not, it will be necessary to consider which of the assets must be sold.

Realisation of assets

The IHT payable on delivery of the account is likely to be the largest expense. Where money has been borrowed from a bank, not only will interest be charged on a daily basis, but an undertaking will have been given for early repayment. It is obviously sensible to discharge this liability as quickly as possible once the grant has been obtained, but the need to borrow often arises in an estate with little cash, the wealth being in other assets. The PRs therefore need to decide with the beneficiaries which assets should be sold to discharge this and other liabilities (see **27.1**). While it may not be possible to effect sales before the grant is obtained, stockbrokers' advice could be taken as to which shares (if any) should be sold so that sales can proceed as soon as the grant is obtained.

In an estate where the instalment option has been exercised, it must be decided how the PRs are to fund payment of the instalments (see **29.2.2**).

Completing the administration

The issue of the grant of representation necessarily produces another peak of activity when steps are taken to collect the deceased's assets. After this, care must be taken to avoid a prolonged trough of inactivity. Assuming the estate is solvent, debts should be discharged as the money is received, legacies should be paid as soon as possible and, if the administration is likely to be prolonged, interim distribution should be made whenever possible to the residuary beneficiaries. All receipts and payments should be recorded in the running estate account as they occur.

When anticipating distributions the solicitor should contact the PRs and beneficiaries in advance to ascertain whether the beneficiaries prefer assets to be transferred to them in specie, or whether they would rather receive cash payments. Where the request is for cash, the CGT implications of any sale should be discussed (see **29.5.4**).

The final step in an administration is the preparation of the estate accounts. By keeping a running account during the administration, the preparation of the accounts should be a straightforward task. Estate accounts are discussed and illustrated in **29.7**.

Chapter 25

ADMINISTRATIVE POWERS OF PRS

25.1 INTRODUCTION

PRs undertaking the administration of an estate must have regard to the powers available to them. The following chapters describe the PRs' duties when collecting the deceased's assets and paying debts and administration expenses. None of these duties can be carried out unless the PRs have adequate powers available to them for the purpose. During the administration of the estate the PRs should exercise their powers in full for the benefit of the deceased's estate.

25.2 DESCRIPTION OF THE POWERS

25.2.1 Administrative powers

Some powers can be described as purely administrative in nature and are available to PRs during the administration period only, for example the power to sell the deceased's property in the due course of administration and the power to employ agents to assist PRs in administering the estate.

25.2.2 Dispositive powers

Other powers can be distinguished as dispositive, because they have some connection with the beneficiaries and their interest in the estate. These include provisions such as TA 1925, ss 31 and 32 and any express power to advance capital from a will trust to a life tenant whose interest is otherwise only in the income of the trust. If a trust arises under the will (or under the intestacy law) these powers are available to the PRs during the administration period and will remain available to the PRs or other persons who, once the estate is administered, continue to hold the property as trustees for the beneficiaries.

25.3 SOURCES OF THE POWERS

In principle the powers available to the PRs derive from the sources mentioned in **25.3.1** and **25.3.2**. If the deceased dies intestate, the PRs have only the implied statutory powers available to them, whereas, if he left a will, the executors may have in addition a number of express powers.

25.3.1 Implied statutory powers

Statutory powers are considered in **25.4** and **25.5** and derive from such statutes as:

(1) AEA 1925, ss 39 to 44;
(2) TA 1925 and TIA 1961.

These statutes provide trustees with various powers which will extend to PRs because trustees are defined to include PRs.

Chapter 25 contents
Introduction
Description of the powers
Sources of the powers
PRs' powers considered in Chapter 10
Other statutory powers
Exercise of powers by PRs

25.3.2 Powers granted by a will

Modification of statutory powers

Many of the statutory powers will be modified by express provision contained within a will (see Chapter 10). If there are no executors who prove the will but the will is proved by administrators with the will annexed, they also have these modified powers available to them.

Additional powers

In addition to modification of statutory powers, a will often grants powers which are not available at law, for example the power mentioned in **25.2.2** to advance capital to a surviving spouse to whom a life interest has been given, or to lend capital to such a person; in the absence of any such express power, the executors have no implied power to advance or lend capital to the surviving spouse.

25.4 PRS' POWERS CONSIDERED IN CHAPTER 10

25.4.1 Will drafting

The desirability of modification or extension of implied powers, and the provision of express powers, has been considered in detail in Chapter 10 in connection with drafting a will. Whether the following powers are available to the PRs at all, or only in modified form, will depend on the terms of the particular will and the circumstances of the estate. These powers are not considered further in this chapter; reference should be made to Chapter 10. If an intestacy arises, only the statutory form of the power will be available to the administrator.

25.4.2 Statutory powers

The most important statutory powers to consider are (with reference to the appropriate paragraphs in Chapter 10) as follows:

(1) TIA 1961 (investment) (see **10.3.2**);
(2) TA 1925, ss 31 and 32 (maintenance and advancement) (see **10.3.5** and **10.3.6**);
(3) AEA 1925, s 41 (appropriation) (see **10.2.2**);
(4) TA 1925, s 19 (insurance) (see **10.2.3**).

25.4.3 Express powers

Express powers most likely to be required are the power:

(1) to advance or lend capital to a life tenant (see **10.3.6**);
(2) to purchase a home for the occupation of a beneficiary (see **10.3.3**);
(3) to accept the receipt of a parent or guardian of a minor beneficiary (see **10.2.4** and **10.3.7**);
(4) to run the deceased's business (see **10.6.3**).

25.5 OTHER STATUTORY POWERS

The following statutory powers are also available during the administration period. In general, it is not thought necessary to expressly extend or modify these powers in a will. They are all available where the deceased has died intestate.

25.5.1 Power to employ agents

TA 1925, s 23(1) empowers trustees and PRs to employ and pay (from the estate) an agent to do any acts (but not exercise any discretion) in connection with the trust or the estate administration. PRs will not be liable for the default of the agent, provided he was employed in good faith. However, lack of care in selection of the agent may render the PR liable for his own breach of duty. Typically this power will be used by PRs to employ estate agents, stockbrokers or bankers to carry out executive functions in relation to the administration, for example PRs may instruct estate agents to sell the deceased's house or stockbrokers to value shares for IHT purposes.

TA 1925, s 23(2) permits the appointment of an agent in respect of any property in the deceased's estate outside the UK.

25.5.2 Delegation by power of attorney

TA 1925, s 25, as amended by the Powers of Attorney Act 1971, s 9, allows trustees and PRs to delegate, by power of attorney, the exercise of any of the powers and discretions vested in them for a period not exceeding 12 months. However, in this case, the PRs remain liable for the acts of the delegate as if they were their own acts.

This provision is often used by PRs who, having obtained their grant, find that they are unable to be involved personally in the administration for some temporary reason, such as absence abroad on business or on holiday. If, before taking out the grant, a long absence is anticipated, the better course of action would be for the PR to renounce his right to a grant or for others to take a grant, reserving power to any absentee executor. It is too late to renounce or reserve power if the grant has already been obtained and, in particular, if the PR has intermeddled in the estate.

25.5.3 Implied indemnity for expenses

TA 1925, s 30(2) permits PRs to reimburse themselves for expenses incurred in the execution of their powers and duties. In connection with this provision, it should be remembered that professional PRs will often have the benefit of a charging clause which allows them to charge profit costs as well as expenses (see **10.6.1**).

25.5.4 Powers of sale and management

In AEA 1925, s 39(1), PRs are given the same powers and discretion in dealing with a deceased's real and personal estate as are enjoyed by trustees of land. This wide provision permits PRs to sell any property in the deceased's estate, and in relation to land gives them the powers of a beneficial owner.

25.5.5 Power to appoint trustees of a minor beneficiary's property

AEA 1925, s 42 provides that, where a minor beneficiary is absolutely entitled to property (under a will or an intestacy), the PRs may appoint a trust corporation or two or more individuals (not exceeding four) to be trustees of the property for the minor. If the PRs transfer the property to the trustees, they may obtain a signed receipt which will be a good discharge to the PRs.

The PRs have no implied authority to pay property to the parent or guardian of the minor beneficiary. If they were to do so they would obtain no proper discharge so that the child, on attaining majority, could require payment from the PRs.

This provision is available to PRs only where the child is absolutely entitled, for example where a will bequeaths 'to Adam a legacy of £1,000', and Adam is aged 9 at the testator's death. Had the legacy been contingent, for example on 'Adam attaining majority', the section would be of no help to the executors. The provision is also available if Adam is entitled to the residue or to a share of it.

25.5.6 Power to postpone distribution

AEA 1925, s 44 provides that PRs are not bound to distribute the estate of the deceased to the beneficiaries before the expiration of one year from the death. By contrast, PRs are required to pay the debts of the testator with 'due diligence' (*Re Tankard* [1942] Ch 69), so it is normal for debts to be paid within one year of the death.

The effect of s 44 is that, although PRs are free to pay legacies or to distribute the residuary estate within one year of the death, they cannot be compelled to do so. Sometimes a will provides: '… and I direct that this legacy be paid within [6] months of my death'. Even in this case the executor cannot be compelled to pay the legacy within 12 months of the testator's death (but see **28.8** for the position relating to the payment of interest on the legacy).

25.6 EXERCISE OF POWERS BY PRS

25.6.1 Fiduciary position

In the same way as trustees, PRs are in a fiduciary position and so must act with the utmost good faith. Unlike trustees, they owe duties to the deceased's estate as a whole and not to the individual beneficiaries. Their function is to administer the estate and to distribute its assets.

25.6.2 Powers of a sole PR

A sole PR (whether an executor or administrator) has all the powers of two or more PRs and, in particular, can give a valid receipt for the proceeds of sale of land to a buyer; by contrast, at least two trustees (or a trust corporation) are required to give a valid receipt for the proceeds of sale of land held in trust.

25.6.3 Powers of two or more PRs

Two or more executors have joint and several authority in relation to dealings in personalty. It is, therefore, possible for one of a number of co-executors to contract to sell the deceased's car, and to bind the estate to sell to the buyer.

The position in relation to realty is different. A contract for the sale of land must be entered into by all proving PRs and they must all convey the legal estate to a buyer (Law of Property (Miscellaneous Provisions) Act 1994, s 16).

Chapter 26

COLLECTING THE DECEASED'S ASSETS

26.1 DUTIES OF THE PRS

As stated in **24.2.1**, the PRs have a statutory duty to collect the real and personal estate of the deceased and to administer it according to the law. The nature of this duty requires the PRs to take stock of the deceased's estate, to consider what assets exist and what steps should be taken to protect them. For example, valuable assets and documents of title (share certificates, land certificates etc) should be moved to a place of safe-keeping (eg the solicitor's strong room) rather than be left in an empty house.

26.1.1 Time-limits

No statutory or other rule provides what is a reasonable period of time in which to collect the assets, or what steps should be taken to collect them. However, PRs should be aware of their potential liability for 'devastavit' as explained in **24.2.2**.

26.2 METHODS OF COLLECTION

In order to collect the property in the deceased's estate, the PRs generally must produce the grant to whoever is holding the various assets, for example to the deceased's bank or building society. If the bank manager is holding share certificates or documents of title to land, these also will be handed over to the PRs once the grant has been produced.

In most cases, an office copy grant will be accepted as evidence of title (see **20.7.3**).

Money collected should be paid into either the PRs' bank account or into the client account held by their solicitor.

Personal chattels are usually collected by taking physical possession of them.

In some cases, a grant is not required to collect certain assets. As explained in **20.6**, it may be possible to realise assets without production of a grant under the Administration of Estates (Small Payments) Act 1965.

26.3 DEVOLUTION OF ASSETS ON THE PRS

26.3.1 Property devolving on the PRs

At law the real and personal estate to which a person is entitled at death generally devolves on the PRs. It is this property which the PRs should collect and administer for the beneficiaries. It is therefore distinguished from other property which passes on the death according to its own rules of succession, as described in **26.3.2**.

Chapter 26 contents
Duties of the PRs
Methods of collection
Devolution of assets on the PRs

26.3.2 Property not devolving on the PRs

Where the deceased had an interest in property which ceased on the death, such property will generally not devolve on the PRs. The following examples illustrate types of property which do not devolve on the PRs and which therefore will not pass under any will or under the intestacy law.

Life interest

> *Example*
> Terry died some years ago having by his will left property to Henry and Ian on trust 'for Andrew for life, remainder for Ben'. Andrew has recently died. Assuming Ben is sui juris, Henry and Ian will transfer the property to him in accordance with the terms of Terry's will.

Joint tenancy

> *Example*
> Alan and Brian own property as beneficial joint tenants at law and in equity. On Alan's death his interest passes by operation of the right of survivorship to Brian the surviving joint tenant.

Policy held in trust for others

As explained in **20.6.3**, any proceeds of an insurance policy written in trust for third parties, or written under the Married Women's Property Act 1882, s 11 for the benefit of the deceased's spouse and/or children, will be paid to the trustees of the policy on proof of death, usually by production of the death certificate. The trustees will then distribute the proceeds among the beneficiaries in accordance with the trusts of the policy.

Pension schemes

Lump sums payable at the discretion of trustees under a pension scheme (eg death in service benefits payable under an occupational pension scheme established by the deceased's former employers) do not devolve on the deceased's PRs and do not form part of the estate for succession purposes. In exercising their discretion as to payment, the trustees will have regard to any 'letter of wishes' given to them by the deceased person during his lifetime; however, they are not bound to give effect to these wishes (see **2.4.4**).

Nominated property

Property which has been made the subject of a nomination by the deceased will pass directly to the nominee on proof of death (see **2.4.2**).

26.3.3 Liability to IHT

Although it can be seen that the deceased's interest in the property in each of the previous examples does not pass under the deceased's will or intestacy, it does not follow that the interest necessarily falls outside the estate for IHT purposes. If, immediately before his death, the deceased had a beneficial interest in the property in question, the value of the interest in the property will be included in the estate for IHT purposes. This matter is considered fully in Chapter 18, but in the context of the examples in **26.3.2** the position is as follows.

Life interest
The deceased is deemed to have a beneficial interest in the whole of the property in the trust. The value of the entire trust property is within the life tenant's estate for IHT purposes.

Joint tenancy
The value of the deceased's interest in property held as joint tenants is within the estate for IHT purposes. Normally this will amount to one half of the value of the entire property (subject to a discount in the case of land).

Policies held in trust and pension schemes
In the case of policies held in trust and pension schemes the deceased does not have a beneficial interest in the property so that no IHT will be payable on the death.

Nominated property
The value of nominated property forms part of the deceased's estate for IHT purposes.

Chapter 27

PAYING THE DECEASED'S FUNERAL AND TESTAMENTARY EXPENSES AND DEBTS

27.1 PRELIMINARY CONSIDERATIONS

27.1.1 Immediate sources of money

As soon as moneys can be collected from the deceased's bank or building society, or realised through insurance policies etc, the PRs should begin to pay the deceased's outstanding debts and the funeral account. Administration expenses, for example estate agents' and valuers' fees, will arise during the course of administration of the estate and will have to be settled from time to time while the administration is proceeding.

27.1.2 Repayment of loan to pay IHT

It may be necessary to raise money to repay a loan from the deceased's bank to pay IHT to obtain the grant. If an undertaking has been given to the bank in connection with the loan, it will probably be a 'first proceeds' undertaking. This means that the PRs must use money first realised by them during the administration to repay the bank. Failure to do so will be a breach of the terms of the undertaking.

27.1.3 Which assets to sell

The PRs must take considerable care when deciding which assets they will sell to raise money for payment of the various outgoings from the deceased's estate. A number of points must be addressed when making their decision including the matters set out below.

Provisions of the deceased's will

The will may include provision as to the part of the deceased's estate from which the debts, funeral account and testamentary and administration expenses should be paid; usually they will be paid from the residue. In the absence of such direction, the PRs must follow the statutory rules for the incidence of liabilities as explained in **27.4**. In any event, it will be generally incorrect for PRs to sell property given specifically by will (eg a gift of the testator's stamp collection to his nephew) unless all other assets in the estate have been exhausted in payment of the debts etc.

The beneficiaries' wishes

Where possible, the wishes of the beneficiaries of the residuary estate should be respected by the PRs. Although the PRs have power to sell any assets in the residuary estate, it is clearly appropriate that the residuary beneficiaries should be consulted before any sale takes place. In general, beneficiaries have clear views as to which assets they desire to be retained for transfer to them; other assets may be sold by the PRs to raise the necessary money, possibly following receipt of professional advice as to particular sales.

Chapter 27 contents
Preliminary considerations
Funeral and testamentary expenses and debts
PRs' duty to pay debts
Protection against unknown claims
Administration of assets: solvent estate
Contrary provision in the will
No contrary provision in the will
The insolvent estate

Tax consequences

Before selling assets, the PRs should consider the amount of any capital gains (or losses) likely to arise as a result of the sale, and the availability of any exemptions etc. Full use should be made of the annual exemption for CGT. If assets are to be sold at a loss (compared to their value at the date of death) CGT loss relief may be available for the PRs, as may 'loss relief' for IHT purposes. An explanation of these reliefs and a discussion of the interaction of IHT 'loss relief' and CGT is contained in **29.5.4**.

27.2 FUNERAL AND TESTAMENTARY EXPENSES AND DEBTS

27.2.1 Funeral expenses

Reasonable funeral expenses are payable from the deceased's estate. In all cases what funeral expenses are reasonable is a question of fact.

27.2.2 Testamentary expenses

The phrase 'testamentary and administration expenses' is not defined in the AEA 1925 but case-law generally considers it to mean expenses incident to the proper performance of the duties of a PR. The phrase will include:

(1) the costs of obtaining the grant;
(2) the costs of collecting in and preserving the deceased's assets;
(3) the costs of administering the deceased's estate, for example solicitors' fees for acting for the PRs, valuers' fees incurred by PRs in valuing the deceased's stocks and shares or other property; and
(4) any IHT payable on death on the deceased's property in the UK which vests in the PRs. All matters relating to the payment and burden of IHT on an estate on death are considered in detail in Chapter 18.

27.3 PRS' DUTY TO PAY DEBTS

The general duty of PRs is to pay the debts incurred by the deceased before death 'with due diligence' having regard to the assets in their hands which are properly applicable for that purpose (*Re Tankard* [1942] Ch 69).

The duty is owed to the creditors and beneficiaries of the estate. Any failure by the PRs to pay the debts with due diligence will cause them to incur liability for any consequent loss suffered by the creditors or beneficiaries. As mentioned in **25.5.6**, there is no rule of law requiring payment of debts within a year, or any other particular time period, but 'due diligence' may indicate that payment should be made as soon as possible after the death.

The duty to pay the creditors cannot be varied by contrary provision by a will. Any attempt to delay payment of creditors in this way would render the particular provision in the will ineffective; for example, if the will stated that debts should be paid no sooner than three calendar months from the testator's death, this would not bind the PRs, nor could it be enforced by the creditors.

27.4 PROTECTION AGAINST UNKNOWN CLAIMS

The general principle that the PRs are liable to beneficiaries and creditors for the unpaid debts and liabilities of the deceased, even if they are unaware of them, means that it is important for the PRs to take steps to protect themselves against such liability.

PRs can obtain statutory protection by advertising for claims in accordance with the TA 1925, s 27.

The following procedure should be followed.

Placing the advertisement
The PR should give notice of the intended distribution of the estate, requiring any person interested to send in particulars of his claim whether as a creditor or as a beneficiary by:

(1) advertisement in the *London Gazette*;
(2) advertisement in a newspaper circulating in the district in which land owned by the deceased is situated; and
(3) 'such other like notices, including notices elsewhere than in England and Wales, as would, in any special case, have been directed by a court of competent jurisdiction in an action for administration'.

A court would normally order the placing of such advertisements as are appropriate to the particular circumstances of the case. Printed forms for the advertisements can be obtained from law stationers.

Time for claims
Each notice must require any person interested to send in particulars of his claim within the time specified in the notice, which must not be less than 2 months from the date of the notice.

Searches in case of land
The PRs should also make searches which the prudent purchaser of land would make in HM Land Registry, HM Land Charges Department and local land charges register as appropriate. The purpose of these searches is to reveal the existence of any liability in relation to the deceased's ownership of an interest in land, for example a second mortgage.

Distribution after notices
When the time-limit in the notice has expired the PRs may distribute the deceased's estate taking into account only those claims of which they have actual knowledge, or which they discover as a result of the advertisements. The PRs are not personally liable for any other claim, but a claimant may still follow the assets into the hands of the beneficiaries who have received them from the PRs.

Early advertisement
In view of the minimum notice period of 2 months, PRs should advertise as early as possible in the administration. If they are executors, they may advertise at any time after the death; if they are administrators, they have the power to advertise at any time after obtaining their grant.

27.5 ADMINISTRATION OF ASSETS: SOLVENT ESTATE

The rules applying to the payment of funeral and testamentary expenses and debts depend on whether the estate is solvent or insolvent. The insolvent estate is considered in **27.8**.

27.5.1 AEA 1925, s 34(3)

Section 34(3) of the AEA 1925 states:

> 'Where the estate of a deceased person is solvent his real and personal estate shall, subject to rules of court and the provisions hereinafter contained as to charges on property of the deceased, and to the provisions, if any, contained in his will, be applicable towards the discharge of the funeral, testamentary and administration expenses, debts and liabilities payable thereout in the order mentioned in Part II of the First Schedule to this Act.'

27.5.2 Significance of s 34(3)

AEA 1925, s 34(3) has an important bearing on the payment of funeral and testamentary expenses and debts from any estate. The following points can be established:

'real and personal estate'
The significance of the phrase 'real and personal estate' is that property in the deceased's estate is made available generally for the purpose of payment of the funeral and testamentary expenses and debts. The PRs are not specifically directed to use any particular type of property, for example the personal estate, in priority to the real estate.

Part II of the First Schedule
Part II of the First Schedule lays out an order which the PRs must follow when deciding which part of the deceased's estate should be used for the purposes of payment of the funeral and testamentary expenses and debts, for example they should generally use assets forming part of the residue before using property given to specific legatees. The order is set out and discussed further in **27.7.2**.

'subject ... to'
The effect of the proviso 'subject ... to' is that the operation of s 34(3) is expressly subject to two important rules or provisions, as follows:

(1) AEA 1925, s 35, which deals with secured debts, ie debts owing by the deceased which are charged on particular items of property, for example a loan secured by legal mortgage on the deceased's house. This section is discussed in **27.7.1**.
(2) Any provisions in the deceased's will which have the effect of varying the provisions implied by AEA 1925, ss 34(3) and/or 35. Clearly, no contrary provision varying the statutory provisions is possible where the deceased has died intestate. In such cases, the terms of ss 34(3) and 35 should be followed by the administrators when administering the assets of the intestate's estate.

27.6 CONTRARY PROVISION IN THE WILL

27.6.1 Clauses showing contrary provision

The need to establish contrary provision to the statutory rules was discussed in **8.3.2**. Specimen clauses can be found in **8.4.5** and in **4.2.2** in Mark King's will (Clause 5) and in **4.3.2** in Julia Gold's will (Clause 6).

Before paying the debts and expenses, the PRs must construe the will (if any) to ascertain whether the testator has indicated the necessary contrary intention to oust the provisions of AEA 1925, ss 34(3) and 35.

Construction of wills is discussed further in **28.2**.

The example below is adapted from a professionally drawn will and illustrates that the PRs may have to construe traditional drafting.

Example: Extract from Tom Smith's will

3. I GIVE all my freehold property situate at and known as 3 Tunsgate Weyford aforesaid to my sister Susan absolutely and I DIRECT that any and all taxes payable by reason of my death in respect of such property and also any mortgage debt or charge affecting such property or any part thereof at the time of my death shall be paid out of the residue of my estate in exoneration of the said property.

4. I GIVE all my estate both real and personal whatsoever and wheresoever not hereby or by any codicil hereto otherwise specifically disposed of (hereinafter called 'my residuary estate') unto my trustees UPON TRUST to pay my debts and funeral and testamentary expenses and all legacies given hereby or by any codicil hereto and any and all taxes payable by reason of my death in respect of property given free of tax and subject thereto UPON TRUST to pay and divide the same equally between ...

27.6.2 Effect of the clauses

The above clauses provide adequate express instructions from Tom Smith as to the payment of debts etc. All outgoings are to be paid from the fund of general residue described as 'my residuary estate'. The operation of such a clause is illustrated in the following example.

Example

Tom's will includes the clauses mentioned above. His sister Susan inherits 3 Tunsgate and his children inherit the residue.

His house is worth £200,000 (subject to a mortgage of £50,000). Debts and funeral and testamentary expenses (including IHT on 3 Tunsgate) amount to £100,000. Residue is £500,000.

Distribution of the estate

	£	£		Beneficiary
House		200,000	to	Susan
Residue		500,000		
less: mortgage	50,000			
debts etc	100,000			
		(150,000)		
		350,000	to	children

27.6.3 Other clauses showing contrary provision

The clauses quoted above contain a trust of the residuary estate with a direction for the payment of outgoings before distribution to the beneficiaries. A will which leaves the residuary estate to a beneficiary 'subject to' or 'after payment of' the funeral and testamentary expenses and debts (but without creating a trust) would also be construed as providing contrary intention varying the implied provisions. (See for example Mark King's will, Clause 5 in **4.2.2**.)

27.6.4 No clause showing contrary provision

In a clear case such as the above example, the PRs need look no further than the terms of the will when deciding the source from which the various outgoings are to be discharged. In cases where there is no express provision in the will, questions of incidence of debts will depend on the relevant rules of law (see **27.7**).

27.7 NO CONTRARY PROVISION IN THE WILL

27.7.1 AEA 1925, s 35(1) – secured creditors

Property subject to a charge
Where the deceased's estate contains property charged with the payment of money then, unless a contrary intention is shown, the property bears the charge. The effect of this rule is that the property passes under the will to the beneficiary subject to the charge which is thus not paid from residue. If Clause 3 in the extract of Tom Smith's will in **27.6.1** had not contained a contrary provision, Susan would have inherited 3 Tunsgate subject to any existing mortgage debt outstanding when the testator died. Using the same facts as in the example in **27.6.2**, the effect would have been as follows:

Distribution of the estate

	£		*Beneficiary*
House	200,000		
less: mortgage	50,000		
	150,000	to	Susan
Residue	500,000		
less: debts etc	100,000		
	400,000	to	children

Had there been no contrary provision shown in Clause 3 of the will, then the mere reference in Clause 4 to payment of 'debts' from residue would not be sufficient to remove the charge from the property. Further words in Clause 4 would be needed to achieve this, such as a clear direction that any mortgage on 3 Tunsgate be discharged from residue instead of by the beneficiary of the property.

> *Example*
>
> ... UPON TRUST to raise and discharge thereout my debts and funeral and testamentary expenses including any mortgage debt or charge affecting my freehold property known as 3 Tunsgate Weyford [in exoneration of the said property] ...

Charges within s 35

Charges within s 35 include charges created by the deceased as well as those arising by operation of law. The following are therefore included:

(1) mortgages, whether legal or equitable, over land owned by the deceased;
(2) an Inland Revenue charge imposed for unpaid IHT; and
(3) a charge imposed by the court on land belonging to a judgment creditor.

Creditors' rights not affected

Section 35 regulates the incidence of secured debts between beneficiaries to determine which property should be used to pay the debts. It does not affect the rights of the creditor, who may pursue whatever remedies are available to him as a secured creditor. If this happens, and the 'wrong' property is used, the doctrine of marshalling will apply as between the beneficiaries to ensure that the debt is borne by the correct beneficiary, and that the beneficiary who is deprived of his property is compensated for the loss.

27.7.2 AEA 1925, s 34(3) – funeral and testamentary expenses and (unsecured) debts

As mentioned in **27.5.1**, s 34(3) establishes that, subject to the provision relating to secured debts in the AEA 1925, s 35(1), the PRs may have recourse to the real and personal property in the deceased's estate in the order set out in Part II of the First Schedule to the Act for the payment of the deceased's funeral, testamentary and administration expenses and debts.

The statutory order in AEA 1925, First Schedule, Part II

'1. Property of the deceased undisposed of by will, subject to the retention thereout of a fund sufficient to meet any pecuniary legacies.
2. Property of the deceased not specially devised or bequeathed but included (either by a specific or general description) in a residuary gift, subject to the retention out of such property of a fund sufficient to meet any pecuniary legacies, so far as not provided for as aforesaid.
3. Property of the deceased specifically appropriated or devised or bequeathed (either by a specific or general description) for the payment of debts.
4. Property of the deceased charged with, or devised or bequeathed (either by a specific or general description) subject to a charge for, the payment of debts.
5. The fund, if any, retained to meet pecuniary legacies.
6. Property specifically devised or bequeathed, rateably according to value.
7. Property appointed by will under a general power, including the statutory power to dispose of entailed interests, rateably according to value.
8. The following provisions shall also apply —
    (a) The order of application may be varied by the will of the deceased ...'

Because these provisions are complex and can lead to difficulties in some cases, they should be excluded when drafting a will (see **27.6**).

Interpretation of the statutory order

PARAGRAPH 1

Undisposed of property includes a lapsed share of residue or the whole of residue if there is no effective gift of residue in the will.

Before using such property for the payment of debts, a fund must be set aside to meet any pecuniary legacies left by the deceased.

Pecuniary legacy is defined in AEA 1925, s 55(1)(ix) to include:

> 'an annuity, a general legacy, a demonstrative legacy so far as it is not discharged out of the designated property, and any other general direction by a testator for the payment of money, including all death duties free from which any devise, bequest, or payment is made to take effect.'

The reference to payment of death duties covers any direction in the will making a gift free of IHT; the IHT on that property will be classed as a pecuniary legacy when determining the order in which assets should be taken to pay the deceased's debts.

PARAGRAPH 2

This covers residue (subject to the retention of a pecuniary legacy fund as above). For the purpose of this paragraph, 'residue' means gross assets less specific gifts.

PARAGRAPH 3

Property specifically given for the payment of debts.

PARAGRAPH 4

Property charged with the payment of debts.

Paragraphs 3 and 4 above may appear difficult to distinguish. They are also very unlikely to arise.

If a testator does give or charge property for the payment of debts, then it is necessary to decide whether:

(1) he has shown sufficient contrary intention to oust the statutory order (see **27.6**), in which case the property given or charged must be used first; or
(2) he did not intend to vary the statutory order, in which case the property falls within paragraphs 3 or 4.

To distinguish between paragraphs 3 and 4, consider the wording of the provision made in the will.

Example
Joe's will states: 'pay my debts from my premium bonds'. Joe has given property for the payment of his debts but has not directed what should be done with any property remaining after those debts have been settled. The premium bonds would fall within paragraph 3.

Example
Tom's will states: 'pay my debts from my National Savings Certificates and give any balance to Dan'. Tom has charged the National Savings Certificates with the payment of debts within the meaning of paragraph 4.

PARAGRAPH 5

This covers the fund set aside under paragraphs 1 or 2.

PARAGRAPH 6

This covers property comprised in specific gifts.

PARAGRAPH 7

This goes beyond the scope of this book and can be ignored.

Application of the statutory order

The examples which follow illustrate the application of the rules in the situations most likely to arise in practice. More complex circumstances would require further consideration of the statutory order.

> *Example 1: Will disposing of whole estate (but no contrary provision)*
>
> In his will, James leaves a specific legacy of jewellery worth £5,000, pecuniary legacies of £2,000 and a gift of residue divisible equally between William and Mary, who both survive James. There is no contrary provision to exclude the statutory order. The residue before debts etc totals £102,000. Debts etc amount to £10,000.
>
> The PRs should pay the debts etc from the residue, after first setting aside enough to pay the pecuniary legacies (para 2 of the order).
>
> If residue is insufficient for the payment of the debts etc, the PRs must then use the pecuniary legacy fund which they have set aside to pay the legacies. Each pecuniary legacy will abate rateably, ie each is reduced proportionately (para 5 of the order).
>
> If the pecuniary legacy fund is also exhausted, the PRs must then use the property specifically given by the will (para 6 of the order).
>
> Distribution on this basis is illustrated below:
>
> | | | |
> |---|---|---|
> | Specific legacy (jewellery) | £5,000 | |
> | Residue (before debts etc) | | £102,000 |
> | pecuniary legacy fund set aside | | £2,000 |
> | | | £100,000 |
> | debts | | £10,000 |
> | | | £90,000 |
>
> Division: W   M
>
>   £45,000   £45,000
>
> (Pecuniary legacies and specific legacy paid in full.)

If the will had contained contrary provision, it would normally have directed payment from residue before its division between the beneficiaries. If so, the manner of distribution of the estate would have been exactly the same as under the statutory order.

Where the statutory order applies, property within paras 3 and 4 of the order is only to be used after property in paras 1 and 2 is exhausted.

Example 2: Partial intestacy (but no contrary provision)

Assume the same facts as in Example 1 except that a partial intestacy arises because Mary has predeceased James and there is no substitutional gift of her share of residue.

In this case the statutory order directs payment of the debts etc from the property within the undisposed of share of residue after first setting aside a pecuniary legacy fund. Only if this is not enough to pay the debts etc will property in another part of the estate be used.

Distribution on this basis is illustrated below:

Specific legacy (jewellery)	£5,000		
Residue (before debts etc)			£102,000
Division	W		M (undisposed of)
	£51,000		£51,000
less pecuniary legacy fund		£2,000	
less debts etc		£10,000	£12,000
			£39,000

If there had been contrary provision in the will, it would probably have provided for payment of debts and legacies before division of residue. In such a case, William's share and Mary's share would each amount to £45,000 (ie £102,000 − £12,000 = £90,000 ÷ 2).

Example 3: Deceased dies intestate

Ingrid has died intestate leaving a spouse and infant children. Her debts etc amount to £50,000 and her estate totals £380,000 (including personal chattels worth £5,000).

In this case, there can be no contrary provision to exclude the operation of the statutory order. The administrators must follow AEA 1925, s 33 when paying the deceased's funeral, testamentary and administration expenses and debts (see **16.2.1**).

	£
Undisposed of estate	380,000
Less debts etc	50,000
	330,000

Distribution of the residue:

	£		*Beneficiary*
Personal chattels	5,000		
Statutory legacy	125,000		
	130,000	to	spouse
Residue	200,000	to	spouse and children (on the statutory trusts)

For details as to how the £200,000 would be divided between the spouse and children, see **16.3.3**.

27.7.3 IHTA 1984, s 211

IHTA 1984, s 211 establishes that, in the absence of any express testamentary direction to the contrary, IHT on any UK property which vests in the deceased's PRs and which was not immediately before the death comprised in a settlement is a testamentary expense. IHT is, therefore, payable out of the residuary estate together with the other testamentary and administration expenses. For a full discussion of the liability and burden of IHT on death, see **18.9** and **18.11**.

27.8 THE INSOLVENT ESTATE

27.8.1 Meaning of insolvency

An estate is insolvent if the assets are insufficient to discharge in full the funeral, testamentary and administration expenses, debts and liabilities. In such cases the creditors will not be paid in full (or at all) and the beneficiaries under the will or the intestacy provisions will receive nothing from the estate.

27.8.2 Possible insolvency

In doubtful cases, the PRs should administer the estate as if it is insolvent. Failure to administer an insolvent estate in accordance with the statutory order is a breach of duty by the PRs. For example, if the PRs pay an inferior debt (according to the order discussed in **27.8.3**) before a superior debt, there is an admission of the existence of sufficient assets to discharge all the superior debts in full. If this is not the case the PRs will be personally responsible to the superior creditors for the shortfall.

27.8.3 Order for distribution

In the case of an insolvent estate which is being administered by the deceased's PRs out of court (this being the most common method of administration) the following order of distribution will apply (Administration of Insolvent Estates of Deceased Persons Order 1986):

(1) reasonable funeral, testamentary and administration expenses have priority; subject to this the following bankruptcy rules apply;
(2) specially preferred debts, for example money belonging to a friendly society which was in the deceased's possession;
(3) preferential debts (ranked equally and abated proportionately), including:

  (a) money owed to Inland Revenue for PAYE deducted from employees' remuneration in the 12 months before the death;
  (b) money owed to HM Customs and Excise for VAT for the 6-month period before the death;
  (c) social security contributions: arrears of Class 1, 2 and 4 contributions for certain periods;
  (d) pension scheme contributions: arrears of state and occupational scheme contributions;
  (e) money owed to employee(s) by way of remuneration: arrears of wages and accrued holiday pay subject to limits;

(4) ordinary debts (ranked equally and abated proportionately);
(5) interest on preferential and ordinary debts;

(6) deferred debts, including loans at variable rates of interest and loans from the deceased's spouse.

27.8.4 Debts which may be proved against the estate

Provable debts include all liabilities, present and future, certain or contingent. If the amount of a debt is uncertain (eg because it is subject to a contingency), its value should be estimated. Statute barred debts cannot be proved.

27.8.5 Secured creditors

Secured creditors, for example those holding a mortgage or charge over the deceased's property, are in a better position than unsecured creditors in that they may:

(1) rely on the security and not prove in the insolvency;
(2) realise the security, ie sell the property by exercising a power of sale as mortgagee or chargee, and then prove for any balance;
(3) value the security, ie not sell the property under the power of sale, but ascertain its value and then prove for the balance;
(4) surrender the security and prove for the whole debt as an unsecured creditor of the estate.

Chapter 28

DISTRIBUTING THE LEGACIES

28.1 INTRODUCTION

Once the funeral, testamentary and administration expenses and debts have been paid, or at least adequately provided for by setting aside sufficient assets for the purpose, the PRs should consider discharging the gifts arising on the death, other than the gifts of the residuary estate. They may also consider making interim distributions to the residuary beneficiaries on account of their entitlement.

28.2 CONSTRUCTION OF THE WILL

When the deceased's PRs are considering payment of legacies they should construe the terms of his will to ascertain the exact nature of the gifts contained in it with a view to giving effect to those gifts. This will involve:

(1) identifying correctly the beneficiaries entitled to the legacies given by the will;
(2) establishing the nature and extent of their entitlement, for example whether the gifts are vested or contingent on attaining a given age or on some other contingency; and
(3) identifying the property in the case of specific gifts since, if the estate does not contain the property given by the will, the gift is adeemed and the beneficiary is not entitled to receive anything.

28.2.1 Construction summons

If problems arise as to the true meaning of the terms of the deceased's will (whether in relation to legacies or otherwise) which cannot be resolved in any other way, the court, on a construction summons taken out by the PRs, should be asked to determine the matter. Normally, application is made in the Chancery Division of the High Court, although the county court has jurisdiction if the deceased's estate is less than £30,000.

The court will construe the will to give effect to the testator's intention as disclosed by the will as a whole, but giving particular expressions and descriptions of people their natural meaning unless the contrary intention appears from the context of the will.

Extrinsic evidence of intention
There are well-established rules allowing the court to take account of extrinsic evidence of the testator's intention in certain situations, for example, where there is a latent ambiguity in a will such as a gift to the testator's nephew Andrew, when he has more than one nephew of that name.

The admissibility of extrinsic evidence has been extended (where the testator dies after 31 December 1982) by the Administration of Justice Act 1982, s 21, which provides that extrinsic evidence, including evidence of the testator's intention, may be admitted to assist the interpretation of a will insofar as:

Chapter 28 contents
Introduction
Construction of the will
Identity of beneficiaries
Classification of gifts
Specific legacies
Pecuniary legacies
Incidence of pecuniary legacies
Time for payment of pecuniary legacies
Intestacy or partial intestacy

(1) any part of it is meaningless; or
(2) the language used in any part of it is ambiguous on the face of it (eg a gift of 'my money'); or
(3) evidence, other than the evidence of the testator's intention, shows that the language used in any part of it is ambiguous in the light of the surrounding circumstances (eg a gift to 'my nephew Andrew' where the deceased has more than one nephew called Andrew, or no nephew by that name but, perhaps, only a great-nephew called Andrew).

Rectification of a will
Administration of Justice Act 1982, s 20 provides that if the court is satisfied that a will fails to carry out the testator's intentions because of:

(1) a clerical error; or
(2) a failure on the part of the draftsman to understand his instructions,

it may order the will to be rectified so as to carry out those intentions.

Applications for rectification must be made within 6 months of the grant, or later if the court grants leave. PRs who distribute after this date, in accordance with the will in its unrectified form, cannot be liable for doing so if the time-limit is extended later, and rectification of the will is ordered.

28.3 IDENTITY OF BENEFICIARIES

As explained in **8.3.3**, a gift (other than a charitable gift) may fail if the beneficiary cannot be identified with sufficient certainty.

Subject to any contrary intention in the will, certain statutory presumptions may assist in identifying beneficiaries in certain situations.

28.3.1 Family Law Reform Act 1987

When identifying family relationships referred to in a will or codicil executed after 3 April 1988, references to any relationship between two persons shall be construed without regard to whether or not the father and mother of either of them, or the father and mother of any person through whom the relationship is deduced, have or had been married to each other at any time (ss 19(1) and 1(1)).

For example, a gift 'to my children' includes both legitimate and illegitimate children of the testator; a gift 'to my grandchildren' includes all his children's children whether or not his children and their children are legitimate.

In the case of wills and codicils executed before 4 April 1988 (but after 31 December 1969), references to children or other relatives of any person generally include any person who is illegitimate or who is related through another person who is illegitimate (Family Law Reform Act 1969, s 15).

28.3.2 Adoption Act 1976

Under the Adoption Act 1976, s 39, an adopted child is treated as the child of his adoptive parents and not of his natural parents.

If the testator makes a disposition by will which depends on the date of birth of a child or children then, by virtue of s 42(2), the disposition shall be construed as if:

'(a) the adopted child had been born on the date of adoption,
(b) two or more children adopted on the same date had been born on that date in the order of their actual births, but this does not affect any reference to the age of a child.'

For example, a gift 'to Joe's children' includes any child that Joe has adopted by the date of the testator's death; if Joe has such a child then and the gift is 'to Joe's children at 21', the adopted child's share vests on his twenty-first birthday (and not by reference to the date of his adoption).

28.3.3 Legitimacy Act 1976

Under Legitimacy Act 1976, s 5(3):

'a legitimated person, and any other person, shall be entitled to take any interest as if the legitimated person had been born legitimate.'

The rule explained in **28.3.2** applies to dispositions which depend on the date of birth of a child, ie a legitimated child is deemed born on the date of legitimation etc but this does not affect any reference to the age of a child (s 5(4)).

28.3.4 Protection of PRs

PRs may find themselves in difficulty if they distribute property in ignorance of the existence of a person who may be entitled as a result of one of the statutory presumptions mentioned above.

Adopted and legitimated persons

The Adoption Act 1976, s 45 and the Legitimacy Act 1976, s 7 contain almost identical provisions protecting (trustees and) PRs.

A PR is not under a duty to enquire, before distributing property, whether, for example, any adoption has been effected or whether any person could be legitimated if such facts could affect entitlement to the property. A PR shall not be liable to any person by reason of a distribution of property made without regard to any such fact if he has received no notice of the fact before the distribution.

The sections do not prejudice the right of any person to follow the property into the hands of the beneficiaries.

Illegitimate persons

There is no statutory protection for PRs in the Family Law Reform Act 1987. PRs should make enquiries of the testators' relatives and known beneficiaries to ensure no potential beneficiary is overlooked. Such enquiries must be conducted with care and tact. PRs should also follow the procedure of TA 1925, s 27 which invites 'any person interested to send ... particulars of his claim'. The s 27 procedure is set out in **27.4**.

Finally, if the PRs consider that they are still at risk, they may take out insurance cover or seek indemnities from the beneficiaries known to them.

Missing beneficiaries

If a beneficiary (known to have existed) cannot be traced, the PRs should take the following steps:

(1) advertise for information in a newspaper circulating in the area where the person was last heard of; and

(2) consider applying for a Benjamin Order (see **24.2.6**); or
(3) seek insurance cover or indemnity from the other beneficiaries.

28.3.5 Class gifts

A class gift is a gift of property to be divided between a group of persons satisfying a given description. For example, '£1,000 to my brother's children' and '£5,000 to my nieces and nephews on attaining 18' are class gifts.

The size of each beneficiary's share depends on the number of persons falling within the class and this may cause difficulties for the PRs when distributing property. For example, if the gift is to be divided between the testator's nephews and nieces, he may have many more nephews and nieces born after his death, but the PRs do not know how much to give each nephew or niece until all are born.

There will be no difficulty in determining the number of members in the class in relation to a gift to the testator's children because all are born or 'en ventre sa mère' (ie conceived but not yet born) at the testator's death. If the testator has included a gift to his grandchildren, it is common to restrict the gift to those grandchildren living at the testator's death (as in Julia Gold's will in **4.3.2**).

In relation to a class gift such as '£1,000 to my brother's children' and the brother is still alive at the testator's death then, in the absence of contrary provision, rules of construction known as 'the class closing rules' must be applied to determine when the class closes and the number of members within it. Details of the rules are outside the scope of this book.

In the case of a gift of a fixed amount to each member of a class (eg '£100 to each of my brother's children') then, in the absence of contrary intention, only those persons alive at the testator's death can take; if there is no member of the class alive at that date, the whole gift fails.

It should be remembered that the Wills Act 1837, s 33 may assist in the construction of a class gift to the testator's children or remoter descendants (see **15.3.6**).

28.4 CLASSIFICATION OF GIFTS

The classification of legacies and devises has been considered in Chapter 8, together with the associated problems such as lapse and ademption (see Chapter 15). These rules should be reconsidered before distribution to the beneficiaries can be effected properly.

Further matters relating to the distribution of specific and pecuniary legacies are considered in **28.5–28.8**.

28.5 SPECIFIC LEGACIES

It is unusual for property given by specific bequest or devise to be needed for payment of the deceased's funeral and testamentary expenses and debts (see Chapter 27). Once the PRs are satisfied that the property will not be so required, they should consider transferring it to the beneficiary, or to trustees if a trust arises, for example if the property is given to a beneficiary contingently on attaining a stated age and the beneficiary has not yet reached that age.

28.5.1 Method of transfer

The method of transferring the property to the beneficiary or trustee will depend on its particular nature. For example, the legal estate in a house or flat should be vested in a beneficiary by a document known as an assent. If the specific legacy is of company shares, a stock transfer form should be used. These, and other matters, relating to transfer of property by the PRs to the beneficiaries are discussed further in **29.6.4**.

28.5.2 Retrospective effect

In the case of specific gifts only, the vesting of the asset in the beneficiary is retrospective to the date of death, so that any income produced by the property, for example dividends on a specific gift of company shares, belongs to the beneficiary. He is not entitled to the income as it arises but must wait until the PRs vest the property in him. As the beneficiary is entitled to the income, he will be liable to be assessed for any income tax due on that income since the death.

Example

John is given 'my 1,000 shares in Alpha Beta Plc' by his aunt's will. A dividend of £80 is paid 3 months after the death. The executors transfer the shares to John by stock transfer form, together with a cheque for £80 (and a tax deduction certificate showing basic rate tax paid on the dividend).

John's income tax position	£
net divided from the executors	80
add – tax credit	20
gross dividend	100

John should add the £100 to his statutory income for the year.

Any costs of transferring the property to a specific legatee, and the cost of any necessary insurance cover taken to safeguard the property, are the responsibility of the legatee who should reimburse the PRs for the expenses incurred (subject to any contrary direction in a will indicating that such expenses should be paid from residue).

28.6 PECUNIARY LEGACIES

Pecuniary legacies, like specific legacies, are unlikely to be required for payment of the deceased's funeral and testamentary expenses and debts. The order in AEA 1925, First Schedule, Part II requires that a pecuniary legacy fund be set aside, so that funeral and testamentary expenses and debts are payable first from the remainder of the estate; if there is insufficient for this purpose then the PRs resort to the pecuniary legacy fund (see **27.7.2**).

28.6.1 Express provision by will for payment of pecuniary legacies

An example of a clause expressly for the payment of pecuniary legacies may be taken from the extract from Tom Smith's will (Clause 4) first mentioned in connection with the payment of debts in **27.6.1**.

The clause reads as follows:

> I GIVE all my estate both real and personal whatsoever and wheresoever not hereby or by any codicil hereto otherwise specifically disposed of (hereinafter called 'my residuary estate') unto my trustees UPON TRUST to raise and discharge thereout my debts and funeral and testamentary expenses and all legacies given hereby or by any codicil hereto and any and all taxes payable by reason of my death in respect of property given free of tax and subject thereto UPON TRUST to pay and divide the same equally between...

The clause should be construed again, this time to ascertain its effect on the payment of pecuniary legacies.

There is clear intention shown by the testator to pay the pecuniary legacies from the fund of general residue described as 'my residuary estate'. If, instead, the clause gave the residuary estate 'subject to' or 'after payment of' the pecuniary legacies, the effect would be the same, that is, the legacies should be paid from the fund of residue before the division of the balance between the residuary beneficiaries.

28.6.2 No express provision in the will

Where there is no intention expressed as to the payment of pecuniary legacies some complex questions of incidence must be addressed. The problem is similar to that which arises in the case of payment of funeral and testamentary expenses and debts, although the law relating to the incidence of pecuniary legacies is more complex. It is, therefore, even more important for the testator to provide express provision in the will as to payment of pecuniary legacies.

28.7 INCIDENCE OF PECUNIARY LEGACIES

The following examples illustrate the principles which apply where the will contains no direction for the payment of the pecuniary legacies. Particular difficulties can arise where there is a partial intestacy, for example where part of a gift of residue fails because one of the beneficiaries dies before the testator and the gift is not saved by another provision in the will. This is addressed in the first example; the second example deals with the more common situation where the will has disposed of residue fully.

28.7.1 Position where there is a partial intestacy

Where there is a partial intestacy, the PRs must consider carefully the following possibilities when determining the appropriate source of funds for the payment of a pecuniary legacy. First, they must determine whether a statutory or an express trust governs the undisposed of share of residue.

Statutory trust: AEA 1925, s 33
AEA 1925, s 33 (referred to in **16.2.1**) imposes a statutory trust over the undisposed of property. It directs the PRs to pay the legacy from a fund set aside out of the proceeds of the sale of this property.

> *Example 1*
> A will leaves a legacy of £1,000 to Angus. Residue of the estate is given to

Bertie as to one half, and Corinne as to the other half. Corinne predeceased the testator and no provision saves the gift from lapse.

If the testator's estate is valued at £100,000 (and if debts are ignored), Bertie will receive £50,000; Corinne's half share will be £49,000, ie her share is used to pay the legacy before the balance is distributed under the intestacy law.

Had the will contained express direction for payment from residue before division between the beneficiaries in the manner referred to in **28.6.1**, Bertie's share and Corinne's share would each amount to £49,500, ie £100,000 − £1,000 = £99,000 ÷ 2.

Express trust contained in the will

If residue is left in the will on an express trust, the statutory trust in AEA 1925, s 33 (discussed in **16.2.1**) will not apply to the administration. This is because AEA 1925, s 33(7) provides that s 33 of the Act is subject to the terms of the testator's will, and the express trust will be construed as excluding the statutory trust. Thus, the PRs are not directed by this section to set aside a fund for the payment of the legacy.

However, the problem confronting the PRs is whether or not the statutory order for payment of debts set out in AEA 1925, First Schedule, Part II (discussed in **27.7.2**) should be followed. The problem arises because the statutory order directs the PRs to set aside a fund for payment of pecuniary legacies (as well as debts) from the lapsed share. However, there are conflicting decisions of equal authority as to whether the PRs should then pay the legacies from this fund rather than from residue generally.

Example 2
The facts are the same as in Example 1 above, but the will contains an express trust. There is no direction for the payment of the legacy given to Angus.

If the PRs pay the legacy from the fund set aside from the lapsed share, this would mean that Corinne's one half share would be reduced to £49,000. If instead they pay the legacy from general residue, both Bertie's one half share and Corinne's one half share would amount to £49,500.

It is evident that the complexity of these provisions and the uncertainty of the law make it essential that a will should contain an express provision as to payment of pecuniary legacies (in the same way as for the payment of debts). In any event, a will should be drafted so as to avoid a lapsed share of residue, for example by including a class gift of the residuary estate or substitutional gifts, as discussed in Chapter 9.

28.7.2 Position where the residue is fully disposed of by the will

Example
A will leaves a legacy of £5,000 to Dawn. There is no direction as to payment of the legacy. Residue consisting of personalty and realty is given by the will to 'Edward if he shall survive me by 28 days'. He does so survive the testator, and residue is, therefore, fully disposed of.

Again the PRs need to determine the fund for payment of the legacy given to Dawn, but in this case the problem is less difficult to resolve. Had the will given the realty and personalty separately, only the personalty (or its proceeds of sale) would have been available for payment of the legacy; the PRs could not have sold realty for this purpose. As the amount of personal estate in residue generally exceeds the amount of any pecuniary legacies, there is normally no problem for the PRs since they will pay the legacies from that source.

However, in this example, as both realty and personalty have been given together, realty (or its proceeds of sale) is available to the executors in the unlikely event that the personalty in the testator's estate is insufficient to pay the legacy. It is still necessary to pay the legacy from the personalty first, with the proceeds of the realty being used afterwards if necessary.

28.8 TIME FOR PAYMENT OF PECUNIARY LEGACIES

28.8.1 The executor's year

The general rule is that a pecuniary legacy is payable at the end of 'the executor's year', ie one year after the testator's death. AEA 1925, s 44 provides that PRs are not bound to distribute the estate to the beneficiaries before the expiration of one year from the death (see **25.5.6**). It is often difficult to make payment within the year and, if payment is delayed beyond this date, the legatee will be entitled to interest by way of compensation. The rate of interest will either be 6 per cent per annum or the rate prescribed by the testator's will. If the testator stipulates that the legacy is to be paid 'immediately following my death', or that it is payable at some future date or on the happening of a particular contingency, then interest is payable from either the day following the date of death, the future date or the date the contingency occurs, as may be appropriate.

28.8.2 Interest payable from the date of death

There are four occasions when, as an exception to the normal rule, interest is payable on a pecuniary legacy from the date of the death. These occur when legacies are:

(1) payable in satisfaction of a debt owed by the testator to a creditor;
(2) charged on realty owned by the testator;
(3) payable to the testator's infant child (historically this was so that provision was made for maintenance of the child, and interest is not payable under this provision if other funds exist for the child's maintenance); or
(4) payable to any child (not necessarily the child of the testator) where the intention is to provide for the maintenance of that child.

28.9 INTESTACY OR PARTIAL INTESTACY

The provisions applicable to beneficiaries on a total or partial intestacy have been considered in Chapter 16. In either of these cases, once the debts and other expenses have been paid or provided for, the PRs should consider distribution of the non-residuary estate, ie the personal chattels and the statutory legacy to the surviving spouse.

Chapter 29

COMPLETING THE ADMINISTRATION AND DISTRIBUTING THE RESIDUARY ESTATE

29.1 INTRODUCTION

Once the PRs have paid the deceased's funeral and testamentary expenses and debts and any legacies given by the will, they can consider distribution of the residuary estate in accordance with the will or the intestacy rules.

The PRs may have made interim distributions to the residuary beneficiaries on account of their entitlements, at the same time ensuring that they have retained sufficient assets to cover any outstanding liabilities, particularly tax.

Before drawing up the estate accounts and making the final distribution of residue, the PRs must deal with all outstanding matters. Such matters relate mostly to adjustments to the IHT liability, but there will also be income tax and CGT to consider.

Statutes on income tax and CGT can be found in the Yellow Tax Handbook, and for more detail on these taxes see Whitehouse. CGT is governed principally by the Taxation of Chargeable Gains Act 1992 (TCGA 1992).

For sources and detail on IHT, see **18.1**.

Chapter 29 contents
Introduction
Adjusting the IHT assessment
Inland Revenue corrective account
IHT clearance certificate
Income tax and CGT
Transferring assets to residuary beneficiaries
Estate accounts

29.2 ADJUSTING THE IHT ASSESSMENT

29.2.1 IHT paid on application for the grant

The IHT payable on the deceased's non-instalment option property must be paid by the PRs before they can apply for the grant (see **18.10.1**). Any adjustment to this property may give rise to additional liability to tax, or to a refund of tax if the amount paid before the grant was obtained is shown to be excessive. The reasons why adjustments may be necessary are considered in **29.2.4**.

29.2.2 IHT by instalments

The PRs may have opted to pay IHT by instalments on the property in the deceased's estate attracting the instalment option. Depending on the time taken to administer the estate, possibly only one of the 10 instalments will have been paid, leaving a continuing liability for the following 9 years. As the PRs are liable to pay this outstanding amount, it is essential that they decide how their liability is to be discharged. Details of the instalment option facility are discussed in **18.10.2**. If any instalment option property is sold, any outstanding IHT becomes due immediately.

29.2.3 IHT on lifetime transfers

If the deceased dies within 7 years of making either a potentially exempt transfer (PET), or a chargeable transfer, IHT (if a PET) or more IHT (if a chargeable transfer) may become payable. For details of the circumstances in which such liability can arise, and the manner of calculation of the tax, see **18.13** and the LPC Resource Book *Pervasive Topics* (Jordans, 1997), Part I.

Liability

Although the general rule is that the donees of lifetime transfers are primarily liable for the tax, the PRs of the donor's estate may become liable if the tax remains unpaid by the donees 12 months after the end of the month in which the donor died. However, the PRs liability is limited to the extent of the deceased's assets which they have received, or would have received in the administration of the estate but for their neglect or default.

In addition, if the deceased gave away property during his lifetime but, having reserved a benefit in that property, such property is treated as part of his estate on death (see **18.9.4**). The donee of the gift is primarily liable to pay the tax attributable but, if the tax remains unpaid 12 months after the end of the month of death, the PRs become liable.

Retention of assets to cover IHT

As PRs can be liable for IHT in relation to lifetime transfers, they should consider carefully whether to retain sufficient assets in the estate with which to discharge any such liability. The amount of this potential liability can be quantified relatively easily in relation to known lifetime transfers (so that adequate funds can be retained). Difficulty will arise should the existence of the transfers, even after extensive enquiries, be unknown to the PRs. As the risk is unknown, it is improbable that the PRs will be able to arrange suitable insurance cover. However, PRs who are solicitors are provided with cover under the Solicitors' Indemnity Fund to the extent that funds are otherwise unavailable.

Other IHT consequences

In addition to the consequences explained above, problems of cumulation may arise. The effect of cumulation of lifetime transfers made within the 7 years before the deceased's death (described in **18.8.2**) is to determine the rate(s) at which the deceased's estate is charged to IHT. Discovery of a previously unknown lifetime transfer may, therefore, give rise to additional liability to tax on the estate, for which the PRs are personally accountable. The possibility of this liability arising should be considered carefully, and funds should be reserved by the PRs where appropriate.

29.2.4 IHT loss relief

Where 'qualifying investments' are sold within 12 months of death for less than their market value at the date of death (ie 'probate value'), then the sale price may be substituted for the market value at death (IHTA 1984, ss 178–189). 'Qualifying investments' include shares or securities which are quoted on a recognised stock exchange at the date of death and also holdings in authorised unit trusts.

There are similar provisions relating to the sale of land within 4 years of the death at a loss (IHTA 1984, ss 190–198).

> *Example 1*
> Terence died 9 months ago. His estate included a holding of quoted shares valued for probate at £10,000 and a house valued for probate at £150,000. His PRs have recently sold both assets: the shares were sold for £9,000 and the house for £135,000.

Provided certain conditions are satisfied, the PRs may substitute the figures of £9,000 and £135,000 (ie the gross sale proceeds) for the original probate values of £10,000 and £150,000 for the shares and house respectively. This action may lead to a repayment of IHT.

If the PRs make several sales of qualifying investments in the 12-month period, the aggregate of the sale proceeds over the whole period must be taken into account when determining whether there has been a loss (or gain) on sale (IHTA 1984, s 179).

Example 2
James died last year leaving shares in Red Plc (probate value £5,000), shares in Blue Plc (probate value £8,000) and shares in Green Plc (probate value £10,000). Two months after his death, the shares in Red Plc were sold for £6,000; a further 3 months later the shares in Green Plc were sold for £11,000; finally, 9 months after his death, the shares in Blue Plc were sold for £4,000. When calculating the loss, the PRs must take the sales of all three holdings into account. They cannot claim a loss of £4,000 on the shares in Blue Plc; instead they may claim relief for an overall loss of £2,000 (taking into account the gains on the other two holdings).

Had an overall gain been made, the Inland Revenue would not have been able to claim extra IHT, but no loss relief could have been claimed on any particular shareholding sold at a loss.

Note that if an overall gain has been made CGT may arise (see **29.5.4**).

Under the IHTA s 179, the relief for qualifying investments may be claimed only on an actual sale. Originally, no relief was available if the shares simply became worthless or were cancelled. New provisions introduced in March 1993 allow relief for qualifying investments which are cancelled without replacement within 12 months of death or are suspended within 12 months of death and remain so on the first anniversary of the death, provided the PRs still hold the shares at the date of cancellation or first anniversary of the death. For IHT purposes, the cancellation or first anniversary will be treated as a deemed sale (and the value of the qualifying investments at that date may be substituted for probate value).

29.2.5 IHT adjustments

Adjustment to the amount of IHT payable on the instalment and non-instalment option property in the estate may arise for a number of reasons including:

(1) The discovery of additional assets or liabilities since the Inland Revenue account was submitted.
(2) The discovery of lifetime transfers made by the deceased within the 7 years before death (as discussed in **29.2.3**).
(3) The reaching of agreement of provisionally estimated values, for example with the shares valuation division of the Inland Revenue (in the case of shares in private companies) or the district valuer (in the case of land). The shares valuation division and the district valuer are official agencies established for the formal agreement of valuations on behalf of the Inland Revenue with PRs and others. Especially in the case of private company shares, but also in the case of land, valuations may require long negotiations and can often delay reaching a final settlement of IHT liabilities.

(4) A tax liability or repayment, in relation to the deceased's income and capital gains before the death, having been agreed between the PRs and the Inland Revenue.
(5) Sales made by the PRs after the deceased's death which have given rise to a claim to the IHT 'loss relief' (see **29.2.4**).
(6) A post-death variation or disclaimer which has resulted in an increase or decrease in the liability to IHT (see Chapter 30).

If substantial additional assets or necessary adjustments come to light, they should be reported immediately to the CTO even if it is known that further amendments are likely and a corrective account is to be delivered later. If the PRs know that further IHT will arise, a payment made on account will prevent further interest running.

29.3 INLAND REVENUE CORRECTIVE ACCOUNT

29.3.1 Corrective account

When all variations in the amount or extent of the deceased's assets and liabilities are known, and all reliefs to which the estate is entitled have been quantified, the PRs must report all outstanding matters to the Capital Taxes Office (CTO). This report is made by way of a corrective account on Form Cap D3, although in a case where there are only minor adjustments to be made a letter will generally suffice. The form is signed by the PRs as disclosing all matters relevant to the IHT position of the estate, but it does not require self-assessment of IHT by the PRs, unlike the original Form IHT 200. An example will be found in Appendix 3. Submission of the form results in the CTO issuing the final IHT assessment.

29.3.2 Final IHT assessment

The assessment should be checked carefully. An example will be found in Appendix 2. If it is correct, the PRs should arrange to pay any further IHT which is due or seek a repayment of any overpaid IHT.

29.4 IHT CLEARANCE CERTIFICATE

29.4.1 Certificate of discharge

The last step for the PRs to take in relation to IHT is to obtain from the CTO a certificate of discharge from any further claim to IHT. If the CTO is satisfied that IHT attributable to a chargeable transfer has been paid they can and, if the transfer is one made on death, they must, give a certificate. The effect of the certificate is to discharge all persons, thus in particular the PRs, from further liability to IHT (unless there is fraud or non-disclosure of material facts). The same certificate also extinguishes any Inland Revenue charge imposed on the deceased's property for the IHT.

29.4.2 IHT Form Cap 30

To obtain the certificate of discharge the PRs complete an application in duplicate on IHT Form Cap 30. This form summarises all particulars relating to the deceased, his estate and the Inland Revenue accounts already submitted, and includes the

PRs' request for a formal certificate of discharge. The CTO will return the form with the certificate endorsed on it. An example of IHT Form Cap 30 with certificate appears in Appendix 3.

In cases where the estate is an 'excepted estate', a certificate is not required because automatic discharge from liability is generally given within 35 days of issue of the grant.

29.4.3 Limited discharge

A full certificate of discharge cannot be issued to the PRs if they are paying the IHT by instalments. However, it is possible in such cases for the PRs to obtain a full certificate of discharge 'save and except' the IHT payable on the instalment option property; once all the IHT has been paid, the PRs should apply for a full certificate.

29.5 INCOME TAX AND CGT

29.5.1 The deceased's liability

Immediately following the death, the PRs must make a return to the Inland Revenue of the income and capital gains of the deceased for the period starting on 6 April before the death and ending with the date of death. Even though the deceased died part way through the income tax year, the PRs, on his behalf, may claim the same reliefs and allowances as the deceased could have claimed had he lived throughout the whole year. Any liability to tax must be paid by the PRs during the administration, and it will represent a debt due at death deductible by them when calculating the amount of IHT. Alternatively, if a refund of tax is obtained this will represent an asset, so increasing the size of the estate for IHT purposes.

Because of the effect on the IHT calculation caused by the deceased's income and CGT position, the outstanding pre-death tax return should be submitted by the PRs as soon as possible after the death. However, it normally takes some time for the return to be processed and in order to avoid delay in obtaining the grant of representation the PRs usually estimate any liability for the purposes of completing the Inland Revenue account (if required) and then submit a corrective account when the exact amount of tax due has been agreed with the Inland Revenue.

29.5.2 The administration period

For each income tax year (or part) during the administration period the PRs must make a return to the Inland Revenue of the income they receive on the deceased's assets, and any gains they make on disposals of chargeable assets for administration purposes, for example to raise money to pay IHT or the pecuniary legacies. These returns for the estate are distinct from the PRs' returns of their own income and capital gains.

29.5.3 Income tax

Calculation of PRs' liability

In calculating any income tax liability on the income of the administration period, the PRs may be able to claim relief for interest paid on a loan to pay IHT. It will be recalled that the PRs must pay IHT on the non-instalment option property in the estate before obtaining a grant. Often they will need to borrow money from a bank for this purpose. If the PRs use this loan to pay the IHT on the deceased's personal property in the UK which devolves on them in order to obtain the grant, income tax relief is generally available to them. As their liability is as representatives of the deceased, the PRs cannot claim a single person's relief or other similar relief to set against the estate income.

Example

PRs receive gross dividend income of £4,000 for a tax year in the administration period. They pay £1,000 interest to the bank on a loan to pay IHT to obtain their grant.

Gross income	£4,000
Less: interest paid	£1,000
Taxable income	£3,000
Less lower rate (20%)	£600
Net income for the beneficiaries	£2,400

Rate of tax

After deducting the relief to which they are entitled, the PRs pay income tax at the lower rate of 20 per cent on dividends and any other savings income, and at 23 per cent on other income. PRs do not pay income tax at any higher rate(s).

Effect of deduction of income tax at source

In many cases the PRs will have no tax to pay since income is often received after income tax at the lower rate has been deducted at source. This will apply to dividends and other savings income. In such cases, if the PRs are to obtain relief for interest they have paid on a loan to pay IHT they must seek a refund of tax from the Inland Revenue.

Example

PRs receive interest of £400 (net) on the deceased's building society account. £100 tax is paid by the building society on the gross interest of £500. The PRs paid £50 interest to the bank on a loan to pay IHT to obtain their grant. There is no other estate income.

	£	Tax paid £	Interest received £
Gross interest	500	100	400
Less: interest paid by PRs	50		
PR's liability	450 × 20% =	90	
Refund due to the PRs from the Inland Revenue		10	

The tax paid (£100) exceeds the PRs' liability (£90). The PRs must seek a refund of £10 from the Inland Revenue. It will make the refund from the £100 already received from the building society.

Beneficiary's income tax liability

Once the PRs' tax position has been settled, the remaining net income will be paid to the beneficiary. The grossed up amount of this income should be included by the beneficiary in his return of income for the income tax year to which it relates.

> *Example*
>
> PRs have completed the administration of an estate and there is dividend and bank deposit account interest which, after payment of lower rate tax by the PRs, amounts to £800. That sum is paid by the PRs to the residuary beneficiary.
>
> When the beneficiary makes his return of income he must declare the estate income grossed up at lower rate (20%), ie £800 × $\frac{100}{80}$ = £1,000.
>
> The PRs will supply the beneficiary with a certificate of deduction of tax, on Form R185E, which the beneficiary should send to his own inspector of taxes as evidence of the payment of the lower rate tax by the PRs.

29.5.4 CGT

No disposal on death

As explained in the LPC Resource Book *Pervasive Topics* (Jordans, 1997), Part I, on death there is no disposal for CGT purposes, so no liability to CGT arises. The PRs acquire all the deceased's assets at their probate value at death. This has the effect of wiping out gains which accrued during the deceased's lifetime so that these gains are not charged to tax. The probate value becomes the PRs' 'base cost' of all the deceased's assets for future CGT purposes.

Sales by the PRs

If the PRs dispose of chargeable assets during the administration of the deceased's estate to raise cash (eg to pay IHT or other outgoings or legacies), they are liable to CGT on any chargeable gains that they make. PRs pay CGT at the uniform rate of 23 per cent (ie the equivalent of the basic rate of income tax) whatever the size of the gains made.

Calculation of liability

When calculating the amount of any chargeable gain, the PRs may deduct from the disposal consideration the incidental costs of disposal (eg stockbroker's commission on sale of shares). In addition, they may deduct a proportion of the cost of valuing the deceased's estate for probate purposes. Calculations may be based either on a scale published by the Inland Revenue or on the actual expenditure incurred if this is higher.

The indexation allowance applies in the same way as for individuals.

The PRs may claim an annual exemption for the tax year in which the deceased died and the following 2 tax years only (if the administration lasts this long). The exemption is the same as for an individual (ie £6,500 for 1997/98). Maximum advantage will be taken from this exemption if the PRs plan sales of assets carefully, so that gains are realised in stages in each of the 3 tax years for which it is available.

Example

PRs need to raise £50,000 to pay administration expenses. The investments they are advised to sell will realise a net gain of £10,000. They have no unused losses.

(1) If all sales occur in the same tax year, their CGT position is as follows:

	£	
gain	10,000	
annual exemption	6,500	
taxable	3,500	at 23% = £805

(2) If the sales are spread evenly over 2 tax years, their CGT position is as follows:

		£
Year 1	gain	5,000
	annual exemption	6,500
	taxable	nil
Year 2	gain	5,000
	annual exemption	6,500
	taxable	nil

Sales at a loss

If the PRs sell assets for less than their value at death, an allowable loss for CGT will arise. This loss may be relieved by setting it against gains arising on other sales by the PRs in the same, or any future tax year, in the administration period. Any loss which is unrelieved at the end of the administration period cannot be transferred to the beneficiaries. In view of this limitation, the PRs should plan sales carefully to ensure they can obtain relief for all losses which they realise. If there is a possibility of losses being unused, the PRs should either plan sales of other assets or consider transferring the assets worth less than their probate value to the beneficiaries (see below).

Interaction of IHT 'loss relief' and CGT

Where the IHT 'loss relief' described in **29.2.4** is claimed, the result for CGT is that the PRs have, effectively, disposed of the shares or the land for neither a gain nor a loss, so that neither liability to tax nor utilisation of losses need be considered.

Example (ignoring indexation allowance etc)

The PRs sell the deceased's holding of 'qualifying shares' for £8,000 at a loss of £2,000 compared to their probate value of £10,000.

(1) IHT loss relief is not claimed:

Disposal consideration	£8,000
Less: base cost (probate value at death)	£10,000
Loss (available to the PRs for CGT)	(£2,000)

Alternatively:

(2) IHT loss relief is claimed:

Disposal consideration	£8,000
Less: base cost (probate value as substituted)	£8,000
Loss/gain (for CGT)	nil

In such cases the PRs must consider whether the estate will benefit more from one relief or the other. They must balance the saving (if any) in IHT at the maximum rate of 40 per cent against foregoing CGT loss relief (by setting the loss against their other chargeable gains) at the maximum rate of 24 per cent. If no IHT is payable on the estate, for example because of the spouse exemption or because the estate falls within the nil rate band, no IHT advantage can be obtained. In such a case, CGT loss relief may be more valuable to the PRs. On the other hand, if the IHT estate rate exceeds the CGT rate of 24 per cent, loss relief for IHT will prove more valuable.

Transfer of assets to the 'legatees'

If, instead of selling assets, the PRs vest them in the legatees, no chargeable gain arises and the legatee is treated as if the PRs' acquisition of the asset had been his acquisition (TCGA 1992, s 62(4)). For CGT purposes, 'legatee' is defined in s 64(2) of that Act and includes any person inheriting under the will or under the intestacy rules. It also includes cases where property is transferred to trustees to hold on trusts which arise on death, for example where the will leaves the residuary estate in trust for the testator's spouse for life with remainder to their children. The transfer by the PRs to the trustees will not give rise to CGT.

The legatee is assumed to acquire the asset transferred to him at its probate value. This 'base cost' of the asset will be relevant to the CGT calculation when the legatee disposes of the asset in the future.

Example

A testator by will leaves his residuary estate to Phil. Among the assets forming residue are 1,000 shares in XYZ plc. Probate value of these was £5,000. Since death they have risen to £10,000. Five years after death Phil sells them for £15,000.

Disposal consideration		£15,000
Less : base cost (probate value)	£5,000	
: indexation allowance (increase in RPI since death)	£500	£5,500
Gain		£9,500
Less annual exemption		£6,500
Chargeable gain		£3,000

The increase in value to £10,000 at the date of the transfer to Phil is not relevant to his CGT position. Likewise, if the shares had fallen in value since the death, this would be ignored when the shares were transferred. However, if he sells the shares for £2,000 less than their probate value his position would be as follows:

Disposal consideration	£3,000
Less base cost (probate value)	£5,000
Loss	(£2,000)

The loss of £2,000 is available to Phil to set against chargeable gains he may have in the same, or any future tax year.

29.6 TRANSFERRING ASSETS TO RESIDUARY BENEFICIARIES

29.6.1 Interim distributions

Once the outstanding tax, legal costs and other matters have been disposed of, PRs should consider transferring any remaining assets to the residuary beneficiaries. In doing so they must remember that payments may have been made already to the beneficiaries as interim distributions on account of their entitlement. If so, these will be taken into account when determining what and how much more should be transferred to those beneficiaries. These interim distributions will also be shown in the estate accounts.

29.6.2 Adult beneficiaries

If the beneficiaries are adults, and have a vested entitlement to property in the residuary estate, their entitlement can be transferred to them. If they have a contingent entitlement, the property cannot be transferred to them but will instead be transferred to trustees to hold on their behalf until the contingency is satisfied.

29.6.3 Minor beneficiaries

If any beneficiaries are under 18 years of age, whether the interest enjoyed is vested or contingent, the property will be held in trust for them until the age of majority is reached or the contingency is satisfied. If a minor beneficiary has a vested interest the PRs may be able to transfer his entitlement to other persons in the manner set out below. If these options are not available for any reason, or if the beneficiary's interest is contingent, the PRs will retain the property (as trustees) for the beneficiary.

Infant receipt clause in a will
The PRs may be able to transfer the property to the beneficiary personally if the will contains an appropriate infant receipt clause as described in **10.2.4**. Generally, a clause of this type will only permit transfer by the PRs if the beneficiary has attained the age of 16 years. In addition it may permit transfer of the property to the beneficiary's parent or guardian from whom the PRs can receive an appropriate receipt.

AEA 1925, s 42
Under AEA 1925, s 42 (see **25.5.5**), the PRs may transfer property to which the beneficiary has a vested entitlement to two trustees, or a trust corporation, to hold until the beneficiary attains majority. Often this provision is used to transfer the property to the beneficiary's parents, providing the PRs with a full discharge.

29.6.4 Transferring property to the residuary beneficiaries

The manner in which the property is transferred to residuary beneficiaries, or to trustees on their behalf, will depend on the nature of the property remaining in the estate.

Personal property
The PRs indicate that they no longer require property for administration purposes when they pass title to it by means of an assent. In general, no particular form of assent is required in the case of personalty, so that often the property passes by

delivery, for example the beneficiary collects from the PRs the property given to him by the will. The beneficiary's title to the property derives from the will; the assent is merely the manner of giving effect to the gift by the PRs.

However, more formal steps must be taken to transfer certain assets to the beneficiaries. For example, special withdrawal or transfer forms are needed for National Savings Certificates and money in national savings accounts. Company shares are transferred by share (stock) transfer form. Although it is not necessary for the PRs to be registered as members of the company before transferring the shares, the PRs must produce their grant to the company as proof of title to the shares. They, as transferors, may transfer the shares 'as PRs of X deceased' to the beneficiary (the transferee), who then applies to be registered as a member of the company in place of the deceased member. Assets such as Premium Bonds cannot be transferred to beneficiaries. They must be surrendered and the cash transferred instead.

Any money remaining in the estate at the end of the administration is transferred by cheque drawn on the PRs' bank account, or the solicitor's client account, depending where the money has been placed during the period of administration.

The same principles apply where PRs are transferring property to beneficiaries under the intestacy rules.

Beneficiaries will discharge PRs from any further liability in relation to their entitlement by giving a signed receipt. The residuary beneficiaries should be asked to sign the estate accounts to signify their approval of the accounts, as well as receipt of their entitlement.

Freehold or leasehold land

PRs vest the legal estate in land in the person entitled (whether beneficially or as trustee) by means of an assent which will then become a document of title to the legal estate. If PRs are to continue to hold property in their changed capacity as trustees under trusts declared by the will, or arising under the intestacy law, an assent will again be appropriate. The PRs should formally vest the legal estate in themselves as trustees to hold for the beneficiaries.

By AEA 1925, s 36(4), an assent must be in writing, it must be signed by the PRs, and it must name the person in whose favour it is made. It then operates to vest the legal estate in the named person. A deed is not necessary to pass the legal estate but PRs must use a deed if they require the beneficiary to give them the benefit of an indemnity covenant. If the title to the land is registered, the assent must be in the form specified by the Land Registration Rules 1925.

Any person in whose favour the PRs make an assent or conveyance may require notice of it to be endorsed on the original grant of probate or administration. In view of this entitlement, it is good practice that the endorsement should be made by the PRs, or solicitors on their behalf, as a matter of routine at the same time as the assent is given. Indeed, if the PRs have made an assent where the title is unregistered in favour of a beneficiary, endorsement is essential for that beneficiary's protection in view of the provisions of AEA 1925, s 36(6) benefiting any later purchaser from the PRs.

If the title to the land is registered, two options are open to the PRs:

(1) they can apply to be registered as proprietor in place of the deceased, in which case they must produce the grant of representation when making the application; or
(2) they can transfer the property by assent without being registered as proprietors themselves, in which case the beneficiary must be given a certified copy of the grant of representation so that he can present it with his application for registration.

As the register is conclusive as to title, the provisions in the AEA 1925 regarding endorsements on the grant are of no relevance.

29.7 ESTATE ACCOUNTS

29.7.1 Purpose of the accounts

The final task of the PRs is usually to produce estate accounts for the residuary beneficiaries. Their task will be considerably eased if they have kept full records of all transactions affecting the estate during the course of its administration (see **24.3**). The purpose of the accounts is to show all the assets of the estate, the payment of the debts, administration expenses and legacies and the balance remaining for the residuary beneficiaries. The balance will normally be represented by a combination of assets transferred to the beneficiaries in specie, and some cash. Approval of the accounts is shown by signature of the residuary beneficiaries on the accounts. In the absence of fraud or failure to disclose assets, their signatures will also release the PRs from further liability to account to the beneficiaries.

29.7.2 Presentation of the accounts

There is no prescribed form for estate accounts. Any presentation adopted should be clear and concise so that the accounts are easily understood by the residuary beneficiaries. If interim distribution payments were made to the residuary beneficiaries during the administration period these must be taken into account and shown in the estate accounts.

29.7.3 Form and content of accounts

Vertical presentation
Estate accounts may be presented vertically, disclosing assets less liabilities etc, and a balance for the beneficiaries, or on a double-sided basis, disclosing receipts opposite the payments. The example set out in Appendix 4 adopts the more usual vertical format. It is customary to use the probate values of the assets for accounting purposes.

Narrative introduction
The accounts generally start with a narrative statement of the date of death, the date of the grant of representation, a summary of the will or succession under the intestacy law and the value of the deceased's gross and net estate. This information is provided to make the understanding of the accounts easier for the beneficiaries.

Capital and income accounts

Normally accounts show capital assets, and income produced by those assets during the administration period, in separate capital and income accounts. In small estates this may not be necessary so that one account showing both capital and income will be sufficient. However, it is always necessary to prepare separate accounts if the will (or the intestacy rules) creates a life or minority interest, since the different interests of the beneficiaries in the capital and income need to be distinguished throughout the period of the trust and when it ends.

Chapter 30

POST-DEATH VARIATIONS AND DISCLAIMERS

30.1 INTRODUCTION

30.1.1 Reasons for using variations and disclaimers

It should not be assumed that the beneficiaries always wish to accept their inheritance under a will or the intestacy provisions. Personal and family reasons may indicate that a different distribution of the deceased's assets among members of the family, or indeed among other beneficiaries, may be more appropriate in the light of the circumstances as they exist at the death. For example, a surviving spouse who inherits the whole of the deceased spouse's estate may wish to make some immediate provision for their children, particularly if the surviving spouse is otherwise adequately provided for; alternatively, children inheriting on a parent's death may wish to ensure greater provision is made for their surviving parent. A will, perhaps drafted many years earlier, may be considered 'out of date' in the manner of its division of the deceased's property between the family; the arbitrary effect of the intestacy rules on the distribution of the estate of someone who dies intestate may be found equally inappropriate.

30.1.2 Taxation advantages

Redistribution of inherited property could be achieved by the beneficiary accepting the property and subsequently giving it to the intended donee. If this was done there would be taxation consequences, some of which might be adverse. The beneficiary, as donor, would be making a PET (potentially exempt transfer) for IHT purposes and a disposal of assets for CGT purposes. Such consequences can be avoided by taking advantage of provisions in the IHT and CGT legislation whereby beneficiaries under a will or an intestacy can alter, for tax purposes, the dispositions of a deceased person's estate. If certain conditions are satisfied, such altered dispositions are 'read back' into the will or the distribution on intestacy, and are treated as though made by the deceased person and taxed accordingly. Use of such provisions can often result in considerable savings of IHT as explained later in this chapter.

30.1.3 Ascertaining the wishes of the beneficiaries

In view of the opportunities available for post-death estate planning through use of variations and disclaimers, it is important that their use be considered at an early stage following the death of a client (see **20.8**).

30.2 DISCLAIMER

30.2.1 Succession aspects

A disclaimer is the rejection by the beneficiary of a gift of property. It is possible to disclaim a benefit under a will and also an entitlement under the intestacy rules. All

Chapter 30 contents
Introduction
Disclaimer
Variation
IHT planning aspects of variations

that is necessary for the disclaimer to be effective is for the beneficiary to indicate the intention to disclaim to the deceased's PRs. No formality is required, although in practice it would be prudent to give notice of disclaimer in writing.

Restrictions on disclaimers

It is not always possible for a beneficiary to disclaim property. As a matter of law:

(1) it will be too late to disclaim the property after some benefit has been derived from it, for example after the beneficiary has lived in a house devised to him, or after the receipt of a dividend from shares given specifically by will;

(2) it is necessary that the beneficiary disclaims the entire gift, ie he cannot disclaim part of the property given to him and retain the remainder of it. Only if the will permits partial disclaimer will this be possible. However, if the will gives the same beneficiary two gifts, he may disclaim one while retaining the other, because each may be considered as a separate gift for the purposes of these provisions.

Devolution of disclaimed property

Control over succession to the property disclaimed does not rest with the original beneficiary. That person merely rejects the benefit. Succession to the property will depend on the type of gift or entitlement which is to be disclaimed. Thus:

(1) If a general or specific legacy is to be disclaimed, the property will fall into and devolve as part of the residuary estate.

(2) If a residuary gift is disclaimed, the disclaimed property will pass under the intestacy law, unless the gift was a class gift when the property will pass to the other members of the class. One consequence of the disclaimed gift passing under the intestacy law is that the same beneficiary, in another capacity, may inherit the property, or a share of it, under the intestacy law. This benefit could also be disclaimed separately.

Example
Andrew by will leaves his residuary estate to his sister Betty who is his only surviving relative. If she disclaims the gift, the property will pass as though Andrew had died intestate. Betty will, therefore, inherit as sister of the whole blood, unless she disclaims this entitlement as well.

(3) If the disclaimer is of an interest under an intestacy, the effect is usually to increase the share of the estate enjoyed by the other members of a class of beneficiaries; if there are no other members in that class, then the gift will pass to the next class which has members in existence. The person disclaiming is not treated as having predeceased the intestate for the purposes of the intestacy rules.

Example
Carol (a widow) dies intestate survived by her only relatives who are her two adult children, David and Ellen. David disclaims his entitlement so that Carol's entire estate passes to her daughter Ellen.

Note that if David had children, they would not benefit under the statutory trusts if he were to disclaim. If he wishes to benefit his children, he should consider a variation (**30.3**).

(4) If the disclaimer is of a limited interest, its effect will normally be to accelerate a subsequent interest.

Example
Under the terms of Edward's will, his estate was left on trust for sale for the benefit of his wife for life, with remainder to his adult children absolutely. If, after Edward's death, his wife disclaims her interest, the gift to the children will accelerate so that they will have an immediate right to the capital.

30.2.2 Taxation aspects

Introduction
The rejection of benefit amounts to a PET for IHT purposes, and to a disposal for CGT purposes, by the beneficiary who disclaims entitlement to the property. However, provided certain conditions are satisfied, the disclaimer will not be treated as a PET nor a disposal, so that neither IHT nor CGT will be of concern to the beneficiary.

IHTA 1984, s 142
If the following conditions are satisfied, the disclaimer will not be treated as a PET and IHT will be calculated as if the deceased had left the property to the person(s) becoming entitled to it once the disclaimer takes effect. To be effective the disclaimer must:

(1) not be made for a consideration in money or money's worth (other than the making of a disclaimer or variation of another disposition on the death);
(2) be made in writing; and
(3) be made within 2 years of the death of the deceased.

A copy of the disclaimer should be sent to the CTO unless it was made before the application for a grant, when a copy should accompany the application.

Example
Felicity's will contains a specific devise of her cottage to her elderly brother George; residue passes to her husband Henry. Although no IHT is payable on residue, the cottage is worth £250,000 so that some IHT is payable.

George decides he has no use for the cottage and is considering disclaiming the gift so that the property will pass instead to Henry.

If George disclaims the gift, and the conditions are satisfied, IHT will not be payable on Felicity's death since her estate then passes entirely to her husband and the whole of it benefits from the spouse exemption.

Additional IHT
If the consequence of the making of the disclaimer is to increase the liability to IHT on the deceased's estate, the PRs must calculate their additional liability and disclose it to the Inland Revenue. There is no requirement for the PRs to consent to the making of the disclaimer, even in cases where more tax becomes payable, for example following a disclaimer by a surviving spouse when the surviving spouse exemption is lost for IHT purposes.

TCGA 1992, s 62

The conditions to be satisfied are the same as those applicable to IHT. If they are satisfied, the disclaimer will not amount to a disposal by the beneficiary. The property will be treated for CGT as if the deceased had left it to the person becoming entitled to it following the disclaimer. As no disposal occurs on death, no CGT is payable, so the disclaimer will not affect the CGT position of the PRs on death.

Position where the conditions for IHT and CGT are not satisfied

Making the disclaimer will have taxation consequences for the beneficiary if the conditions above are not satisfied. These are illustrated in the context of the previous example.

Example

If George decides to accept the gift and then gives the cottage to Henry, there will be no alteration to the tax position in Felicity's estate but he runs the risk of IHT on the PET if he dies within 7 years of giving away the cottage. Also, CGT could become payable on the disposal if the cottage has increased in value significantly since Felicity died. The indexation allowance and the annual exemption will help to reduce any gain but the exemption for the principal private residence may not be available if George has another property which is his main residence.

30.3 VARIATION

30.3.1 Succession aspects

The principal difference between a variation and a disclaimer is that, by using a variation, the beneficiary controls the destination of the property. It is a direction by the beneficiary to the PRs to transfer some or all of the property subject to the variation to a particular person or persons who may or may not be beneficiaries already under the will or intestacy rules. It is equivalent to a gift inter vivos by the beneficiary to another person. The beneficiary is not restricted as to the circumstances when he may enter into a variation, for example a variation is available:

(1) if a benefit has been enjoyed from the property, for example by receiving income from it;
(2) after it has been transferred to the beneficiary by the PRs;
(3) after the deceased's estate is fully administered;
(4) in part, ie part of a gift may be varied and the remainder retained by the beneficiary.

30.3.2 Taxation aspects

As in the case of disclaimers, it is necessary to consider the position of both the beneficiary contemplating making the variation and the PRs of the deceased's estate. Often the principal reason for making the variation is an overall tax saving, particularly of IHT, and the relative positions of all concerned must be borne in mind when planning any variation. An illustration is provided in **30.4**.

As the beneficiary entering into the variation is effectively making a gift of the property, questions of IHT and CGT arise in the same way as they arose in relation to disclaimers. The variation will amount to a PET for IHT purposes, and a disposal for CGT purposes by the beneficiary. However, if certain conditions are satisfied, the variation will not be treated as a PET or a disposal, so that no liability to IHT or CGT will arise for the beneficiary.

IHTA 1984, s 142

If certain conditions are satisfied, the variation will not be treated as a PET by the beneficiary. IHT will be calculated as if the deceased had left the property to the person entitled to it as a result of the variation.

The three basic conditions mentioned in **30.2.2** in relation to disclaimers also apply to variations. In addition to satisfying these conditions, the person making the variation (the beneficiary) must give written notice of election to the Inland Revenue within 6 months of the variation (or such longer time as the Inland Revenue may permit). A copy of both the variation and the election must be sent to the CTO unless they were made before the application for a grant, when copies should accompany the application.

> *Example*
> Ian's will leaves a specific legacy of shares worth £200,000 to his cousin Jane and it divides his residuary estate equally between Kate and Lionel, two of the three children of his late brother Michael. Jane has no need for the gift of the shares, preferring instead that all three of Michael's children should benefit. A disclaimer would not achieve her objective since only Kate and Lionel, as residuary beneficiaries, could benefit.
>
> If Jane enters into a variation of the legacy, and the conditions are met (including the election), the IHT liability in Ian's estate will be unaltered since, in effect, one chargeable beneficiary (Jane) is to be substituted by three (Michael's children).

Additional IHT

If the variation increases the liability of the deceased's estate to IHT, the PRs must join in the election. They may refuse to do so only if they hold insufficient assets to discharge the additional tax. For example, if a spouse (an exempt beneficiary) enters into a variation redirecting property to children (non-exempt beneficiaries) there may be additional IHT to pay since the spouse exemption is lost once the variation is made. If the PRs have already distributed the majority of the assets, they may have insufficient remaining to discharge the additional IHT and so may decline to join in the election.

No IHT election

If no written election is given by the beneficiary, or any of the other conditions is not satisfied, the variation will not comply with the conditions of the IHTA 1984, s 142, and will be treated as an inter vivos gift by the beneficiary, ie a PET for IHT purposes. This is illustrated in the context of the previous example.

> *Example*
> If Jane fails to make the election or divides her gift between the three children outside the time-limit, she has made PETs (in total in excess of the nil rate band) with potential liability to IHT if she dies within 7 years. She is also making a disposal of the shares for CGT, with possible liability to tax if they have increased in value since the date of death beyond the amount of the indexation allowance and her annual exemption.

To elect or not to elect for IHT?
Generally, it will be considered beneficial to make an election since there can then only be one charge to IHT in relation to the property which is the subject of the variation. This will occur when it passes from the deceased's estate to the 'new beneficiary'. If no election is made two charges can arise: the first when the property passes under the will or the intestacy to the original beneficiary; the second if that beneficiary dies within 7 years of the gift to the donee (the new beneficiary). As there is no obligation to elect, the relative advantages and disadvantages flowing from an election should always be considered.

TCGA 1992, s 62
The conditions to satisfy are the same as those for IHT, including the election; however, there is no equivalent provision requiring the PRs to join in the election. If the conditions are met, the variation will not amount to a disposal by the beneficiary. The property will be treated for CGT as if the deceased had left it to the person becoming entitled to it following the variation.

To elect or not to elect for CGT?
For CGT, the making of the variation will be a disposal by the beneficiary unless an election is made. It is clear that, if an election is made, no liability occurs either on the variation (because of the election) nor on the death (because there is no disposal on death). The beneficiary should only consider not making the election if that will be of some advantage to him. For example, he might decide not to make an election where the disposal would result in a loss which he could set against other gains, thereby saving CGT. If the gain (after allowing for inflation) does not exceed the annual exempt amount (£6,500 in 1997/98) there would appear to be no purpose in the beneficiary making the election.

Note that it is possible to elect in different ways for CGT and IHT. The beneficiary must decide which election(s) to make (if any).

30.4 IHT PLANNING ASPECTS OF VARIATIONS

30.4.1 Planning a variation

The wish to reduce the tax burden on a death generally governs whether a post-death variation should be made. However, family and personal considerations may give rise to equally compelling reasons for a variation, for example the wish to redirect some property to another member of the family who is otherwise inadequately provided for, or who is not provided for at all. Clearly, full instructions are needed so that appropriate arrangements may be made.

30.4.2 Full use of the IHT nil rate band

The most likely occasion when a variation can achieve a significant saving in IHT is where the nil rate band has not been fully used, for example where an entire estate has been left to a surviving spouse and is therefore exempt. The exemption from tax is superficially attractive but may result in a 'bunching' of estates, and thus an increased liability to tax on the death of the second spouse when the assets in the combined estates pass to the children. If the surviving spouse's position is such that the inherited property can be made the subject of variation, it may be possible to effect a considerable reduction in the overall IHT burden on the family and, in particular, the children.

Example 1
Willemena (W) owns assets worth £250,000 and her husband, Harold (H), owns assets worth £50,000. They have one child, Chloe. W dies, leaving all her estate to H. He dies later leaving all his estate to Chloe.

There will be no IHT on W's death (spouse exemption) but, on H's death, IHT will be charged on £300,000 passing to Chloe (H's estate combined with W's estate). IHT on £300,000 is £34,000 (£215,000 @ 0%; £85,000 @ 40%).

Example 2
The facts are the same as Example 1 above except that, within 2 years after W's death, Harold varies her will by giving a legacy of £175,000 to Chloe, residue to himself. He complies with the necessary IHT and CGT conditions for a variation. For IHT and CGT purposes, W's will is read as though she had left £175,000 to Chloe (covered by her IHT nil rate band) and residue to H (exempt).

On H's death, he leaves Chloe £125,000 (ie £75,000 inherited from W and his own £50,000). This falls within his IHT nil rate band.

A tax saving of £34,000 has been made.

Ideally (from an IHT point of view) W's will should have been in the terms of Example 2 above (see **12.4**). However, it might be unrealistic to expect W to have made a will in these terms since H may have needed their combined estates.

Appendix 1

RODNEY PARKS DECEASED

ATTENDANCE NOTE

Jenkins & Co
Bank Chambers
Newton
Blankshire

Attending Miss P. Dixon and Mrs P. Collyer

Rodney David Parks of 6 Camp Road, Newton, Blankshire died on 3 November 199– in St. Ann's Hospital, Newton. He was 84 years old.

Assets:	£
National Savings Certificates	3,000
Bank account	6,432
Arrears of pension	68

Debts:	
Telephone	37
Funeral account	650

Mr Park's will made when he lived at Downside Villas, Newton, appoints his sister, Elsie Dixon to be his executrix and leaves his estate equally between his two adult nieces Pauline Dixon and Patricia Collyer. Elsie Dixon died 5 years ago and the nieces have agreed that Patricia should act as administratrix; her address is The Old Smithy, School Lane, Newton.

Appendix 1

Oath for Administrators with the Will

IN THE HIGH COURT OF JUSTICE
Family Division

Extracting Solicitor ...Jenkins & Co......................................
Address ..Bank Chambers Newton Blankshire............

* "Principal" or "District Probate". If "District Probate" add "at _____".

† If necessary to include alias of deceased in grant, add "otherwise (alias name)" and state below which is true name and reason for requiring alias.

(¹) "I" or "We". Insert the full name, place of residence and occupation or, if none, description of the deponent(s).

The* DISTRICT PROBATE Registry AT WINCHESTER

IN the Estate of† RODNEY DAVID PARKS

deceased.

(¹) I Patricia Collyer of The Old Smithy School Lane Newton Blankshire

(2) Or "do solemnly and sincerely affirm".

(3) Each testamentary paper must be marked by each deponent, and by the person administering the oath.

(4) "With one, two (or more) Codicils", as the case may be.

(5) If exact age is unknown, give best estimate.

(6) Where there are separate legal divisions in one country, the state, province, etc., should be stated.

(7) Complete both blanks. When either such interest arises, two grantees may be required unless a trust corporation is applying.

(8) Delete "no", if there was settled land vested in deceased which remained settled land notwithstanding his death.

(9) If there was settled land such land may be included in the scope of the grant, but the settlement must be identified and all the applicants must show that they are also entitled to a grant in respect of the settled land.

(10) Here state manner in which all prior rights are satisfied, e.g., residuary legatees/devisees must show that no executors were appointed, or that those appointed either died before deceased or survived him and have since died without taking probate, or that they have renounced probate, or have failed to take a grant after being cited so to do *(the order authorising a grant to citor being quoted)*.

(11) "I am" or "we are" and state title of applicants to the grant, including their relationship to the deceased only if necessary to establish title or identification.

(12) If there was settled land and the grant is to include it, insert "including settled land", but, if the grant is to exclude the settled land, insert "save and except settled land".

(13) Complete this paragraph only if the deceased died on or after 1 April 1981 and an Inland Revenue Account is not required; the next paragraph should be deleted.

(14) The amount to be inserted here should be in accordance with the relevant figure shown in paragraph 1 of the PEP list.

(15) The amount to be inserted here should be in accordance with the relevant figure shown in paragraph 2 of the PEP list.

(16) Complete this paragraph only if an Inland Revenue Account is required and delete the previous paragraph.

make Oath and say (²) that
(¹) I believe the paper writing now produced to and marked by (³) me to contain the true and original last Will and Testament (⁴)

of† RODNEY DAVID PARKS

of 6 Camp Road Newton Blankshire

formerly of Downside Villas Newton Blankshire

deceased,

who died on the 3rd day of November 19 9,

aged 84 years (⁵) domiciled in (⁶) England and Wales

and that there is (⁷) no minority and (⁷) no life interest in the estate of the said deceased; and that to the best of my knowledge, information and belief there was (⁸) [no] land vested in the deceased which was settled previously to his death (and not by his Will (⁴)) and which remained settled land notwithstanding his death (⁹)

and (¹) I further make Oath and say (²) that (¹⁰)

Elsie Dixon the sole executrix named in the will predeceased the deceased

that (¹¹) I am one of the residuary beneficiaries named in the will

; and that
(¹) I will (i) collect, get in and administer according to the law the real and personal Estate (¹²) of the said deceased; (ii) when required to do so by the Court, exhibit on oath in the Court a full inventory of the said Estate, (¹²) and when so required render an account of the administration of the said Estate to the Court; and (iii) when required to do so by the High Court, deliver up the grant of letters of administration with Will annexed to that Court; and that to the best of my knowledge, information and belief.

(¹³) [the gross estate passing under the grant does not exceed (¹⁴) £ 180,000 , and the net estate does not exceed (¹⁵) £ 10,000 , and that this is not a case in which an Inland Revenue Account is required to be delivered]

~~(¹⁶) [the gross estate passing under the grant amounts to £ and the net estate amounts to £~~ ~~].~~
*

SWORN by PATRICIA COLLYER the above-named }
Deponent }
}
at }
}
this day of 19 }

Before me,

A Commissioner for Oaths/Solicitor.

Appendix 2

ALISTAIR DAVIS DECEASED

ATTENDANCE NOTE   23/8/199–

Alistair John Davis died last night. He was a sales executive for a local company.

Address: 53 The Mews, Salthouse Lane, Weyford, Blankshire (purchased in 1976).

Date of Birth: 18 January 1930

No will.

Surviving relatives:
wife – Susan Ann Davis
son – Peter Frank Davis of 3 Fishbourne Road, Weyford
daughter – Katy Louise Brown of the Old Rectory, Twistleton, Cheshire.
(Mrs Brown is disabled and does not wish to be involved in the administration.)

Assets:	£
500 British Telecom plc shares	1,750.00
Current account with Lloyds Bank	837.62
Halifax Building Society account	47,279.18
Prudential life insurance cover	100,000.00
National Savings Certificates	5,000.00
The Mews (owned jointly with Susan)	180,000.00
Debts:	
Barclaycard	866.23
Otterbourne Funeral Directors	1,000.00

Appendix 2

Inland Revenue Account for Inheritance Tax

This Account is for use only for an original grant where the deceased died on or after 18 March 1986 and was domiciled in the United Kingdom, and
- the whole of the estate is situated in the UK
- the deceased within seven years of the death neither made any lifetime transfers of value chargeable with Inheritance Tax nor had any interest in settled property
- the net estate after exemptions and reliefs does not exceed the Inheritance Tax threshold at the death
- the gross estate before exemptions and reliefs does not exceed **twice** the Inheritance Tax threshold at death.

If the deceased died before 18 March 1986 or you need any further help or information, contact the Capital Taxes Office where the staff will be pleased to help you.

Before you start to fill in this Account, read the Guidance Notes in booklet IHT 210. The marginal notes on this Account refer to the relevant paragraphs of the booklet. They will help you to fill it in quickly and correctly. If you need more space use a separate sheet of paper showing to which section of the Account it relates.

Insert 'Principal', or the name of the District and 'District'

In the High Court of Justice Family Division (Probate), The WINCHESTER **Registry**

Solicitor(s) or Agent(s)

Please give your full name and address including postcode, using capital letters, even if the DX code is given

LOWE SNOW & CO
HIGH STREET
WEYFORD
BLANKSHIRE
WY12HA

Please give the full name and title of the deceased using CAPITAL letters

In the estate of
Surname
DAVIS
Title and Forenames
MR ALISTAIR JOHN

Show, for example, 9 January 1993 as 09 Jan 1993

Date of birth 18 JAN 1930   **Date of death** 23 AUG 199-

Marital Status
Married ☐ Single ✓ Divorced ☐ Widowed ☐

Surviving relatives
Husband ☐ Wife ✓ Child(ren) ✓ Parent(s) ☐

All communications concerning Inheritance Tax will be sent to the solicitors or agents unless the executors or administrators request otherwise

DX Code
1234 WEYFORD

Your reference
Cj/WPA

Domicile
England and Wales ✓ Scotland ☐ N. Ireland ☐

Address

You may wish to give the name of the person dealing with this estate

Contact

Telephone
WEYFORD 0678

Fax

Give the last known usual address of the deceased including postcode

53 THE MEWS
SALTHOUSE LANE
WEYFORD
BLANKSHIRE WY2 3FX

If available, please give this information

Tax District and reference
WEYFORD 1 ref 13579

National Insurance No
D/468

Please give the occupation of the deceased

Occupation
SALES EXECUTIVE

Date of Grant (For official use only)

Executors or intending administrators

*Give the full names and **permanent** addresses including postcode of the executors or intending administrators*

SUSAN ANN DAVIS
53 The Mews
Salthouse Lane
Weyford
Blankshire WY2 3FX

PETER FRANK DAVIS
3 Fishbourne Road
Weyford
Blankshire WY2 3LL

IHT202(1993)

Nominated and Joint Property

You must answer these first two questions

Note 7
If 'Yes', please give full particulars below

Did the deceased nominate any Savings Bank Account, Savings Certificates or other assets in favour of any person? Yes [ ] No [✓]

Note 8
If 'Yes', also answer the following questions

Was the deceased joint owner of any property of any description or did the deceased hold any money on a joint account? Yes [✓] No [ ]

On a separate sheet of paper state for each item of joint property
- the name(s) of the other joint owner(s) — SUSAN ANN DAVIS
- when the joint ownership began or when the joint account was opened — 1976

Note 9
- by whom and from what source the joint property was provided and if it or its purchase price was contributed by more than one of the joint owners, the extent of the contribution made by each — equally by co-owners

Note 10
- how any income was dealt with and enjoyed — N/A

If 'Yes' include the value below

Did any joint property pass by survivorship? Yes [✓] No [ ]

If 'Yes' include the value as part of the Free Estate

Did any joint property pass under the deceased's Will or intestacy? Yes [ ] No [✓]

Nominated and Joint Property

All claims for exemptions or reliefs should be made on Page 4

Particulars of the property | **Gross value at date of death**

53 The Mews – freehold property | 90,000

See Note 24 and first paragraph of Note 46 before continuing

Deceased's share of liabilities in respect of the property

Name of creditor	Description of liability	Amount
		NONE

Carry the net value forward to Page 4 Box A

Net value A 90,000

Free Estate

Note 13

All claims for exemptions or reliefs should be made on Page 4

All the property of the deceased in respect of which the grant is required

Property without the Instalment Option

Gross value at date of death

Notes 14, 15 and 16

Stocks, shares, debentures and other securities, as set out on IHT 40 quoted or listed in the Stock Exchange Daily Official List and others, except those qualifying for the instalment option | 1,750
500 BT plc shares @ 350p per share

Note 17 Premium Savings Bonds and National Savings Certificates (including interest) | 5,000

Cash and cash at Bank or Savings Bank, a building society, a co-operative or friendly society, including interest to the date of death, as statement attached | 48,116
[Statement would show Lloyds and Halifax accounts]

Note 20 Policies of insurance and bonuses thereon (if any) on the life of the deceased, as statement attached | 100,000

Saleable value of policies of insurance and bonuses (if any) on the life of any other person, as statement attached |

Income Tax repayable |

Carried forward | 154,866

Property without the Instalment Option - continued

Brought forward 154,866

Note 21
Please attach a valuation if one has been obtained

Household and personal goods, including pictures, china, clothes, books, jewellery, stamp, coin and other collections, motor cars, boats etc

Sold, realised gross

Unsold, estimated

Note 22
Please state the name and date of death of the testator or intestate

Interest in an unadministered estate

Other assets not included above or as instalment option property

Carry the total forward to Page 4 Box B

Total **B** 154,866

Liabilities at the date of death and funeral expenses

Notes 24, 25 and 26

Name of creditor	Description of liability	Amount
Barclaycard	credit card	866
Otterbourne	funeral account	1,000

Note 27
Carry the total forward to Page 4 Box E

Total **E** 1,866

Property with the Instalment Option

Gross value at date of death

Note 28 — Land and buildings as described on IHT 37 attached

Note 29 — Business interests (state nature of business)
- Net value of deceased's interest in business, as statement or balance sheet attached

Note 30
Please give the name of the firm
- Net value of deceased's interest as a partner in the firm of

as statement or balance sheet attached

Note 31 — Stocks, shares, debentures and other securities as set out on form IHT 40
- which gave the deceased control of the company
- other unquoted shares or securities.

Carry the total forward to Page 4 Box C

Total **C** NONE

Liabilities

Note 32

Name of creditor	Description of liability (and property on which charged)	Amount

Carry the total forward to Page 4 Box F

Total **F** NONE

Probate Summary

Aggregate Gross Value
which in law devolves on and vests in the personal representatives of the deceased, for and in respect of which the grant is to be made

					Totals
B	154,866				
+ C	none	=	D	154,866	

Deduct liabilities

E	1,866			
+ F	none	=	G	1,866

Net estate for Probate purposes D - G = H 153,000

Tax Summary

Nominated and joint property (net) A 90,000

As box **H** above + H 153,000 = J 243,000

Notes 42, 43, 44 and 45

Deduct exemptions and reliefs

Nature	Net value	Amount £		
Spouse exemption	House 90,000 Statutory legacy 125,000 Half residue 14,000	90,000 139,000	= K	229,000

Net estate for tax purposes J - K = L 14,000

Note 55

Declaration

Tick the appropriate box

I/We wish to apply for a
- Grant of Probate ☐
- Grant of Letters of Administration ✓
- Grant of Letters of Administration with Will annexed ☐
- Grant _____ ☐

To the best of my/our knowledge and belief all the statements made and particulars given in this Account and its accompanying schedules are true and complete.

I/We have made the fullest enquiries that are reasonably practicable in the circumstances to ascertain the value of all assets, interests, liabilities, etc.

The deceased within 7 years of the death neither made transfers of value chargeable with Inheritance Tax (ie no transfers of value that were not covered by the IHT exemptions nor any gifts, subject to a reservation to the donor).

The estate at the death did not include any property situate outside the UK.

The deceased did not have an interest in settled property at the death nor had within 7 years of death an interest in settled property or settled any property.

Notes 56 and 57

I/We understand that the issue of the Grant does not imply acceptance by the Inland Revenue of any of the statements or values included in this Account.

Warning

An executor or intending administrator who fails to make the fullest enquiries that are reasonably practicable in the circumstances may be liable to penalties.

You may be liable to penalties or prosecution if you fail to disclose, in this Account and in your answers to the questions on Page 2 all the property in respect of which tax may be payable.

SUSAN ANN DAVIS	Name	
	Signature	
	Date	

PETER FRANK DAVIS	Name	
	Signature	
	Date	

Appendix 2

Oath for Administrators

IN THE HIGH COURT OF JUSTICE

Family Division

Extracting Solicitor: Lowe Snow & Co
Address: High Street Weyford Blankshire WY1 2HA

The* DISTRICT PROBATE Registry AT WINCHESTER

IN the Estate of†

ALISTAIR JOHN DAVIS deceased.

(¹) We MRS SUSAN ANN DAVIS of 53 The Mews Salthouse Lane Weyford Blankshire and MR PETER FRANK DAVIS of 3 Fishbourne Road Weyford Blankshire

make Oath and say (²)
that* ALISTAIR JOHN DAVIS
of 53 The Mews Salthouse Lane Weyford Blankshire

deceased

died on the 23rd day of August 199-

aged 6- years (³) domiciled in (⁴) England and Wales
Intestate (⁵)

~~(⁶) or any other person entitled in priority to share in h—— estate by virtue of any enactment~~ and that (⁷) no minority (⁷) but a life interest arises under the intestacy; and that to the best of our knowledge, information and belief there was (⁸) [no] land vested in the said deceased which was settled previously to his death and which remained settled land notwithstanding his death (⁹)

And (¹) We further make Oath and say (²)
that (¹⁰) we are the (¹¹) lawful widow and son and two of the persons entitled to share in the estate

of the said Intestate,

and that (¹) we will (i) collect, get in and administer according to the law the real and personal Estate (¹²) of the said deceased; (ii) when required to do so by the Court, exhibit on oath in the Court a full inventory of the said Estate (¹²) and when so required render an account of the administration of the said Estate to the Court; and (iii) when required to do so by the High Court, deliver up the grant of letters of administration to that Court; and that to the best of our knowledge, information and belief

~~(¹³) [the gross estate passing under the grant does not exceed (¹⁴) £————, and the net estate does not exceed (¹⁵) £————, and that this is not a case in which an Inland Revenue Account is required to be delivered]~~

(¹⁶) [the gross estate passing under the grant amounts to £ 154,866 and the net estate amounts to £ 153,000].
*

SWORN by SUSAN ANN DAVIS the above-named
Deponent

at

this day of 19

Before me,

A Commissioner for Oaths/Solicitor.

SWORN by PETER FRANK DAVIS the above-named
Deponent

at
this   day of   19

Before me,

                A Commissioner for Oaths/Solicitor.

Appendix 3

ROSEMARY JONES DECEASED

ATTENDANCE NOTE

Rosemary Penelope Jones died on 4 June 199–. Her will contained the following provisions:

(a) Executor: Harold Prior (solicitor) of Bank Chambers, Weyford

(b) Legacies: £10,000 to NSPCC (a registered charity)

all her shares in RJP Designs Ltd to her son Daniel

residue to her daughters Tamsin and Dorcas in equal shares.

She was born on 14 November 1950 and is survived by her husband, Tim, and the 3 children.

The estate consists of:	£
Freehouse house 'Languards', Weyford (owned jointly with her husband Tim and bought in 1990)	300,000
10% Treasury Stock 2008	155,000
10,000 Fictional plc shares @ £6.80	68,000
Britannia Building Society account (inc accrued interest)	12,000
Midland Bank current account	2,500
Premium Bonds	10,000
Personal chattels (inc car)	15,000
Life insurance in trust for Tim	250,000
20% shareholding in RPJ Designs Ltd (shares registered in the name of Penny Jones)	200,000
Debts:	
Income tax (weyford 1 district ref 7/59321)	700
Thomson's garage	600
Pitmans Undertakers	1,200

Appendix 3

Inland Revenue Account for Inheritance Tax

This Account is for use only where the deceased died on or after 18 March 1986 and was domiciled in the United Kingdom.

If the deceased died before 18 March 1986 or you need any further help or information, contact the Capital Taxes Office where the staff will be pleased to help you.

Before you start to fill in this Account, read the Guidance Notes in booklet IHT 210. The marginal notes on this Account refer to the relevant paragraphs of the booklet. They will help you to fill it in quickly and correctly. If you need more space use a separate sheet of paper showing to which section of the Account it relates.

Insert 'Principal', or the name of the District and 'District'

In the High Court of Justice Family Division (Probate), The PRINCIPAL **Registry**

Please give your full name and address including postcode, using capital letters, even if the DX code is given

Solicitor(s) or Agent(s)

PRIOR & PRIOR
BANK CHAMBERS
WEYFORD
BLANKSHIRE
W1 3QT

In the estate of

Please give the full name and title of the deceased using CAPITAL letters

Surname: JONES

Title and Forenames: MRS ROSEMARY PENELOPE

Show, for example, 9 January 1993 as 09 Jan 1993

Date of birth: 14 NOV 1950   Date of death: 04 JUN 199-

Marital Status
Married ☐   Single ✓   Divorced ☐   Widowed ☐

Surviving relatives
Husband ✓   Wife ☐   Child(ren) ☐   Parent(s) ✓

All communications concerning Inheritance Tax will be sent to the solicitors or agents unless the executors or administrators request otherwise

DX Code
4321 WEYFORD

Your reference
CJ/App 2

Domicile
England and Wales ✓   Scotland ☐   N. Ireland ☐

You may wish to give the name of the person dealing with this estate

Contact

Give the last known usual address of the deceased including postcode

Address
LANGUARDS
WEYFORD
BLANKSHIRE
WY1 6FL

Telephone
WEYFORD 1230

Fax

If available, please give this information

Tax District and reference
WEYFORD 1 7/59321

Please give the occupation of the deceased

Occupation
Company Director

National Insurance No
J/641

Date of Grant (For official use only)

Executors or intending administrators

*Give the full names and **permanent** addresses including postcode of the executors or intending administrators*

HAROLD PRIOR
BANK CHAMBERS
WEYFORD
BLANKSHIRE WY1 3QT

IHT 200(1993)

	Section 1 - Lifetime gifts or transfers of value		
You must answer *all* the questions in this section	**Did the deceased within 7 years of death**	Yes	No
Note 1	make any gift, settlement, or other transfer of value? (See Note 1 as to the transfers you should not include)	☐	✓
Note 2	pay any premium on a policy of life assurance not included on Page 4 Section 3A of this form? `Policy dated 14 June 1980. £250,000 payable to husband`	✓	☐
Note 3	cease to be entitled to any beneficial interest in possession in settled property?	☐	✓
Note 4	**Did the deceased at any time on or after 18 March 1986 dispose of any property by way of gift where**	Yes	No
	possession and enjoyment of the property was not bona fide assumed by the donee?	☐	✓
	the property was not enjoyed to the entire exclusion of the deceased?	☐	✓
	any benefit was retained by contract or otherwise?	☐	✓

Details of lifetime gifts or transfers of value

Please enter in chronological order details of each lifetime gift or transfer of value. You should deduct any exemptions or reliefs due (See Note 5). Enter the chargeable value showing how you have calculated this

Date of disposition	To whom given (name and address)	Description of asset(s) at date of transfer	Value

Carry the total chargeable value of lifetime transfers to Page 10 Box A unless the property given was subject to a reservation retained by the deceased at the date of death, in which case it should be included in Section 5 on Page 8

Total chargeable value of gifts made within 7 years of death ☐

Show on a schedule details of all gifts made within 7 years of the earliest transfer but do not carry the value of these gifts to Page 10 (See Note 54).

		Yes	No
Note 6	**Superannuation benefits** Was any provision, apart from State Pension, made by the deceased, the deceased's employers or otherwise for retirement, pension, or other superannuation benefits?	☐	✓
	If 'Yes' were any benefits payable, or dispositions made as described in Note 6?	☐	✓

For Official use only

Appendix 3 311

Section 2 - Nominated and Joint Property

You must answer the first two questions in this Section

Note 7
If 'Yes', please give full particulars in Section 2A

Did the deceased nominate any Savings Bank Account, Savings Certificates or other assets in favour of any person? Yes [ ] No [✓]

Note 8

Was the deceased joint owner of any property of any description or did the deceased hold any money on a joint account? Yes [✓] No [ ]

On a separate sheet of paper state for each item of joint property

- the name(s) of the other joint owner(s)   TIM JONES
- when the joint ownership began or when the joint account was opened   1990

Note 9
- by whom and from what source the joint property was provided and, if it or its purchase price was contributed by more than one of the joint owners, the extent of the contribution made by each   Equally by co-owners

Note 10
- how any income was dealt with and enjoyed.   N/A

If 'Yes' include the value in Section 4A or 4B
Was any joint property situated outside the UK? Yes [ ] No [✓]

If 'Yes' include the value in Section 2A or 2B if the property was situated in the UK
Did any joint property pass by survivorship? Yes [✓] No [ ]

If 'Yes' include the value in Section 3A or 3B if the property was situated in the UK
Did any joint property pass under the deceased's Will or intestacy? Yes [ ] No [✓]

Section 2A - Nominated and Joint Property without the Instalment Option

Particulars of the property | Gross value at date of death

Note 11
All claims for exemptions or reliefs should be made in Section 6 on Page 9

Deceased's share of liabilities in respect of the property

See Note 24 and first paragraph of Note 46 before continuing

| Name of creditor | Description of liability | Amount |

Net Value   NONE

Carry the net value forward to Page 10 Box 1

Section 2B - Joint Property with the Instalment Option

Particulars of the property | Gross value at date of death

All claims for exemptions or reliefs should be made in Section 6 on Page 9

Freehold property - Languards (one half)   150,000

Deceased's share of liabilities in respect of the property

See Note 24 and first paragraph of Note 46 before continuing

| Name of creditor | Description of liability | Amount |

NONE

Net Value   150,000

Carry the net value forward to Page 10 Box 8

Note 12
Is tax to be paid by instalments? Yes [ ] No [✓]

For Official use only

Section 3 – Free Estate in the UK

All the property of the deceased in respect of which the grant is required

Section 3A – Property without the Instalment Option

Note 13 — All claims for exemptions or reliefs should be made in Section 6 on Page 9

Notes 14, 15 and 16

	Value at date of death
Stocks, shares, debentures and other securities as set out on IHT 40: quoted or listed in the Stock Exchange Daily Official List except so far as included in Section 3B 10% Tr Stock 2008 £5,000 10,000 Fictional plc @ 680p £68,000	223,000
others, except so far as included in Section 3B	
Uncashed dividends and interest received, dividends declared, and interest accrued due to the date of death in respect of the above investments, as statement attached	
Premium Savings Bonds	10,000

Note 17

National Savings Certificates including interest to the date of death	
Bank accounts including interest to the date of death, as statement attached Midland current a/c	2,500
Money with the National Savings Bank, a building society, a co-operative or friendly society, including interest to the date of death, as statement attached Britannia Building Soc	12,000
Cash (other than cash at banks, etc)	
Money out on mortgage including interest to the date of death, as statement attached	

Note 18

Debts due to the deceased including interest to the date of death (except book debts included in section 3B) as statement attached	
Rents including apportionment of rents of the deceased's own real and leasehold property to the date of death	

Note 19

Income arising, but not received before the death, from real and personal property in which the deceased had a life or other limited interest

Please state the source

	Accrued
	Apportioned
Any other income, apportioned where necessary, to which the deceased was entitled at the date of death (for example pensions, annuities, director's fees, etc), as statement attached	

Note 20

Policies of insurance and bonuses thereon (if any) on the life of the deceased, as statement attached	
Saleable value of policies of insurance and bonuses (if any) on the life of any other person, as statement attached	
Amounts payable under private health insurance schemes	
Income Tax repayable	

Note 21 — Please attach a valuation if one has been obtained

Household and personal goods, including pictures, china, clothes, books, jewellery, stamp, coin and other collections, motor cars, boats etc	
Sold, realised gross	
Unsold, estimated	15,000

Note 22 — Please state the name and date of death of the testator or intestate

Interest in an unadministered estate

Carried forward	262,500

For Official use only

Appendix 3 313

Section 3A - Property without the Instalment Option - continued

	Brought forward	262,500

Note 23
Please state how the deceased acquired the interest and the estimated value at the date of the deceased's death

Interest in expectancy

Other personal property as listed below or as statement attached

Carry the total forward to the Probate Summary on Page 11 Box L

Gross value of property without the Instalment Option	262,500

Liabilities at the date of death and funeral expenses

See Note 24 and first paragraph of Note 46 before continuing

Note 25

Name of creditor	Description of liability	Amount
Inland Revenue	Income tax	700
Thomson's Garage	Repair bill	600

Note 26

Funeral expenses

Pitmans	1,200

Note 27
Carry the total forward to the Probate Summary on Page 11 Box Q

Total liabilities	2,500

Carry the net total forward to Page 10 Box 2

Value of property without the Instalment Option less liabilities	260,000

For Official use only

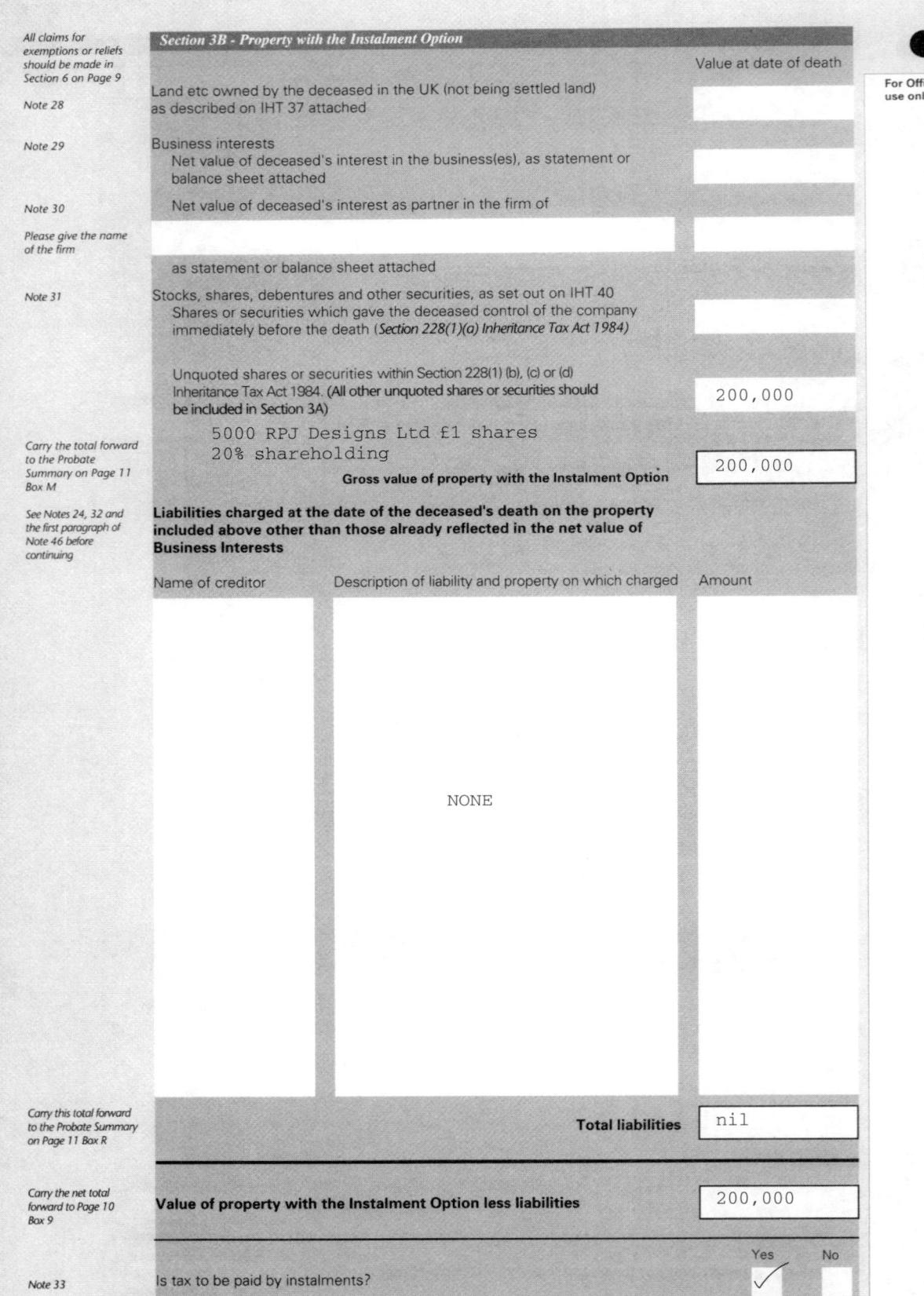

Appendix 3 315

Section 4 - Foreign Property

Note 34

Section 4A - Property without the Instalment Option

Note 35

All claims for exemptions or reliefs should be made in Section 6 on Page 9

Particulars of the property | **Value at date of death**

NONE

Gross Value

Note 36

Liabilities in respect of the property above or due outside the UK

Name and address of creditor | Description of liability | Amount

NONE

Total liabilities

Carry the net total forward to Page 10 Box 3

Value of property without the Instalment Option less liabilities | NIL

Section 4B - Property with the Instalment Option

Note 35

All claims for exemptions or reliefs should be made in Section 6 on Page 9

Particulars of the property | **Value at date of death**

NONE

Gross Value

Liabilities in respect of the property above or due outside the UK

Name and address of creditor | Description of liability | Amount

NONE

Total liabilities

Carry the net total forward to Page 10 Box 10

Value of property with the Instalment Option less liabilities | NIL

Note 37 Is tax to be paid by instalments? Yes ☐ No ✓

Section 5 - Settled Property and Gifts with Reservation

Note 38

All other property to which the deceased was beneficially entitled or was treated as beneficially entitled.

*You **must** answer the question opposite*

Was the deceased, at the date of death, entitled to a life interest, annuity or other interest in possession in settled property whether as beneficiary under a settlement or otherwise? See Note 39.

Yes [ ] No [✓]

Note 39

If so, please state below the name(s) of the settlement(s), the trustees and their solicitors.

Note 40
Please note that the value of any property within Section 5 must be included on Page 10 even if you are not liable for the tax on that property.
Enter the value in Box 15 and/or Box 16 unless you are paying tax on delivery, in which case enter it in Box 4 and/or Box 11.

All claims for exemptions or reliefs should be made in Section 6 on Page 9

Section 5A - Property without the Instalment Option

Particulars of the property — Value at date of death

Liabilities in respect of the property above — Amount

Carry the net value forward to Page 10 Box 4

Property on which tax is being paid now on delivery of this Account — Net value: nil

Carry the net value forward to Page 10 Box 15

Property on which tax is not being paid now — Net value: nil

Section 5B - Property with the Instalment Option

Particulars of the property — Value at date of death

All claims for exemptions or reliefs should be made in Section 6 on Page 9

Liabilities in respect of the property above — Amount

Carry the net value forward to Page 10 Box 11

Property on which tax is being paid now on delivery of this Account — Net value: nil

Carry the net value forward to Page 10 Box 16

Property on which tax is not being paid now — Net value: nil

Note 41

Is tax to be paid by instalments?   Yes [ ] No [✓]

For Official use only

Section 6 - Exemptions, Exclusions and Reliefs against Capital

See Notes 42, 43, 44 and 45

Property without the Instalment Option on which tax is being paid on delivery of this Account

Property in Sections: 2A, 3A, 4A, and 5A

Description of property and Section of Account in which included	Nature of relief claimed	Net value of property	Amount of relief claimed
section 3A	charity exempt	10,000	10,000

Carry this total forward to Page 10 Box 6

Total of reliefs etc — 10,000

Property with the Instalment Option on which tax is being paid on delivery of this Account

Property in Sections: 2B, 3B, 4B, and 5B

Description of property and Section of Account in which included	Nature of relief claimed	Net value of property	Amount of relief claimed
2B - house	spouse exempt	150,000	150,000
3B - shares	BPR @ 100%	200 000	200 000

Carry this total forward to Page 10 Box 13

Total of reliefs etc — 350,000

Property on which tax is not being paid on delivery of this Account

Property in Sections: 2B, 3B, 4B, 5A and 5B

Description of property and Section of Account in which included	Nature of relief claimed	Net value of property	Amount of relief claimed

Carry this total forward to Page 10 Box 18

Total of reliefs etc

Section 7 - Liabilities within Section 103, Finance Act 1986

If the reply to either question is 'Yes' see Note 46

In the case of any liability for which a deduction has been taken in this Account

	Yes	No
did the consideration for any such debt or incumbrance incurred or created on or after 18 March 1986 consist of property derived from the deceased?		✓
was the consideration given by any person who was at any time entitled to, or amongst whose resources there was at any time, any property derived from the deceased?		✓

Any deduction claimed may be disallowed for Inheritance Tax purposes

Calculation of Inheritance Tax

The tax calculated to be due is payable prior to lodging the application for the grant.
The Account will be fully examined after the grant has been issued.

Summary for determining the chargeable estate

Note 47

You may use the reliefs box to show against which property a particular exemption, exclusion or relief has been taken

Section 1 Total of chargeable transfers from Page 2   **A** nil

Part 1. Property without the Instalment Option

Section	Net Total	Reliefs	Value after Reliefs
2A	1		
3A	2 260,000	10,000	
4A	3		
5A	4		
Sub-total	5 260,000	6 10,000	7 250,000

Bring forward the totals from Sections 2A, 3A, 4A, 5A and 6

Part 2. Property with the Instalment Option

2B	8 150,000	150,000	
3B	9 200,000	200,000	
4B	10		
5B	11		
Sub-total	12 350,000	13 350,000	14 nil

Bring forward the totals from Sections 2B, 3B, 4B, 5B and 6

Part 3. Other Property on which tax is not being paid on this Account

5A	15		
5B	16		
Sub-total	17	18	19

Bring forward the totals from Sections 5A, 5B and 6

                Box 5 + 12 + 17   Box 6 + 13 + 18   Box 7 + 14 + 19

Totals   610,000   360,000   **B** 250,000

Aggregate chargeable transfers **A + B** = **C** 250,000

Calculation of Tax

Note 48

Tax on **C**
on first £ 215,000   nil

Plus
balance of £ 35,000   @   40 % =   14,000

                                            Total   14,000

There will be no tax chargeable on A unless it exceeds the date of death threshold

Less tax on **A** at death rate

on first £

Plus
balance of £   @   % =

                                            Total

Note 49
Please attach a schedule showing how you have calculated the relief

Less Quick Succession Relief

Total tax chargeable on **B** above = **D** 14,000

Apportionment of tax payable on this Account

Note 50

From Box 7 opposite

Any capital figure multiplied by $\frac{D}{B}$ gives the proportion of tax assessable on the capital

Property without the Instalment Option £ 250,000 × $\frac{D}{B}$ = 14,000

Note 51
Please attach a schedule showing how you have calculated the relief

Less reliefs against tax other than Quick Succession Relief

Net tax **E** 14,000

Note 52
Tax becomes due 6 months after the end of the month during which the death occurred. Unpaid tax including tax being paid by instalments carries interest from and including the day after the due date irrespective of the reason for the late payment

Carry this total forward to Box F below

Add interest on net tax from ___ 19 ___ to ___ 19 ___
___ years ___ days @ ___ % =

Total tax and interest on property without the Instalment Option **F** 14,000

That part of Box 14 opposite on which tax is to be paid now either in full or by instalments

Property with the Instalment Option £ ___ × $\frac{D}{B}$ =

Less reliefs against tax other than Quick Succession Relief

Net tax **G**

Add interest on net tax from ___ 19 ___ to ___ 19 ___
___ years ___ days @ ___ % =

Note 33

Include the date the last instalment became due

Instalments ___ tenths of net tax **H**

Add interest on instalments now assessed from: ___ 19 ___ to ___ 19 ___
___ days @ ___ % =

If the due date for the second or subsequent instalment has now passed and interest relief is not appropriate, add here interest on the whole of the net tax on property with the Instalment Option up to the due date of the last instalment

Add interest on whole of net tax on instalment property from ___ 19 ___ to ___ 19 ___
___ years ___ days @ ___ % =

Carry this total forward to Box J below

Total tax and interest on property with the Instalment Option **J**

Tax Summary

For official use only

EDP ___

Financial Services Office

Total tax and interest - Property without the Instalment Option **F** 14,000

Total tax and interest - Property with the Instalment Option **J**

Total tax and interest payable now on this Account **K** 14,000

Signature of Solicitor(s) or agent(s) for the applicant(s) ___ Date ___

If tax is payable, send the Account for receipting to Inland Revenue Financial Services Office **by post** at Barrington Road Worthing West Sussex BN12 4XH or by DX 90950 Worthing 3 or take it **by hand** to Room G21 West Wing Somerset House Strand London WC2

Probate Summary

Aggregate Gross Value
which in law devolves on and vests in the personal representatives of the deceased, for and in respect of which the grant is to be made.

Section 3A **L** 262,500

Section 3B **M** 200,000

Only include at N general power property

Section 5 **N**

Total to be carried to the Probate papers **P** 462,500

Deduct

Section 3A, total of liabilities and funeral expenses **Q** 2,500

Section 3B, total of liabilities **R**

Net estate for Probate purposes **S** 460,000

Declaration

Note 55

Tick the appropriate box

I/We wish to apply for a
- Grant of Probate ✓
- Grant of Letters of Administration ☐
- Grant of Letters of Administration with Will annexed ☐
- Grant of _____ ☐

To the best of my/our knowledge and belief all the statements made and particulars given in this Account and its accompanying schedules are true and complete.

I/We have made the fullest enquiries that are reasonably practicable in the circumstances to ascertain the value of all assets, interests, liabilities etc.
- Where it has been possible to obtain exact values these have been included.
- Where exact values have not been obtained the values included are the best estimates which could be made on the information available, and I/We undertake, as soon as the final values are obtained, to deliver a further Account, and to pay any additional tax and interest for which I/we may be liable.

I/We have aggregated on Pages 10 and 11 the value of chargeable gifts and settled property.

So far as the tax on property disclosed in this Account may be paid by instalments, I/we elect to pay or not to pay by instalments as indicated in the Sections, and I/we understand that interest may be payable on unpaid tax in accordance with the statutory rules.

Notes 56 and 57

I/We understand that the issue of the Grant does not imply acceptance by the Inland Revenue of any of the statements made or values included in this Account.

Warning

An executor or intending administrator who fails to make the fullest enquiries that are reasonably practicable in the circumstances may be liable to penalties.

You may be liable to penalties or prosecution if you fail to disclose, in this Account and in your answers to the questions on Pages 2, 3, 8 and 9, all the property in respect of which tax may be payable.

Name	HAROLD PRIOR
Signature	
Date	25 JULY 199
Name	
Signature	
Date	
Name	
Signature	
Date	
Name	
Signature	
Date	

Appendix 3

Oath for Executors

IN THE HIGH COURT OF JUSTICE

Extracting Solicitor ...... Prior & Prior ....

Family Division

Address ..Bank Chambers Weyford WF1 3QT......

† "Principal" or "District Probate". If "District Probate" add "at.................".
* If necessary to include alias of deceased in grant add "otherwise (alias name)" and state below which is true name and reason for requiring alias.
(1) "I" or "We". Insert the full name, place of residence and occupation, or, if none, description of the deponent(s), adding "Mrs", "Miss", as appropriate, for a female deponent.

The†   PRINCIPAL PROBATE   Registry

IN the Estate of*   ROSEMARY PENELOPE JONES   deceased.
Otherwise PENNY JONES

(¹) I HAROLD PRIOR
of Bank Chambers Weyford Blankshire WF1 3QT

(2) Or "do solemnly and sincerely affirm".
(3) Each testamentary paper must be marked by each deponent, and by the person administering the oath.
(4) "with one, two (or more) Codicils", as the case may be.

make Oath and say (²)   that
(¹) I believe the paper writing now produced to and marked by (³) me
to contain the true and original last Will and Testament (⁴)
of* ROSEMARY PENELOPE JONES otherwise PENNY JONES
of Languards Weyford Blankshire
~~formerly of~~
                                                                        deceased

(5) If exact age is unknown, give best estimate.
(6) Where there are separate legal divisions in one country, the state, province, etc., should be specified.
(7) Delete "no", if there was land vested in deceased which remained settled land notwithstanding his or her death.
(8) Settled land may be included in the scope of the grant provided the executors are also the special executors as to the settled land; in that case the settlement must be identified.

who died on the   4th   day of   June   199~~-~~
aged   4-   years (⁵) domiciled in (⁶)   England and Wales
and that to the best of   my   knowledge, information and belief there was (⁷) [no]
land vested in the said deceased which was settled previously to h~~er~~   death (and
not by ~~her~~ Will (⁴)   )
and which remained settled land notwithstanding h~~er~~   death (⁸)

~~And (¹) further make oath and say (²)~~
~~that notice of this application has been given to~~

(9) Delete or amend as appropriate. Notice of this application must be served on all executors to whom power is to be reserved unless dispensed with by a Registrar under Rule 27 (3).
(10) "I am" or "we are". Insert relationship of the executors to the deceased only if necessary to establish title or identification.
(11) "The sole", or "the surviving", or "one of the", or "are the", or "two of the", etc.

~~the executor(s) to whom power is to be reserved, [save~~   ~~]. (⁹)~~

And (¹) I further make Oath and say (²)
           that (¹⁰) (¹¹) I am the sole

                                                                                                    Execut or
named in the said will

(12) If there was settled land and the grant is to include it, insert "including settled land" but, if the grant is to exclude the settled land, insert "save and except settled land"

and that (^{1}) I will (i) collect, get in and administer according to the law the real and personal estate (^{12}) of the said deceased; (ii) when required to do so by the Court, exhibit on oath in the Court a full inventory of the said estate (^{12}) and when so required render an account of the administration of the said estate to the Court; and (iii) when required to do so by the High Court, deliver up the grant of probate to that Court; and that to the best of my knowledge, information and belief

(13) Complete this paragraph only if the deceased died on or after 1 April 1981 and an Inland Revenue Account is not required; the next paragraph should be deleted.

~~(^{13}) [the gross estate passing under the grant does not exceed (^{14}) £~~ , ~~and the net estate does not exceed (^{15}) £~~ ~~, and that this is not a case in which an Inland Revenue Account is required to be delivered]~~

(14) The amount to be inserted here should be in accordance with the relevant figure shown in paragraph 1 of the PEP List.

(^{16}) [the gross estate passing under the grant amounts to £ £462,500 and the net estate amounts to £ £460,000].

(15) The amount to be inserted here should be in accordance with the relevant figure shown in paragraph 2 of the PEP List.

* The true name of the deceased was Rosemary Penelope Jones but the deceased owned certain shares in RPJ Designs Ltd registered in the name of Penny Jones

(16) Complete this paragraph only if an Inland Revenue Account is required and delete the previous paragraph.

N.B. The names of all executors to whom power is to be reserved must be included in the Oath.

SWORN by Deponent HAROLD PRIOR the above-named

at

this day of 19 ,

Before me,

A Commissioner for Oaths/Solicitor.

Appendix 3

 **Inland Revenue Capital Taxes Office**

CTO reference

Corrective Account for Estate Duty, Capital Transfer Tax or Inheritance Tax

- Use this form when too much or too little tax/duty has been paid on the Inland Revenue account or affidavit.
- If a return of tax/duty is applied for, evidence in support of the claim should be furnished.
- It remains a general requirement that estate duty accounts should be sworn but the Commissioners, if they think fit, may dispense with an oath in corrective accounts which lead to the payment of further duty. This form must therefore be sworn in all return of duty cases. Otherwise the form may be signed. However, if it is necessary for the form to be sworn it will be returned.

Person to whom any communications should be sent

Name ......HAROLD PRIOR, PRIOR & PRIOR..............

Address ..BANK CHAMBERS..............

Post Town ..WEYFORD..............

County ......BLANKSHIRE..............   Postcode ...WF2 4BC..............

Reference ...CJ/APP 2..............

Telephone no. ..Weyford 1230..

~~Transferor~~/Deceased/~~Settlement~~   ROSEMARY PENELOPE JONES
Date of ~~birth~~/death/~~settlement~~   4 JUNE 199
Title, chargeable transfer or chargeable event, etc, to which this corrective account relates   As executor of the deceased's estate

(1) Insert name and address of signatories

I/~~We~~ (1)   HAROLD PRIOR of Bank Chambers Weyford Blankshire

state as follows:—

1. The particulars contained on pages 2, 3 and 4 and any attached schedules are a full statement of all known additions and amendments to the details already supplied in the original account or affidavit and any subsequent corrective assessments.

(2) Delete "other than" if no further amendments

2. To the best of my/~~our~~ knowledge and belief no further amendments are necessary ~~other than~~ (2).

3. The particulars given above and the statements in the foregoing paragraphs are true.

(3) Complete only if the person(s) delivering the account paid the overpaid tax/duty

4. ~~Any overpaid tax/duty may be returned to (3)~~

~~whose receipt shall be sufficient discharge for the same.~~

Signed by the above named   HAROLD PRIOR

capacity   Executor

date   10 December 199

Signed by the above named

capacity

date

Signed by the above named

capacity

date

Signed by the above named

capacity

date

Warning   If you fail to verify personally that the statements in this account are true and complete you may make yourself liable to prosecution or penalties.

Cap D3

Property without the instalment option

● Amendments to exemptions and reliefs should be shown separately on page 4 of this account

Assets previously omitted or to be adjusted		Value as last previously shown £	Value as now corrected £
Weyford Building Society (inc interest to date of death)		–	2,500
	Totals		2,500
		Adjustment	
Overall increase (+) or decrease (–) in assets to be carried forward to summary on page 4		+ 2,500	–

Liabilities previously omitted or to be adjusted		Amount as last previously shown £	Amount as now corrected £
Wessex Gas	Gas supplied	–	100
Barclay Card	Account	–	400
	Totals		500
		Adjustment	
Overall increase (+) or decrease (–) in liabilities to be carried forward to summary on page 4		+ 500	–

Please state here the circumstances in which the corrections are considered to have become necessary:

Assets and liabilities discovered subsequently to submission of IHT 200

Appendix 3

Property with the instalment option

● Amendments to exemptions and reliefs should be shown separately on page 4 of this account

Assets previously omitted or to be adjusted		Value as last previously shown £	Value as now corrected £
RPJ Designs Ltd		200,000	220,000
	Totals	200,000	220,000
		Adjustment	
Overall increase (+) or decrease (−) in assets to be carried forward to summary on page 4		+ 20,000	−

Liabilities previously omitted or to be adjusted		Amount as last previously shown £	Amount as now corrected £
None			
	Totals		
		Adjustment	
Overall increase (+) or decrease (−) in liabilities to be carried forward to summary on page 4		+	−

The instalment facility ceases to be available for otherwise qualified property which has been sold (or, in the case of land subject to estate duty, mortgaged). Details of any dealings with property in respect of which the instalment option has been exercised should be given.

Value of shares agreed with shares valuation division

Summary of amendments to estate

Property without the instalment option — from page 2

	Increase in estate £	Decrease in estate £
Increase in assets	2,500	
Decrease in assets		
Increase in liabilities		500
Decrease in liabilities		

Property with the instalment option - from page 3

	Increase in estate £	Decrease in estate £
Increase in assets	20,000	
Decrease in assets		
Increase in liabilities		
Decrease in liabilities		
Totals	**22,500**	**500**

Amendments to exemptions and reliefs

Property in respect of which exemption or relief is claimed	Nature of exemption or relief	Amended net value of property on which exemption or relief is claimed (before deduction of that exemption/relief)	Corrected amount of exemption or relief now claimed
Property without the instalment option None		£	£
		Totals of reliefs and/or exemptions	
Property with the instalment option 20% shareholding RPJ Designs Ltd	BPR @ 100%	£ 220,000	£ 220,000
		Total of reliefs and/or exemptions	220,000

Page 4

Appendix 3

Inland Revenue Capital Taxes Office
Calculation of Inheritance Tax — Non Instalment Option Property

Name of Deceased: Mrs ROSEMARY PENELOPE JONES
Date of Death: 04/06/9-
CTO Reference: X123456/96Q
Title: Free estate
Entry: A/NIOP-1/2
Your Reference:

MESSRS PRIOR & PRIOR
DX 4321
WEYFORD

Calculation of Tax

		£
on Aggregate Chargeable Transfer	F	252,000.00
first £ 215,000.00		NIL
balance £ 37,000.00 @ 40 %		14,800 00
Total Tax Chargeable	J	14,800 00

Summary of Estate

Total of chargeable lifetime transfers* **A** Nil

Non Instalment Option Property (as last shown)

On the Inland Revenue Account ✓
or Calculation dated

Previous Value: 250,000.00

Amendments
Non Instalment Option Property
  Weyford Building Society (new)   + 2,500.00
  Liabilities (new)   -   500.00

		£
Value now taxable here	B	252,000.00
Instalment Option Property Tax shown separately on IHT 302	C	nil
Total value this title B + C =	D	252,000.00
Aggregate Chargeable Transfer A + D =	F	252,000.00

Apportionment of Tax

Tax on B = $\frac{B}{F-A} \times J$ = 14,800 00
less tax on IRA or Calculation dated = 14,000 00
Tax payable/repayable = 800 00

*Interest from 01/12/1996
        to 15/12/1996 = 0 93
* See IHT4 for rates

Tax & interest payable/repayable 800 93

Money applied from Deposit
Deposit No(s)   Date received

Repayment(s) being applied here

To be paid/repaid 800 93

Unless this sum is paid promptly, additional interest may be payable.

If you need help with this calculation, please telephone

at   ext   Date

Our telephone numbers are shown overleaf

Summary

Capital value on which you are now paying tax at this title is £ 252,000

The amount of tax and interest now payable/repayable is £ 800 93

Notes

For statistical use only

* **A** No tax is payable on the chargeable lifetime transfers because their total does not exceed the tax threshold in force at the date of death. The total of lifetime transfers has to be added to the value of all property at this title to calculate the tax on the total death estate.

IHT 301A   10/93

Appendix 3

Application for clearance certificate

**Inheritance Tax Act 1984 S239(2) or
Finance Act 1975 Schedule 4 Para 25(2) or
Finance Act 1894 S 11 (2)**

CTO reference (if known)

HAROLD PRIOR
PRIOR & PRIOR
BANK CHAMBERS
WEYFORD
BLANKSHIRE

Your Reference
CJ/APP 2

Telephone No.
Weyford 1230

Name and address of the person to whom we should send this certificate

Please read these notes before you fill in this form

- Do not send this form to us until you believe that it will not be necessary to change the amount of the tax or duty paid.

- Fill in section A or B or C (one only) and sections D, E and F. Tick 'Yes' and 'No' boxes as appropriate.

- Only trustees may normally apply for a certificate in respect of a lifetime transfer that becomes chargeable.

- Agents may not sign this form on behalf of executors, administrators or trustees.

- Please send the completed form in **duplicate** to the Capital Taxes Office dealing with the estate.

- Ferrers House, PO Box 38, Castle Meadow Road, Nottingham NG2 1BB
  DX 701201 Nottingham 4
  Tel: 0115 974 2400 Fax: 0115 974 2432

- Charles House, 375 Kensington High Street, London W14 8QH
  DX 42159 West Kensington
  Tel: 0171 605 9800 Fax: 0171 610 4470

- Dorchester House, 52-58 Great Victoria Street, Belfast BT2 7QL
  DX 2001 NR Belfast 2
  Tel: 01232 315556 Fax: 01232 331001

- Mulberry House, 16 Picardy Place, Edinburgh EH1 3NB
  Tel: 0131 556 8511 Fax: 0131 556 9894

A   Liability arising on death

Full name of deceased: ROSEMARY PENELOPE JONES

Date of death: 4th June 199-

Title under which the property is taxable: WILL OF DECEASED
(eg. 'Will of Deceased')

B   Liability in respect of a chargeable lifetime transfer

Full name of transferor (ie. in the case of settled property   N/A
the person entitled to the interest in possession):

Date of birth: Date of death (if applicable):

Details of that transfer including date of transfer:

C   Liability in respect of a settlement without an interest in possession

Full title and date of settlement: N/A

Date of chargeable event:

Details of that event:

Cap 30

D **The property or value transferred in respect of which this application is made to be included in the**

Original Account(s)/Inventory(ies) dated 25/07/9-

Corrective Account(s)/Inventory(ies) dated 10/12/9-

Calculation(s) of tax dated 05/01/9-

Have there been changes since these were submitted or issued ?   Yes ☐   No ☑

If 'Yes', give details.

E **Except as mentioned at D above, to your knowledge**

- is there any other property (at a title other than in Section A overleaf), passing or taxable on the death of the deceased ?   Yes ☐   No ☑

- have there been any previous chargeable transfers ?   Yes ☐   No ☑

- have there been any previous events on which tax was chargeable or which may affect the amount of tax chargeable ?   Yes ☐   No ☑

If 'Yes'. give details on a separate sheet, and ensure before you apply that the value of this other property/transfer has been determined for IHT purposes.

F **Declaration**

To the best of my/our knowledge and belief the information given is correct.
I am/ We are not aware of any other information which I/we should disclose.
I/We apply for a statutory certificate of discharge.

HAROLD PRIOR

EXECUTOR
10 JANUARY 199-

Name
Signature
Capacity*
Date

Name
Signature
Capacity*
Date

* Capacity i.e. executor, administrator, trustee

Certificate

The Commissioners of Inland Revenue discharge the above named applicants from any further claim for tax or duty on the value attributable to the property specified at D on the occasion specified at A/B/C.

Signed by
For and on behalf of the Commissioners

Signature
Date

- This certificate does not itself constitute a determination of values of individual items for any Revenue purpose. In particular the issue of the certificate does not necessarily mean that values have been "ascertained" or that values may be taken to be market values for Capital Gains Tax within the provisions of Section 274 and Paragraph 9, Schedule 11, Taxation of Chargeable Gains Act 1992.

- A certificate is not valid in certain circumstances, such as in the case of fraud or failure to disclose material facts or where further tax becomes payable as a result of an instrument of variation - see Section 239(4) Inheritance Tax Act 1984.

You can get prints of this form from the Capital Taxes Offices at the addresses shown overleaf

Appendix 4

FREDERICK SMITH DECEASED

Mr Frederick Smith, late of the Oaks, Links Road, Hixley died on 28 June 199–, aged 62. Probate of his will was granted out of the Principal Probate Registry on 15 August 199– to Mr William Old and Mr Brian Smith, the executors named in the will.

By his will, the testator bequeathed the following legacies:

(1) £2,000 to Mrs Angela Smith
(2) £2,000 to Dr Michael Carling.

After payment of these legacies and all debts and funeral and testamentary expenses, the residue was given to the testator's brother, Mr Brian Smith.

The net estate for probate purposes amounted to £221,000. The IHT on the estate amounted to £2,400. This has been paid and a Certificate of Discharge obtained.

Estate capital account

Assets (at probate value)	£	£
The Oaks, Links Road, Hixley		140,000.00
ABC Plc 10,000 Ord. shares		40,000.00
Contents of house and personal effects		22,000.00
Halifax Building Society	9,900.00	
Interest to date of death	100.00	10,000.00
All risks Life Co. Plc – life policy		20,000.00
Lloyds Bank, Hixley		
Current Account		1,500.00
Deposit Account	4,980.00	
Interest to date of death	20.00	5,000.00
Cash in House		10.00
GROSS ESTATE		**238,510.00**
Less Debts : Mortgage Halifax Building Society	15,000.00	
: Barclaycard	1,000.00	
Funeral expenses	1,510.00	17,510.00
NET ESTATE		**221,000.00**
Less Administration Expenses		
: valuers fees	500.00	
: legal fees	1,500.00	
Inheritance Tax	2,400.00	4,400.00
		216,600.00
Legacies		
Mrs Angela Smith	2,000.00	
Dr Michael Carling	2,000.00	4,000.00
Residue : Mr Brian Smith		212,600.00

Estate income account

	£
ABC Plc Dividend	250.00
Interest received	
Halifax Building Society – to close account	130.00
Lloyds Bank, Hixley – to close account	50.00
	430.00
Less	
Lloyds Bank, Hixley Interest on loan to pay IHT	30.00
	400.00
Balance : Mr Brian Smith	400.00

Beneficiary's account

Mr Brian Smith

	£
Residue due to you per Capital Account	212,600.00
Income due to you per Income Account	400.00
	213,000.00
Represented by:	
Retained by you	
Cash in house	10.00
Transferred to you	
ABC Plc, 10,000 Ord. shares	40,000.00
The Oaks	140,000.00
Contents of house and personal effects	22,000.00
Interim payments made to you	6,000.00
Balance now due to you	4,990.00
	213,000.00

Appendix 5

EXTRACTS FROM THE NON-CONTENTIOUS PROBATE RULES 1987 (AS AMENDED)

Rule 12   Evidence as to due execution of will

(1) Subject to paragraphs (2) and (3) below, where a will contains no attestation clause or the attestation clause is insufficient, or where it appears to the registrar that there is doubt about the due execution of the will, he shall before admitting it to proof require an affidavit as to due execution from one or more of the attesting witnesses or, if no attesting witness is conveniently available, from any other person who was present when the will was executed; and if the registrar, after considering the evidence, is satisfied that the will was not duly executed, he shall refuse probate and mark the will accordingly.

(2) If no affidavit can be obtained in accordance with paragraph (1) above, the registrar may accept evidence on affidavit from any person he may think fit to show that the signature on the will is in the handwriting of the deceased, or of any other matter which may raise a presumption in favour of due execution of the will, and may if he thinks fit require that notice of the application be given to any person who may be prejudiced by the will.

(3) A registrar may accept a will for proof without evidence as aforesaid if he is satisfied that the distribution of the estate is not thereby affected.

Rule 13   Execution of will of blind or illiterate testator

Before admitting to proof a will which appears to have been signed by a blind or illiterate testator or by another person by direction of the testator, or which for any other reason raises doubt as to the testator having had knowledge of the contents of the will at the time of its execution, the registrar shall satisfy himself that the testator had such knowledge.

Rule 14   Evidence as to terms, condition and date of execution of will

(1) Subject to paragraph (2) below, where there appears in a will any obliteration, interlineation, or other alteration which is not authenticated in the manner prescribed by section 21 of the Wills Act 1837, or by the re-execution of the will or by the execution of a codicil, the registrar shall require evidence to show whether the alteration was present at the time the will was executed and shall give directions as to the form in which the will is to be proved.

(2) The provisions of paragraph (1) above shall not apply to any alteration which appears to the registrar to be of no practical importance.

(3) If a will contains any reference to another document in such terms as to suggest that it ought to be incorporated in the will, the registrar shall require the document to be produced and may call for such evidence in regard to the incorporation of the document as he may think fit.

(4) Where there is a doubt as to the date on which a will was executed, the registrar may require such evidence as he thinks necessary to establish the date.

Rule 15 Attempted recovation of will

Any appearance of attempted revocation of a will by burning, tearing, or otherwise destroying, and every other circumstance leading to a presumption of revocation by the testator, shall be accounted for to the registrar's satisfaction.

Rule 16 Affidavit as to due execution, terms, etc, of will

A registrar may require an affidavit from any person he may think fit for the purpose of satisfying himself as to any of the matters referred to in rules 13, 14 and 15, and in any such affidavit sworn by an attesting witness or other person present at the time of the execution of a will the deponent shall depose to the manner in which the will was executed.

Rule 17 Wills proved otherwise than under section 9 of the Wills Act 1837

(1) Rules 12 to 15 shall apply only to a will that is to be established by reference to section 9 of the Wills Act 1837 (signing and attestation of wills).

(2) A will that is to be established otherwise than as described in paragraph (1) of this rule may be so established upon the registrar being satisfied as to its terms and validity, and includes (without prejudice to the generality of the foregoing) –

　(a) any will to which rule 18 applies; and

　(b) any will which, by virtue of the Wills Act 1963, is to be treated as properly executed if executed according to the internal law of the territory or state referred to in section 1 of that Act.

Rule 20 Order of priority for grant where deceased left a will

[For the full text of this rule see **22.3**.]

Rule 22 Order of priority for grant in case of intestacy

[For the full text of this rule see **22.4**.]

Rule 25 Joinder of administrator

(1) A person entitled in priority to a grant of administration may, without leave, apply for a grant with a person entitled in a lower degree, provided that there is no other person entitled in a higher degree to the person to be joined, unless every other such person has renounced.

(2) Subject to paragraph (3) below, an application for leave to join with a person entitled in priority to a grant of administration a person having no right or no immediate right thereto shall be made to a registrar, and shall be supported by an affidavit by the person entitled in priority, the consent of the person proposed to be joined as administrator and such other evidence as the registrar may direct.

(3) Unless a registrar otherwise directs, there may without any such application be joined with a person entitled in priority to administration –

　(a) any person who is nominated under paragraph (3) of rule 32 or paragraph (3) of rule 35;

　(b) a trust corporation.

Rule 27   Grants where two or more persons entitled in same degree

(1) Subject to paragraphs (1A), (2) and (3) below, where, on an application for probate, power to apply for a like grant is to be reserved to such other of the executors as have not renounced probate, notice of the application shall be given to the executor or executors to whom power is to be reserved; and, unless the district judge or registrar otherwise directs, the oath shall state that such notice has been given.

(1A) Where power is to be reserved to executors who are appointed by reference to their being partners in a firm, and not by their names, notice need not be given to them under paragraph (1) above if probate is applied for by another partner in that firm.

(2) Where power is to be reserved to partners of a firm, notice for the purposes of paragraph (1) above may be given to the partners by sending it to the firm at its principal or last known place of business.

(3) A registrar may dispense with the giving of notice under paragraph (1) above if he is satisfied that the giving of such a notice is impracticable or would result in unreasonable delay or expense.

(4) A grant of administration may be made to any person entitled thereto without notice to other persons entitled in the same degree.

(5) Unless a registrar otherwise directs, administration shall be granted to a person of full age entitled thereto in preference to a guardian of a minor, and to a living person entitled thereto in preference to the personal representative of a deceased person.

(6) A dispute between persons entitled to a grant in the same degree shall be brought by summons before a registrar.

(7) The issue of a summons under this rule in the Principal Registry or in a district probate registry shall be notified forthwith to the registry in which the index of pending grant applications is maintained.

(8) If the issue of a summons under this rule is known to the registrar, he shall not allow any grant to be sealed until such summons is finally disposed of.

Rule 46   Additional personal representatives

(1) An application under section 114(4) of the Act to add a personal representative shall be made to a registrar and shall be supported by an affidavit by the applicant, the consent of the person proposed to be added as personal representative and such other evidence as the registrar may require.

(2) On any such application the registrar may direct that a note shall be made on the original grant of the addition of a further personal representative, or he may impound or revoke the grant or make such other order as the circumstances of the case may require.

Appendix 6

FAMILY DIVISION PRACTICE DIRECTION OF 19 APRIL 1988

(1) Parts I and III of the Family Law Reform Act 1987 came into force on 4 April 1988.

(2) Where the deceased died (a) intestate on or after 4 April 1988 or (b) died leaving a will or codicil dated on or after 4 April 1988 containing dispositions which refer to relationships between two persons, then any question of entitlement to a grant of representation will be determined in accordance with the provisions of s 1 of the 1987 Act whereby references in the Act or any instrument made after the coming into force of s 1 to any relationship between two persons shall be construed without regard to whether or not the father or mother of either of them, or the father and mother of any person through whom the relationship is deduced, have or had been married to each other at any time, unless the contrary intention appears. Where the applicant is the spouse of the deceased the present terminology in use should continue to be adopted, ie 'The lawful widow [or husband]', but otherwise it will no longer be necessary to describe an applicant's relationship to the deceased as either 'lawful' or 'natural'. When clearing off prior claims, there is no need to describe the same as either 'lawful' or 'natural'.

(3) By ss 18 and 21 of the 1987 Act presumptions are created whereby (i) a person whose father and mother were not married to each other at the time of his birth shall be presumed not to have been survived by his father or by any person related to him only through his father and (ii) a deceased person shall be presumed not to have been survived by any person related to him whose father and mother were not married to each other at the time of his birth or by any person whose relationship with him is deduced through such a person, unless the contrary is shown. The applicant's title, as sworn to in the oath, will be taken as sufficient to rebut any such presumption. Evidence of paternity will not be required except in exceptional circumstances.

(4) The following tables set out the appropriate wording to be used in oaths:

Clearing off	Wording
	Swear that deceased died:
	a bachelor
Spouse	a spinster
	a widower
	a widow
	a single man
	a single woman
Children or other issue	without issue

Parents	[or] parent	
Brother or sister and their issue	[or] brother or sister of the whole [or half] blood or their issue	or any other person entitled in priority to share in his [or her] estate by virtue of any enactment
Grandparents	[or] grandparents	
Uncles and aunts and their issue	[or] uncle or aunt of the whole [or half] blood or their issue	

Applicant's relationship	Description	
Spouse	lawful husband	and only person [now] entitled to the estate (if so)
	lawful widow	
Child*	son	and only person [or one of the persons] entitled to [share in] the estate
	daughter	
Grandchild* with stirpital interest	son [or daughter] of C D the son [or daughter] of the said deceased who died before the said deceased	and only person [or one of the persons] (etc)
Parent	mother [or father]	

*Adopted children or grandchildren should be described as 'the lawful adopted son [or daughter] (etc)'

19 April 1988

C F TURNER
Senior Registrar

INDEX

Abatement
    debts, of, in insolvent estate   27.8.3
    order of   15.9
Accountant
    executor or trustee, as   10.6.1
Accounts
    estate, *see* Estate account
Accumulation rules   15.10
Ademption   8.4.1, 15.2
    basic rule   15.2.1
    beneficiary's position   28.2
    drafting will, and advice on   8.4.1
    nature of asset, changes in   15.2.2
    shares, and   15.2.2
    will 'speaking from death', and   15.2.3
Address
    testator, of   4.2.3, 5.1
Administration
    grant de bonis non   22.7.3
    grant of letters of   1.6.3, 22.5.2
Administration of estate   24.1 *et seq*
    accounting records   24.3.2, 24.3.3
    accounts, duty to keep   24.3.1, 24.3.4, *see also* Estate account
    administration period   24.1.2, 29.5.2
    assets
        collection of   24.1.1
        realisation of   24.4.2, 26.2
        see also Personal representative
    completion of   24.4.2, 29.1 *et seq*
    expenses of   27.1.1, 27.2.2
        insolvent estate   27.8.3
        solvent estate   27.5.1
    file management   24.4.1
    investing and managing, *see* Investment; Investment business
    powers and duties of personal representatives, *see* Personal representatives
    stages of   24.1.1
    time organisation, importance of   24.4.2
    work comprising   19.2
Administration period   24.1.2, 29.5.2
Administrator
    see also Personal representative
    appointment of   1.5.2, 22.4
        'clearing off'   22.4.2, 23.4
        order of priority   22.4.1
    beneficial interest in estate, need for   22.4.3
    child of deceased as   22.4.1
    clearing off   22.4.2, App 6
    entitlement to act   22.4.1
    grant to   1.6.3, 22.5.2
    minors acting as   22.4.4
    number of   22.4.6
    oath for   22.4, 23.4
        relationship with deceased, statement of   23.4
        specimens   23.4, App 2
    renunciation   22.4.5
Administrator with will annexed   1.6.2, 20.2.2
    see also Personal representative
    appointment   22.3.2
        'clearing off'   22.3.2, 23.3, App 6
        order of priority   22.3.2
    entitlement to act   22.3.1, 23.3
    minors acting as   22.3.3
    number of   22.3.4, 23.3
    oath for   22.1.1, 23.3
        life or minority interest created   23.3
        specimen   23.3, App 1
    renunciation   22.3.5
Adopted child   16.6.2, 28.3.2
    date of birth, and   28.3.2
    parents of, construction of   28.3.2
    personal representatives, and   28.3.4
    wording for, in oath   23.4, App 6
Advancement
    power of   10.3.6, 25.2.2
Advertisement
    personal representatives, by   24.2.5, 27.4, 28.3.4
Affidavit of due execution   20.7.2
Age
    minimum, to make will   2.2, 13.2.1
Agent
    employment by personal representative   25.5.1
Agricultural property relief   12.4.2, 18.7.2, 18.13.1
Alteration to will   11.2, 13.6
    affidavit of plight and condition   20.7.2
    basic rule   13.6.1
    codicil confirming   13.6.1
    doctrine of dependent relative revocation   13.6.4
    initialling   13.6.1, 13.6.3
    invalid, effect   13.6.4
    practical safeguard   13.6.3
    presumptions   13.6.2
Ambiguity
    will, in   3.2, 3.3.1, 3.3.2, 28.2.1
Annuity
    pecuniary legacy, as   27.7.2
Apportionment   10.5
Appropriation
    power of   10.2.2, 25.4.2
Assent   28.5.1, 29.6.4
Asset
    see also Chattel; Land; Property
    additional, effect of discovery of   29.2.5
    change in nature of   15.2.2
    collection of   24.4.2, 26.1 *et seq*, *see also* Personal representative

Asset cont
   details of, for probate   20.4.1
   devolution to personal representatives   26.3
   insolvent estate, and   27.8
   misappropriation of   24.2.2
   realisation of   24.4.2, 27.1.3
      payment of inheritance tax, for   21.1.3, 24.4.2
      without a grant   20.6.1, 26.2
   recording of   24.4.2, *see also* Inland Revenue account
   safeguarding   20.3.4, 24.2.2
   sale of, by personal representatives   24.4.2, 27.1.3
   solvent estate, and   27.5
   valuable   20.3.4
   valuations   20.4.4, 21.1.2
      jointly owned   21.1.2
   value of, preserving   24.2.2
   wasting of, liability   24.2.2
Attendance note   13.5.5, Apps 1,2,3
Attestation clause   4.2.3, 13.3.2, 13.4.3
   affidavit of due execution where faulty   20.7.2
   codicil, for   4.4.2, 4.4.3
Aunt
   administrator, as   22.4.1

Bank
   executor or trustee, as   6.5, 6.8, 10.6.1
   loan from, for payment of inheritance tax   21.1.3, 27.1.2
Bank account
   not an 'investment'   19.2.1
   valuation of, for inheritance tax   18.5.3, 21.1.2
Bankrupt
   grant of probate, and   6.6
Bankruptcy rules
   application to insolvent estate   27.8.3
Beneficiary
   administrator, as   22.3.2
   adoption, and, *see* Adoption
   adult   29.6.2
   capital advance   10.3.6
   child as, *see* Child; Minor
   claim by   27.4
   class gift   8.3.3, 28.3.5
      lapse of   15.3.5
   consultation with, by trustees   10.4.2
   contingent interest   10.3.1
   control of trustees   10.3.8
   death before testator   8.3.1, 8.3.3, 15.3
   description in will   8.3.3
   disclaimer   15.8, 30.1, 30.2
      tax, and   30.1.2
      see also Disclaimer
   entitlement of   28.2
      ascertaining prior to grant   20.4.2
   failure of gift to   8.3.3, 15.3
   family provision claim, and
      agreement with claimant   17.1.3
      financial resources of   17.2.4
      physical or mental disability of   17.2.4
   home for, purchase of   25.4.3
   income tax   28.5.2, 29.5.3
   identity of   8.3.3, 15.6.2, 28.2, 28.3
      ascertaining, for grant   20.4.2
      extrinsic evidence as to   28.2.1
      family relationships, construing   28.3.1
      statutory presumptions   28.3, App 6
   illegitimacy   28.3.1
   income tax liability   29.5.3
   interest in possession, with   10.4
   legacy, *see* Legacies
   legitimacy   28.3.3
   loan from, for payment of inheritance tax   21.1.3
   maintenance   10.3.5
   minor, *see* Minor
   missing or unknown   20.4.3, 24.2.6, 28.3.4
   occupation, right of   10.4.3
   protection of personal representatives   28.3.4
   residuary, *see* Residuary estate
   solicitor, as   11.1.3, 13.3.2
   spouse of, as witness   13.5.2, 13.5.3
   variation by, effect   30.3.1
   tax, and   4.2.3
   tracing   24.2.6, 27.4
   transfer to   27.1.3, 28.5.1, 29.5.4, 29.6
   unadministered estate, remedy of   22.8.2
   vesting of asset in, retrospective effect   28.5.2
   wishes
      disclaimer, and   30.1.3
      cash or in specie payment, as to   24.4.2
      sale of assets, and   27.1.3
   witness to will, effect   13.5.2, 13.5.3
Benjamin order   24.2.6, 28.3.4
Bequest, *see* Legacy
Blind person
   testator   13.3.2
   witness   13.5.1
Body
   disposal of, wishes on   2.3.6, 5.3
   donation for medical research or education   5.3
Bona vacantia   16.2.2, 16.6.3
Borrowing
   payment of inheritance tax, for   21.1.3
      repayment   27.1.2
Brother
   administrator, as   22.4.1
   entitlement on intestacy   16.2.2, 16.4.2
Building society account
   details of, for probate etc   20.4.1
   grant of representation not required, circumstances for   20.6.1

Building society account *cont*
  inheritance tax
    payment of, out of   21.1.3
    value for   18.5.3
  not an 'investment'   19.2.1
Burial
  directions for   2.3.6, 5.3, 20.3.2
Business
  details of, in Inland Revenue account   21.5.4
  personal representatives' powers   10.6.3, 25.4.3
Business property relief   12.4.2, 18.7.1, 18.13.1

Capacity, *see* Testamentary capacity
Capital
  trustees' powers to advance   10.3.6, 25.2.2
Capital gains tax
  administration period, in   29.5.2
  death, no disposal on   29.5.4
  deceased, liability of, return for   29.5.1
  disclaimer, and   30.2.2
  disposal of assets, on   27.1.3, 29.5.4, 30.1.2, 30.2.2
  gift as disposal for   12.3.3
  inheritance tax loss relief, interaction with   29.5, 29.5.4
  liability, calculation of   29.5.4
  transfer of assets to legatees, on   24.4.2, 29.5.4
  variation, and   30.3.2
Capital Taxes Office
  clearance from   29.4
Cash
  beneficiary paid by   24.4.2
  grant of representation, and   20.6.1
  personal representative holding   26.2
Caveat   22.8
  entering of, effect, and response to   22.8.1
Caveator   22.8.1
Charge
  creditor with, secured   27.8.5
  property with   27.7.1
Charging clause   6.7.2, 10.6.1
Charity
  gift to
    cy-près doctrine, and   8.3.3
    drafting   8.3.3
    example   4.4.2
    specimen clause   8.3.3
    uncertainty, and   15.6.2
  inheritance tax exemption   18.6.2, 18.13.1
    claiming in Inland Revenue account   21.5.7
  valid receipt for money   4.4.3, 8.3.3
Chattel
  gift of, *see* Legacy
  grant not required, circumstances when   20.6.1
  personal, statutory definition   8.4.1, 16.3.3
  personal representative collecting   26.2

Child
  adopted   16.6.2, 28.3.2
    administrator, wording for   23.4
    date of birth, construction of   28.3.2
  birth of, and will drafting   3.2
  contingent gift   9.2.2
  describing or naming   9.2.2
  family provision claim by, *see* Family provision
  gift to
    considerations   8.3.3, 9.2.2
    meaning   28.3.1
    substitutional provision implied by statute   15.3.6
  grandchild, substitution for   9.1.2
  guardian for, *see* Guardian
  illegitimate   16.6.2, 28.3.1
  legacy for, interest on   28.8.2
  legitimated   28.3.3
  maintenance of   10.3.5
  receipt from   10.3.7
    specimen clause   10.3.7
    validity   8.3.3
  substitution provision   9.2.2, 15.3.4, 15.3.6
  trust for   2.3.2, 7.4, 9.1.2
Citation   22.8
  types of   22.8.2
Citor   22.8.2
Class gift   8.3.3, 28.3.5
  lapse of   15.3.5
Clauses
  commencement clause   5.1
  numbering of   3.3.3
Club
  gift to   8.3.3
Codicil
  attestation clause   4.4.3
  commentary on   4.4.3
  effect   3.7.2
  example of   4.4.1–4.4.3
  purpose and use of   3.7.1, 11.2
  republication of will by   3.7.2
  testimonium   4.4.3
  validity   3.7.1
Cohabitee
  claim for family provision   17.2.2, 17.8, 17.11.1
  deaths after 1 Jan 1996, applies to   17.8
Commencement clause   5.1
Conflict of interests   11.1.3
Construction summons   28.2.1
Contentious probate business
  caveat, after   22.8.1
Contents   3.1 *et seq*
  absence of knowledge, proving   13.3.2
  affidavit as to knowledge of   20.7.2
  testator's knowledge and approval   2.2, 4.2.3, 13.3.2, 13.3.3
Contingent interest   2.3.1, 4.3.3, 8.3.3, 9.1.2
  substitutional gift to child, as   9.2.2
  trust of residue arising   10.3.1

Corneal grafting
   clause in will   5.3
Creditor
   see also Debt(s)
   duty of personal representatives to pay
      25.5.6, 27.3
   interest, where legacy in satisfaction of debt
      28.8.2
   judgment   27.7.1
   missing or unknown, personal representatives'
      liability and   20.4.3
      protection, methods of   27.4, 28.3.4
   secured   27.7.1, 27.8.5
   unsecured   27.7.2
Cremation
   request for   5.3, 20.3.2
Criminal conviction
   person with, incapacity to take grant of probate
      6.6
Cy-près doctrine   8.3.3

Damaged will   14.3.3
Death
   age at, and date of, on oath form   23.2
   beneficiary, of   8.3.1, 8.3.3, 15.3
   executor, of   22.7.1
   intestate   1.2.2, *see also* Intestacy
   partially intestate   1.2.3, *see also* Intestacy
   personal representative, of   22.7.1
   solicitor's action on   20.3
   testate   1.2.1, *see also* Will
   two or more, order of   15.3.2, 16.7
   will taking effect on   2.1.2, 15.2.3
Death certificate   20.3.6, 20.7.4
Debt(s)
   abatement of gifts to pay   15.9
   apportionment of, between income and capital
      10.5.3
   charged on specific property   8.3.2, 8.4.6,
      27.7.1, 27.6, 27.7.2
   deferred   27.8.3
   details of, for grant of probate   20.4.1
   discharge of   24.4.2, 27.1 *et seq*, *see also*
      Testamentary debts and expenses
   inheritance tax, and
      deductible for   18.5.4
      Inland Revenue account, in   21.3.4, 21.4.4
      owing to deceased   18.5.3
   insolvent estate, order of payment in   27.8.3
   preferred   27.8.3
   provision for, in will   8.3.2, 9.1.4, 27.1.3, 27.6
   secured   27.5.2, 27.7.1
   solvent estate, order of payment in   27.7.2
   statute barred   27.8.4
   unsecured   27.7.2
Deceased
   death certificate for   20.3.6, 20.7.4
   identification of, in oath   23.2
   income and capital gains tax liability   29.5.1
   names/aliases   23.2
Dependent relative revocation, doctrine of
   13.6.4, 14.3.1, 14.3.3
Destruction   14.3.3
Devastavit   24.2.2
   liability for   24.2.3, 26.1.1
   relief from   24.2.4
Devise
   see also Gift; Legacy
   meaning   8.1
   specific   8.4.6
Disability
   executor under   22.2.2
   person under, *see* Child; Minor
   testator and, *see* Testamentary capacity
Disclaimer   15.8, 30.1, 30.2
   delay   30.2.1
   devolution of property disclaimed   30.2.1
   effect of   20.8, 29.2.5
   formalities for   30.2.2
   limited interest, of   30.2.1
   lodging   20.7
   partial   30.2.1
   restrictions on   30.2.1
   succession after   30.2.1
   taxation, and   30.1.2, 30.2.2
   time for   30.2.2
   wishes of beneficiaries, ascertaining   30.1.3
Disposal of body
   directions about   2.3.6, 5.3, 20.3.2
Dispute
   grant of representation, over   22.8
Distribution   28.1 *et seq*
   beneficiaries, identification of   28.2, 28.3, *see
      also* Beneficiary
   construction summons   28.2.1
   intestacy, on   28.9
   interim   24.4.2, 28.1, 29.1
   pecuniary legacies   28.6
   postponement, power of   25.5.6
   specific legacies   28.5
   time for   27.4, 28.2.1, 28.8.1
Dividend
   personal representatives' duty to account for
      21.5.4
Divorce
   deaths after 1 Jan 96   14.3.2, 15.5
   drafting of will, and   3.2, 15.5
   effect on will of   14.3.2
   intestacy, and   16.3.1
   lapse of gift on   14.3.2, 15.5
   spouse appointed as executor, effect on   6.4,
      14.3.2, 22.2.2
   testator's, effect of   14.3.2
Document
   grant of representation, for   20.7, *see also*
      Grant of representation
   incorporated into will by reference   8.4.3
   safe-keeping of, after death   20.3.4, 26.1

Domicile outside UK
   Inland Revenue account form for   21.1
Donor card   5.3
Drafting will   3.3, 3.4
   aims   3.2
   anticipation of future problems   4.3.3
   capital letters   3.3.3
   codicils   3.7
   commencement   5.1
   desired result, to achieve   3.3.6
   disposal of body, directions on   5.3
   family provision legislation, and   17.1.2, 17.10
   form and content, examples of   4.2–4.4
   inheritance tax, and   11.3.3, 11.4.4, 12.1, 12.2.4 *et seq*, 18.6.3
   numbers   3.3.3
   powers for executor   10.7.2, 25.3.2, 25.4.1
   precedents, use of   3.4
   punctuation   3.3.2
   revocation clause   5.2
   silence, problem of   3.3.5
   style   3.3, 4.2.4
   stylistic alternatives versus legal alternatives   3.3.4
   trust, whether required   3.6, 6.2, 10.7.3
   validity, essential requirements for   13.1 *et seq*

Employee
   wages etc owing to, insolvent estate   27.8.3
Estate
   inheritance tax, and
      definition for   18.4.1
      identifying for   12.2.1
      property outside   12.4.3
      see also Inheritance tax
   will, and   2.4, 15.2.3
Estate account
   draft   24.4.2
   form and content of   29.7.3
   interim distributions, on   29.6.1
   preparation of   24.3, 24.4.2, 29.7
   presentation of   29.7.2
   purpose of   29.7.1
Estate administration   19.1, 19.2
   see also Administration of estate; Investment business; Personal representative; Solicitor
Execution
   attendance note of   13.5.5
   check on executed document   13.5.5
   codicil, of   4.4.2, 13.4.3
   formalities for   13.4
      attestation clause   4.2.3, 13.3.2, 13.4.3
      signature   2.1.1, 13.4.1
      summary of   13.4.2
      witnesses   13.4.1
      writing, in   13.4.1
   place for   13.5.5
   presumption of due   13.4.3, 20.7.1
   procedure for   13.5.5
   suspicious circumstances   13.3.2
   undue influence, etc   13.3.2
Executor
   see also Personal representative
   appointment   1.5.2, 2.3.2, 6.1 *et seq*
      clause in will   4.2.3
      failure   6.6
      reasons for   6.1
      specimen clauses   6.6
      spouse, of, and subsequent divorce   6.4, 14.3.2
   assignment not possible   22.7.2
   bank as   6.5, 6.8
   breach of duty   24.2.2, 24.2.3
      will clause excusing   24.2.4
   capacity to act   22.2.2, 22.8.1
   chain of representation   22.7.2, 22.7.3
   charging clause   6.7.2, 10.6.1
   choice   2.3.2, 6.5, 6.7.1
      advice on   6.5, 11.4.1
   costs   6.6
   death of   22.7.1
   disability, under   22.2.2, 22.8.1
   entitlement to act   22.2.1, 23.2
   expenses   6.6
   firm as, drafting points   6.7.1
   former spouse, as   22.2.2
   general   6.4
   grant of probate, entitlement to   20.2.2
   individual as   6.6
   intermeddling   22.2.3, 25.5.2
   literary   6.4, 22.6.2
   mental incapacity   22.2.2
   minor, as   22.2.2
   notice to non-proving executors when power reserved   23.2
   number of   6.4, 22.2.1, 22.2.4
   oath for   22.1.1, 22.2, 23.2
      'marking will'   23.2.1
      names and addresses, on   23.2
      specimen   23.2, App 3
      swearing or affirming   23.2
   power reserved   22.2.4
   powers granted in will   10.7, 25.3.2, 25.4
   professional   6.5, 6.7
   Public Trustee as   6.9
   renunciation   22.2.3
   signing the will and codicils   23.2.1
   sole   25.6.2
   solicitor as   6.5, 6.7
      firm appointed   6.7.1
      professional conduct obligations, and   6.7.1
   statutory powers, extension of   2.3.4, 10.1.2, 25.3.2
   substitute, provision for   6.4, 6.6
   suitability   6.6
   trust corporation as   6.8

Executor *cont*
  trust corporation as *cont*
    pros and cons   6.8.1
  trustees, dual capacity as   6.3, 6.6
Executor's year   28.8.1

Family provision   17.1 *et seq*
  acquisition of property for transfer, order for 17.8.1
  advice on, when making will   11.4.5, 17.1.2, 17.10.1
  anti-avoidance   17.9
  child of deceased, claim by   17.5
  child of family, claim by   17.6
  claim (generally)   17.2 *et seq*
    persons who can make   17.2.2
    settlement between beneficiaries to preclude 17.1.3
    time-limit for   17.2.1, 17.10.3
  claimant
    acting for   17.10.3
    conflict of interest, avoidance of   17.10.1, 17.10.2
    conduct of   17.2.4
    deceased's moral obligations towards 17.2.4
    financial resources, obligations, and needs of 17.2.4
    physical or mental disability of   17.2.4
  cohabitee, claim by   17.10.1
    age, etc, and contribution made   17.4
    deaths after 1 Jan 96, applies to   17.8
  former spouse, claim by   17.4
  grounds for claim   17.2.3
  inheritance tax, and   17.8.3, 17.8.5, 17.10.3
  lump sum order   17.8.1, 17.8.3
  marriage settlement variation   17.8.1
  'net estate', meaning   17.8.2
  orders
    available to court   17.8.1
    burden of, where falling   17.8.4
    effect of   17.8.3
    inheritance tax consequences   17.8.5
    net estate of deceased, against   17.8.2
  periodical payments order   17.8.1
  person being maintained by deceased, claim by 17.7
  personal representatives, acting for   17.1.2, 17.10.2
  property against which order can be made 17.8.2
  'reasonable financial provision'
    common guidelines on   17.2.4
    standards for judging   17.2.3
  size and nature of estate, account of   17.2.4
  spouse (surviving), claim by   17.3
  standing search   17.11
  statement by testator explaining why no provision   17.10.1
  time-limit for claim   17.2.1
  transfer or settlement of property   17.8.1
Fee
  probate, for   20.7, 21.4.5, 22.1.3, 23.5
  solicitor's, for being personal representative 27.2.2
Financial services, *see* Investment business
Flat
  specific devise of   8.4.6
Foreign property
  disposal of, by will   11.3.4
  Inland Revenue account, and   21.2.1, 21.2.2, 21.5.5
Friendly Society
  debt owed to, insolvent estate   27.8.3
  money in, grant may not be necessary 20.6.1
Funeral
  see also Body
  arrangements   20.3.3
  expenses
    Inland Revenue account, in   21.4.4, 21.5.4
    payment of   24.1.1, 27.2.1, 27.5.2, 27.7.2
    provision in will for   8.3.2, 9.1.4, 27.6
    statutory order for payment   27.7.2

Gift
  abatement   15.9
  ademption of   2.1.2, 8.2.1, 8.4.1
  charity, to, *see* Charity
  child, to, *see* Child
  class   8.3.3, 28.3.5
    lapse of   15.3.5
  classification   28.4
  contingency, failure of   15.4
  contingent   2.3.1, 4.3.3, 8.3.3, 9.1.2
  devise, *see* Devise
  disclaimer   15.8, 30.2, *see also* Disclaimer
  distribution of   28.1 *et seq*
    beneficiaries, identification of   28.2, 28.3, *see also* Beneficiary
    construction summons   28.2.1
    intestacy, on   28.9
    pecuniary legacies   28.6
    specific legacies   28.5
  divorce, effect of   15.5
  failure of   2.1.2, 8.3.1, 8.3.3, 15.1, 15.3
  free of tax   8.3.2, 18.6.3, 18.11.2
  income from, rules   10.5.4
  institution, to   8.3.3
  lapse   2.1.2, 15.3
    basic rule   15.3.1
    class gifts   15.3.5, 15.3.6, 28.3.5
    divorce, on   15.5
    joint tenants, gift to   15.3.5
    order of deaths when close together 15.3.2
    residue, falling into   15.3.1
    statutory substitutional provision   15.3.6

Gift *cont*
  lapse *cont*
    substitutional gifts   15.3.4
    survivorship   9.2.1, 11.3.2, 15.3.3
    tenants in common, gift to   15.3.5
    two or more people dying together   15.3.2
  legacy, *see* Legacy
  money, of   4.2.3
  receipt for   8.3.3
  rejection of   30.2
  residue, of, *see* Residuary estate
  retrospective effect, specific gifts   28.5.2
  shares, of   8.4.5
  solicitor, to   11.1.3
  specimen clauses   8.3.3
  spouse, to, *see* Spouse
  substitutional   4.3.3, 9.1.1, 15.3.4, 15.3.6
  tax, subject to   8.3.2
  types of   8.2
  uncertainty   8.4.1, 15.6
  vested   8.3.3
Grandchild
  administrator, as   22.4.1
  gift to, construction of   28.3.1
  substitution of, provision for   9.1.2, 9.2.3, 15.3.6
Grant de bonis non administratis   22.7.3
Grant of representation
  admissibility of will   20.7.1
  application   20.7
    inheritance tax paid on   18.10.1, 29.2.1
    place for   20.5.1, 20.7, 23.2
  cessate grant   22.6.4
  chain of representation, and   22.7.2, 22.7.3
  citation to accept or refuse grant   22.8.2
  clearing off person with prior right   22.8.2
  cost of obtaining   27.2.2
  death certificate copies   20.3.6, 20.7.4
  disclaimer, and   20.8
  documents to be lodged   20.7
    Inland Revenue account, *see* Inland Revenue account
  due execution of will, affidavit of   20.7.2
  effect of   22.5
  issue of   23.5
  knowledge and approval, affidavit as to   20.7.2
  letters of administration, of   1.6.3, 22.5.2
  letters of administration with will annexed, *see* Administrator with will annexed
  limited   22.6, 22.6.1
    minor, for use of   22.6.4
    property, to   22.6.2
    settled land, to   22.6.3
  lost will   20.7.2
  minor
    grant for the use of   22.6.4
  need for   20.6
  oath supporting application, *see* Oath
  obtaining   20.4 *et seq*
    assets and liabilities, details of   20.4.1
    beneficiaries, details of   20.4.2
    cost of   27.2.2
    inheritance tax payment   18.10.1, *see also* Inland Revenue account
    missing and unknown creditors and beneficiaries, and   20.4.3
    probate papers   20.4.4
  office copies of, as evidence of title   20.7.3, 26.2
  plight and condition, affidavit as to   20.7.2
  prevention of issue of   22.8.1
  probate, of, *see* Probate, grant of
  production of   20.7.3, 26.2
  realisation of assets without   20.6
  requirement to obtain   1.6
  simple administration   1.6.3
  types of   1.6, 22.5
  variation, and   20.8
Guardian
  appointment   2.3.3, 7.2 *et seq*
    specimen clause   7.4
  choice of   7.4
  death of parent, and   7.3
  need for   7.1

Hotchpot
  abolition of rules   16.1.4
House
  assent to vest legal estate in beneficiary   28.5.1
  beneficiary, purchase for   25.4.3

Illegitimate person   16.6.2, 28.3.1
  personal representatives, and   28.3.4
Income
  apportionment   10.5.1, 10.5.4
  beneficiary, on specific gift   28.5.2
  interest in, divided from capital interest   10.3.1
  trustees' powers as to use of   10.3.5
Income tax
  administration period, in   29.5.2
  beneficiary, liability of   28.5.2, 29.5.3
  deceased, liability of, return for   29.5.1
  deduction at source   29.5.3
  personal representatives, liability of   29.5.3
  relief, on interest on loan account   21.1.3, 29.5.3
Indemnity
  personal representatives, for   25.5.2, 28.3.4
Infant receipt clause   4.2.3, 8.3.3, 29.6.3
Inheritance tax (general)   18.1 *et seq*
  adjustment to assessment   29.2
  agricultural property relief   12.4.2, 18.7.2
  annual exemption   18.13.2
  application for grant, paid on   29.2.1
  business property relief   12.4.2, 18.7.1

Inheritance tax (general) cont
  capital gains tax, interaction with, see Capital gains tax
  certificate of discharge 29.4.1
  chargeable transfer, charged on 18.2
  charity, and 4.4.3, 18.6.2, 18.13.1
  clearance certificate 29.4
  corrective account 29.3.1, 29.4.2, App 2
  cumulation 12.2.3, 18.8.2, 29.2.3
  death, on, see Inheritance tax on death
  disclaimer, effect of 30.2.2
  estate, for purposes of 12.2.1, 18.4
    property outside 2.5, 12.4.3, 18.4.4
  estimating 12.2, 24.4.2, see also 'planning' below
  excluded property 18.4.4
  exemptions
    annual 18.13.2
    charity 18.6.2, 18.13.1
    death, on 12.2.2, 18.6, 18.13.1
    gift in consideration of marriage 18.13.2
    lifetime transfers and death, applying on 18.13.1
    lifetime transfers only, applying to 18.13.2
    normal expenditure out of income 18.13.2
    partially exempt transfers 18.6.3
    small gifts 18.13.2
    spouse, see 'spouse exemption' below
    use of 12.3.1
  family provision order, effect of 17.8.3, 17.8.5, 17.10.3
  final assessment 29.3.2
  foreign property and double taxation 11.3.4
  Form Cap 30 (corrective account) 29.3.1, 29.4.2, App 2
  free estate, meaning 21.3.3
  funding of 21.1.3, 24.4.2, 27.1, 27.1.2
  gift in will, and 4.2.3, 4.3.3, 8.3.2
  house 8.4.6
  Inland Revenue account, see Inland Revenue account
  instalment, paid by 18.10.2, 29.2.2, 29.4.3
  insurance policies 2.5
  intestacy, on 16.3.4, 16.3.5
    life interest, redemption of 16.3.5
  joint property 2.5, 11.3.3, 18.4.1, 26.3.3
  life assurance policy, and 12.4.3
  life interest, and 12.4.1, 18.4.2, 18.6.1
    Inland Revenue account, details in 21.5.6, 21.5.7
  lifetime transfers 12.3, 18.2.1, 18.13, 29.2.3
    advice and planning 11.3.3
    discovery of, after Inland Revenue account 29.2.3, 29.2.5
    effect of 12.2.3
    exemptions and reliefs 12.3.1, 18.2.1, 18.13
    liability for tax on 29.2.3
    use of 12.1, 12.3
    within seven years of death 12.2.3, 18.8.2, 18.13.4, 28.2.3
  limited discharge 29.4.3
  loss relief 27.1.3, 29.2.4, 29.2.5
    interaction with capital gains tax 29.5.4
  marriage, gift in consideration of 18.11.2
  nil rate band, use of 12.3.2, 12.4.1, 30.4.2
  nominated property 2.5, 18.4.1, 21.4.2, 26.3.3
    Inland Revenue account, in 21.4.3, 21.5.3
  normal expenditure out of income 18.13.2
  payment 20.4.4, 29.2
    adjustment of assessment 29.2
    apportionment 21.5.9
    Inland Revenue account, with 21.1.3, 21.6, 24.4.2
    loan for 21.1.3, 27.1.2
  pension benefits 2.5, 12.4.3, 26.3.3
  planning 11.3.3, 11.4.4, 12.1, 12.2.4 et seq, 18.6.3
  post-date variation
    effect of 30.3.2
    planning aspects 30.4
  potentially exempt transfers 12.3.2, 18.2.1, 18.9.4
    death within seven years of, effect of 18.8.2, 18.13.4
    disclaimer by beneficiary, as 30.1.2, 30.2.2
    meaning 18.2.1
    variation by beneficiary, and 30.3.2
  preparation of, time for 24.4.2
  property
    deceased's, meaning of 18.4.1
    excluded from estate 18.4.4
    related 18.5.5
    reservation, subject to 12.3.2, 18.4.3, 18.9.3, 29.2.3
    trust, subject to 18.4.2
  quick succession relief 18.8.4
  reliefs 12.2.2, 18.13.2, 18.13.3, 29.2.4
  repayment of loan to pay 27.1.2
  residuary estate, paid from 8.3.2, 27.7.3
  settlement, for purposes of 9.2.1, 18.4.2
  spouse exemption 12.2.2, 12.3.1, 18.6.1
    lifetime gift, and 18.13.1
    nil rate band, and 12.3.2, 12.4.1
  survivorship clause, and 9.2.1, 18.6.1
  tapering relief 18.8.2, 18.13.2, 18.13.4
  testamentary expense, as 27.2.2, 27.7.3
  transfer of value, definition 18.2.1
  unpaid, Inland Revenue charge imposed 27.7.1
  variation, and 30.3.1
Inheritance tax on death 18.2.2
  assets, valuation of 18.5.1–18.5.5
  burden of 18.11
    meaning 18.11.1

Inheritance tax on death *cont*
  burden of *cont*
    personal representatives, and   18.11.2, 18.11.3
    trustees, and   18.11.3
  calculation of tax   18.3, 18.8
    adjustments to   29.2.5
    cumulation   18.8.2, 29.2.3
    estate rate   18.8.3
  chargeable transfers within seven years of death, effect   18.3.5
  'due date'   18.3.5
  estate
    basic valuation principle   18.5.1–18.5.3
    debts and expenses, deduction of   18.5.4
    definition   18.4.1
    gross   21.2.1
    identification of   18.3.1, 18.4
    property outside   18.4.4
    property within   18.4.1–18.4.3, 26.3.3
    related property rule   18.5.5
    reservation, property subject to   12.3.2, 18.4.3, 18.9.3, 21.5.2, 21.5.6
    trust property included in   18.4.2, 18.6.1
    valuation of   18.3.2, 18.5
  'estate rate' of tax   18.8.3
  example of   18.12
  exemptions, application of   18.3.3, 18.6
  free of tax   8.3.2, 18.6.3, 18.11.2
  interest   18.10.1, 18.10.2, 21.1.1
  liability for   18.9
    adjustment to   29.2, 30.2.2, 30.3.2
    meaning   18.9.1
    personal representatives, of   18.9.2, 18.9.4, 18.10, 18.11.1, 18.11.2
    sale of instalment option property, on   18.10.2, 29.2.2
    trustees, of   18.9.3, 18.11.3
  loss relief   29.2.4, 29.5.4
  nil rate band   18.3.5
  non-settled property   18.9.2
  quick succession relief   18.8.4
  rate of tax   18.3.5, 18.8.1
  settled property   18.9.3
  time for payment   18.10
    instalment option property   18.10.2
    non-instalment option property   18.10.1
  transfer of value on   18.2.2
  two or more people dying together   18.4.6
Inland Revenue
  charge   27.7.1
  repayment or liability, agreed with personal representatives, effect   29.2.5
Inland Revenue account   20.4.3, 20.7
  completion of   20.4.4, 21.1 *et seq*
  corrective account   29.3, App 2
  delivery of   21.1.1
  excepted estate   21.1, 21.2.1
    criteria for   21.2.1
  Form IHT 200   21.2.3, 21.5 *et seq*
    calculation of tax   21.5.9, App 2
    criteria for use   21.2.3
    debts, recording   21.3.4
    declaration   21.3.9, 21.5.11
    exemptions, exclusions and reliefs   21.5.7
    figures, presentation of   21.3.5
    foreign property, section on   21.5.5
    free estate, section on   21.5.4
    instalments, property with option   21.5.4
    instalments, right to pay by   21.5.3
    layout   21.3.2
    liabilities   21.5.4, 21.5.8
    lifetime gifts, section on   21.5.2
    nominated and joint property, section on   21.5.1, 21.5.3
    personal details   21.3.1
    probate summary   21.3.8, 21.5.10
    property vesting in personal representatives, value   21.5.10
    reservation of benefit, details of   21.5.2, 21.5.6
    Schedules   21.3.6
    settled property, details of   21.5.6
    specimen   App 2
    superannuation benefits, details of   21.5.2
    totals   21.3.7
  Form IHT 202   21.2.2, 21.4 *et seq*
    contents of, diagram   21.4
    criteria for use of   21.2.2
    debts in   21.3.4, 21.4.4
    declaration   21.3.9, 21.4.7
    delivery to probate registry   21.4.7
    figures, presentation of   21.3.5
    free estate, section on   21.4.4
    layout   21.3.2
    nominated and joint property, section on   21.4.2, 21.4.3
    personal details   21.3.1
    probate summary   21.3.8, 21.4.5
    property vesting in personal representatives, value   21.4.5
    Schedules   21.3.6
    specimen   App 1
    tax summary   21.4.6
    totals   21.3.7
  free estate
    meaning   21.3.3
    section in Form IHT 202 on   21.4.4
  instalment option property, and   21.1.1, 21.3.2
  inventory of assets, as   21.1.1
  liability of personal representatives for contents   21.3.9
  nature of   21.1.1
  payment of tax with   21.6
    funds for   21.1.3
  purpose of   21.1.1
  requirement for   21.1, 21.1.1, 21.2
    oath form, completion of, and   23.2

Inland Revenue account *cont*
   types of   21.1
   valuations
      general principles   21.1.2
      jointly owned assets   21.1.2
Insolvent estate
   meaning   27.8.1
   payment of debts in   27.8
      debts proved against   27.8.4
      order for distribution   27.8.3
      possible insolvency   27.8.2
      secured creditors   27.8.5
Instructions   11.1 *et seq*
   carrying out   11.5
   confirmation of   6.8.2, 11.1.2
   conflict of interests   11.1.2
   personal representative, from   20.1, 20.2.1, 20.2.3 *et seq*
   Professional Conduct of Solicitors, guidelines   11.1.2, 11.1.3
   property details   11.3
   solicitor's role in   11.1, 11.3.2, 11.3.3
      duty of care   11.1.6
   tax, and   12.1 *et seq*
      consideration of alternatives, and   11.4.4, 12.1
      estimate   11.3.3, 12.2
Insurance
   life policy, *see* Life assurance policy
   power of personal representatives   10.2.3, 25.4.2
Intention
   testator, of   13.3, *see also* Testator
Interest (money)
   inheritance tax, on   18.10.1, 18.10.2, 21.1.1
   pecuniary legatee, to   28.8.1
      payable from date of death   28.8.2
      rate, etc   28.8.1
Intestacy   16.1 *et seq*
   administrator of estate   2.3.2, *see also* Administrator
   bona vacantia   16.2.2, 16.6.3
   brothers and sisters   16.2.2, 16.4.2, 16.6.1
   cohabitee, and   17.10.1
   cousins   16.2.3
   deaths, two or more, occuring together   16.7
   debts, payment of   16.2.1, 27.7.2
   distribution on   16.2 *et seq*, 28.9
   entitlement on   16.2.2
      disclaimer of   30.2.1
   grandparent, entitlement   16.2.2, 16.6.1
   implied powers of personal representatives   25.3.1
   inheritance tax on   16.3.4, 16.3.5
      life interest, redemption of   16.3.5
   issue, entitlement of   16.2.2, 16.3.2
      adopted or illegitimate, no spouse   16.6.2
      meaning of 'issue'   16.3.2
      no surviving spouse   16.6.1
      statutory trusts for   16.3.4
   life interest, right to redeem   16.3.5
   'living', meaning of   12.2.3
   matrimonial home, spouse's right   16.3.6, 16.4.3
   meaning   1.2.2, 16.1.1
   nephews and nieces   16.2.3
   no surviving spouse   16.2.2, 16.6
   parent, entitlement   16.2.2, 16.4.2, 16.6.1
   partial   1.2.3, 16.1.2
      debts, payment of   27.7.2
      drafting to prevent   4.3.3
      effect   16.1.2
      meaning   16.1.2
      pecuniary legacies, source of funds for   28.7.1
   personal chattels, meaning   16.3.3
   property passing on   2.4, 16.1.3
   residuary estate, meaning   16.2.1
   rules, avoiding   2.3.1
   spouse, entitlement on   16.2.2, 16.3, 16.4.1, 16.5
      appropriation of matrimonial home, right to   16.3.6, 16.4.3
      deaths after 1 Jan 96   16.3.3, 16.5
      life interest   16.3.3, 16.3.5
      meaning of 'spouse' for   16.3.1
      no other close relatives   16.5
      spouse and issue survive   16.3.3
      spouse but no issue   16.4
      statutory legacy   16.3.3, 16.4.1
      survival period for   16.7
   statutory trusts, imposition of   16.2.1–16.2.3, 16.3.4, 16.6.1
   total   16.1.1
Investment(s)
   see also Share(s)
   meaning   19.2.1, *see also* Investment business
   power to make, personal representatives'   10.3.2, 25.4.2
   wasting, hazardous or unauthorised   10.5.2
Investment business   19.1 *et seq*
   advice
      beneficiaries, to   19.4
      given in course of profession   19.2.3
   assets which are 'investments'   19.2.1
   dealing   19.2.2
   'dealing as principal'   19.2.3
   discrete, avoiding   19.2.4, 19.3, 19.4
   excluded activities   19.2.3
   incidental activity, as   19.3
   managing   19.2.2–19.2.4
      'administrative management' of assets   19.2.2
   meaning   19.2, 19.2.4
   permitted third party   19.3, 19.4
   solicitor
      compliance with Solicitors' Investment Business Rules   19.1 *et seq*
      'packaged products'   19.3
      personal representative, as   19.2.3, 19.3

Joint property
   see also Joint tenants
   death, passing on   2.4.1, 11.3.2, 26.3.2
      no grant required   20.6.2
   family provision order against   17.8.2
   inheritance tax, and
      details of   21.4.2, 21.4.3
      estate includes   18.4.1, 26.3.3
   realisation without grant   20.6.2
   survivorship, right of   11.3.2, 20.6.2, 26.3.2
   tax, and   2.5
      valuation for   21.1.2
Joint tenants   2.4.1, 11.3.2
   lapse of gift to   15.3.5
   survivorship, and   11.3.2, 20.6.2, 26.3.2
Jurat
   executor's oath, on   23.2

Land
   see also Devise; House
   charge imposed by court on   27.7.1
   gift of   8.1
   inheritance tax, and
      instalment option for   18.10.2
      loss relief   29.2.4, 29.5.4
      value for   18.5.3
   not an 'investment'   19.2.1
   personal representatives' powers
      purchase of, as to   10.3.3
      sale of, as to   25.5.4, 25.6.3
   proceeds of sale of, receipt for   25.6.2
   specific devise of land   8.4.6
   transfer to residuary beneficiary   29.6.4
   trust, held on   9.1.3, 9.2.4, *see also* Trust of land
   valuation of, for inheritance tax   21.1.2, 29.2.4, 29.2.5
Lapse   15.3
Legacy
   see also Gift
   charging clause treated as   6.7.2
   demonstrative   8.2.3
   divided by agreement   8.4.4
   drafting of clause for   4.2.3
   free of tax   8.3.2, 18.6.3, 18.11.2
   general   4.2.3, 8.2.2
      disclaimed, effect   30.2.1
   generic specific   4.2.3
   meaning   8.1
   payment of   24.4.2
      time for   25.5.6
   pecuniary   4.2.3, 4.3.3, 8.2.4
      distribution of   28.6
      examples of   4.2.2, 4.3.2
      express provision for payment of   28.6.1
      interest on   28.8.1, 28.8.2
      meaning   8.2.4, 27.7.2
      no express provision for payment of   28.6.2, 28.7
      partial intestacy, on   28.7.1
      payment, time for   28.8
      residue disposed of by will, where   28.7.2
      source of funds for   28.7
      time for payment   28.8
   shares, of   8.4.5
   specific   4.2.3, 8.2.1, 8.4
      ademption, doctrine of   8.2.1, 8.4.1, 15.2
      beneficiaries to decide division   8.4.4
      certainty   8.4.1, 15.6
      costs, who bears   8.4.2
      describing   8.4.1
      disclaimed, effect   30.2.1
      distribution of   28.5
      meaning   8.2.1
      number of small   8.4.3
      property, identity of   8.4.1
      retrospective effect   28.5.2
      shares of   8.4.5
      transfer, method of   28.5.1
Legatee, residuary
   see also Residuary estate
   administrator, as   22.3.2
   asset vested in, capital gains tax and   29.5.4
   meaning   29.5.4
   personal representative of, as administrator   22.3.2
Legitimated person   28.3.3
   personal representatives, and   28.3.4
Letters of administration   1.6.3
   with will annexed   1.6.2, 20.2.2
Liabilities
   see also Debt(s); Testamentary debts and expenses
   recording of   24.4.2, *see also* Inland Revenue account
Life assurance policy   2.4.3
   benefit, ownership of   2.4.3
   death, and proceeds of   2.4.3
   estate, outside   12.4.3
   inheritance tax, and   12.4.3
      Inland Revenue account section on   21.5.2
      valuation of, for   21.1.2
   Inland Revenue account, declaration in   21.5.2
   investment, as   19.2.1
   mortgage debt, covering   8.4.6
   realisation without grant of representation   20.6.3
   tax, and   2.5
   trust, held on, no grant for   2.4.3, 20.6.3, 26.3.2
Life interest
   apportionment, and   10.5
      exclusion of rules   10.5.5
   capital advance to life tenant   10.3.6, 25.2.2, 25.4.2, 25.4.3

Life interest cont
    death of life tenant   26.3.2
    inheritance tax, and   12.4.1, 18.4.2, 18.6.1
        Inland Revenue account, details in   21.5.6, 21.5.7
    trust of residue, and   9.1.2
    two personal representatives required, where created   22.3.4, 23.3, 23.4
    will drafting considerations   10.7.4
Lost will   20.7.2

Maintenance
    trustees' power of   10.3.5, 25.4.2
Management
    personal representatives' powers of   25.5.4
Marriage
    annulment   14.3.2, 15.5
    forthcoming, will made in expectation of   5.1, 14.3.2
        marriage to another   14.3.2
        specimen clause   14.3.2
    gift on, inheritance tax, and   18.13.2
    revocation of will by   14.3.2
    settlement, variation of   17.8.1
    void   14.3.2, 15.5
    will conditional on   14.3.2
Matrimonial home
    intestacy, on   16.3.6, 16.4.3
Medical research
    donation of body for   5.3, 20.3.2
Minor
    see also Child
    absolute entitlement   25.5.5
    administrator, as   22.4.4
    administrator with will annexed, as   22.3.3
    executor, as   6.6, 22.2.2
    grant for the use of   22.6.4
    infant receipt clause   4.2.3, 8.3.3
    married   10.2.4
    minority interest created, executors for   22.3.4, 23.3, 23.4
    personal representatives' power to accept receipt from   10.2.4, 25.4.3
    trust for   2.3.2, 9.1.2, 10.3.1, 25.5.5, 29.6.3
    witness, as   13.5.1
Missing will   14.3.3
Mistake
    oath, in   23.5
    will, in   13.3.2, 28.2.1
Money, see Cash
Mortgage
    creditor with, secured   27.8.5
    devise of property subject to   8.4.6
    property subject to   27.7.1
Mutual wills   14.2
    revocation, and   14.2

National Savings
    grant of representation not required, circumstances   20.6.1
    not an 'investment'   19.2.1
    payment of tax from   21.1.3
Negligence
    solicitor, of   11.1.6, 13.5.4, 17.11.3
Nominated property
    death, passing on   2.4.2, 20.6.2, 26.3.2
    tax, and   2.5
    value for inheritance tax purposes   26.3.3
        Inland Revenue forms, details in   21.4.2, 21.4.3, 21.5.3
Non-contentious probate business   20.5
    court's involvement   20.5.3
    meaning   20.5.2
    registry for   20.5.1
    Rules, extracts   App 5

Oath
    administrator, for   22.4, 23.4
        example   23.4
    administrator with will annexed   22.3, 23.3
        'clearing off' executor etc   22.3.2, App 6
        example   23.3
    application for grant of representation supported by   22.1
    completion of   23.5
    executor, for   22.2, 23.2
        example   23.2, App 3
        'marking' will   23.2.1
    lodging of   20.7
    mistake in   23.5
    preparation of, time for   24.4.2
    solicitor's name and address on, use   23.2
    stop notice   23.5
    swearing or affirming of   22.1.3
    types of   22.1.1
Organ transplant
    clause in will   5.3

PAYE
    debt to Inland Revenue, as, insolvent estate   27.8.3
Parent
    death of, effect on appointment of guardian   7.3
    intestacy, entitlement on   16.2.2, 16.4.2, 16.6
Parental responsibility   7.2, 7.3
Partner
    executors, as   6.7.1
Pecuniary legacy   4.2.3
Pension benefits
    death, passing on   2.4.4, 20.6.3, 26.3.2
    estate, outside   12.4.3, 26.3.2
    grant, whether required   20.6.3
    Inland Revenue account, details in   21.5.2
    tax, and   2.5, 12.4.3
    trust, in   2.4.4, 26.3.2

Pension scheme payments
   insolvent estate, as debt due from   27.8.3
Periodical payments order   17.8.1
Perpetuity rules   15.10
Personal representative
   accounting records   24.3.2, 23.2.3
   accounts, requirement to keep   24.3.1, 24.3.4
   administration work   19.1, 19.2
   administrator, *see* Administrator;
      Administrator with will annexed
   advertisement by   24.2.5, 27.4, 28.3.4
   agent, employment of   25.5.1
   appointment   1.5.2, 2.3.2
   appropriation of assets   10.2.2, 25.4.2
   assets, collection of   24.1.1, 26.1 *et seq*
      costs of   27.2.2
      duty   24.2.1, 26.1
      methods of   26.2
      time-limits   26.1.1
   assets, sale of, necessity for   24.4.2, 27.1.3
   authority before grant   20.2.2
   beneficiary, and
      failure to take account of   24.2.6
      unknown, failure to pay   24.2.5, 27.4
      see also Beneficiary
   breach of duty by   24.2.2–24.2.4
   business of deceased, powers as to   10.6.3, 25.4.3
   capital gains tax liability   29.5.4
   chain of representation   22.7.2, 22.7.3
   claims from beneficiaries   27.4
   dealings by   19.2, 19.2.3
   death of   22.7.1
   debts, *see* 'expenses and debts, payment' *below*
   delay by   25.5.6, 26.1.1
   delegation   25.5.1, 25.5.2
   devastavit   24.2.2–24.2.4, 26.1.1
   devolution of assets on   26.3
      inheritance tax, liability to   26.3.3
      property not devolving on   26.3.2
      real and personal property   26.3.1
   distribution of estate   28.1 *et seq*, 29.1 *et seq*
      Benjamin order   24.2.6, 28.3.4
      power of postponement   25.5.6
      time for   27.4, 28.2.1, 28.8.1
   duties of   1.5.1, 15.1, 24.1.1, 25.1
      assets of deceased, collection of   24.2.1, 26.1
      breach of   24.2.2–24.2.4
      missing beneficiaries, and   24.2.6, 28.3.4
      oath, set out in   23.2
      powers for carrying out   25.1
   executor, *see* Executor
   expenses of
      charging clause for   6.7.2, 10.6.1
      implied indemnity for   25.5.2
   expenses and debts, payment
      assets, sale of, for   27.1.3
      contrary provision in will   27.6
      duty   25.5.6, 27.3
      funeral expenses, *see* Funeral expenses
      incurred by deceased   25.5.6, 27.3
      inheritance tax   27.2.2, 27.7.3
      insolvent estate, in, *see* Insolvent estate
      no contrary provision in will   27.7
      repayment of loan to pay inheritance tax   27.1.2
      secured creditors   27.7.1
      sources of money   27.1.1
      testamentary, *see* Testamentary debts and expenses
      time for   25.5.6, 27.3
      unsecured debts   27.7.2
   family provision claim, and   17.1.2, 17.10.2
      personal liability if early distribution   17.10.2
   financial services, and, *see* Investment business
   grant of representation, *see* Grant of representation
   income tax liability   29.5.3
   indemnity for   25.5.2, 28.3.4
   inheritance tax, liability for   18.9.2, 18.9.4, 18.10, 18.11.1, 18.11.2
      due date   18.10.1
      gifts with reservation of benefit, on   18.9.4, 29.2.3
      payment, time for   18.10
      potentially exempt transfers, on   18.9.4
      protection of   18.9.4
      retention of assets for   29.2.3
   insurance
      for   28.3.4, 29.2.3
      power of   10.2.3, 25.4.2
      reimbursement of cost   28.5.2
   intermeddling   22.2.3, 25.5.2
   investment, power of   10.3.2, 25.4.2, *see also* Investment business
   liability (general)
      personal   24.2.2, 24.2.3, 24.3.6
      protection against   24.2.5, 28.3.4
      relief from   24.2.4
   maintenance and advancement, power of   10.3.5, 10.3.6, 25.4.2
   maladministration by   24.2.2
   meaning   1.5.2
   meeting with solicitor, preliminary   24.4.2
   minor, receipt from   10.2.4
   misappropriation of assets   24.2.2
   number of   1.5.1, 20.2.2
   persons who may be   1.5.1, 20.2.2
   power of attorney, delegation by   25.5.2
   powers   10.1, 25.1 *et seq*
      administrative   25.2.1
      dispositive   25.2.2
      distribution, to postpone   25.5.6
      exercise of   25.6
      express   25.4.3
      extending by will   10.1.2 *et seq*, 25.3.2
      fiduciary exercise of   25.6.1
      implied statutory   25.3.1

Personal representative *cont*
  powers *cont*
    intestacy, on   25.3
    selection of, in will   10.7
    sole PR, of   25.6.2
    sources of   25.3
    statutory   10.1.1, 25.4.2, 25.5
    trust, under, *see* Trustee
    two or more PRs, of   25.6.3
    types of   25.2
    will drafting, and   10.2.1, 10.7, 25.4.1
    will, granted by   25.3.2
  property vested in, burden of tax   18.11.2
  protection of   24.2.5, 28.3.4
  records   24.3
  role   1.5.1
  sale and management, powers   25.5.4
    signature of withdrawal/transfer forms by   20.4.1
    time for   24.4.2
  sole   25.6.2
  solicitor
    as, *see* Solicitor
    instruction of, by   20.2.1, 20.2.3
  tax returns, for deceased's liability   29.5.1, 29.5.2
  time-limits   25.5.6, 26.1.1
  trustee, as   10.3, *see also* Trustee
  'trustee' includes   10.1.1
  trustees of minor beneficiary's property, power of appointment   25.5.5
Personalty
  see also Chattels
  powers of personal representatives as to   25.6.3
  transfer to residuary beneficiary   29.6.4
Post-death variations
  effect of   20.8, 29.2.5
  inheritance tax planning aspects   30.4
  reasons for using   30.1.1
  succession aspects   30.3.1
  taxation
    advantages   30.1.2
    aspects of   30.3.2
  wishes of beneficiaries, ascertaining   30.1.3
Postponement
  distribution, of   25.5.6
Power of attorney   25.5.2
Precatory trust   8.4.3
Precedents
  use of   3.4
Preferred debts   27.8.3
Premium bond
  grant of representation not required, circumstances   20.6.1
  not an 'investment'   19.2.1
  payment of tax with   21.1.3
Principal Registry of Family Division   20.5.1, 20.7
Privileged will   5.2

generally   13.2.1
Probate, grant of   1.6.1
  see also Grant of representation
  admission of will to   20.7.1
  capacity to take out   6.6
  effect   22.5.1
  general   6.4
  oath for   20.4.4, *see also* Oath
  special   6.4
Probate business
  non-contentious
    conducting   20.5.1
    court, assistance of   20.5.3
    meaning   20.5.2
Probate practice
  meaning   20.9
Probate registry
  application to, office for   20.5.1, 20.7, 23.2
  standing search   17.11
Property
  see also Asset
  details of, taking   11.3.1
  disposal before death   2.1.2
  divided interests   10.3.1
  foreign, *see* Foreign property
  gifts of, freedom of donor   17.1
  intestacy, passing on   16.1.3
  joint, *see* Joint property
  nominated, *see* Nominated property
  not capable of passing by will or intestacy   1.3, 2.4.1–2.4.4
    tax, and   2.5
  passing by will   2.4, 15.2.3
  pension benefits   2.4.4
  related, inheritance tax, and   18.5.5
  settled, *see* Settlement
  solicitor securing, after receiving instructions   20.3.4
  succession, advice on   11.3.2
  transfer of, family provision claim   17.8.1
  uncertain   15.6.1
Public benefit
  gift for, and inheritance tax   18.6.2
Public Trustee
  executor, as   6.9
Punctuation
  will drafting, and   3.3.2

Quick succession relief   18.8.4, 21.5.9

Realty
  see also Land
  legacy charged on, interest on   28.8.2
  powers of personal representatives as to   25.6.3
Receipt
  charity, from   4.4.3, 8.3.3
  minor, from   4.2.3, 8.3.3, 10.3.7

Rectification
  will, of   28.2.1
Relative
  executor, as   6.6
  intestacy, entitlement on   16.2.2
Residuary estate   4.2.3, 8.2.5
  absolute interest in
    adult beneficiary, with substitution of another adult   9.2.4
    example   9.2
    failure of gift to spouse, reasons   9.2.2
    specimen clauses   9.2.4
    substitutional gifts   9.2.2, 9.2.3, 9.2.4
    surviving spouse, to   9.2.1, 9.2.2, 9.2.4
    survivorship clause   9.2.1
  assets in, transfer of   29.6
  children
    remainder to   9.3.2
    substitutional gift to   9.2.2
  contingent interests   9.1.2, 9.2.4, 10.5.4, 10.5.5
  debts and expenses, payment out of   8.3.2, 9.1.4, 27.6.1
  disclaimer of gift, effect   30.2.1
  distribution of   29.1 *et seq*
    interim   24.4.2, 28.1, 29.1
  drafting matters
    avoiding partial intestacy   9.1.1
    trust, whether required   9.1.2
    type of trust   9.1.3
  grandchildren, substitutional gift to   9.2.3, 9.3.2
  land   29.6.4
  lapsed gift falling into   15.3.1, 16.1.2
  legacies, express provision for   9.1.4
  life interest in   9.1.2, 9.3
    example   9.3, 9.3.2
    remainder to children   9.3.2
    spouse, to   9.3.1
  meaning   8.2.5
  minor beneficiary   9.1.2
  personalty   29.6.4
    apportionment rules, and   10.5.2
  property, transfer of   29.6.4, 29.6
  tax, subject to   8.3.2, 27.7.3
  transfer of assets in   29.6
  trust, *see* Trust
Revocation   14.1 *et seq*
  clause   14.3.1, 14.3.3
  codicil
    by   14.3.1
    effect on   14.3.3
  dependent relative, doctrine of   14.3.1, 14.3.3
  destruction and part destruction   14.3.3
  express   14.3.1
  implied   14.3.1
  later will, by   14.3.1
  marriage, by   14.3.2
  mutual wills doctrine, and   14.2
  presumption of, when lost etc   14.3.3
  revocation clause, *see* Will

Sale
  capital gains tax, on   29.5.4
  personal representatives' powers of   25.5.4
Securities, *see* Share(s)
Security
  effect of   27.7.1, 27.8.5
Settlement
  family provision claim, order for   17.8.1
  grant of representation limited to   22.6.3
  inheritance tax, and   18.4.2, 18.9.3
    Inland Revenue account, in   21.5.6
  oath form, and   23.2
  strict, end of   9.1.3, 23.2
Share(s)
  business and agricultural property relief   18.7
  certificate, safe-keeping of   26.1
    production of grant for   26.2
  details of deceased's holdings, for probate   20.4.1
  dividends, apportionment of   10.5.4
  gift of   8.4.5
    change in nature of   15.2.2
  inheritance tax
    Inland Revenue account, details in   21.5.4
    instalment option on   18.10.2
    'qualifying investment' loss relief   29.2.4
    value for   18.5.3, 21.1.2, 29.2.4, 29.2.5
  investment, as   19.2.1
  private company, investment business exclusion for   19.2.3
  transfer of   28.5.1
Sister
  administrator, as   22.4.1
  entitlement on intestacy   16.2.2, 16.4.2
Social security contributions
  insolvent estate, payment of   27.8.3
Sole trader
  business of, arrangements on death   10.6.3
Solicitor
  beneficiary
    as   11.1.3, 13.3.2
    duty of care to   13.5.4
  conflict of interest   11.1.3
  dealing in investments, by   19.2.2, 19.2.3
  delay by   24.4
  executor, as   1.5.1, 6.5, 6.7
    firm, appointment of   6.7.1
    professional conduct obligations, and   6.7.1
    see also 'personal representative' *below*
  family provision, and
    advice to testator on   17.1.2, 17.10.1
    claimant, acting for   17.10.3
    conflict of interest, and   17.10.1, 17.10.2
    negligence   17.10.3

Solicitor *cont*
  family provision, and *cont*
    personal representatives, acting for 17.10.2
  fees, as personal representative 27.2.2
  gift to 11.1.3, 13.3.2
  incorporated practice 6.7.1
  instructions, first steps after receiving 20.3
  instructions (generally), *see* Instructions
  insurance cover 29.2.3
  investment by, *see* Investment business
  meeting with personal representatives, first 24.4.2
  name and address on oath form 23.2, 23.3, 23.4
  negligence 11.1.6, 13.5.4, 17.11.3
  organisation of probate work 24.4
  personal representative
    advising on family provision legislation 17.1.2, 17.10.1
    as 1.5.1, 6.5, 6.7, 10.6.1, 19.2.3, 19.3, 20.2.1
    instructions from 20.1, 20.2.1, 20.2.3 *et seq*
  role of 11.1
  succession, advice on 11.3.2
  tax advice 11.3.3, 11.4.4
  trustee, as 6.7.2, 10.6.1
  undertaking for repayment of loan for payment of tax 21.1.3, 27.1.2
  will drafting 3.3, 11.4
    advising client 3.3.4, 3.3.6, 10.7.1, 17.1.2, 17.11.1
    duty of care 11.1.6
    reading and explaining will to client 13.3.3
    see also Drafting will
Spouse
  absolute gift of residue to 9.2.1
  conditional gift to 9.2.1
  divorce, *see* Divorce
  family provision application, *see* Family provision
  former, as executor 6.4, 14.3.2, 22.2.2
  inheritance tax exemption 12.4.1, 18.6.1, 18.13.1
  intestacy, and, *see* Intestacy
  life interest, *see* Life interest
  marriage, *see* Marriage
  residue, gift to
    absolutely 9.2.1
    life interest 9.3.1
  substitutional gift where gift fails 15.5
  survivorship 9.2.1
Standing search
  probate registry, of 17.11
Superannuation benefits
  see also Pension benefits
  Inland Revenue account, in 21.5.2
Survivorship
  beneficiary, clause for 9.2.1, 15.3.3
  Inland Revenue account, and 21.4.2, 21.4.3
  joint tenancy, and 11.3.2, 26.3.2

Taxation
  see also Capital gains tax; Income tax; Inheritance tax
  estate, property falling outside 2.5
  will drafting, role in 1.4
Tenants in common
  grant of representation, and property held as 20.6.2
  lapse of gift to 15.3.5
Testamentary capacity
  basic rule 13.2.2
  medical report as to 11.1.4, 13.2.3, 20.7.2
  query as to, on application for grant 20.7.2
  requirement of, for valid will 2.2
Testamentary debts and expenses 8.3.2, 9.1.4, 24.1.1, *see also* Debts; Personal representatives
  insolvent estate 27.8
    doubtful cases, procedure 27.8.2
    meaning of insolvency 27.8.1
    order 27.8.3
  meaning 27.2.2
  payment of 27.1 *et seq*
    considerations for 27.1.3
    funds for 27.1
    sale of assets for 27.1.3
  solvent estate 27.5.1
  statutory order for payment in 27.7.2
Testate
  meaning 1.2.1
Testator
  address 4.2.3
  age of 2.2, 13.2.1
  blind 13.3.2
  capacity, *see* Testamentary capacity
  death of, *see* Death; Deceased
  identity 4.2.3, 4.3.3, 5.1
  illiterate 13.3.2
  intention 13.3
    construction summons, and 28.2.1
    contents, knowing and approving, *see* below
    demonstration of 5.1
    extrinsic evidence of 28.2.1
    general 13.3.1
    specific 13.3.2
  knowledge and approval of contents 2.2, 4.2.3, 13.3.2, 13.3.3
    affidavit as to 20.7.2
  signature 2.1.1, 4.2.2, 4.3.2, 13.4.1
Testimonium 4.4.3
Title
  evidence of, office copy of grant as 20.7.3
Transfer of property
  family provision claim, on 17.8.1
  inheritance tax on, *see* Inheritance tax

Transmission
    office of executor, of   22.7.2
Transplant
    organ, of, on death   5.3
Treasury Solicitor   22.4.3
Trust
    end of   6.3
        beneficiaries' power   10.3.8
    inheritance tax
        creation of, in will, and   18.6.1
        property subject to, and   18.4.2
    intestacy, imposed on by statute   16.2.1, 28.7.1
    life assurance policy, under   2.4.3, 26.3.2
    land, of, see Trust of land
    property held on, devolution of   26.3.2
    residue, of   9.1.2, 9.1.3, 9.3.1, 10.3.1, 27.6.3, 29.6
        whether required for   9.1.2
    whether required   3.6, 6.2, 9.1.2
    will drafting, and   3.6, 6.2, 10.7.3, 10.7.4
Trust corporation
    executor, as   6.5
    trustee, as   10.6.2
Trust of land   10.4
    beneficiaries' powers   10.4.1–10.4.3
    land, of
        end to trust for sale   9.1.3
        personal representatives, and   10.3.3
        valid receipt for proceeds   6.4
        occupation by beneficiary   10.4.3
        partial intestacy, on   28.7.1
Trustee
    administrator as   2.3.2
    appointment   2.3.2
        beneficiaries' power   10.3.8
        dual capacity   6.3
        personal representatives, by   25.5.5
        specimen clauses   6.6
    charging clause   10.6.1
    choice   6.5–6.9
        advice on   11.4.1
    consultation duty   10.4.2
    dealings, by   19.2.3
    executors, dual capacity as   6.3
    individual as   6.5
    inheritance tax liability   18.9.3, 21.5.6
    maintenance and advancement   10.3.5, 25.2.2
    minor beneficiary's property, of   25.5.5
    need for   6.2
    number of   6.4
    personalty, power as to   9.1.3, 10.3.4
    powers of
        examples of   4.3.2, 10.3.1 et seq
        extending by will   10.1.2, 10.3
        selection of, by testator   10.7
        statutory   10.1.1
    professional
        charging clause   6.7.2, 10.6.1
        legal and practical considerations   6.7.1

Public Trustee as   6.9
settled property, liability for tax on   18.9.3
solicitors as
    charging clause   6.7.2, 10.6.1
    legal and practical considerations   6.7.1
statutory powers, extending   2.3.4
transfer of property to   29.6.3
    capital gains tax and   29.5.4, 29.6.2
trust corporation as   6.5, 10.6.2
    drafting and advice   6.8.3
    legal and practical considerations   6.8.1
    professional conduct consideration   6.8.2
trust funds, investment of   10.3.2
Trustee Savings Bank account
    grant of representation not required, circumstances   20.6.1

Uncle
    administrator, as   22.4.1
Undertaking
    repayment of loan for payment of tax, for   21.1.3, 27.1.2
Undue influence   13.3.2
Unincorporated association
    gift to, specimen clause   8.3.3
Unit trust
    investment, as   19.2.1
Unmarried father
    parental responsibility, and appointment of guardian   7.2

Validity   1.1, 2.1, 11.1.3, 13.1 et seq, 13.4.1
    challenging   22.8.1
    practical safeguards   13.5.5
    requirements for   3.2, 13.1
Valuation
    assets, of   20.4.4, 21.1.2
    costs of   27.2.2
Value added tax
    debt in insolvent estate, as   27.8.3
Variation   20.7, 20.8, 29.2.5, 30.3, 30.4
    availability of   30.3.1
    succession after   30.3.1
    tax
        advantages   30.3.2
        planning for   30.4
    written notice of election   30.3.2

Will
    admissibility   20.7.1
    alteration to, see Alteration
    ambiguity in   3.2, 3.3.1, 3.3.2, 28.2.1
    attestation clause   4.2.3, 13.3.2, 13.4.3
        affidavit of due execution where faulty   20.7.2
    codicil, for   4.4.2, 4.4.3
    codicil, see Codicil

Will *cont*
   construction summons   28.2.1
   damaged   14.3.3
   date   4.2.3, 4.3.3, 5.1
   debts, express provision for   8.3.2, 9.1.4, 27.1.3
      effect of   27.6
      time for payment, effect   25.5.6, 27.3
   destruction of   14.3.3
   document incorporated into by reference   8.4.3
   drafting, *see* Drafting will
   due execution, presumption of   13.4.3, 20.7.1
   examples   4.2.2, 4.3.2, 4.4.2
   executor, powers granted to   10.7, 25.3.2, 25.4, *see also* Executor
   existing, check on   11.2, 20.3.1
   force, fear, fraud or undue influence, made under   13.3.2
   form   3.5
      examples   4.2, 4.3, 4.4
   formalities of   *see* Execution
   gift by, *see* Devise; Gift; Legacy
   instructions to solicitor, *see* Instructions
   intention to make, *see* Testator
   lodging of, with probate registry   20.7
   lost   20.7.2
   mistake in   13.3.2, 28.2.1
   planning, and tax issues, *see* Inheritance tax
   property passing by   2.4, 15.2.3
   proving, *see* Probate, grant of
   reasons for making   2.3
   rectification of   28.2.1
   review of   11.4.6
   revocation clause   4.2.3, 4.3.3, 5.2, 14.3.1
      reason for   5.2
   revocation of, *see* Revocation
   signature   2.1.1, 4.2.2, 4.3.2, 13.4.1
   structure   3.5
   taking effect ('speaking') from death   2.1.2, 15.2.3
   tax, importance of   1.4, 2.3.5, *see also* Inheritance tax (general): planning
   testamentary capacity, *see* Testamentary capacity
   testator, *see* Testator
   validity, *see* Validity
Witness
   beneficiary, or spouse of, as   13.5.2, 13.5.3, 15.7
   capacity   13.5.1
   charging clause, and   6.7.2
   choice, advice to testator on   13.5.4
   execution, summary of formalities for   13.4.2
   independence of   13.5.2
   requirement for   13.4.1
   signature of   13.4.1
   solicitor's firm, from   13.5.2